Every
GOOD AND

EVIL ANGEL
in the Bible

Every

GOOD AND

EVIL ANGEL

in the Bible

LARRY RICHARDS

Illustrated by

Paul Richards

THOMAS NELSON PUBLISHERS

Nashville

Published in Nashville, Tennessee, by Thomas Nelson, Inc.

Library of Congress Cataloging-in-Publication Data

Richards, Larry, 1931–
    Every good and evil angel in the Bible / Larry Richards.
      p.   cm.
    Includes index.
    ISBN 0-7852-1263-9
    1. Angels—Biblical teaching.   2. Demonology—Biblical teaching.
  I. Title.
  BS680.A48R53   1997
  235′.3—dc21   97-14577
                                                   CIP

Printed in the United States of America

1 2 3 4 5 6 7 8—02 01 00 99 98 97

CONTENTS

INTRODUCTION

Why the current fascination with angels? It's rooted in the fact that we human beings are aware of a spiritual realm which lies beside or beyond our own. Somehow we sense that this world cannot be all there is, that the meaning of our existence can't be summed up in the few brief decades we live here on earth. It's no wonder, then, that so many people today are fascinated by angels and demons, if not with God Himself. Stories of angel encounters and of demonization open up the "world beyond" to our speculation.

But it isn't necessary to speculate or wonder about angels and demons. The Bible contains solid information about both the bright and the dark beings. As we explore everything the Bible says about angels and demons, our curiosity will be satisfied—and our faith will be strengthened as well.

The very word "angel" tells us so much about these special beings. The Hebrew word, *mal'ak,* emphasizes the fact that angels are God's agents who represent the One who sends them. Similarly the Greek word, *angelos,* represents angels as divine messengers, ambassadors sent by God. Scripture tells us that these ever-living beings were created by God to serve as ministers to us, the heirs of God's salvation (Heb. 1:14). As His ministers, angels direct our attention to God, not to themselves. And what the names and ministries of angels tell us about the Lord is exciting indeed. These spirit beings, who are not bound by the natural laws that limit humans, symbolize God's active involvement in our lives. What do angels do?

- They come to reassure us and offer hope.
- They come to give us guidance and direction.

- They come to call us to special missions.
- They come to rescue us from some great danger.

While at times angels appear as radiant beings, very often angels come in the guise of ordinary men. It was as ordinary men that the two "investigating" angels visited Sodom before its destruction. And it was as an ordinary man that the Old Testament's premier angel, the Angel of the Lord, visited Gideon to commission him to deliver God's people. While we can't begin to imagine how often angels walk among us today, some of the contemporary stories included in this book remind us that God still sends out His angel messengers, and so reveals another facet of His great love.

Angels have also been involved in salvation history's pivotal events. Hosts of angels witnessed the creation of our universe. Angels were involved in the miracles that won Israel's release from slavery in Egypt. Angels observed the giving of the Law at Mount Sinai, and angels administered Old Testament Law. Angels announced the Savior's birth. Angels ministered to Jesus at Gethsemane the night before His crucifixion. Angels rolled the stone away from the empty tomb where Jesus had been buried, and they announced His resurrection to the women who came there that first Easter Sunday morning.

The angels who touch our lives today have witnessed the unfolding of God's purposes across the millennia, and they have seen how deeply God cares for you and me.

But there is a dark side to the spiritual universe as well. The Bible tells how Satan led a great rebellion against God and how a host of angels sided with him against God. These dark angels, the demons of the New

Testament, are the hidden beings who lay behind history's pagan deities and who lie behind today's practitioners of the occult. Scripture testifies to their intense hostility toward God and the human beings God loves. Yet the demonic holds no terror for believers today, for Jesus is supreme. Just as Jesus cast out demons in New Testament times, today too demons are unable to resist His authority.

As we explore everything the Bible says about Satan and his fallen legions, we'll discover what we need to know in order to understand and to resist demonic influences.

So what will you gain as you join me in exploring everything the Bible says about angels and demons? You'll get answers to your questions about the supernatural. You'll learn principles for discerning between encounters with angels and encounters with demons. You'll discover how to distinguish between true and false accounts of angel appearances. You'll gain fresh insights into familiar passages of Scripture. You'll find your faith in God stimulated as you realize how committed He truly is to our human family.

And, perhaps, you'll be prepared for an angel encounter of your own!

❖

CHAPTER 1

ANGEL WITH AN ATTITUDE:

SATAN AT WORK IN THE WORLD

Genesis 1—3

Angels fascinate us. There's something special and attractive about these bright beings so often portrayed with white wings and golden halos. Most of the angel stories we've heard, whether from the Bible or as told by someone relating a contemporary angel encounter, remind us that angels are both friendly and good.

Two of the angels named in Scripture are Gabriel and Michael. The last two letters of their names, *-el,* stand for "God." The name Gabriel means "strength of God," and Michael means "who is like God." The names of these two angels remind us that most angels are wonderful creatures who are close to the Lord and reflect His own desire to do us good.

But there's a dark side to the first angel we meet in Scripture. We know him as Satan, or the devil, and he is one of only four persons on the scene as Genesis begins: God, who created the universe; Adam and Eve, human beings shaped by God in His image; and Satan—an intruder, an angel with an attitude.

THE SETTING   *(Genesis 1—3)*

The first three chapters of Genesis, featuring only these four beings, raise some of the most basic questions in our own lives—and answer them:

- Where do we come from?
- What is unique about us compared to other creatures?
- What is God's attitude toward us?
- Why does the world have so much evil?
- Is this world, this life, all there is?

All these questions come up sharply when Satan intrudes into a garden called Eden.

CREATION   *(Genesis 1)*

The first chapter of Genesis pictures God creating our universe. With a burst of unimaginable power He spreads a vast expanse, and then with loving care God focuses His attention on a single planet hung in endless space. Step by step, God lovingly shapes this planet, forming seas and dry land, enriching it with an assortment of vegetation, and filling its skies and valleys and seas with an infinite variety of living creatures. And when the planet has been enriched and beautified, as the culminating act of creation God announces His intent to create humankind "in Our own image, according to Our likeness" (1:26 NKJV).

In this way the Bible introduces the first Person identified in Scripture: God. To this point we know little about God. We know that He exists and that He is the source of our universe. We know He has unimaginable power. From the design of our planet, we know something of His wisdom, His love of beauty, and His appreciation for what is good. We will learn something else that is important—God has a special concern for the human creatures He will soon place on the planet He has shaped and beautified.

ADAM AND EVE   (Genesis 2)

The second and third persons introduced in Scripture are Adam and Eve. Our first impression of them underlines the specialness of these creatures. Genesis describes God's means of creating every other thing as His spoken word: "God said," and what He spoke came into existence. Yet Genesis 2 says that God stooped to fashion Adam from the "dust of the ground" and then, bending near, He breathed "into his nostrils the breath of life" (2:7). Later, Eve was fashioned from Adam's rib, an act that Adam understood to mean that she shared of his own essential identity (2:21–23). And what an identity that is!

Humankind's special relationship with God (*Genesis 1:26–27*). Two Hebrew words are linked in Genesis 1:26–27. When God expressed His intent to create human beings, He said, "Let Us make man in Our image [*selem*], according to Our likeness [*dᵉmut*]." When linked together, these two words become a technical theological phrase which asserts that, like God, human beings are *persons*. We share those attributes of God which set us apart from other creatures: a full measure of intellect and memory, the ability to feel, a sense of beauty, the capacity to love and be loved, the potential for creativity, the responsibility of choosing between good and evil. It's for this reason that, while we cannot compare God to human beings, we can only grasp our true identity by seeing ourselves as beings cre-

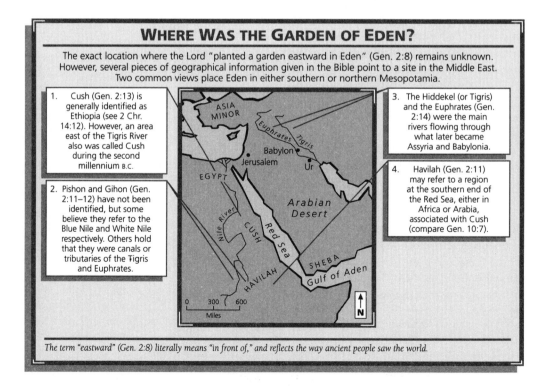

WHERE WAS THE GARDEN OF EDEN?

The exact location where the Lord "planted a garden eastward in Eden" (Gen. 2:8) remains unknown. However, several pieces of geographical information given in the Bible point to a site in the Middle East. Two common views place Eden in either southern or northern Mesopotamia.

1. Cush (Gen. 2:13) is generally identified as Ethiopia (see 2 Chr. 14:12). However, an area east of the Tigris River also was called Cush during the second millennium B.C.

2. Pishon and Gihon (Gen. 2:11–12) have not been identified, but some believe they refer to the Blue Nile and White Nile respectively. Others hold that they were canals or tributaries of the Tigris and Euphrates.

3. The Hiddekel (or Tigris) and the Euphrates (Gen. 2:14) were the main rivers flowing through what later became Assyria and Babylonia.

4. Havilah (Gen. 2:11) may refer to a region at the southern end of the Red Sea, either in Africa or Arabia, associated with Cush (compare Gen. 10:7).

The term "eastward" (Gen. 2:8) literally means "in front of," and reflects the way ancient people saw the world.

ated in His image. The key to understanding human identity is not to be found in our supposed links with animal-like ancestors, but rather in our personhood, which forever links us to God.

Life in Eden (Genesis 2). At first, life in Eden preserved and enriched the link between God and man. There, God fashioned Eve from Adam's substance, and Adam realized that they both shared God's image and a common identity as human beings. There too Adam and Eve explored their potential as persons made in God's image. The garden's trees were "pleasant to the sight and good for food" (2:9). The first couple discovered their capacity to appreciate beauty. They were placed in the garden "to tend and keep it" (2:15). Adam and Eve discovered the joy of personal accomplishment to be found in work. They were also shown a tree in the garden from which they were not to eat (2:16–17).

The forbidden tree (Genesis 2:15–17). God's reason for planting one tree in Eden from which the first pair was not to eat is often misunderstood. To truly be persons like God, persons rather than mere puppets, Adam and Eve had to be given the opportunity to make a responsible moral choice, for God is a moral Person who exercises choice. The forbidden tree was necessary, even though it provided an opportunity for the fourth person we meet in these early chapters of Genesis to shatter the peace and harmony of Eden. The forbidden tree provided an opportunity for an intruder to drive a wedge between the first human beings and the God who formed them and loved them.

SATAN: THE ANGEL WITH AN ATTITUDE

SATAN AS SERPENT   *(Genesis 3:1)*

The intruder came in the guise of a serpent. Scripture later identifies this "serpent of old" as "the Devil and Satan" (Rev. 12:9; 20:2). Jewish and Christian commentators seem to agree that while it was the serpent who spoke, it was Satan who harnessed this creature and acted through it. Genesis described the serpent as "more cunning [shrewd] than any beast of the field" (Gen. 3:1). Satan chose his representative carefully. The New Testament claims, "Satan himself transforms himself into an angel of light" (2 Cor. 11:14). Satan hardly wanted Adam and Eve to see him as he was. How much better for him to choose the form of a serpent, an animal which had a reputation for being shrewd (Gen. 3:1).

———————————— ❖ ————————————

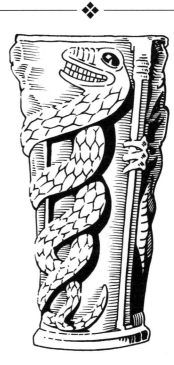

ANGELORE

SERPENTS IN ANCIENT NEAR EAST LORE

In the Ancient Near East serpents were associated with life, wisdom, and chaos, all themes linked with Genesis 3. More sinister, the Hebrew letters that spell "serpent" are used in a verb that means "to practice divination," an occult practice linked in Scripture with demonic powers. So Satan, demons, and serpents are closely linked in many early pagan religions.

———————————— ❖ ————————————

So the serpent in Eden was Satan in disguise. But larger questions arise:

- What is Satan's origin?
- Where did he come from?
- What is he like?
- What is his relationship with God and with humanity?

SATAN'S ORIGIN IN THE SPIRITUAL REALM   (Genesis 1—2)

God created the material universe (Genesis 1). The first question Satan's appearance in Eden raises is, Where did he come from? Genesis 1 describes God's creation of the material universe and its living inhabitants. But it mentions nothing about a being like Satan. For that answer we have to look elsewhere in Scripture. When we do, we discover that the material universe is *not* all there is.

The spiritual realm has always existed (Genesis 1:1). This is clear from Genesis 1, which opens with the affirmation, "In the beginning God." Before there was a physical universe, God existed. Before there was matter, there was a realm beyond matter inhabited by the Lord. Genesis 1 tells us nothing specific about this realm but does imply its existence. It would be strange indeed if God were not able to populate that nonmaterial realm which we call the "spiritual."

God populated the spiritual realm with angels (Psalm 148:1–6). The Bible clearly indicates that God populated the spiritual realm with beings we call angels. Psalm 148:1–6 calls on "all His angels" and "all His hosts" to praise the Lord, along with sun, moon, and stars, for "He commanded and they were created." Job calls the angels "sons of God"—a Hebrew idiom which indicates direct creation by God—and says that they "shouted for joy" at the creation of the earth (Job 38:7). So while we do not know exactly when the spiritual realm was populated, the Bible clearly suggests it was before the creation of our material universe. Thus Satan, a member of that spiritual realm, existed before the birth of our

race, and his appearance in the Garden of Eden, though unexpected, can be explained.

SATAN IS IDENTIFIED AS AN ANGEL WHO SINNED (Ezekiel 28; Isaiah 14)

Who is Satan, and why would he slip into Eden to visit Adam and Eve? The answer is found in two bold prophetic passages, one in the book of Ezekiel and one in the book of Isaiah.

Interpreting Ezekiel 28 and Isaiah 14. In both passages the prophets begin by addressing a contemporary political figure, and then they suddenly shift their focus to look directly at a shadowy figure who stands behind the human ruler. This pattern is common in biblical prophecy. A prophet's focus is on a present event or personality, when suddenly his viewpoint shifts, and he sees beyond the present into the past or the future. The present event or personality serves as a lens through which the prophet sees a common theme worked out on a far grander scale. For instance, Joel's experience of a plague of locusts served as a lens through which the prophet saw a vision of history's end, with vast armies flowing over the Holy Land and bringing total devastation (see Joel 1—3).

In Ezekiel 28 the prophet addressed the "prince of Tyre." Tyre was a wealthy city-state on the Mediterranean coast, whose citadel was constructed on an island and whose sea-approaches were protected by the era's strongest fleet. The prophet announced God's judgment on Tyre's leader, whose power generated such pride that he confused himself with deity. Suddenly, the image of the proud prince of Tyre shimmered, and Ezekiel saw, as if through a bright haze, and then addressed a figure identified as the "king of Tyre"—a spiritual being who stood behind the prince of Tyre and whose character was reflected in him.

Ezekiel's prophecy against the prince of Tyre became the lens through which the prophet looked back, before the creation of our universe, and saw a vision of the original beauty, the fall, and the resultant character of a powerful angel whose pride and rebellion against God overshadowed that of Tyre's human ruler.

Satan was once a powerful and good angel (*Ezekiel 28:12b–15a*). In this passage the "king of Tyre" is identified as an angel of the highest order, called a "cherub." The prophet, speaking God's words (28:12), said:

> You were the anointed cherub who
>   covers;
> I established you;
> You were on the holy mountain* of
>   God;
> You walked back and forth in the
>   midst of fiery stones;
> You were perfect in your ways
>   from the day you were created,
> Till iniquity was found in you.
>
> *Ezekiel 28:14, 15*

Satan's sin corrupted him (*Ezekiel 28:16–19*). This high angel, this cherub, was perfect when God created him. But then, inexplicably, he was corrupted from within ("iniquity was found in you"). The passage goes on to describe this inner corruption in terms of a pride that stimulates violence and rebellion.

> By the abundance of your trading
> You became filled with violence
>   within,
> And you sinned;
> Therefore I cast you as a profane
>   thing
> Out of the mountain of God;
> And I destroyed [expelled] you, O
>   covering cherub,
> From the midst of the fiery stones.
> Your heart was lifted up because of
>   your beauty;

> You corrupted your wisdom for the
>   sake of your splendor.
>
> *Ezekiel 28:16–17*

Satan's sin is defined by Isaiah (*Isaiah 14:12–15*). Isaiah provides more details about Satan. Isaiah was addressing the king of Babylon, when suddenly his perspective shifted and he spoke to a fallen being named "Lucifer." This, Satan's original name, means "morning star," or "day star," and is often paraphrased as "light bearer." Isaiah's vision was of the past and depicted Satan's fall, but Isaiah also indicated Satan's ultimate destiny: He "shall be brought down to Sheol, / To the lowest depths of the Pit" (14:15). One day God will judge the now evil angel.

Most importantly, however, Isaiah's words provide insight into Satan's character and his essential motivation.

> How you are fallen from heaven,
> O Lucifer, son of the morning!
> How you are cut down to the
>   ground,
> You who weakened the nations!
> For you have said in your heart;
> 'I will ascend into heaven,
> I will exalt my throne above the stars
>   of God;
> I will also sit on the mount of the
>   congregation
> On the farthest sides of the north;
> I will ascend above the heights of the
>   clouds,
> I will be like the Most High.'
> Yet you shall be brought down to
>   Sheol,*
> To the lowest depths of the Pit.
>
> *Isaiah 14:12–15*

We can learn much about Satan from Ezekiel and Isaiah. When we consider these two

---

* In biblical symbolism, "mountain" frequently stands for government or rule. Satan originally had a significant role in God's government of His universe.

* *Sheol* is the Hebrew word for the grave, the abode of the dead.

prophetic passages, we learn several important things about Satan:

- Satan is a created being. He was originally one of a powerful type of angelic beings called cherubim.
- Satan, an angelic being, belongs to the spiritual realm rather than the material creation.
- Satan was created perfect, and thus was holy, completely in harmony with God's intent and will.
- Satan sinned—iniquity was found in him.
- Satan's sin seems to have been one of pride, according to the accusation in Ezekiel. This is more clearly indicated by the five "I will" statements in Isaiah 14. What Satan demanded was the right to *live independently of God*—to ascend into heaven and to be god, not only for himself, but also to rule others! These "I wills" set Satan against his Creator, for he demanded a role to which no creature has a right.
- Implicit in Satan's corrupt desire is not only pride, but rebellion against God, rejection of His ways, and hostility to His plans and purposes.

Satan exhibits a hostile attitude toward human beings. Even at this early stage in Genesis, we can clearly see that when Satan intruded into the Garden of Eden and began his conversation with Eve, he truly was an angel with an attitude.

Satan's attitude and character were forged in the fires of rebellion against God. His intent now is to thwart God's plans and purposes. His disposition toward humanity is the opposite of God's. If God loves our race and seeks only our good, Satan cares nothing for us. His only interest in the first pair was to enlist them as pawns in his struggle to break free of God's dominion and live a life independent of God's moral constraints.

Knowing something of Satan, who expressed himself through the serpent, we can expect that he intended nothing good when he struck up a conversation with Eve.

SATAN TEMPTED EVE   (Genesis 3)

Satan intruded into the Garden of Eden with the specific intention of getting Adam and Eve to sin and thus to adopt his attitude of rebellion against God.

SATAN'S STRATEGY IN TEMPTING EVE   (Genesis 3:1b–5)

As we examine the conversation between Satan and Eve, we sense something of Satan's subtlety. He told no direct lie to Eve, but through half-truth and innuendo Satan led Eve to doubt the Lord and ultimately to adopt his own attitude. We can sense more of Satan's basic approach to temptation by looking carefully at the conversation recorded in Genesis 3:1–5, noting the tone of voice adopted by each speaker.

Satan: [*his tone one of surprise, shock*] "Has God indeed said, 'You shall not eat of every tree of the garden?' "

Eve: [*her tone defensive*] "We may eat the fruit of the trees of the garden; but of the fruit of the tree which is in the midst of the garden, God has said, 'You shall not eat it, nor shall you touch it, lest you die.' "

Satan: [*his tone at first one of utter amazement*] "You will not surely die" [*then changing to one of encouragement*] "For God knows that in the day you eat of it your eyes will be opened, and you will be like God, knowing good and evil."

Satan sought to distort Eve's view of God (*Genesis 3:1b–2*). Satan's first question was especially subtle. God told Adam, "Of every tree of the garden you may freely eat." The one exception was "the tree of the knowledge of good and evil" (2:16). Satan shifted the emphasis from God's generous provision of "every tree" to draw Eve's attention to the one tree from which she and Adam were not to eat. Adam and Eve had reason to appreciate God's generosity in providing so profusely. Satan's first remark encouraged them to focus on the prohibition, to cast the Lord as harsh and repressive.

Eve adopted Satan's perspective (*Genesis 3:2–3*). Eve's response shows that Satan's poison had already begun to work. She told him that they may eat the fruit of the trees in the garden, but she left out the word "every," which emphasized God's bounteous supply. Eve also added to God's original prohibition. She told the serpent that God had said "nor shall you touch it," which God did not say at all. Eve had unconsciously begun to adopt Satan's distorted interpretation of God's actions, which ignored evidence of His love and threw doubt on His deep concern for human beings.

Satan questioned God's word (Genesis 5). Satan's next statement has an unusual word order in Hebrew, which creates ambiguity. The listener must decide whether the phrase means "Certainly you will not die" or "It is not certain that you will die." Was Satan directly contradicting God, or was he raising a doubt about the warning God gave when He placed this one restriction on the first pair? The ambiguity was certainly intended, and Eve could take Satan's words whichever way she chose. But either way, doubt about the reliability of God's word had been planted.

Satan suggested an attractive alternative (Genesis 3:4, 5). Satan went on to suggest that God had a reason for the restriction other than concern for His creatures. Satan promised Eve that when the fruit of the tree is eaten, "your eyes will be opened, and you will be like God, knowing good and evil" (3:5).

Satan took the name of the tree, the Tree of the Knowledge of Good and Evil, and argued that what the name implied would be good for Adam and Eve rather than harmful! Adam and Eve would "know good and evil" if they ate. They would gain knowledge they presently did not have—and then, Satan said, "you will be like God."

Satan's goal is to enlist rebels! How striking it is that here we see reflected Satan's own passionate desire and original sin. Satan's five "I wills" expressed his drive for an independent existence—a drive to replace God as the authority in his life and to become his own authority. This is exactly what Satan now held out before Eve. "Violate God's command and

assert your independence! Eat, deny your creatureliness, and claim your place as a being with a right to live your life as you please, without reference to God or His moral standards. Eat and be free!"

Eve chose to rely on her senses rather than on God's word (Genesis 3:6a). Eve's response to Satan was to examine the tree. It seemed "good for food." The fruit smelled delicious. It was "pleasant to the eyes." It looked beautiful.

Today too people tend to rely on their senses rather than on Scripture. If something feels good or is enjoyable, they assume it must be good, even though God's word tells us that a thing that seems so good to us is really harmful. One of Satan's consistent strategies is to get people to choose on the basis of appearances and feelings and to reject the clear moral guidance provided in Scripture.

Eve's choice imitated Satan's own rebellion (Genesis 3:6b). Most appealing of all to Eve was the fact that the tree was "desirable to make one wise." Eve wanted to be more than she had been, more than God intended her to be. This was exactly what Satan himself had desired! Underlying the rebellion of both Satan and Eve was a desire for independence from God. People still mistakenly take that independence for "freedom," never realizing that it is only in allegiance to God and His will that any creature can find fulfillment.

RESISTING SATAN'S STRATEGY TODAY

Characteristics of Satan's strategy. From this story early in Genesis, we learn much about Satan's strategies as he seeks to influence us today. And we learn how to resist Satan's temptations successfully. When tempting us, Satan will:

1. raise doubts about the reliability of God's Word;
2. portray God as oppressive and restrictive;
3. cast doubt on God's motives;
4. urge us to act and "to see for ourselves";
5. create a desire for the forbidden;

6. question the consequences of disobedience;
7. appeal to our pride and to our desire to be independent and to do whatever *we* think best.

Countering Satan's strategy. To resist these strategies of Satan, we as believers need to:

1. know and rely completely on God's Word;
2. maintain confidence in God's goodness and generosity;
3. trust that God's commands are motivated by love and truly do define what is best for us;
4. remember that we need not touch a fire to know that it burns;
5. keep our desires focused on that which is noble, just, pure, lovely, of good report, virtuous, and praiseworthy (Phil. 4:8);
6. heed the warnings of consequences which God's love has moved Him to provide;
7. remember that God is God and that we are His creatures; and therefore
8. reject every temptation to act independently of His will.

Genesis tells us that Eve was taken in by Satan and fell into the same trap as that fallen angel. Like Satan, Eve chose to act independently of God, and Adam quickly followed her lead. How suddenly the two learned the difference between good and evil. How tragic that knowledge was!

SATAN AND EVIL

SATAN AS THE "EVIL ONE" (*John 17:15*)

One of Satan's names is "the evil one" (John 17:15; 1 John 5:18). The name "Satan" means "adversary"—the enemy of God and humanity. It's clear in Genesis 3 that God's command not to eat the fruit of the forbidden tree was intended to protect Adam and Eve from knowing "good and evil," and that Satan was just as intent on drawing them into an act which would enlist them on his side in a struggle between good and evil. But what *is* evil?

BIBLE BACKGROUND:

ISHTAR AND GILGAMESH

How well does Satan succeed in twisting human beings' perception of God? In Tablet IV of the Babylonian *Epic of Gilgamesh,* dating some 2,000 years before Christ, the goddess Ishtar fell in love with the human Gilgamesh, who recounted the ways that Ishtar had mistreated former lovers. Ishtar flew into a rage and determined to smash him!

Gilgamesh to Ishtar:

> For Tamumz, the lover of thy youth,
> Thou hast ordained wailing year after year.
>> Having loved the dappled shepherd-bird,
>> Thou smotest him, breaking his wing,
>> In the groves he sits, crying "My wing!"
>> Then thou lovedst a lion, perfect in strength;
>> Seven pits and seven thou didst dig for him.
>> Then a stallion thou lovedst, famed in battle;
>> The whip, the spur, and the lash thou ordainst for him.

Rejected by Gilgamesh, Ishtar appealed to her parents for power to exterminate him.

> When Ishtar heard this,
> Ishtar was enraged and [mounted] to heaven.

Forth went Ishtar before Anu, her father,
To Antrum, her mother, she went and
    [said]:
"My father, Gilgamesh has heaped insults
    upon me!
Gilgamesh has recounted my stinking deeds,
My stench and my foulness."
. . . .
"My father, make me the Bull of Heaven
    [that he smite Gilgamesh]!
If thou dost not
I will smash [the doors of the nether world],
I will [raise up the dead eating alive]
So that the dead shall outnumber the
    living!"

The Bible preserves a portrait of God as consistent, just, loving, and forgiving; but Satan's attempt to corrupt and distort humanity's image of deity clearly bore fruit in other ancient cultures!

THE DEFINITION OF EVIL

The basic Hebrew word for evil is *ra'*, which can be translated as either "evil" or "bad." The family of words constructed on this root are used throughout the Old Testament to focus on two aspects of evil. As a moral term, *ra'* identifies actions which violate God's intentions for created beings. As a descriptive term, *ra'* is used of the consequences of doing evil—the tragedy and distress, the physical and emotional harm that come as a result of wrong moral choices. In taking and eating the fruit of the forbidden tree, Adam and Eve did evil, and they immediately began to experience, and thus in an experiential sense to "know," the evil consequences of their choice.

THE CONSEQUENCES OF DOING EVIL FOR HUMANITY
(Genesis 3:3–4)

Biological death. Satan had cast doubt on God's warning that the first pair would die the very day they ate the forbidden fruit. Although Genesis says that Adam lived 930 years, the processes of biological death set to work immediately.

Death as separation from God. But "death" in Scripture also serves as an image for separation from God (see Eph. 2:1–3). In choosing to live independent lives, Adam and Eve stepped out of the moral realm of good, where they had naturally and gladly submitted to God's will, into a realm where they operated independently of Him; and, separated from God, they began to experience the evil consequences of their choice.

Guilt and shame *(Genesis 3:7, 8).* Immediately Adam and Eve recognized that they were naked. The freedom they once had to relate to each other without any need for shame was stripped away (3:7). When they heard the sound of God walking in Eden, they fled from Him. Their innocence was replaced by a terrifying sense of guilt (3:8).

Broken relationships *(Genesis 3:11–13).* When Adam and Eve were confronted by God, each blamed the other—and even blamed God—rather than accept responsibility for their act (3:11–13). The loving and supportive relationship Adam and Eve once had was corrupted by selfishness, and they were set at odds against each other, as well as against God. All this was an expression of the spiritual death they experienced in their fall.

Death passed to the human race *(Romans 5:12; Genesis 4—6).* Romans 5 tells us that "through one man [Adam] sin entered the world, and death through sin, and thus death spread to all men, because all sinned." The next chapters of Genesis illustrate the impact of evil upon human experience.

The first pair, now separated from God and spiritually dead, passed on that spiritual state to their offspring. Intent on living the independent life, their son Cain became jealous of his brother Abel and murdered him (Gen. 4:1–8). Their descendant, Lamech, broke God's pattern for marriage by marrying two women; he then tried to justify his murder of a man who had merely injured him

(Gen. 4:19–24). Many hundreds (or thousands) of years later, God's evaluation of the human race was that "every intent of the thoughts of his [humanity's] heart was only evil continually" (Gen. 6:5).

SATAN'S CONTINUING THREAT TO HUMANITY

THE THREAT GROWING OUT OF HUMANITY'S FALL

Satan introduced our race to evil. The sequence of events in Genesis, beginning with the appearance of Satan in Eden, helps us understand this dark angel and also helps us understand the underlying nature of evil itself. Evil is not the mere absence of good; it is not an abstract idea. Evil is bluntly practical; it is something that is expressed in a person's relationship with God and with other human beings. Evil is what we do when we choose a course of action that is wrong because it violates God's intentions for us. *Evil is anything a creature does independently of God's will.* And evil also encompasses all the tragic results that always ensue from such choices.

Satan infected humanity with his own moral corruption. Where did evil originate? In a cosmic sense, evil originated in the heart of the angel Lucifer. There pride was born, and he rebelled against his own identity as a creature, demanding independence from God. In that moment, Lucifer became Satan—an implacable enemy of God, an angel with an attitude.

The early chapters of Genesis reveal that that angel slipped across the boundary between the spiritual and material realms to trick our first parents into adopting his attitude. And he succeeded. In choosing to act independently of God, in rejecting their identity as creatures and demanding a prerogative reserved for God, Adam and Eve cut our race off from God and doomed us to wander in a moral wilderness where every misstep leads to tragedy and personal disaster.

THE CONTINUING THREAT TRACED THROUGH THE SCRIPTURES

Satan was not finished when he led Adam and Eve into sin. He appears in Scripture frequently, always as the implacable enemy of God and of human beings. Most often Satan's efforts are directed against God's chosen people in an attempt to thwart God's plans. Also, Satan typically works through other angels who followed him in his rebellion, fallen angels best known as the "demons" of the Gospels.

Satan in the Pentateuch (Genesis—Deuteronomy). God chose to work through the family of a man named Abraham in order to ultimately bless and redeem our race. At one time, Abraham's descendants spent four hundred years as slaves in Egypt. They were also corrupted by the religion of Egypt. God delivered Abraham's descendants, the Israelites (the Jewish people), from slavery and gave them His Law, a wonderful revelation of what constitutes a godly life. The Israelites did not leave Egypt unscathed. Leviticus 17:7 makes it clear that Satan's forces were behind the religion of Egypt—just as they are behind all pagan religions—and that Egypt's religion had influenced many of the Jews. The verse says, "They shall no more offer their sacrifices to demons, after whom they have played the harlot."

Satan in the Historical Books (Joshua—Esther). Satan is mentioned by name only in 1 Chronicles 21:1, where he directly attacked Israel through King David. However, the Israelites' repeated turning aside from God to practice pagan religions is directly attributed to the influence of Satan's angels in Psalms 106 and 109:6.

The awful impact of Satan's influence through pagan religions is powerfully depicted in Psalm 106.

But they mingled with the Gentiles
And learned their works;
They served their idols,
Which became a snare to them.

They even sacrificed their sons
And their daughters to demons,
And shed innocent blood,
The blood of their sons and
    daughters,
Whom they sacrificed to the idols
    of Canaan;
And the land was polluted with
    blood.

Psalm 106:35–38

The vulnerability of the Israelites to pagan religions ultimately led God to punish them and to send them into captivity in Babylon. Surely Satan has proved himself to be no friend of God's people—or humankind in general!

Satan in the Poetic Books *(Job—Song of Solomon).* The Psalms portray Satan's indirect attack on God's people through pagan religions.

The book of Job tells of a direct attack on a true believer. God permitted Satan to bring disaster after disaster upon a man named Job, who continued to trust the Lord even though he could not understand why God would let such terrible things happen to him. Satan's total lack of concern for human suffering and his active hostility to those who trust in God are both powerfully revealed in the first two chapters of Job.

Satan in the Major Prophets *(Isaiah—Daniel).* The Bible's revelation of a personal being named Satan has enabled commentators to identify the supernatural being behind the human rulers of Tyre and Babylon. These passages also provide special insight into Satan's origin and character, as well as into the origin of evil in a universe created by a God who is wholly good.

Daniel 10 adds a new dimension to Satan's activity as the prophet caught a glimpse of an invisible war waged in the spiritual realm between the angelic forces of God and of Satan. In the last chapters of Daniel the invisible war spills over onto earth, and political leaders energized by demons struggle to exterminate God's people.

Satan in the Minor Prophets *(Hosea—Malachi).* Most of the Minor Prophets lived and ministered during the same period of time covered by the Historical Books. They stood against the moral corruption and idolatry of their times and called God's people back to Him. Their struggle was against the demonic forces of Satan which were behind the pagan religions and ways they preached against. Satan is mentioned by name only in Zechariah 3, where he opposed the band of Jews who had returned to the Holy Land from captivity in Babylon.

Satan in the Gospels *(Matthew—John).* It is clear from the direct involvement of Satan and the increased activity of demons that the devil marshaled his forces to stand against Christ during His incarnation. The Gospels reveal much about Satan's ability to oppress human beings, to cause disease, and even to control individuals who open themselves to satanic influence. In every direct confrontation between Satan and Jesus, the devil was defeated by the Lord. However, Satan's grip on God's people was made evident in their ultimate rejection of Jesus as the Messiah: the Crucifixion.

Satan in the book of Acts. Satan's intensified activity continued as he worked to corrupt the Christian church from within (5:3; 13:10) and to prevent people from responding to the gospel (26:18). Satan's opposition to the gospel continues to this day.

Satan in the Epistles *(Romans—Jude).* The letters of instruction written by the leaders of the early church provide Scripture's clearest teachings about Satan and his methods of attacking believers and how believers can withstand those attacks. There is no doubt that Satan is a personal being, an individual who leads other fallen angels in a struggle against God and who is openly hostile to God's people. Understanding and acting on the teachings of the New Testament letters is vital if we are to avoid the traps set by this evil angel, if we are to break free of the attitudes he encourages in us, just as he encouraged them in Eve so long ago.

Satan in Revelation. The book of Revelation depicts the final triumph of God over evil in the entire universe. As history draws to a close, the warfare that had been limited to the spiritual realm will spill over into our world, as visible demonic forces are released. But Satan's frantic struggle is in vain: Satan and the angels who have followed him are condemned to eternal punishment by God, never to trouble humanity again.

But all this lies ahead. We need to return to Eden, where Satan introduced our race and world to evil, in order to see how God responded to Satan's apparent victory.

GOD'S RESPONSE TO SATAN'S SUCCESS IN EDEN

God did not respond to Satan's achievement by turning against the human race. On the contrary, God set in operation a plan to redeem humankind! Our confidence in this wonderful truth is rooted in what the Bible tells us about human beings and about God.

GOD CONTINUED TO CARE FOR HUMAN BEINGS

We still bear God's image and likeness (Genesis 9:6; James 3:9). One of the most basic questions human beings have asked is Who are we? What makes human beings unique?

We continue to give evidence of God's image and likeness. In the last hundred years, of course, the cultural notion that human beings somehow evolved from previous living creatures, which themselves originated in random combinations of simple compounds, has come to be commonly accepted. This has made possible theories which explain wrong moral choices, and even criminal behavior, as simply a residue of mankind's "animal origin"—never mind the fact that animals hardly behave toward their own as human beings do. But no animal origin theory can explain our capacities to appreciate beauty, to create and invent, or to love selflessly on occasion.

We sense the existence of a spiritual realm. The fact that human beings are aware of a spiritual realm may be one cause for the current fascination with angels and demons, if not with God Himself. Somehow we sense that this world cannot be all there is, that the meaning of our individual existences cannot be found or summed up in the few brief decades we live here on earth. There simply must be more to life, more to existence, than this. Stories of angels and demons seem to open up the world beyond to our speculation.

We seek ultimate answers in the spiritual realm. The Bible's revelation of the spiritual realm which lies beside or beyond ours affirms what we sense intuitively. Scripture strikingly unveils events and personalities in that spiritual realm and thereby explains much of what happens to us here and now!

We wonder, Where does evil came from? How can a world that is so good be filled at times with such suffering and tragedy? The Bible has an answer. An angel called Lucifer once sinned in the spiritual realm, and evil was born within him.

GOD CAME TO THE AID OF ADAM AND EVE   (Genesis 3:8–22)

As we return to Genesis 3, we make the amazing discovery that the God whom Adam and Eve had rejected did not abandon them!

God took the initiative (Genesis 3:8, 9). Our first indication of God's continuing love is that after the fateful choice had been made, God went looking for Adam and Eve (3:8, 9). They hardly looked for Him—they now feared Him.

God covered their nakedness (Genesis 3:21). Our second indication of God's continuing love is that God, after spelling out the consequences of the first pair's choices (Gen. 3:14–19), made "tunics of skin, and clothed them" (3:21). This has often been pointed to as history's first sacrifice, for the life of animals was taken to provide a covering that made it possible for the first human beings to stand in

God's presence. Adam and Eve declared their independence, but God was unwilling to let them go on alone. He was intent on remaining with them, to be there should they turn back to Him.

These creatures, these persons—who alone in all of creation had been made in God's own image and likeness—were precious to the Lord. They were too precious for Him

to abandon, in spite of the fact that by choosing independence they had abandoned Him.

God sent Adam and Eve from Eden (*Genesis 3:22–24*). Our third indication of God's continuing love is that He was determined to keep Adam and Eve from taking "also of the tree of life" to "eat, and live forever." So God sent Adam and Eve out of the garden. The Bible says, "He drove out the man," but adds that "He placed cherubim at the east of the garden of Eden, and a flaming sword which turned every way, to guard the way to the tree of life."

It's easy to misunderstand this verse. God didn't send Adam from the garden to punish him, but to protect him. How horrible an endless life would have been for the first pair! As millennium after millennium rolled on, Adam and Eve would be forced to witness the awful results of their choice in the cruelty and the suffering, the wars and the miseries, that life was destined to bring to creatures unwilling to live in submission to God.

God's angel guards our way home (*Genesis 3:24*). The cherubim, of the same order of powerful angels as Satan, were not placed to the east of Eden in order to keep Adam *away from* the Tree of Life, but to *keep the way open* for him and for us.

Satan corrupted the human race, but neither he nor any dark angel we meet—in Scripture or in man's imagination—will ever be able to isolate us from God's redeeming love. God's angels guard the way home, and God's own Son acted in history to open completely, for you and me, the way to eternal life.

CHAPTER 2

THE MYSTERY ANGEL:

THE ANGEL OF THE LORD IN HEBREW HISTORY

Genesis 16; Exodus 3; additional Old Testament passages

aint Gemma Galgani (1878–1903) claimed to see her guardian angel constantly. They spoke together and prayed together. At age 22, Gemma was surprised to learn that not every Christian sees their guardian angel, as she herself did.

There's no indication in Scripture that every believer can expect to encounter angels. In fact, Scripture's next mention of an angel encounter after Eden doesn't occur until Genesis 16, many years after Satan's appearance to Eve in the Garden of Eden (see chapter 1).

When the next angel appears, it is to a young and pregnant Egyptian slave woman, who was slumped in despair in the desert. The young woman, named Hagar, was fleeing in fear from Abraham's wife and, though she was traveling toward Egypt, she had nowhere to turn. It's no wonder that her heart seemed about to break from hopelessness.

THE ANGEL OF THE LORD

What is special about this angel encounter is not only its setting, but the fact that the angel who appeared to Hagar is truly the Bible's Mystery Angel. He is called the "Angel of the Lord," and he appears frequently in the

Old Testament. There's something very special about each of these occurrences, and something even more special about the angel's identity.

THE ANGEL OF THE LORD: SCRIPTURE'S PREMIER "GOOD" ANGEL

Let's note first of all that the Bible's angel stories establish a spiritual realm lying above or alongside the material. Just as God created the material universe and populated it with living creatures, so God created beings to live in the spiritual realm. Satan is one of those beings, an angel of an order called cherubim. But Satan became proud and rebelled against God. His attitude of pride and rebellion infected Adam and Eve and, through them, our race.

In Genesis 16 we meet a being who is identified as the Angel of the Lord—a being from the same spiritual realm as that of Satan, but who is "of the Lord," an angel who does not act independently, but who acts in complete harmony with the will of God.

Satan is Scripture's premier "bad" angel. We can best begin to understand the Angel of the Lord by viewing him as Scripture's premier "good" angel.

THE ANGEL OF THE LORD DISPLAYED SPECIAL KNOWLEDGE   *(Genesis 16:8)*

Not only do we learn a number of things about angels from Hagar's brief encounter with the Angel of the Lord, we also confront the mystery of this angel's unique identity. Notice in the Genesis 16 (NKJV) text:

And He [the Angel of the Lord] **said, "Hagar, Sarai's maid. . . ."** *This angel knew exactly who Hagar was, both her name and her identity as Sarah's maid. While we cannot see into the spiritual realm, angels can view what is happening in our realm.*

"where have you come from, and where are you going?" *The question was not asked out of ignorance, but with an intent to involve Hagar in a conversation that would engage her mind and heart. The angel succeeded, for Hagar answered,*

"I am fleeing from the presence of my mistress Sarai." *Hagar did not answer the second question. She was fleeing from Sarah, not heading toward any particular destination. How like Hagar we often are!*

THE ANGEL OF THE LORD SPOKE WITH GOD'S OWN AUTHORITY *(Genesis 16:9–12)*

The Angel of the LORD said to her, "Return to your mistress, and submit yourself under her hand" (v. 9). *This is not a suggestion, but a command. This angel spoke for and with the authority of God. Note that this command provided guidance. Hagar did not know where she was going or what to do, but the angel knew what she was to do (return) and how she was to go about doing it (accept the submissive role appropriate to her position in the family).*

Then the Angel of the LORD said to her, "I will multiply your descendants exceedingly, so that they shall not be counted for multitude" (v. 10). *The Angel of the Lord can guarantee the future! The words "I will" assumed not just knowledge of the future, but actual control of the future insofar as Hagar's child was concerned.*
The Angel of the Lord then proceeded to confirm Hagar's pregnancy, to name her child, and to describe her son's future.

THE ANGEL OF THE LORD MIGHT HAVE BEEN GOD CLOAKED AS AN ANGEL *(Genesis 16:13)*

Then she called the name of the LORD who spoke to her, You-Are-the-God-Who-Sees; for she said, "Have I also here seen Him who sees me?" (v. 13). *Hagar, recognizing this angel's inherent authority, identified him not as an angel, but as the Lord himself! Hagar was convinced that the Angel of the Lord was more than an angel, that in meeting him she met God cloaked in angelic form.*

The Angel of the Lord might be a theophany. Hagar's conclusion, that her experience of the Angel of the Lord was a theophany—an appearance of God in human or angel form—has been accepted by many Bible scholars. Others argue that the Angel of the Lord is one of the special "named" angels of Scripture, one who is so intimate with God that his words can be considered those of God Himself. While other angels who appear to human beings display knowledge of what happens in the material realm and serve as God's messengers, no other angel makes promises as if he were God Himself. Only the Angel of the Lord makes first person pronouncements about the future, such as "I will multiply your descendants" (see also Judg. 2:1).

This, of course, is why the Angel of the Lord truly is a mystery angel. Is he simply an angelic high ambassador, who carries out his commission by speaking for God in the first person in order to underline the certainty of his promises? Or is the Angel of the Lord an earthly visitation of God Himself cloaked as an angel?

Some verses distinguish between the Angel of the Lord and God. On the one hand, the Bible seems to suggest that the Angel of the Lord and God are distinct. In Zechariah 1:12 the Angel of the Lord prayed to the "LORD of hosts" for the city of Jerusalem. Later (Zech. 3:1–2), the Angel of the Lord seems to speak to a separate person he calls "Lord." How can more than one being be "the Lord"?

Many passages identify the Angel of the Lord as God. On the other hand, in many of his appearances throughout sacred history this angel is presented as the Lord Himself, as the writer of Genesis apparently does in 16:3. It was the Angel of the Lord who appeared to Moses in the burning bush (Ex. 3:2), yet the text almost immediately states that "God" spoke to Moses (Ex. 3:4) and quotes Him as saying, "I am the God of your father—the God of Abraham, the God of Isaac, and the God of Jacob" (Ex. 3:16). The being who commissioned Gideon to save his people is identified as the Angel of the Lord in Judges 6:12, and as the Lord in 6:14. It is also significant that while the New Testament mentions "*an* angel of the Lord," the Old Testament's "*the* Angel of the Lord" is absent. The strong implication is that in most cases the Angel of the Lord is indeed the Lord Himself, cloaked in a way that permits human beings to experience His presence.

What is more, the appearances of the Angel of the Lord are closely linked with a significant feature of the Old Testament: the unique covenant promises which God made to one man.

GOD'S COVENANT WITH ABRAHAM

To understand the significance of the appearances of the Angel of the Lord, we need to understand the special relationship that God established with a man named Abram, whom we know better as Abraham.

GOD MADE COVENANT PROMISES   (Genesis 12:1–3)

God's relationship with Abraham has its roots in Genesis 12. There we're told that God appeared to a man named Abram and told him to leave the city of Ur and go to a land God would show him. Genesis 12 also records a series of stunning promises, which are so significant that they give shape and form to the entire Old Testament. God told Abram:

I will make you a great nation;
I will bless you

And make your name great;
And you shall be a blessing.
I will bless those who bless you,
And I will curse him who curses
   you;
And in you all the families of the
   earth
   shall be blessed.

Genesis 12:2, 3

A little later God adds, "To your descendants I will give this land" (12:7). (We know this land today as Israel or Palestine.) These promises were soon formalized as a contract guaranteed by God. The name for this contract is b^{e}rit, or covenant (Gen. 15:1–16).

In one sense, the rest of the Old Testament is the story of how God has been faithful to those promises, which culminate in Jesus Christ. As we will see, the Angel of the Lord plays a significant role in guaranteeing the covenant promises.

THE RECIPIENT OF THE COVENANT PROMISES

Today Abram is better known as Abraham, and his descendants as the Jews—the "chosen people" of the Old Testament. However, some 4,000 years ago Abraham was simply a wealthy merchant in the city-state of Ur. He traded everything he had for flocks and herds to become a wanderer after God in a beautiful but underpopulated district known as Canaan. Abraham was very much like many thousands of others in the wealthier classes of the ancient world. Why, then, would God choose to make promises to Abraham?

It's common to assume that God chooses to bless individuals because they are in some way better or have higher morals than others. Joshua later reminds Abraham's descendants of God's words: "Your fathers, including Terah, the father of Abraham and the father of Nahor, dwelt on the other side of the River in old times; and they served [worshiped] other gods" (Josh. 24:2). When God first approached Abraham he was, like others, an

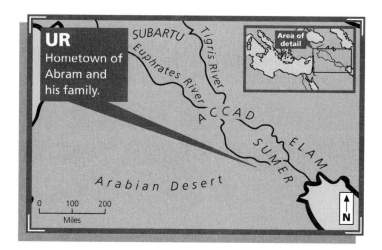

UR
Hometown of Abram and his family.

SUBARTU

Euphrates River

Tigris River

Area of detail

ACCAD

ELAM

SUMER

Arabian Desert

0   100   200
Miles

N

idolater in rebellion against the true God; yet God chose to love him and give him the wonderful promises we've just read.

In a sense, the question Why Abraham? is really Why anyone? Why would God make great and wonderful promises to any member of a race that has rebelled and declared independence from Him? Yet God did make promises to Abraham, and in Christ God has made promises to you and me—not because we are better than others, but simply because God has chosen to love us. When we respond to God's promises with simple faith, as Abraham did, all the wonderful promises made in Christ become ours.

THE PROBLEM OF ABRAHAM'S CHILDLESSNESS (Genesis 16:1–6)

The fulfillment of God's promise to Abraham depended on his having children—and Abraham and Sarah had none. In another encounter with God, the Lord told Abraham, "To your descendants *I have given* this land" (Gen. 15:18; italics mine). The verb tense reminds us that God's promises, once made, are as good as kept! But Abraham was eighty-five years old at the time the words in Genesis 15 were spoken, and his wife Sarah, then 75, was barren.

The human solution (Genesis 16:1–3). The reference to descendants certainly troubled Abra-

ham and his wife. How could God keep His promise to give the land to their descendants when they had no children?

Abraham and Sarah seem to have struggled with this problem for some time. Finally, after they had been in Canaan for ten years (16:3), Sarah suggested a solution. She would give her maid, Hagar, to Abraham as a surrogate wife! Abraham could impregnate Sarah's Egyptian slave, and any child Hagar bore would legally be Sarah's and Abraham's!

BIBLE BACKGROUND:
WAS SARAH'S SOLUTION IMMORAL?

Well-established custom regulated situations in which a childless wife provided her husband with a servant surrogate in order to have children by her. Here are several relevant quotes from ancient documents which span two millennia.

Hammurabi's Code, #146: "When a free man married a priestess and she gave a female slave to her husband and she has then borne children, if later that female slave has claimed equality with her mistress because she bore children, her mistress may not sell her; she may mark her with the slave-mark and count her among the slaves."

A text from Nuzi: "If Gilimninu will not bear children, Gilimninu shall take a woman of N/Lullu land as a wife for Shennima."

In an Assyrian marriage contract: "Laqipum took Hatala, the daughter of Enissru. In the country Laqipum shall not take another, but in Ashshur he may take a priestess. If within two years she has not procured offspring for him, only she may buy a maidservant and even later on, after she procures somehow an infant for him, she may sell her wherever she pleases."

In a Neo-Assyrian text: "If Subetu does not conceive and does not give birth, she may take a maidservant as a substitute in her position she may place her. Subetu will [thus] bring sons into being and the sons will be her sons. If she loves [the maidservant] she may keep her. If she hates her she may sell her."

The weakness of the human solution (Genesis 16:4–6). There's no indication that either Abraham or Sarah asked the Lord to approve their plan. Sarah simply urged Abraham to adopt their culture's approach and so solve the problem. They undertook to resolve the mystery of how God would provide descendants by taking care of things for Him!

This decision was rooted in an attitude which Satan spread to our race. We human beings want to be independent, we want to work things out our way; and if God isn't willing to meet our timetable, too often we'll go ahead without Him.

At first, the solution Sarah came up with seemed to work. In fact, her solution has even affected rabbinic rulings. According to one school of rabbis, if a couple is childless after ten years—the length of time Abraham and Sarah lived childless in Canaan (Gen. 16:3)—they may, or even must, divorce so the husband can marry again and procreate! But in the historical context, Sarah's solution was clearly flawed. Yes, Hagar became pregnant, but her pregnancy introduced deep hostilities into the family.

The consequences of the human solution (Genesis 16:4–6). The Bible tells us that Hagar showed contempt for Sarah. It was clear that Abraham was able to sire children, so Sarah

must be responsible for the couple's childlessness. The fact that Hagar was an Egyptian probably intensified her contempt for her barren mistress. A number of indicators—including the variety of amulets intended to increase fertility discovered by Egyptologists, and the popularity of the hippopotamus fertility goddess Taweret—underscore the importance that Egyptian women placed on having children. In fact, they yearned for as many as possible, and we have a document from one husband who boasted that his wife had borne him 70! Hagar might have been Sarah's slave, but the fact that she had conceived and Sarah could not made Hagar superior in her own eyes.

For her part, Sarah resented Hagar and her attitude. And Sarah began to blame Abraham (16:5). Now it was *his* fault, even though the plan had been Sarah's all along.

Following the precedents of the time, Abraham reminded Sarah that Hagar's primary identity was as her slave, not his surrogate wife (16:6). Thus, Sarah had a legal right to treat Hagar as she wished—and the text tells us that "Sarah dealt harshly with her." In fact, Sarah treated Hagar so harshly that she fled into the wilderness in despair. It was in the wilderness near Canaan's border with Egypt, by a "spring on the way to Shur," that the Mystery Angel, "the Angel of the LORD," appeared and spoke to the lonely and frightened Egyptian girl.

THE SIGNIFICANCE OF THE ANGEL'S NAME   (Exodus 3:1–15)

Genesis 16 contains the first mention in Scripture of the Angel of the Lord, that mysterious figure who appears again and again through the Old Testament era. Hagar's experience is closely linked with the other encounters; but before we can see the link, we need to know the significance of the angel's name.

THE SPECIALNESS OF THE NAME "LORD" (YAHWEH)

The Old Testament makes reference to an "Angel of God" only six times. In one passage the angel identifies himself as "the God of Bethel" (Gen. 31:11, 13). Three of the six occurrences of the phrase "Angel of God" are in passages where the angel is also called the Angel of the Lord (Judg. 6:20; 13:6, 9). Reference to the "Angel of the Lord" occurs 68 times in 64 verses! Why is "Angel of the Lord" preferred to "Angel of God?"

In the Old Testament, the Hebrew word for "God" is 'el. This is a term peoples throughout the Ancient Near East used to designate deity. However, where we find the English word "Lord" in the Old Testament, the Hebrew text has a very different word, which is comprised of four letters and pronounced as in English "Yahweh" (or Jehovah). This name is so special, so sacred, that orthodox Jews read "Adonai" or use the word "Hashem," which means, "the Name," rather than pronounce it.

THE MEANING OF "LORD" (Exodus 1—3)

The true meaning of this unique name is explained in the third appearance of the Angel of the Lord in Scripture.

Abraham's descendants were enslaved in Egypt (Exodus 1:8–22). Centuries had passed since God made his great promises to Abraham. Abraham and Sarah did have a son together, named Isaac. When a famine struck Canaan, Abraham's great-grandchildren moved to Egypt. There, safe within the borders of one of the ancient world's major powers, Abraham's descendants multiplied. In time, their numbers became so great that the pharaoh of Egypt felt threatened and decided to enslave the Jewish people. Almost four hundred years after their entry into Egypt, the Jewish people—worn out by toil and oppression—cried out to the God of their forefathers. God responded by giving a dream to a man named Moses—a dream of winning freedom for his distressed brothers and sisters.

God chose Moses to rescue Abraham's descendants (Exodus 2—3). The story of Moses is one of the most familiar stories told in Scripture. We know how he was adopted by Pharaoh's daughter and educated as a prince. We know that when Moses tried to follow his dream he was forced to flee Egypt. And we know that for 40 years Moses led the simple life of a shepherd in the wilderness of Sinai, his dream dead.

God revealed Himself to Moses (Exodus 3:1–6). One day Moses saw a bush engulfed in flames; it burned brightly, but was unconsumed. When Moses approached, the Angel of the Lord spoke to him from the midst of the flames (3:2). The voice, now identifying Himself as the "God of your father" (3:6), called Moses back to his dream and commissioned Moses to confront Pharaoh and demand that Israel be freed from bondage.

However, 40 years of tending sheep in the wilderness had done more than cause Moses' dream to die; it drained Moses of his confidence, and it left him humbled and empty. So Moses objected: "Who am I that I should go to Pharaoh, and that I should bring the children of Israel out of Egypt?" (Ex. 3:11).

God responded by promising to be with Moses in the coming adventure, but Moses still hesitated. What could he say when he came to Egypt to tell his people of his mission? What could he tell them about this God of their fathers? Who would believe Moses' claim that God had spoken to him?

God revealed the meaning of the name "Lord" (Exodus 3:13–14). God's answer is found in one of the most significant verses in the entire Bible: "I AM WHO I AM. . . . Thus you shall say to the children of Israel, 'I AM' has sent you' " (3:14).

The name God announced was the name Yahweh (or Jehovah). It is constructed on the root of the Hebrew verb "to be," and is therefore translated "I AM" here. However, there is more to this special name of God than a mere statement of existence. The name Yahweh is God's *personal name,* it is not a noun which serves as a designation for "God" ('el is the Hebrew noun for "God" or "god"). Like other personal names in Scripture, "Yahweh" reveals something about the essence, nature, and character of the individual who bears it.

Perhaps the best way to paraphrase the meaning of God's name is to say that Yahweh means "The God Who Is Always Present." Our God was present at the Creation—indeed, He is the Creator. Our God was present with Adam and Eve in the Garden and protected them even after they sinned. God was present with Abraham and gave him wonderful promises. Now God tells Moses that He, the God of history past and history yet to come, is present with him also, and God will be present as Moses confronts Egypt's ruler and leads Israel out of the land of servitude. "This is My name forever," God told Moses (Ex. 3:15). This is the way that God is to be known and experienced by His people, as One Who Is Always Present. He is the I AM, here right now, and He is always involved in the lives of His people.

God will demonstrate that He is always present (*Exodus 3:19–21*). The Lord told Moses that He will perform wondrous miracles in order to free Israel. God explained that even though he had spoken to Abraham and Isaac and Jacob, "by My name LORD [Yahweh] I was not known to them" (Ex. 6:3). It's not that the name Yahweh is not to be found in Genesis; it is there (Gen. 16) in the name of the "Angel of the Lord" (the Angel of Yahweh).

God's point is that while Israel's forefathers had believed in Him, they had not experienced Him as the children of Israel were about to. The miracles that were to win Israel's freedom would leave no doubt that God truly *was* "present." God was there, acting for His people in totally unmistakable ways.

Today, we are to remember the name that God says is His "forever." The God who showed Himself present when He freed Israel from slavery is present with us now! And we too are to experience Him as One Who Is Present—present and active in our lives.

Perhaps the significance of the name given the Angel of Yehovah is this: He is the Angel of the Lord's Presence (see Isa. 63:9). He is the Angel who expresses the active involvement of God in the affairs of those to whom He appears.

YAHWEH AND THE COVENANT WITH ABRAHAM

Gerard Van Groningen notes that the name Yahweh:

particularly stresses the absolute faithfulness of God. God had promised the patriarchs that he would be their God, and that he would be with them, would deliver and bless them, keep them, and give them a land as a place of service and inheritance. Moses is told by God that Israel is about to behold and experience the unchangeableness of God as he steadfastly and wonderfully remembers his word and executes it to the fullest degree. . . . Yahweh, then, is the name par excellence of Israel's God. As Yahweh he is a faithful covenant God who, having given his Word of love and life, keeps that Word by bestowing love and life abundantly on his own (*Baker Encyclopedia of the Bible, Vol. 2,* p. 884).

Since Yahweh is the name of God most closely associated with the carrying out of His covenant promises, it is not surprising that when the Angel of the Lord appears, his involvement in the situation has a direct, and sometimes dramatic, link to God's covenant with Abraham and his descendants. We trace this feature of the Angel's appearances throughout the Old Testament beginning on page 23. However, let us first give consideration to another important matter with respect to God's personal name, one which will be especially significant in the New Testament.

THE RELATIONSHIP OF YAHWEH AND JESUS

Theologians have long been aware that God the Son is the person of the Trinity most closely linked to God's self-revelation. Hebrews 1:2 reminds us that while God spoke to human beings in many ways in earlier times, He "has in these last days spoken to us by His Son."

Jesus as the Word (John 1:1–3). In the first chapter of his Gospel, John affirms that Jesus is the *Logos,* the Greek term for "Word." Through John the *Logos* is revealed to *be* God (1:1–3). What's more, the Word is the second person of the Trinity, who became incarnate in Jesus. As John says, "the Word became flesh and dwelt among us, and we beheld His glory" (1:14).

In pre-Christian rabbinic thought, the sages began to realize that since God is personal, some personal mediator was necessary if humankind was to know God in a personal way. The Aramaic term *Memra,* meaning "word," was chosen for this mediator, and the belief developed that the *Memra* had created the world, had appeared to Abraham and Moses, and had worked the miracles that freed Israel from Egypt. In this, rabbinic thought was close to the special revelation about the Mediator given by the apostle John.

Jesus claimed to be the Lord (John 8:58). Since Christ is the eternal Word, the eternal expression and revelation of God's person, many theologians argue that the Old Testament name "Yahweh" specifies the second person of the Trinity—Jesus, the Son, the eternal Word.

Christ himself seems to support this view. John 8 records a lengthy dialogue Jesus had with some antagonistic Pharisees. During the course of their debate, Christ boldly confronted those influential men, who had a reputation for scrupulously keeping the letter of the Law. As the confrontation continued, the Pharisees claimed Abraham as their father. Jesus refuted their claim, stating that they followed their father the devil, since they lived independent lives outside of God's will. Otherwise, they would have heard and responded to God's words spoken by Jesus.

Challenged by the Pharisees, who understood this to be a claim of superiority over Abraham, Jesus announced that Abraham had looked forward to His coming and added, "Most assuredly, I say to you, before Abraham was, I AM" (8:58). Was Jesus really claiming to be the I AM, Yahweh of the Old Testament? His listeners

clearly understood Him this way. John says that they "took up stones to throw at Him" (8:59).

Stoning was a method of execution in that society. In a first-century rabbinic interpretation of Jewish Law, a group which was so incensed by a religious crime that they could not help themselves could legally execute the guilty person—without trial! The Pharisees were ready to kill Jesus for the crime of blasphemy. It was clearly blasphemy for a human being to claim to be God!

At least it would have been blasphemy for any other human being to make that claim. Jesus could make such a claim because He was God come in human flesh. Jesus could claim to be the I AM of the Old Testament, the covenant-keeping, faithful Yahweh of sacred history—because He was.

The Angel of the Lord as a preincarnation visitation of earth by Christ. So the mystery about the Old Testament's Mystery Angel deepens, or is perhaps solved. Was the Angel of the Lord Yahweh Himself appearing cloaked as an angel? And if so, was the Angel of the Lord an appearance of Christ before His incarnation as Jesus of Nazareth? Yes, it is possibly, even probably, so. An awareness of this adds even more significance to each appearance of the Angel of the Lord in the Old Testament. He is the Lord Himself, cloaked as an angel, and personally present to see that His covenant promises to Israel are faithfully fulfilled.

OLD TESTAMENT APPEARANCES OF THE ANGEL OF THE LORD

There is much to learn from a study of the appearances of the Angel of the Lord to human beings. We need to examine each Old Testament account individually.

THE ANGEL OF THE LORD APPEARED TO HAGAR
(Genesis 16)

God's compassion. Since Hagar was only an Egyptian slave in the household of Abraham and not a member of his family, she was not a recipient of God's covenant promises. Yet God still cared for the lost and lonely Egyptian girl. The angel's words, "the LORD has heard your affliction" (Gen. 16:11), show that God cared then and cares today about people who experience hurt, those outside the household of faith, as well as those within.

The angel's words to Hagar provided the direction and guidance she needed, and Hagar heeded his words. We can never assume that God is indifferent to the needs of any human being. He is present, with words of direction and guidance for everyone who is willing to hear.

The covenant connection (*Genesis 21:13*). At the same time, there is a link to God's covenant with Abraham in this appearance. Hagar was pregnant with Abraham's son, Ishmael. Some 15 years later, Hagar and her teenage son were sent away from the tents where Abraham and Sarah lived with their own son, Isaac. Still, God promised Abraham,

"I will also make a nation of the son of the bondwoman, because he is your seed" (21:13).

God's original promises to Abraham included a commitment to make of him a great nation, to bless him, and to make his name great. Today, the descendants of Ishmael—the Arab peoples—together with Jews and Christians look back and honor Abraham as their father. Abraham is considered a great man by the adherents of three great world religions—Islam, Judaism, and Christianity.

The meaning of the Angel of the Lord's appearance for Israel and for us. The Angel of the Lord not only showed compassion for Hagar; he also showed how committed God is to fulfilling every covenant promise He made. We can count on the Lord to do more for us than we can ask or imagine.

THE ANGEL OF THE LORD APPEARED TO ABRAHAM
(Genesis 22:22, 23)

God tested Abraham's faith in His trustworthiness (*Genesis 22:1–2*). When Isaac, the son of Abraham and Sarah, was nearly grown, God commanded Abraham to sacrifice Isaac on Mount Moriah (where Solomon later erected the Jerusalem temple; 2 Chron. 3:1). We can hardly imagine the thoughts that must have swirled about in Abraham's mind. How unlike God this was! How could God order the death of the son through whom He intended to fulfill the covenant promises?

The covenant connection (*Genesis 22:3–13*). Abraham obeyed and led his son Isaac to the place God had ordained for the sacrifice. Along the way, we are given a significant insight into Abraham's faith in God. Although Abraham's first reaction was one of surprise and uncertainty, by the time he drew near Mount Moriah, some three days' journey from his camp, he was convinced that God would somehow solve the problem. He told the men

The Angel of the Lord and Hagar.

traveling with him to wait, and said, "Stay here with the donkey; the lad and I will go yonder and worship, and *we will come back to you*" (22:5; emphasis added). Hebrews 11:19 suggests that Abraham spoke this way because he had absolute confidence that "God was able to raise him [Isaac] up, even from the dead." Abraham knew that God would keep the promises He had made, whatever it took.

When the two reached the top of the mountain, Abraham laid out the implements for sacrifice and bound his son. Just as Abraham was about to plunge a knife into Isaac, "the Angel of the LORD called to him from heaven" and said, "Do not lay your hand on the lad, or do anything to him." Then Abraham looked up, saw a ram caught in a thicket, and offered up the ram in place of his son (22:11–13).

This event foreshadows Christ's sacrifice on Calvary (John 3:16). How significant it is that God did not demand the ultimate sacrifice from Abraham, but that He Himself provided an animal to take the place of Isaac. Nevertheless, if God was to fulfill His covenant promise to bless all the peoples of the earth through Abraham's descendants, there is one whom He *could not* spare. The Bible tells us: "For God so loved the world that He gave His only begotten Son, that whoever believes in Him should not perish but have everlasting life" (John 3:16). What God would not permit Abraham to sacrifice—his son—God Himself sacrificed—for us.

The meaning of the Angel of the Lord's appearance for Israel and for us. God had been present with Abraham, in all his turmoil and uncertainty, from the outset. Even before the Angel of the Lord acted at the critical moment, Abraham was sure that God would somehow keep the promises He had made. As the centuries passed, Israel could look back on this event and, no matter how dark the day, remain confident that God would remain faithful to Abraham's descendants.

God is present with us in our turmoil. He is with us in our uncertainty. How wonderful

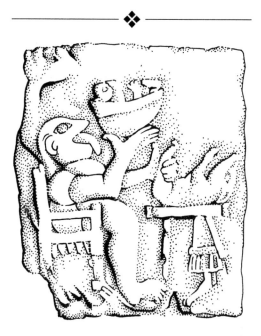

BIBLE BACKGROUND

This drawing from a carved relief found at Pozo Moro shows the bloodthirsty Canaanite god Mot. As he grasps a pig with his left hand, Mot has his head thrown back to swallow a child stuffed into a bowl. The scene reminds us of the deity's words reported in a Canaanite myth: "My soul longs to kill, to kill. My desire is to kill many. Behold, my two hands hold food. Behold they are greedy." What a contrast to Scripture's covenant God of love as He revealed Himself in His appearance to Abraham and Isaac as the Angel of the Lord!

to know that we, too, can trust God fully, and that the God Who Is Always Present will, at the right moment, reveal His solution to our problems!

THE ANGEL OF THE LORD
APPEARED TO MOSES
(Exodus 1—3)

The covenant connection (Exodus 1:15, 16). When the Angel of the Lord appeared to Moses, the Israelites were enslaved in Egypt.

Pharaoh was so committed to the extermination of the Israelites as a people that he issued a command that all Hebrew males should be killed as soon as they were born. These slaves were the descendants of Abraham, to whom God had made binding promises. Surely He must act!

The angel revived Moses' dream (*Exodus 3:7–10*). Moses' youthful dream of freeing the Israelites had died, and his confidence drained, during his 40 years of tending sheep in the wilderness; but the Angel of the Lord again called Moses to that very task and gave the dead dream new life. He also replaced Moses' dwindled self-confidence with fresh confidence in the Lord.

The angel promised God's active presence (*Exodus 3:12–20*). At this time, God revealed His personal name to Moses and announced that this was the name by which His people are to know Him forever. What's more, God promised His active involvement: Through a series of miracles He would bring Israel out of Egypt and prove how committed He was to keeping His covenant promises. The descendants of Abraham were not destined to live as a slave people. God fully intended to keep His promises by freeing the Israelites and giving them the land promised to Abraham's offspring.

The meaning of the Angel of the Lord's appearance for Israel and for us. Forever after, Israel was to look back on the Exodus as the defining moment when God redeemed them and made them His people. In a significant way, the Israelites define God by His delivering them from Egypt. No wonder God is so often called "Redeemer" and "Deliverer" in the Old Testament!

Today the God Who Is Always Present can call our dreams to life long after we have given them up for dead. The Lord has committed Himself to us in Christ and, as we focus on who He is and on His powerful presence with us, we can face the future with restored confidence—restored because our confidence is no longer in ourselves or our abilities, but in the power of a God who is present with us every moment of every day.

THE ANGEL OF THE LORD APPEARED TO BALAAM
(*Numbers 22:22–35*)

The covenant connection (*Numbers 22:1–6*). Balaam was a pagan seer, or prophet. As Israel traveled from Egypt toward the promised land, Balak, the ruler of a nation through which Israel needed to pass, hired Balaam to curse Israel. However, among the covenant promises God had made to Israel was His commitment to bless and not curse (Gen. 12:2). Although Balaam was warned by God in a dream not to go (Num. 22:12), he was greedy for the gold he'd been offered. After begging for permission a second time, Balaam set out to meet Balak and fulfill the commission.

The Angel of the Lord confronted and limited Balaam (*Numbers 22:22–35*). Along the way, Balaam's donkey balked three times, which infuriated the pagan prophet. Balaam's eyes were then opened and he saw the Angel of the Lord standing in the way with a drawn sword, ready to kill him. Terrified, Balaam confessed, "I have sinned"; and he offered to go back home if the angel was displeased with him (22:34). Balaam's words were hypocritical. He already knew God did not want him to go to Balak, but Balaam had made his choice. So the Angel of the Lord permitted Balaam to go on and warned him that he must speak only words that God would give him.

The reason for the appearance of the Angel of the Lord at this time was the warning. God intends to bless His covenant people, and no curse directed against them will stand. When Balaam finally arrived and attempted to curse Israel, he was compelled by fear to speak the words that God had given him— words of blessing—which infuriated the king who had hired him.

Balaam attempted to turn God against His people (*Numbers 31:16*). Balaam was still intent on winning the king's gold. Numbers 31:16 tells us that Balaam advised the king to set young women near the Israelite camp to seduce the men and lead them into idolatry. Balaam believed that God would then be forced to turn on His people and destroy them. Instead, the Lord purged the camp of the idolaters (Num. 25:1–11), and He remained completely faithful to His covenant with Abraham.

This is the second time the Angel of the Lord appeared to a pagan (see p. 23), and again the encounter is clearly associated with God's covenant promises. The Angel of the Lord did not turn Balaam back, for God does not override the will of humans. However, the angel made it very clear to Balaam what God's will was and placed restrictions on what Balaam could do, even if he still insisted on his own way; and Balaam, intent on material gain, did just that. In the end, all of his attempts to sabotage Israel failed, and Joshua 13:22 tells us that when Israel invaded his homeland, Balaam was killed.

The meaning of the Angel of the Lord's appearance for Israel and for us. God is present with those who do not believe, as well as with those who do. He speaks to the consciences of human beings in an attempt to limit their behavior, but God does not force anyone to do what is right. When anyone decides to harm God's people, however, God will become actively involved on their behalf. As for the Balaams around us, there are consequences that invariably follow for anyone who chooses his own way rather than God's.

There are also consequences for believers who insist on their own way. Yet the God who remained faithful to Israel, despite their vulnerability to Balaam's plot, remains committed to you and to me.

THE ANGEL OF THE LORD APPEARED TO SINFUL ISRAEL
(Judges 2:1–7)

God was with His people, and their invasion of Canaan was successful. God kept His promises, but the people of God had neither obeyed the Lord's command to drive out all the peoples who had settled in the land, nor had they rooted out the pagan religions.

The covenant connection. When the Angel of the Lord appeared to an assembly of the Israelites, it was to explain the consequences of their failure to obey God. The original inhabitants of Canaan left in the land by the Israelites would be "thorns" in their side, and the Canaanite gods would be a "snare" to them (Judg. 2:3).

This angel encounter was pivotal if Israel was to understand the limits of its rights under the covenant. Judges 2 tells us that none of the predicted disasters came for some time, "so the people served the LORD all the days of Joshua, and all the days of the elders who outlived Joshua" (2:6, 7). Later, when the people did turn aside to worship pagan deities, God permitted enemy nations to invade the land and oppress His people. The God Who Is Always Present, Yahweh, remained with Israel to discipline them, as well as to bless them.

The meaning of the Angel of the Lord's appearance for Israel and for us. This appearance of the Angel of the Lord reminded the Israelites that any generation of Abraham's descendants would be blessed *if they remained faithful to God.* God's covenant promises remain in force until the end of time, but sin can rob any given generation, or individual, of the blessings that the covenant provides. When Israel groaned under oppression, none were to assume that God had abandoned His covenant people or to accuse God of unfaithfulness to His word. God's covenant promises remain in force, whatever individuals, or even the whole nation, might do.

Today also, God's presence assures His total involvement in our lives. He is committed to us. God not only supervises the outcome when we choose to obey, the Lord also imposes the consequences when we choose to disobey, but in either case, God Himself will never leave us or forsake us (Heb. 13:5).

THE ANGEL OF THE LORD APPEARED TO GIDEON
(Judges 6:11–22)

The covenant connection. In the decades that followed God's announcement of the consequences of Israel's failure to purify the land of idolatry, Israel often turned away from the Lord to worship other gods. Invariably, foreign enemies invaded Israel and oppressed God's people until they turned back to Him. When Israel did turn back, God provided them with deliverers, called "judges." Gideon became one of those judges.

The Angel of the Lord appeared to an insignificant individual *(Judges 6:11–15).* When the Angel of the Lord appeared to Gideon, he was an insignificant farmer, who threshed a few stalks of grain in a sunken winepress for fear that marauding Midianites would see him and take the grain away. Gideon was also a person who doubted the Lord, for when the angel appeared, he asked, "O my Lord, if the LORD is with us, why then has all this happened to us? And where are all His miracles which our fathers told us about?" (6:13).

The Angel of the Lord addressed Gideon as a "mighty man of valor," stunning the frightened young farmer. Despite Gideon's fears and his hesitation, God guided Gideon step by step, and Gideon became the savior of his generation. Once again, God proved faithful to His covenant promises.

The meaning of the Angel of the Lord's appearance for Israel and for us. The God Who Is Always Present understands our weaknesses—and our potential. Gideon wondered where God's miracles were. One of the greatest miracles of all is that the Lord can call and enable weak individuals to do great things for Him. None of us should need miracles as proof that God is always present with us. He is. When we hesitate, the Lord will encourage us. When we are willing to follow, He will lead us step by step to victory. The angel who commissioned Gideon also commissions us, and it is the Lord's presence that enables us to succeed.

THE ANGEL OF THE LORD APPEARED TO MANOAH AND HIS WIFE   *(Judges 13—16)*

The covenant connection. This appearance of the Angel of the Lord also took place during the age of the judges. At that particular time, the Philistines—who had mastered the secrets of smelting and working iron—dominated Palestine and forced the Israelites into the poorest regions. The Angel of the Lord promised Manoah and his wife a son and, at their request, gave them careful instructions concerning how the son was to be brought up (Judg. 13:3, 13–21). Their son, Samson, was to become history's strongest man. Once again, God was about to intervene on behalf of His covenant people.

Samson failed to follow the Lord closely. Tales of Samson's legendary strength have captivated generations of boys and girls. Samson grew up and became a judge in Israel, but he proved willful and unresponsive both to his parent's guidance (cf. Judg. 14:3) and to God's will. Even so, the God who gave Samson his strength enabled him to win many battles against the Philistines.

The meaning of the Angel of the Lord's appearance for Israel and for us. Sometimes God works through flawed individuals. This is particularly helpful to remember when we look at our children and see their faults. We need to follow the example of Manoah and seek instruction from God for rearing our sons and daughters. We also need to remember that the God Who Is Always Present is with us as we bring children into the world and as we seek to bring them up to be godly individuals. Even when our efforts seem to fail, and our children willfully go their own way, we can find comfort and reassurance in the fact that God is present with us—and with them.

THE ANGEL OF THE LORD APPEARED TO KING DAVID
(2 Samuel 24; 1 Chronicles 21:12–18, 30)

After the age of the judges, God set kings over Israel. The greatest of Israel's kings was David, who united the tribes under a central government, unified worship, defeated Israel's enemies, and expanded the size of the territory occupied by the Israelites some ten times.

Although we know David as a deeply spiritual and godly individual, he was not flawless.

The covenant connection. One of David's flaws was revealed when he decided to number Israel, an act which seems to have implied a reliance on numbers rather than on the Lord. Since 2 Samuel 24:1 tells us that the Lord was angry with Israel, it appears that Israel had also begun to rely on military might rather than on the Lord.

When God's prophet let David choose between punishments for his and the nation's unfaithfulness, David chose a plague to be administered by God Himself. David reasoned, "Please let me fall into the hand of the LORD, for His mercies are very great" (1 Chron. 21:13).

The Angel of the Lord stopped the plague (1 Chronicles 21:14–18, 26). God did strike Israel with a plague, but when the destroying angel (see chapter 3) was about to strike Jerusalem, the Angel of the Lord stopped the slaughter. He stood between heaven and earth with a sword drawn, waiting (21:15, 16).

David confessed his sin (1 Chron. 21:17), and God commanded him to erect an altar on the future site of Solomon's temple, where years earlier Abraham had come to sacrifice Isaac (21:18). So David built an altar there and offered sacrifices for sin, "burnt offerings," and sacrifices signifying restored fellowship, "peace offerings" (21:26).

The meaning of the Angel of the Lord's appearance for Israel and for us. As Israel had been shown in the days of the judges, only faithfulness to the Lord could provide the nation with a present experience of the covenant blessings. Even when Israel was unfaithful, God's punishments were not intended to destroy; instead, they were intended to turn God's people away from their sin and lead them back to the place of blessing.

Earlier appearances of the Angel of the Lord underscored God's faithfulness to His covenant promises and established the fact that sin prevents individuals or generations from experiencing covenant blessings. Through David's experience with the Angel of the Lord, Israel learned that confession of sin and sacrifice could restore the nation to a healthy relationship with their ever present God.

It's important to remember that the God Who Is Always Present is with us when we sin. Nothing is hidden from Him, not even motives we struggle to disguise. Although God judges sin, He is never deaf to our appeals. Christ offered the ultimate sacrifice for sins, and so the New Testament promises, "If we confess our sins, He is faithful and just to forgive us our sins and to cleanse us from all unrighteousness" (1 John 1:9).

Like David, we are to be in awe of God and His displeasure, unlike David, we ought never hesitate to approach Him, but should be confident that He will welcome us and forgive.

THE ANGEL OF THE LORD APPEARED TO ELIJAH   *(1 Kings 19:7; 2 Kings 1:3, 15)*

The covenant connection. Elijah is perhaps the Old Testament's premier prophet. He ministered at a time when worship of the Lord was threatened with extinction, while a particularly virulent form of Baal worship was actively promoted by King Ahab and Queen Jezebel. The Angel of the Lord appeared to Elijah three times during this critical period, and Elijah stood, seemingly alone, against the rising tide of paganism that was engulfing Israel.

The Angel of the Lord's first appearance to Elijah *(1 Kings 19)*. The first time the Angel of the Lord appeared to Elijah was after his great victory over hundreds of prophets of the pagan god Baal. This victory lead the people of Israel once again to acknowledge the Lord as the one true God (1 Kings 18:27–40). When the victorious prophet was threatened by Queen Jezebel, he was filled with terror and fled (19:1–4). Finally, utterly exhausted, Elijah collapsed and fell asleep. The Angel of the Lord gently woke him and provided food and drink to strengthen him so that he could continue his flight (19:5–8). Later, the Lord spoke to His despondent, depressed prophet and led him back to his ministry.

The Angel of the Lord's second appearance to Elijah *(2 Kings 1:1–8)*. When the Angel of the Lord appeared to Elijah the second time, he told Elijah to pronounce God's sentence of death on King Ahaziah, the son of Queen Jezebel (1:3). Despite the danger involved in confronting an absolute ruler who wielded power over life and death, Elijah sent the message as he had been commanded.

The Angel of the Lord's third appearance to Elijah *(2 Kings 1:9–17)*. Ahaziah reacted as we might expect: He sent soldiers to bring Elijah to him. These soldiers were destroyed by fire from heaven in answer to Elijah's prayer, as was a second group of 50. The captain of the third group of 50 soldiers sent after Elijah fell on his knees and begged for his life and for the lives of his soldiers. The Angel of the Lord told Elijah not to be afraid, but to go and confront the King. Elijah boldly restated God's judgment, and Ahaziah died.

What an important role the angel of God's presence played in Elijah's life! When Elijah despaired, the Angel of the Lord strengthened him. When Elijah lacked direction, the Angel of the Lord gave him a mission. When that mission seemed to endanger Elijah's life, the Angel of the Lord guaranteed his safety.

Through the ministry of Elijah the immediate threat of Baal worship was turned back, and the people of Israel once again acknowledged the Lord. Our Covenant-keeping God had intervened at the critical moment.

The meaning of the Angel of the Lord's appearances to Elijah for Israel and for us. We are reminded once again of the faithfulness of God to His word. At the same time, we need to remember that the God Who Is Always Present can play many roles in our lives, just as He did in Elijah's. He can and will gently lift us up when we're down, give us purpose when our lives seem empty, and protect us as we do His will.

THE ANGEL OF THE LORD DESTROYED AN ASSYRIAN ARMY
(2 Kings 19:35; Isaiah 37:36)

The covenant connection (2 Kings 18:9–37). In 701 B.C., the fortress cities on the border of Judah had been destroyed, and Jerusalem lay helpless before an invading Assyrian army. The nation was in danger of being wiped out, and any survivors were to be torn from the promised land.

When an Assyrian ambassador demanded Israel's surrender and ridiculed their God, King Hezekiah prayed that the Lord would intervene. He did, and that night the Angel of the Lord put to death 185,000 Assyrians. The Angel of the Lord had judged Israel's enemies and ensured the survival of God's people. As stated in the covenant promises, "I will bless those who bless you, / And I will curse him who curses you" (Gen. 12:3).

Those two aspects of the covenant are celebrated in two psalms. Psalm 35:5, 6 calls on God to judge His people's enemies, saying:

Let them be like chaff before the
   wind,
And let the angel of the LORD chase
   them.
Let their way be dark and slippery,
And Let the angel of the LORD pursue
   them.

Psalm 34:7 describes the role of the Angel of the Lord from the believer's perspective.

The angel of the Lord encamps all
   around those who fear Him,
And delivers them.

The meaning of the Angel of the Lord's appearance for Israel and for us. Throughout history—and to the present day—God has guaranteed the survival of the Jewish people. Our Lord, the One Who Is Always Present, surrounds us also with His love, and He protects us from our enemies.

THE ANGEL OF THE LORD APPEARED TO ZECHARIAH
(Zechariah 3:5; 12:8)

The covenant connection. The disobedience of the Jewish people brought about a devastating invasion. The people of Israel were carried away to Babylon in captivity. Years later, a small company of Jews returned to reestablish a Jewish presence in the Holy Land. Even after the remnant returned, however, they were unable to reestablish Jewish nationhood.

The Angel of the Lord's appearance to Zechariah (Zechariah 3). During those days, the prophet Zechariah was given visions to encourage the Jewish people. Although the time for the full restoration of the nation had not yet arrived, the Angel of the Lord promised that a day would come when the offices of priest and king would be combined in a single person—and that person would fully restore God's people (3:5, 6). Christians see Jesus in this ancient prophecy, for He is identified in the New Testament both as our High Priest, and as the King of kings.

The Old Testament's last mention of the Angel of the Lord is found in Zechariah 12:8, where the prophet looks forward to a day when "the LORD will shield those who live in Jerusalem, so that the feeblest among them will be like David, and the house of David will be like God, like the Angel of the LORD going before them" (NIV).

The meaning of the Angel of the Lord's appearance for Israel and for us. The word spoken by the Angel of the Lord to Israel was "Not yet, but one day." Centuries would pass while Israel awaited the fulfillment of God's covenant promises, but the Angel of the Lord's word to Zechariah still stimulated hope.

It's the same for us today. We wait for Jesus to return, and we are not discouraged as we wait. We know that God is faithful to His promises, and that every promise He has made to us He will surely keep.

SUMMARY

What then can we say about the Angel of the Lord, Scripture's premier "good angel"? The biblical evidence suggests that the Angel of the Lord is, in fact, an appearance of God Himself cloaked in the form of an angel.

The identification of this angel with the name "Yahweh" (or "Jehovah") suggests that each of his appearances is intimately linked with God's covenant promises and with the abiding presence of God Himself with His people.

Christ's identification of Himself with the "I AM" of the Old Testament provides strong evidence that the Angel of the Lord may in fact be Christ, God's eternal Son, appearing in angel form prior to His incarnation as Jesus. Indeed, there is no mention of the Angel of the Lord after the birth of Jesus.

The intimate connection of the Angel of the Lord with God's covenant promises takes on fresh meaning if the Angel of the Lord is indeed the preincarnate Christ. Jesus became flesh to fulfill the promise God made to Abraham, that "in you all the families of the earth shall be blessed" (Gen. 12:3). Christ died on the cross, and rose again, to open the door to all for a personal relationship with God. When we respond to the invitation of the gospel to trust Jesus as Savior, we become members of the company of believers who have a covenant relationship with God. From the beginning, that relationship has been based on simple trust in the faithfulness of a God who has always been, and always will be, faithful to His word.

What a joy it is, then, to see in this angel of the Old Testament a prefiguration of the promises God makes to us today. In the God Who Is Always Present we, like Hagar, have direction and guidance. Like Abraham, we have hope in uncertainty and turmoil. Like Moses, we have our dreams revitalized. Like Gideon, we have the strength we need to overcome our weaknesses. Like Elijah, we have encouragement in disappointment, a mission to give direction to our lives, and support in our moments of despair. Like David, we have the assurance of forgiveness when we sin; like Hezekiah, the guarantee of protection from our enemies; and like Zechariah's community, the certain confidence that God's good future lies ahead for us.

CHAPTER 3

LAW AND ORDER ANGELS:

INSTRUMENTS OF GOD'S JUDGMENT

Genesis 18—19; Exodus 7—12; additional Old & New Testament passages

A March 1993 Gallup survey showed that 76 percent of the teenagers in the United States believe in the existence of angels. The number of teenagers who believe angels exist has steadily increased in the 15 years since the survey was first taken in 1978, when only 64 percent affirmed such a belief. Our era exhibits a marked fascination with angels matched only by the Middle Ages.

When we read modern stories about angel visitations, many are similar to one reported by Brad and Sherry Steiger in their book, *Angels Over Their Shoulders* (p. 87), published in 1995. Two young sisters, ages eight and four, fell into a river and were carried away by the swift current. The pastor of a nearby church heard their mother's screams and hurried to the shore as a man fishing in a boat rushed to the girls' rescue. It seemed certain that the girls would drown, but when the fisherman finally reached them, the little girls were floating calmly, as if "somehow supported from underneath." Dr. Larson, the pastor, reported that men and women watching from the riverbank saw a beautiful person in white supporting the girls until the fisherman caught up with them. The girls insisted an angel had kept them from sinking and described their rescuer in "vivid detail."

In most reports of angel encounters in the past two decades, angels have appeared as rescuers who protect an individual from some great peril. This certainly is in line with Scripture's portrait of angels as guardian spirits sent by God to serve believers. There's no doubt that every believer is indebted to guardian angels for protection from hazards of which they were completely unaware. However, there is another, perhaps surprising, aspect of angelic activity in our world.

WHEN ANGELS VISITED ABRAHAM
(Genesis 18, 19)

An unexpected aspect of angelic ministry can be discovered in the story of Abraham's encounter with the Lord when He was accompanied by two "Law and Order Angels." The incident is reported in Genesis 18 and 19.

ABRAHAM WELCOMED ANGELS "UNAWARE" *(Genesis 18:1–5)*

Then the LORD appeared to him [Abraham] by the terebinth trees of Mamre, as he was sitting in the tent door in the heat of the day. So he lifted his eyes and looked, and behold, three men were standing by him; and when he saw them, he ran from the tent door to meet them, and bowed himself to the ground, and said, "My Lord, if I have now found favor in Your sight, do not pass on by Your servant. Please, let a little water be brought, and wash your feet, and rest yourselves under the tree. And I will bring a morsel of bread, that you may refresh your hearts. After that you may pass by, inasmuch as you have come to your servant."

Genesis 18:1–5 (NKJV)

THE ANGELS APPEARED TO BE ORDINARY MEN   *(Genesis 18:2)*

Several things are notable in this opening scene. Both the Lord and His two companions were cloaked in human form. When Abraham noticed them, he saw what appeared to be "three men." In fact, they looked like ordinary travelers, their feet dusty from walking in sandals over the open fields and dirt paths of Canaan.

ABRAHAM OFFERED HIS VISITORS HOSPITALITY *(Genesis 18:3–5)*

Abraham's reaction does not suggest that he recognized his visitors; rather, it was a tra-

ditional form of hospitality offered to strangers in the Ancient Near East. Hospitality was deeply rooted in that culture, so offering and accepting hospitality had deep significance.

The host who fed a visitor became obligated to protect the visitor from every evil while in his territory. The familiar phrase from the Twenty-third Psalm, "You prepare a table before me in the presence of my enemies" (v. 5), is an expression of the wonderful confidence that David found through his relationship with the Lord. God had invited David into His presence and prepared a table before him. The Lord, David's host, would surely protect David from all his enemies!

So Abraham acted in character as a good host, offering hospitality to three strangers, unaware of who his visitors would soon reveal themselves to be. The author of Hebrews was alluding to this incident when he wrote, "Do not forget to entertain strangers, for by so doing some have unwittingly entertained angels" (Heb. 13:2).

ONE VISITOR WAS THE LORD HIMSELF   *(Genesis 18:9–20)*

Abraham realized that one of his visitors was the Lord Himself. The Lord confirmed

ANGELORE

WHAT DO ANGELS LOOK LIKE?

Artists have tended to depict angels as lovely women or as healthy infants, called cherubs. In fact, angels are sexless (see Matt. 22:30). However, in every report in Scripture of angels appearing in human form, they are described as men (see Gen. 18, 19; Judg. 13:16; Matt. 28:2, 3; Luke 24:4).

And the LORD said, "Because the outcry against Sodom and Gomorrah is great, and because their sin is very grave, I will go down now and see whether they have done altogether according to the outcry against it that has come to Me; and if not, I will know." Then the men [the two accompanying angels] turned away from there and went toward Sodom, but Abraham still stood before the LORD.

Genesis 18:20–22

UNDERCOVER ANGELS

Although surveillance is not an activity we generally associate with angels, it is clear that God sent His angels in the guise of men to investigate the cities of Sodom and Gomorrah.

THE ANGELS' MISSION: INVESTIGATE SODOM
(Genesis 18:20–22)

But why should the angels investigate Sodom? The text tells us that "the outcry against" Sodom and Gomorrah was "great." This expression indicates that many people had been harmed by the citizens of these cities, and so they complained to heaven. What had happened in Sodom was no single incident in which there was one victim; rather, there was an established pattern of behavior which had victimized many. There is no question that the people of these cities were involved in serious sin, and God was fully aware that their sin was "very grave."

Why did God send the angels to investigate? These messengers of God were His representatives sent to discover whether the citizens of Sodom "have done altogether according to the outcry against it." The angels were to enter the town to see if they would be treated as previous visitors had been. The investigating angels were undercover agents. The way in which God's undercover agents were treated would clearly and unmistakably reveal the true character of those the angels had been sent to investigate.

His earlier promise and announced that Sarah, Abraham's aged and childless wife, would soon bear his son.

When the visitors stood to leave, Abraham, a courteous host intent on honoring his guests, "went with them to send them on the way" (18:16). Then the Lord stopped and told Abraham what He was about to do.

LOT OFFERED THE ANGELS HOSPITALITY (Genesis 19:1–3)

Chapter 19 of Genesis describes what happened next. It was near evening when the two angels entered the city of Sodom. The text says that Lot, a nephew of Abraham who settled in Sodom some years before because of the economic opportunities there, was "sitting in the gate." This phrase is used in the Old Testament to indicate a person of influence. The elders of a community took their seat at the gates of the city (see Deut. 22:15) to serve as judges and moral authorities (see Ps. 69:12). So Lot, undoubtedly a wealthy man at this time, was recognized as an important significant citizen of Sodom.

Lot's reaction when he saw the two strangers enter the city's gates was much like Abraham's in Genesis 18. Lot hurried to offer hospitality to the two visitors. At first, the two investigating angels refused: "We will spend the night in the open square" (19:2). But Lot insisted, and like a good host, he prepared a fine meal for them. Then the men of Sodom revealed their true character—precisely what the angels had come to investigate.

THE MEN OF SODOM INTENDED HOMOSEXUAL RAPE (Genesis 19:4–5)

The men of the city, the men of Sodom, both old and young, all the people from every quarter, surrounded the house. And they called to Lot and said to him, "Where are the men who came to you tonight? Bring them out to us that we may know them *carnally.*" Genesis 19:4, 5

The italicized word, "carnally," is not in the Hebrew text, but it is not really needed. One of the basic meanings of the Hebrew verb "to know" is "to have sexual intercourse." We see this meaning clearly in Genesis 4:1, which says "Adam knew his wife, Eve, and she conceived." Adam had sexual intercourse with Eve, and that act produced a child. Familiarity with this use of the verb "to know" leads to the conclusion that the men of Sodom, then,

were intent on subjecting two visitors to their town to homosexual rape.

It's clear from the Scriptures and other ancient documents that in the biblical world homosexuality was not considered an "alternative lifestyle" for consenting adults. Old Testament Law, dating over half a millennium after Abraham, commanded that a man "shall not lie with a male as with a woman," and added that "it is an abomination" (Lev. 18:22). The Middle Assyrian Code of Tiglath-Pileser I, rooted in the earlier law code of Hammurabi, stated: "If one citizen has homosexual relations with another, then the sentence, following due process, is castration" (Article 20).

The issue at stake in Sodom was far more than sex between two adults of the same gender. The issue here was the violation by an entire community of one of the most basic values to be found in any society: values reflected in the custom of hospitality. The stranger must be welcomed and cared for, because that is how we show respect for persons created in the image of God. Strangers in Sodom were treated worse than animals; they were to be used and discarded, rather than respected.

The fact that every man, young and old, from every quarter of the city, eagerly joined in the attempted rape of the angels shows that Sodom was a completely corrupt society, whose citizens were driven by a passion for perverted sex to violate the rights and the person of any victim who might come near. The investigating angels' experience demonstrated the corruption of Sodom beyond any shadow of a doubt.

UNDERCOVER ANGELS TODAY?

We have no certain knowledge that God sends investigating angels into our world today. Yet it may be that Hesiod, an ancient Greek, was near the truth when he wrote, "Three times ten thousand immortal watchers does Zeus possess on the all-nourishing earth for men, who observe decisions of law and unwholesome deeds and go about the whole earth clothed in air" (*Erga*, 252f.). Surely the Jews who lived two centuries before Christ were sensitive to this ministry of angels. In a book of the Pseudepigrapha, angels are quoted as saying, "Therefore we come and make known all sin . . . before the Lord, which is done in heaven and earth and in light and in darkness and everywhere" (Jubilees 4:6). Investigating angels indeed!

UNDERCOVER ANGELS AND JUSTICE

ABRAHAM'S CONCERN FOR THE INNOCENT   *(Genesis 18:23–33)*

When God first informed Abraham of his intention to investigate and then punish Sodom and the other cities of the plain, Abraham expressed concern. "Would You also destroy the righteous with the wicked?" Abraham asked (18:23).

On the surface, this question is an affront to God, for it suggests that God might act unjustly. Yet, in the ensuing conversation between Abraham and God, God promises Abraham that He would not destroy the cities if even ten righteous persons were found there. This prayer and what follows is crucial for our understanding of the work of Law and Order Angels, whom we meet throughout Scripture.

When the angels visited Sodom, and the entire male population of the city turned out to demand that Lot turn the two visitors over to them, Lot faced the crowd and pleaded with them. He was committed to fulfilling the host's duty of protecting his guests, whatever the cost to him. Even when the men of Sodom threatened to "deal worse with" Lot than with the angels, Lot stood his ground (Gen. 19:9). Lot was saved only because the two angelic visitors dragged him into his house and then blinded Sodom's citizens so they couldn't find the door. At this moment, the angels announced to Lot that they were about to destroy Sodom, for "the LORD has sent us to destroy it."

GOD'S PROVISION FOR INNOCENT LOT *(Genesis 19:12–22)*

The angels urged Lot to warn his daughters' future husbands and to prepare to leave.

Lot's prospective sons-in-law took the warning as a joke, but Lot and his family made preparations. As morning drew near, Lot, his wife, and his two daughters linked hands, and the angels led them outside the city (19:16). One of the angels urged Lot to hurry to the nearby city that would be his new home, for he could not do anything until Lot arrived there (19:22). When Lot arrived in the little city named Zoar, the angels acted and "Then the LORD rained brimstone and fire on Sodom and Gomorrah, from the LORD out of the heavens" (19:24).

Abraham had begged God to be merciful and spare the cities of the plain if only ten righteous persons should be found there, but God showed an even greater concern. Before the fires fell, God made sure that His angels rescued the family of the one righteous man in Sodom, the one man in the entire population who had not fallen into that community's sinful way.

As we read the Scriptures further, we'll discover that God frequently uses angels to administer justice and to punish, but we need to remember the rescue of Lot. While God's justice calls out Law and Order Angels to investigate sin and administer punishment, God's love and concern for individuals is greater than Abraham had imagined. As moral judge of the universe, God could not spare the sinful cities, but He did see to it that the righteous did not perish with the wicked. In His wrath, God always remembers mercy.

LAW AND ORDER ANGELS AT SODOM

THE DESTRUCTION OF SODOM *(Genesis 19:23–28)*

The location of Sodom. People have wondered about the location of the five cities of the plain, especially the leading communities of Sodom and Gomorrah. Where were they? Where are their remains now? From the details given in Scripture, their location has been fixed in or near the valley where the Dead Sea now lies. Most scholars assume that the five cities lie underneath the waters of the Dead

Sea, but archaeologist Willem C. van Hattem, writing in the spring 1981 issue of *Biblical Archaeologist* (pp. 87–93), argues that five ruins which lie a few miles south of the Dead Sea and whose destruction dates from around 2200 B.C., the traditional date of Abraham, are probably the cities of Genesis 19. In his description of the ruins, van Hattem writes: "Of note, too, is the evidence of severe burning on many of the stones."

How Sodom was destroyed (Gen. 19:24). While the exact location of the cities remains uncertain, their destruction is no mystery. The valley in which the cities stood lies on a major geologic fault line, making it as vulnerable to earthquakes as California. The valley itself contained asphalt, a highly flammable material. Thus, an earthquake there would fill the air with explosive material; and if this asphalt were to be ignited by lightning, fire would fall from the heavens and destroy all life in the cities of the plain. Apparently, that is what happened as soon as Lot was safe. The Law and Order Angels, agents of God's moral governance of the universe, acted; and the people of Sodom, Gomorrah, and the other corrupt cities of the plain were completely destroyed.

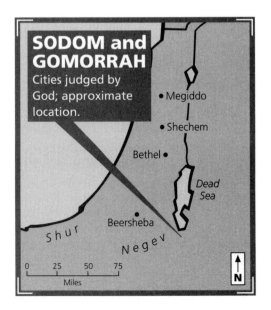

SODOM and GOMORRAH
Cities judged by God; approximate location.

Megiddo
Shechem
Bethel
Dead Sea
Beersheba
Shur
Negev

0   25   50   75
Miles

N

The pattern revealed in Genesis 19. The story told in Genesis 18 and 19 introduces us to the ministry of angels as investigators and executors of God's judgment against sin. It is always important to study carefully the first reference to any recurring theme in Scripture. In most cases, the first occurrence of a theme gives us a framework for understanding the other passages in which that theme reoccurs. So what do we learn from the two chapters that introduce angels as upholders of moral order in God's universe?

- God is fully aware of sins that cry out for punishment.
- God remains patient until sin is "very grave" and *requires* punishment. God did not act until every man in Sodom proved to be corrupt.
- God may send angels as undercover agents to demonstrate the extent of the corruption that requires punishment.
- God *preserves* the righteous when punishing the sinful. Lot lost his wealth, but not his life.
- Angels may serve as the agents who implement God's decree to punish.
- The function of Law and Order Angels is not to discipline (correct, instruct) sinners; Law and Order Angels *punish sin*. By the time Law and Order Angels are involved, the hope of repentance is past.

Where does Scripture describe other Law and Order Angels in action? How do those incidents fit the framework evident in Genesis 19?

OTHER JUDGMENTS EXECUTED BY LAW AND ORDER ANGELS

LAW AND ORDER ANGELS WERE INVOLVED IN THE PLAGUES UPON EGYPT   (Exodus 7—12)

The cause of the judgment (Exodus 1:8–16). Abraham's grandson, Jacob, led his small family into Egypt. A terrible famine had struck the

Middle East, and only Egypt had a supply of stored grain to ensure the nation's survival. Jacob's son, Joseph, who had been sold into slavery by his jealous brothers, was responsible for saving Egypt. Joseph correctly interpreted a dream God had given to Pharaoh which foretold the famine, and Joseph then rose to become the chief administrator of Egypt. With Pharaoh's blessing, Joseph settled his father, his brothers, and their families on prime Egyptian land.

The descendents of Abraham stayed in Egypt for some four hundred years, during which time their number increased to nearly two million. For at least the last one hundred years of that period, however, Abraham's descendants were enslaved and set to forced labor under harsh foremen. Then the children of Israel cried out to God for help. Their prayers were answered in one of the most pivotal moments in sacred history. God provided an eighty-year-old deliverer, Moses, and He unleashed a series of devastating plagues on Egypt which ravaged the land and the people who had oppressed the Israelites. Ultimately, the proud Pharaoh was humbled and forced to let his slaves go. The Israelites had been rescued by unmistakable acts of divine power, and the Egyptians were punished for the decades they had oppressed the Jewish people.

The involvement of angels (Psalm 78). Psalm 78 celebrates the wonders God performed "when He worked His signs in Egypt" (v. 43). Verse 49 tells us: "He cast on them [the Egyptians] the fierceness of His anger, / Wrath, indignation, and trouble, / *By sending angels of destruction among them*" [emphasis added]. Just as God had used angels to punish Sodom and Gomorrah in the time of Abraham, He used angels to bring about the plagues of punishment which shattered Egypt in Moses' day.

A passage in Exodus suggests that an angel was directly involved in the final plague, in which the eldest son in every Egyptian household was killed in a single night. The Israelites were instructed to mark their doors with the

An angel called "the destroyer" carried out the final plague against Egypt—but spared the Israelites.

blood of a sacrificed lamb, and they were promised that when the Lord saw the blood, He would pass over that door, "and not allow the destroyer to come into your houses to strike you" (Ex. 12:23). This incident is referred to in the New Testament. Hebrews 11:28 identifies the divine agent as "he who destroys." It seems clear in light of the reference to "angels of destruction" in Psalm 78 that "the destroyer"—"he who destroys"—is a Law and Order Angel commissioned to punish Egypt for decades of unremitting, unrepented sin against God's people.

LAW AND ORDER ANGELS WERE INVOLVED IN A PLAGUE THAT STRUCK THE ISRAELITES ON THE WAY TO CANAAN (Numbers 11)

The cause of the judgment. After the Israelites left Egypt, God led them into the Sinai desert. They camped at Mount Sinai, where God gave Moses the Ten Commandments, in which He etched a lifestyle that would forever separate the Jews from all the other peoples of the world. When that was done, Moses led the people toward Canaan, the land God had promised to Abraham's descendants.

For some reason, however—even though that generation had seen the miracles God worked to win their freedom, and even though God daily provided them food and direction—the hearts of the Israelites were filled with bitterness rather than gratitude, and with doubt rather than faith. The Hebrew phrase translated "complain," which sets the tone for the events recorded in Numbers 11, indicates an angry, bitter hostility. Despite all that God had done to show His love, the Israelites remained bitter over the fact that all they had to eat was a special food, called "manna," which the Lord provided daily. They gave in to an "intense craving" for "the fish which [they] ate freely in Egypt, the cucumbers, the melons, the leeks, the onions, and the garlic" (11:5).

It's important to remember that this attitude is one the Israelites had displayed almost as soon as they had been given their freedom. Complaints broke out after just three days of travel (Ex. 15:22) and quickly intensified (see Ex. 16). Despite the fact that the Israelites had seen God work wonders for them, had watched an Egyptian army drown in the same sea through which they had passed safely, and had observed an awesome display of God's power at Mount Sinai, this generation was totally unwilling to revere or trust Him.

The involvement of angels (1 Corinthians 10:10). At last God acted. He provided the people with a gigantic flock of quail, the "meat" they had demanded. "But while the meat was still between their teeth, before it was chewed, the wrath of the LORD was aroused against the people, and the LORD struck the people with a very great plague" (Num. 11:33). Looking back on this event, the apostle Paul says in 1 Corinthians 10:10 that "some of them also complained, and were destroyed by the destroyer." Psalm 78, which identifies the "destroying angels" as those who brought the plagues on Egypt, also refers

specifically to this incident (vv. 21–25), and says that God was angry with those who complained "Because they did not believe in God, / And did not trust in His salvation" despite all He had done for them.

LAW AND ORDER ANGELS WERE INVOLVED IN ISRAEL'S CONQUEST OF CANAAN (Exodus 23:23; 33:2)

The cause of the judgment. God commanded the Israelites to exterminate the peoples of Canaan, whom they were to supplant (Deut. 7:22, 23; 9:3). This is thought to pose one of the great moral objections to the character of God as represented in the Old Testament.

There is no doubt that God told the Israelites to exterminate or drive out the peoples of Canaan. Many passages in the Old Testament express God's command to the Israelites to "utterly destroy" the peoples of Canaan (see Deut. 7:22, 23; 9:3). How, people ask, can a loving God permit, much less demand, genocide?

The answer is found in Genesis 15:13–16, which reports what the Lord said to Abraham in a vision. God told Abraham that his descendants would live as strangers for some four hundred years in a land where they would be afflicted. God also told Abraham that He would punish the nation that oppressed them. Just as the Lord had said, the land of Egypt was judged and then punished by the terrible and devastating plagues described in Exodus 7—12. But in Abraham's vision God went on to promise that Abraham's descendants would "return here." The text explains that the years in Egypt were required "for the iniquity of the Amorites [was] not yet complete" (15:16).

One reason why Israel was set aside in Egypt and made to wait is that the extermination of the peoples of Canaan could only be justified as a response to the complete corruption of their culture, just as the destruction of Sodom was delayed until the cities of the plain were completely corrupted by their peculiar sin.

Today, we know much about Canaanite culture through the recovered hymns and legends of the people who lived there at the time of the Israelite invasion. For instance, we know about the bloody character of the Canaanite gods and goddesses; we know about the ritual prostitution the Canaanites practiced and the corrupt rites they performed. The destruction of the Canaanites *was an act of divine judgment,* a punishment merited by fully matured sin.

The involvement of angels. Two passages in Exodus clearly indicate that angels fought alongside Israel in their attack on Canaan.

For My Angel will go before you and bring you in to the Amorites and the Hittites and the Perizzites and the Canaanites and the Hivites and the Jebusites; and I will cut them off. Exodus 23:23

And I will send My Angel before you, and I will drive out the Canaanite and the Amorite and the Hittite and the Perizzite and the Hivite and the Jebusite. Exodus 33:2

God's Law and Order Angels went before God's people and acted through them to root out and destroy a culture whose sinful practices we can hardly imagine today.

LAW AND ORDER ANGELS WERE INVOLVED IN GOD'S JUDGMENT ON ISRAEL IN DAVID'S DAY
(2 Samuel 24; 1 Chronicles 21)

The cause of the judgment. We are told in 2 Samuel 24 that "the anger of the LORD was aroused against Israel." We are not told why the Lord was angry, but typically this phrase is associated with idolatry and the Israelites' unfaithfulness to their covenant with God. When David took a census of Israel's fighting men, which suggests that David himself was about to rely on numbers rather than on the Lord, David was given a choice of three punishments: the nation could experience seven years of famine, its armies could be defeated and pursued for three months, or God could send a three-day plague. David, aware of God's merciful nature, chose the plague.

The involvement of angels (2 Samuel 24:15–16). During the first day of the plague,

70,000 people died. David was given a vision of a destroying angel, with sword raised to strike Jerusalem. According to verse 16,

And when the angel stretched out His hand over Jerusalem to destroy it, the LORD relented from the destruction, and said to the angel who was destroying the people, "It is enough; now restrain your hand."

David was wise to choose the punishment he did. Out of compassion God cut short the angel's mission.

LAW AND ORDER ANGELS DESTROYED AN ASSYRIAN ARMY
(2 Kings 19; 2 Chronicles 32; Isaiah 36)

The cause of the judgment. The same story is told in each of these chapters. When the army of the Assyrian ruler Sennacherib threatened Jerusalem, King Hezekiah begged for God's intervention.

In a fascinating passage, Isaiah calls Assyria the "rod of [God's] anger," sent to punish His sinful people. However, Assyria was not willing to be limited to this mission; instead, "it [was] in his heart to destroy." Overcome by arrogance and conceit, the Assyrians ridiculed the God of the Jews and bragged that He was powerless to help His people (see Isa. 10:5–11).

The angel involvement. In response to King Hezekiah's prayer, "the LORD sent an angel who cut down every mighty man of valor, leader, and captain in the camp of the king of Assyria" (2 Chron. 32:21). Isaiah and 2 Kings report that 185,000 men in the Assyrian army died, and Sennacherib was forced to return to Assyria.

Sennacherib's own court records have been recovered, and while he boasts of taking 200,150 Jewish prisoners and shutting Hezekiah up in his city "like a bird in a cage," he never claims to have taken Jerusalem. The records are silent about the loss of his army, but that is not surprising since conquerors do not boast about their defeats. It is interesting, however, that the Greek historian Herodotus reports that Sennacherib did suffer massive losses—supposedly due to field mice who ate the army's weapons and left the men exposed to destruction by an unnamed enemy.

LAW AND ORDER ANGELS WILL BE ACTIVE AT HISTORY'S END
(Matthew 13:41, 42; 2 Thessalonians 1:7–9)

The cause of the judgment. When Jesus spoke of His future return to earth, He stated that the conditions then will be like those in the days of Noah, when "every intent of the thoughts of [humankind's] heart was only evil continually (Matt. 24:36–39; see Gen. 6:5). As the end of history draws near, once again society will be corrupt, ignoring God and His ways.

The involvement of angels. Jesus spoke of His return and stated that at the end of the age He would "send out His angels, and they will gather out of His kingdom all things that offend, and those who practice lawlessness, and will cast them into the furnace of fire" (Matt. 13:41, 42). In 2 Thessalonians, Paul also describes the impact of Christ's return on those who have not chosen the way of faith:

The Lord Jesus [will be] revealed from heaven with His mighty angels, in flaming fire taking vengeance on those who do not know God, and on those who do not obey the gospel of our Lord Jesus Christ. These shall be punished with everlasting destruction from the presence of the Lord and from the glory of His power.

Even this description pales before the punitive role assigned to angels in the book of Revelation, where both Scripture and history are drawn to a close (see Revelation 22).

Although these are terrible and unsettling images, it's important to remember a principle we saw illustrated in Genesis 19. God does not judge hastily. He waits until sin matures and totally corrupts a society, until there is no hope of reform. Today, our God gives all an invitation to turn to Him before the judgment comes. God eagerly waits to welcome us home—He puts off the Day of Judgment to give everyone a chance to experience His love.

LAW AND ORDER ANGELS AT THE DEATH OF HEROD AGRIPPA I (Acts 12)

The cause of the judgment. The Herod in this chapter is the grandson of Herod the Great. He was set on the throne of Judea by the Roman emperor Caligula, and he was later given additional lands by the Roman emperor Claudius, a childhood friend.

Although he owed his crown to Rome, Agrippa eagerly sought the support of his Jewish subjects. The Jewish Mishna relates how this king of Edomite stock showed his respect for the Scriptures by standing as he read from Deuteronomy 17 at a celebration of the Feast of Tabernacles.

King Agrippa received it [the holy book] standing and read it standing, and for this the Sages praised him. And when he reached "Thou mayest not put a foreigner over thee which is not thy brother," his eyes flowed with tears; but they called out to him, "Our brother art thou! Our brother art thou! Our brother art thou!"

When Herod sensed the hostility of the Jewish leaders to the followers of Jesus, he had the apostle James executed and the apostle Peter imprisoned. An angel released Peter before he too could be killed.

The angel involvement (Acts 12:20–23). The angel's intervention did not end with Peter's release. Josephus, a first-century Jewish historian, gives an account of Herod Agrippa's death in his *Antiquities* (XCIX, 343–50 [vii.2]), which corroborates the story in Acts: When Herod was hailed as a god by the people of Tyre, "immediately an angel of the Lord struck him, because he did not give glory to God. And he was eaten by worms and died" (Acts 12:23).

The cause of Agrippa's death was probably intestinal roundworms. Clusters of these worms, which grow to a length of ten to fourteen inches, can block the intestines and cause severe pain. The sufferer will vomit worms or, in an advanced case, will die an excruciatingly painful death. Josephus gives us a graphic description: Herod "was overcome with intense pain. . . . Exhausted after five straight days by the pain in his abdomen, he departed this life in the fifty-fourth year of his life and the seventh of his reign."

The Law and Order Angel who released Peter from prison was also God's agent of justice who executed His judgment on Herod and condemned him to a painful death.

The chart summarizes the involvement of Law and Order Angels in God's moral governance. Cultures entrenched in evil were wiped out. Egypt was punished for oppressing God's people for decades. Selective judgments against Israel prevented or delayed the nation's tilt toward sin. Enemies who threatened to exterminate God's people had armies destroyed. Herod was executed by an angel when he threatened the early church. All of these events should serve as warnings to people today, for they illustrate God's commitment to intervene in our world when judgment simply cannot be put off any longer.

LAW AND ORDER ANGELS IN REVIEW

The role of Law and Order Angels in the operation of God's moral universe doesn't correlate with the image most people have of angels or their activities. Contemporary angel stories typically feature angels intervening to warn, protect, or rescue—and these are valid ministries of angels. Such stories are also reported in Scripture and, since God's angels are active today, we need to be careful not to discount modern reports of angel encounters. At the same time, we make a mistake if we picture either God or His angels as little more than servants, eager to help us when we're in need.

Law & Order Angels Summary

Passages	Who is judged	Nature of the sin	The punishment
Genesis 19	Sodom, cities of the plain	Culture corrupt; shown by homosexual rape	The culture was destroyed by fire
Exodus 1, 7—12	People of Egypt	Prolonged enslavement of Israelites	Egypt was devastated by plagues; eldest sons killed
Numbers 11	Unbelieving Israelites	Refused to trust God, who had freed His people and shown His presence	Many died in a "great plague"
Exodus 23, 33; Genesis 15:13–16; Deuteronomy 9:3	Peoples of Canaan	The culture was religiously and morally corrupt; threatened purity of Israel's faith	Culture wiped out or people driven from Canaan
2 Samuel 24; 1 Chronicles 21	Citizens of Israel	Shift from relying on God to relying on military might by king and people	70,000 killed in a plague before David confessed and sacrificed
2 Kings 19; 2 Chronicles 32; Isaiah 36	King and army	Assyrians massacre Jews, intend to take Jews from the promised land	185,000 of the Assyrian army killed by an angel
Matthew 13:41, 42; 2 Thessalonians 1:7–9	Unbelievers on earth at Jesus' return	Sin has matured as in Noah's day; persecution of believers	Angels execute God's vengeance (see chapter 22)
Acts 12	Herod Agrippa	He executed John, threatened the survival of the church; accepted worship as god	Angel struck him with fatal infection of roundworms

The Bible's stories of Law and Order Angels remind us that we live in a moral universe—a universe where right and wrong are realities, and where God, though rich in mercy, does not hesitate to punish when a society or an individual becomes entrenched in sin.

God is especially likely to judge when sin threatens His covenant people. Angels served as God's agents to punish Sodom for its corruption and Egypt for its oppression of God's people. Angels aided the Israelites in their conquest of Canaan, and angels were active in the extermination of the peoples whose corrupt culture threatened Israel's relationship with the Lord. Angels were God's agents to punish those who were spiritually unresponsive both in the Exodus generation and in the time of David. Angels stopped the Assyrian army that threatened to wipe out Judah. An angel executed God's judgment on a ruler set on pleasing his citizens by trying to stamp out the early church. Additionally, angels will be active when Christ returns to judge our earth and to establish righteousness.

Despite the finality of these judgments, we sense more of the grace of God in every story. God does not rush to judgment. God does not send angels on missions of punishment until every avenue of redemption has been explored. God withholds judgment and punishment until humankind's own actions force Him to act. When we recognize both God's commitment to mercy and His unalterable resolution to judge sin, we can only be amazed with Paul that some "despise the riches of His goodness, forbearance, and long-suffering" (Rom. 2:4). What a wonderful "goodness of God" delayed punishment is! And how vital it is that we let God's patience lead us to repentance, to moral and spiritual renewal, and to the discovery of His forgiving love!

ANGEL ENCOUNTERS:

MEN, VOICES, AND RADIANT BEINGS

Genesis 16—32; additional Old & New Testament passages

Saint Teresa of Avila, the great Catholic mystic, described one of her angel encounters this way:

It pleased the Lord that I should sometimes see the following vision. I would see beside me, on my left hand, an angel in bodily form—a type of vision I am not in the habit of seeing, except very rarely. It pleased the Lord that I should see this angel in the following way. He was not tall, but short, and very beautiful, his face so aflame that he appeared to be one of the highest types of angel who seem to be all afire. They must be those who are called cherubim; they do not tell me their names but I am well aware that there is a great difference between certain angels and others, and between these and others still, of a kind I could not possibly explain.

Saint Teresa goes on to describe a golden spear with which the angel seemed to pierce her.

When he drew it out . . . he left me completely afire with a great love of God. The pain was so sharp that it made me utter several moans; and so excessive was the sweetness caused me by this intense pain that one can never wish to lose it, nor will one's soul be content with anything less than God. It is not bodily pain, but spiritual, though the body has a share in it—indeed a great share. So sweet are the colloquies of love which pass between the soul and God that if anyone thinks I am lying I beseech God, in His Goodness, to give him the same experience (Malcom Godwin, *Angels,* 1990, p. 178).

Saint Teresa had no doubt that what she experienced was an angel encounter. The being she saw in her vision seemed "aflame," and the result of the encounter was an intense, and even painful, heightening of her love for God. As we read the Bible, we discover fascinating reports of angel encounters; many of the reports provide details about the angel's appearance, and most angel encounters have a distinctive impact on the lives of those who experience them.

ANGELORE

BRIGHT, SHINING ANGELS

Most angels described in Scripture seem to appear in human form, but some appear as bright and shining beings (cf. Ezek. 1:7; Dan. 10:6; Luke 24:4).

The tradition is found in many languages and is reflected in the singular term, "El," which has as one of its root meanings "shining" or "radiant."

Sumerian	**El**	"brightness, shining"
Akkadian	**Ilu**	"radiant one"
Babylonian	**Ellu**	"the shining one"
Old Welsh	**Ellu**	"a shining being"
Old Irish	**Aillil**	"shining"

| English | **Elf** | "shining being" |
| Anglo-Saxon | **Aelf** | "radiant being" |

Does the appearance of a bright, shining being guarantee that the experience is a visit by one of God's angels? Not at all, for 2 Corinthians 11:14 warns us that "Satan himself transforms himself into an angel of light!"

JACOB'S ANGEL ENCOUNTER AT BETHEL   (Genesis 28)

THE SETTING
(Genesis 27:1—28:5)

Jacob made a truly big mistake: He had alienated his brother, Esau, and Esau was a man of action. Years earlier, Jacob got Esau to trade his birthright—the right to inherit the covenant promises God made to their grandfather, Abraham—for a bowl of stew. The fact that Esau was willing to make the trade revealed how little he valued the Lord's promises. Even so, when Esau remembered how his brother had taken advantage of his hunger, he was resentful.

More recently, the brothers' mother had actually helped Jacob, her favorite, trick their father, Isaac, into giving Jacob (the younger son) the blessing intended for Esau (the eldest). By stealing his brother's blessing, Jacob turned Esau's antagonism into active hostility, and Esau had been heard to mutter that when his father died, he intended to kill Jacob. So the parents quickly sent Jacob to a distant country to find a wife among relatives who lived there.

THE ENCOUNTER
(Genesis 28:10–13a)

On the way to his relatives' home, Jacob was frightened and exhausted. Lying under the open sky, his head pillowed on a rock, Jacob had a vision of angels. The story is told in Genesis 28.

So he [Jacob] 'came to a certain place and stayed there all night, because the sun had set. And he took one of the stones of that place and put it at his head, and he lay down in that place to sleep. Then he dreamed, and behold, a ladder was set up on the earth, and its top reached to heaven; and there the angels of God were ascending and descending on it. And behold, the LORD stood above it, and said, "I am the LORD God of Abraham your father and the God of Isaac" Genesis 28:11–13a NKJV.

Jacob's dream *(Genesis 28:12)*. People have seen angels either with their natural eyes, when the angels are cloaked in human form, or in visions, when angels appear in their spiritual form. Jacob's experience was of the second kind: In his dream Jacob saw angels passing back and forth on a "ladder" (literally, a "stairway" or "ramp") between the spiritual and material realms. Angels clearly can bridge the gap between the two realms!

God spoke to Jacob *(Genesis 28:13a)*. The focus of Jacob's dream shifted very quickly. The vision of angels receded into the background as Jacob's gaze was drawn to a Being standing above the ramp, a Being who identified Himself as "the LORD God."

From this point to the end of Genesis 28, no reference is made to angels. Jacob's attention is fixed completely on the Lord and what He has to say. There's a healthy reminder here. Yes, the Bible has much to say about angels, but Scripture is always focused on the Lord Himself—thus, our focus is to be upon Him also. We study angels not for their own sake, but to learn more about the God who sends angels to us. We can and should appreciate the ministry of angels, but we ought to give thanks to God, for He is the One who directs them to care for us.

God's purpose in the encounter *(Genesis 28:13b–15)*. The Lord had a clear purpose in giving Jacob this vision of angels passing between heaven and earth. God was preparing Jacob to hear a reaffirmation of His covenant. "I am the LORD God of Abraham your father and the God of Isaac; the land on which you lie I will give to you and your descendants" (28:13). With this restatement of His promise to Abraham, the Lord made a special, personal

Jacob's dream at Bethel.

promise to Jacob: "Behold, I am with you and will keep you wherever you go, and will bring you back to this land; for I will not leave you until I have done what I have spoken to you" (28:15).

Jacob's response to the encounter (*Genesis 28:17–22*). Jacob's initial response was one of awe and fear (28:17), but then he made a vow.

If God will be with me, and keep me in this way that I am going, and give me bread to eat and clothing to put on, so that I come back to my father's house in peace, then the LORD shall be my God. And this stone which I have set as a pillar shall be God's house, and of all that You give me I will surely give a tenth to You. Genesis 28:20–22

Rabbi Sholomo Riskin, chief rabbi of Efrat and dean of the Ohr Tora institutions, observed in the "Shabbat Shalom" column of

the *Jerusalem Post* (December 9, 1989) that Jacob's statement

is not conditional. It is pure prayer: I will believe, Jacob is saying, no matter what transpires, and if the Lord [Elohim] will protect and clothe me, and I'll return to my father's house in peace. "Then shall the Lord [JHVH] be my God [Elohim] . . ." and I'll be able to worship You not only as the God of justice and power but as the personal God of love and compassion.

The effect of the encounter in Jacob's life (*Genesis 28:21b–22*). Jacob's vision of angels compelled belief and also served as the setting for a message delivered by God Himself. Jacob's first response of awe and fear led to the realization that God was now, and would continue to be, with him. The long-term impact of this encounter was that Jacob committed himself to worship the Lord and serve Him.

Like Saint Teresa's vision, the vision given to Jacob resulted in a heightened awareness of God and deepened love for Him.

Before we analyze other reports of angel visitations in Scripture, we need to understand more about angels themselves.

WHO OR WHAT ARE ANGELS?

In chapter 1 we observed that the angel encounters reported throughout the Bible confirm the fact that there are two realms, the material and the spiritual. The spiritual realm is home to God and the angels; the material realm is home to human beings and to all living things on earth. While we cannot pass from one realm to the other, evil angels (like Satan) and good angels (like the Angel of the Lord) can cross into our realm and act in it!

THE BIBLE CLEARLY TEACHES THAT ANGELS EXIST

There can be no question that the existence of angels is presupposed in the Bible. In the Old Testament (NKJV), the word "angel" appears 15 times in the Books of Moses, 13 times in the Historical Books, 8 times in the Poetical Books, and 17 times in the Prophets. Angels are mentioned much more frequently in the New Testament (NKJV): 30 times in the Gospels, 16 times in Acts, 30 times in the Epistles, and 74 times in Revelation. In addition, angels are called "living creatures" 23 times, cherubs or cherubim 10 times. Two angels, Gabriel (Dan. 8:16; 9:21; Luke 1:19, 26) and Michael (Dan. 10:13, 21; 12:1; Jude 9; Rev. 13:7), are identified by name. God's angels are called "spirits" 4 times (in the NKJV) and "holy ones" 10 times (in the NIV). The phrase "heavenly hosts" is applied to angels once (in the NKJV), but God is called "Lord of hosts" (that is, commander of heaven's angelic armies) no less than 281 times in the Old Testament. These 535 biblical references are all to God's angels and do not include the many references to Satan and the dark angels who follow him.

Scripture refers to angels in other ways also. The Bible uses the word "stars" symbolically to refer to angels, as in Job 38:72. In Psalm 89:6, angels are called *bene elim* ("sons of the mighty"), a name that emphasizes their great strength. In Psalm 103:20, David cried out, "Bless the LORD, you His angels, / Who excel in strength." The name "sons of the mighty" is surely appropriate, for Scripture depicts angels as performing feats impossible for human beings.

Another name for angels is *bene 'elohim,* "sons of God" (Job 1:6; 2:1; 38:7). The phrase "son of" is often used idiomatically in Hebrew to indicate the class to which one belongs. For instance, the phrase "son of man" emphasizes the fact that the one described is truly, or merely, a human being. Even the term *'elohim,* normally translated "God," is applied to angels in Psalm 8:5 and in descriptions of an experience such as Jacob's (Gen. 35:7; see also Dan. 3:25). In such cases, the expressions "sons of God" or "gods" simply mean "supernatural beings." These texts emphasize the fact that angels belong to the realm of the supernatural, not the realm of the natural.

ANSWERS TO OUR QUESTIONS ABOUT ANGELS MUST BE DRAWN FROM MANY DIFFERENT BIBLE PASSAGES

Despite the many references to angels in the Bible, no single passage develops a theology of angels or tries to answer all our questions about them. Instead, we must examine all of the references in order to come up with answers to the questions people ask. Here are some of the typical questions—and their answers.

Can we see angels? Not normally. Colossians 1:16 speaks of Christ as the Creator of all things in heaven and on earth, visible or *invisible.* We cannot see the spiritual realm with our eyes. Neither Moses nor the Israelites saw the Law and Order Angels who brought destruction to Egypt. No one saw the angel who struck Herod. When Elisha was protected by

ANGELORE

DO ANGELS HAVE WINGS?

Artists portray angels, both good and evil, as beings with wings. Even the "Christmas angel" figures that top our Christmas trees are winged. But do angels really have wings? Two special classes of angels, seraphim and cherubim, are described as winged (Isa. 6:2, 6; Ezek. 1:5–8). Although other angels are said to "fly" (Dan. 9:21; Rev. 14:6, 7), Fred Dickason notes that "they do not have material wings, for wings are for planing or flapping in flight for bodies with weight. Since angels are spirits, they have no weight. They certainly could move without physical wings" (C. Fred Dickason, *Angels Elect & Evil*, 1995, 42).

an army of angels, he had to pray that his servant's eyes would be opened before the servant was able to see the mountainside filled by a fiery angelic army, which stood between the prophet and the enemy (2 Kings 6:17). Even though angels are normally invisible to us, they *are* present.

Where do angels come from? The Bible makes it clear that angels are created beings. John 1:1–3 teaches that Christ's own creative acts were the source of everything that exists; the text specifically says that "without Him nothing was made that was made." The psalmist recognized this by calling on the visible and invisible creation to praise its Creator:

> Praise the LORD!
> Praise the LORD from the heavens;
> Praise Him in the heights!
> Praise Him, all His angels;
> Praise Him, all His hosts!
> Praise Him, sun and moon;
> Praise Him, all you stars of light!
> Praise Him, you heavens of heavens,
> And you waters above the heavens!
> Let them praise the name of the
>   LORD,
> For He commanded and they were
>   created.
>
> *Psalm 148:1–5*

When were angels created? John Calvin, in his *Institutes*, criticized those who "stir up questions concerning the time or order in which they [angels] were created." All that we can say is that the spiritual realm was populated with angels before the creation of the material universe. The Lord asked Job where he was when He designed the earth and laid its foundation, "When the morning stars sang together, / And all the sons of God [angels] shouted for joy?" (Job 38:7).

How are angels like human beings? It is a mistake to assume that angels in their uncloaked form "look like" people. We simply do not know. However, in many ways angels seem to be very much like human beings. They clearly are individuals, as we are. Angels have curiosity and intellect. First Peter 1:12 describes them as eagerly studying the events that transpire on earth in order to learn more about God's plan as it is worked out in history and in our lives. Angels are often described as engaged in conversation with human beings (see Dan. 10; Luke 1:27–38). Angels also have emotions. They rejoice in heaven over the salvation of individual sinners (Luke 15:10). Angels also have free will—that is, they can recognize options and make choices—as can be seen in the heavenly counsels described in 1 Kings 22 and Job 1. Like us, angels are individuals. Two angels—Michael and Gabriel—are given personal names, and the Bible speaks of multitudes of individual angels gathering on special occasions (see Luke 2:13). In these respects, angels and humans are not so different. Angels and humans are certainly enough alike that they can understand and communicate with each other.

How do angels differ from human beings? There are so many differences that it is difficult to list them. Angels have continued to exist since the time of their creation—they do not die (Luke 20:36). Their lives span millennia, and in that time they have come to understand us far better than we understand them.

As citizens of the spiritual realm, angels have experienced God directly; thus, they know Him in ways that we do not. God's angels are distinctive in that they remained faithful to the Lord when Satan rebelled, and apparently they have been confirmed in that faithful state. There is no biblical evidence to indicate that holy angels can still fall; they do God's will as perfectly as is possible for created beings (Ps. 103:20). Because God's angels always act in harmony with God's will, they are called His holy ones (Ps. 89:5, 7, NIV).

Angels are also called spirits (Heb. 1:14). The bodies of angels—whatever they may be—are not corporeal. Still, the fact that angels are individuals who can move from place to place indicates that their identity is organized and localized in some way. We have no notion what the actual bodies of angels look like; we know only that when angels appear to human beings, they are most often cloaked in human form.

Unlike humans, angels are sexless (Matt. 22:30). God created human beings as male and female. Because God created the ranks of angels in their entirety at one time, and because angels do not die (Luke 20:36), they have no need to procreate.

How do angels differ from God? It's extremely important not to become so engrossed with angels that we confuse their traits and abilities with those of God. Angels are created beings, and God is their Creator. God is omnipresent; that is, He is everywhere at once. Angels are limited spatially; angels can only be in one place at a time. God's angels are dependent; they depend upon God for direction and for their very existence. Most important, God's angels are His agents; their mission is to carry out God's will. God's angels do not act independently.

We are not told whether God's angels have any affection for us, but we are assured that God Himself loves us dearly. Although angels have powers far greater than ours, we are not to rely on angels. Instead, we are to depend on the God who sends angels to help us and who protects us in other ways as well.

What basic information about angels do we possess? We can sum up the basic information about God's angels provided in the Bible in this way. God's angels are spirits, beings who were directly created by God. Like human beings, angels are individuals. We know nothing about the bodies of angels, other than that when they have visited earth, they appeared to be ordinary—or, in some instances, extraordinary—human beings. Nevertheless, angels are active in our world in ways we cannot see. Our consideration of God's Law and Order Angels in chapter 3 indicated that angels do much of their work "behind the scenes," without appearing to us at all. God's angels, who have remained faithful to Him since their creation, serve Him in the material realm *and* in the spiritual realm.

ANGEL ENCOUNTERS TODAY

Jacob had no trouble recognizing the angels as they passed back and forth between earth and heaven in his vision. Yet biblical accounts of angel visitations make it clear that angels may visit us when we are completely unaware. Hebrews 13:2 recalls Abraham's visitation by three angels and exhorts: "Do not forget to entertain strangers, for by so doing some have unwittingly entertained angels." Abraham's three visitors looked like ordinary travelers to him. Lot and the men of Sodom had a similar impression of the angels who appeared to them. Nothing obvious marked those angels as supernatural visitors.

At times, of course, angels have appeared to people as very *unusual men.* The two men who appeared at Jesus' tomb after His resurrection wore "shining garments" (Luke 24:4). Daniel described an angel who appeared to him as "a certain man" and went on to say that "his face [was] like the appearance of lightning, his eyes like torches of fire, his arms and feet like burnished bronze in color, and the sound of his words like the voice of a multitude" (Dan. 10:6). There was no mistaking *this* supernatural being!

However, it is possible to be mistaken about angel visitations. Paul warned that "Satan himself transforms himself into an angel of light" (2 Cor. 11:14). What a person takes as a visit from an angel may not be a visit from one of God's angels at all! So it's important not to assume that every supernatural visitation is by an angel sent from God, nor should we assume that every experience we take to be an angel encounter actually is one. It is possible that an angel encounter is imaginary, just as it is possible that a dream may simply be a dream rather than a vision.

———————— ❖ ————————

ANGELORE

ANGELIC COMFORT

ileen Elias Freeman, the founder of the AngelWatch Network, tells about how an angel comforted her as a child (*Touched by Angels,* 1994, p. 39). After the death of her grandmother, Eileen began to have fears that turned into terror at the sight of familiar toys and ob-

jects in her room. While she was in bed one night, Eileen saw a mist-like cloud appear and take on the shape of a man's face, with large, dark, and compassionate eyes. She sat up straight in bed and heard a voice say, "Don't be afraid, Eileen. Your grandmother is not in a cold and dark grave. She is happy in heaven with God and her loved ones." When Eileen asked, "Who are you?" she was told, "I am your guardian angel. Always remember, there is nothing to be afraid of."

———————— ————————

Eileen Elias Freeman further reports (pp. 87–93) on angel visits in our time, and she provides several "points of discernment" that she believes will reduce confusion over whether or not an angel encounter is genuine. According to her list:

1. Angel encounters don't leave us with feelings of anxiety or fears we can't quite name.
2. Angels don't leave us confused.
3. Angels don't try to force us into anything.
4. Angel messages point to the Sender and away from the messenger.
5. We must always examine the fruits of any angelic encounter or message in our lives and the lives of those around us.
6. Test anything that seems like an angelic message against what is known to be true, wise, and filled with love and light.
7. An angelic encounter leaves us changed for the better in some way, great or small.
8. Angelic encounters don't have hurtful consequences for those around us.
9. Any being we can summon at will, whether with or without accompanying rituals, is probably (*certainly!*) not an angel.

This list is helpful in some ways, and it raises an important question: What are the characteristics of real angel encounters? The best way to answer this question is to catalogue and then carefully examine the angel encounters reported in Scripture to see what we can learn. In what follows, the focus will be on incidents in which individuals or groups *interacted with* angels. We will look at each of these encounters to discover to whom the angel(s) appeared, the form they appeared in, the purpose of the appearance, the immediate response of the person(s) to the encounter, and the outcome of the encounter. The results of this investigation will give us a grid we can use to think more carefully about what the Bible teaches, and it will provide criteria we can use to evaluate any personal experience we may regard as an angel encounter.

ANGEL ENCOUNTERS THROUGHOUT THE SCRIPTURES

For the purposes of this study, we will limit ourselves to incidents in which individuals or groups encountered and interacted with God's good angels, including the Angel of the Lord.

ANGEL ENCOUNTERS IN THE PENTATEUCH
(Genesis—Deuteronomy)

The first five books of the Old Testament were written by Moses around 1400 B.C. With the exception of Genesis, the Pentateuch focuses on events during Moses' life, which spanned 120 years. Most of the reports of angel encounters in the Pentateuch are located in Genesis.

Genesis is a seminal book which describes the origins of our universe and of humankind; it also defines God's unique relationship with the Jewish people, established by the covenant He made with Abraham. Most of the angel encounters described in Genesis have a direct or an indirect relationship to this covenant, and several of those encounters serve to establish the transmission of the covenant from Abraham to his son, Isaac, and to Isaac's son, Jacob. Eight of the ten angel encounters reported in the Pentateuch probably took place within a one-hundred-year period, from around 2000 to 1900 B.C.

1. Genesis 16. Hagar was pregnant and fled from the tents of Abraham and Sarah. The text says that "the Angel of the LORD found her," which may imply that he met Hagar in the guise of an ordinary traveler. The Angel of the Lord made promises concerning her son, Ishmael, and sent her back to her life as Sarah's slave. Hagar later realized that she had "seen him" (16:13), which again suggests the angel appeared cloaked as an ordinary person. Only afterward did Hagar understand the encounter to have been with the Angel of the Lord himself. Hagar returned to Sarah as commanded, and gave birth to Abraham's son, Ishmael (16:15).

2. Genesis 18. The Lord, accompanied by two angels, visited Abraham. All three appeared to be ordinary men, and we must assume that the Lord took on His cloak as the "Angel of the Lord" (18:1–3). The Lord announced that Sarah would bear Abraham's son "about this time next year" (18:10; NIV).

The Lord also revealed His intent to investigate Sodom (18:17–21). Abraham implored God not to destroy the innocent with the wicked, and God promised to spare the city if ten righteous persons could be found in it (18:23–33).

3. Genesis 19. Two of the angels who visited Abraham entered Sodom, still appearing to be ordinary travelers. Lot offered them hospitality (19:1–3). The men of the city gathered, intent on the homosexual rape of the visitors (19:4–11). The angels revealed that God had sent them to destroy Sodom and to rescue Lot and his family. Lot believed the angels, but was hesitant (19:12–15). The angels physically removed Lot and his family from Sodom (19:16); they then destroyed Sodom and four other sinful cities of the plain (19:24–25).

4. Genesis 21. Ishmael, about 17 years old, teased three-year-old Isaac (21:8). Sarah insisted that Abraham send Ishmael and his mother, Hagar, away. Abraham resisted, but God confirmed that as His will (21:12–13). Hagar and Ishmael wandered in the desert until their water was gone and they were dying. This time, Hagar heard the voice of the "angel of God" calling from heaven (21:17). The an-

gel of God told Hagar not to fear and showed her a source of water nearby (21:19). Hagar and Ishmael were saved, and Ishmael became the father of the Arab peoples.

5. Genesis 22. The Lord told Abraham to offer Isaac as a sacrifice on Mount Moriah (22:1–2). Abraham was about to kill his son when the Angel of the Lord called to Abraham from heaven and stopped him (22:10–11). Abraham saw a ram caught in a thicket and offered it in place of his son. The Angel of the Lord again called to Abraham from heaven and reconfirmed the covenant promises, assuring the obedient patriarch of His continual blessing (22:15–18).

6. Genesis 28. In a dream, Jacob saw angels passing back and forth over a ladder (a *ramp*) that bridged the gap between the material and spiritual realms (28:12). There is no hint here that the angels seemed to be either ordinary or extraordinary men, so Jacob apparently saw the angels in their natural, luminous form. The Lord confirmed Jacob's inheritance of His covenant with Abraham (28:13, 14) and

added to that some personal promises. God would go with Jacob and keep him. God would bring Jacob back to Canaan and not leave him (28:15). Jacob's initial reaction was one of awe and fear (28:16); he then responded to God's promises by committing himself to the Lord (28:20–22).

7. Genesis 31. The Angel of God spoke to Jacob in a dream (31:11) and identified himself as the "God of Bethel" (31:13). The Lord showed Jacob how to gain large flocks and herds at the expense of his uncle Laban, who had cheated him for 20 years (31:10, 12). God then told Jacob to return to Canaan. Jacob followed the Lord's instructions and set out for Canaan (31:20).

8. Genesis 32. As Jacob traveled toward Canaan, "the angels of God met him." It would seem that these angels appeared in their natural, luminous form, as they had at Bethel earlier (Gen. 28), for the text tells us "when Jacob saw them" he said "this is God's camp" (32:1, 2). We are not told the reason for this angel encounter, but the name Jacob gave the site, Menanaim, or "double camp," is suggestive. Jacob stopped there as he prepared for the reunion with his brother Esau. It's important to remember that when the two brothers last saw each other 20 years earlier, Esau was intent on killing Jacob. It may well be that the appearance of the angels was intended to encourage Jacob, who was obviously afraid, by reminding him of God's promises, presence, and protection.

9. Exodus 3. The Angel of the Lord appeared to Moses in a burning bush (3:2). Moses' first reaction was one of curiosity (3:3). As the dialogue with God developed, Moses was told that he was to go back to Egypt and free his people. Moses was reluctant and fearful (3:11), so the Lord told Moses in detail what would happen when he returned to Egypt (3:12–22). In the end, Moses obeyed and became Israel's great deliverer and lawgiver.

10. Numbers 22. After God warned the pagan seer Balaam in a dream not to accept a king's commission to curse Israel, Balaam did so anyway (22:2–21). The Angel of the Lord blocked the pagan prophet's path on the road. The donkey on which Balaam rode could see the angel, but Balaam could not. God then opened Balaam's eyes and he saw the Angel of the Lord standing there with sword drawn (22:31). This was no cloaked angel; it was unmistakably a supernatural being. Balaam "fell flat on his face" (22:31). God gave him permission to continue on and said, "only the word I speak to you, that you shall speak" (22:35). When Balaam later tried to curse Israel, all he could utter were words of blessing (Num. 23, 24). After this failure to earn his fee, Balaam advised the king who hired him to use young women to seduce the men of Israel and lead them into idolatry, the assumption being that then God Himself would be forced to curse His people (31:16). Balaam's greed overcame his awe of the Angel of the Lord, and he defied God's clear instruction that he was to bless, rather than curse, Israel. Balaam later was killed when Israel invaded his homeland (Josh. 13:22).

ANGEL ENCOUNTERS IN THE HISTORICAL BOOKS   (Joshua— Esther)

The Historical Books span a period of about a thousand years, from Israel's conquest of Canaan under Joshua (c. 1400 B.C.), to the deportation of the Jews from the promised land by Babylonians (596 B.C.) and their return seven decades later, to the end of Nehemiah's governorship of Jerusalem (around 430 B.C.). During this thousand-year period, only six unmistakable angel encounters are reported!

1. Judges 2. The Angel of the Lord appeared to the Israelites gathered at Gilgal some years after their conquest had established their domination of Canaan. Each tribe was given its own district and told to drive out any Canaanites who remained, for while organized resistance had ended, there were still cities and lands occupied by the original inhabi-

tants. Some tribes simply failed to drive out the enemy (Judg. 1:19, 21), while others let the defeated enemy stay to pay tribute or to serve as slaves (Judg. 1:35). The Angel of the Lord appeared to announce the consequences of Israel's lack of trust and disobedience (2:1–3). The reaction of the people was to weep, to confess their sin, and to offer sacrifices (2:4). While weeping after being rebuked may at times be little more than self-pity, a godly sorrow can lead to repentance (see 2 Cor. 7:8–10). This is apparently what happened here, for "the people served the LORD all the days of Joshua, and all the days of the elders who outlived Joshua" (Judg. 2:7).

2. Judges 6. The days of the judges were marked by history repeating itself. The Israelites would turn aside to worship pagan deities; God would use foreign oppressors to discipline Israel. The people would turn back to God, and God would then send a military–political–religious leader called a "judge."

Judges 6 reports that the Israelites did evil and "so the LORD had delivered them into the hand of Midian for seven years" (6:1). After the Israelites turned back to the Lord, the Angel of the Lord appeared to a young man named Gideon (6:12). The dialogue makes it clear that the angel was cloaked as an ordinary human being in this encounter. The angel called Gideon a "mighty man of valor" (6:12) and said that Gideon would defeat the Midianites (6:14, 15). Gideon was skeptical, and he pointed out that God had not done anything for His people recently (6:13). Gideon "perceived that He was the Angel of the LORD" only after the angel had

put out the end of the staff that was in His hand, and touched the meat and the unleavened bread; and fire rose out of the rock and consumed the meat and the unleavened bread. And the Angel of the LORD departed out of his sight. Judges 6:21

Gideon was terrified, but God spoke to him and reassured him (6:23).

Throughout the rest of this familiar story, Gideon continues to dialogue with God and to receive His directions. Whatever the means of communication, there is no hint that it is mediated through an angel encounter.

3. *Judges 13*. Late in the period of the judges, the Angel of the Lord appeared to the childless wife of a man named Manoah. He announced that she was to have a son, who from birth was to be set apart to God (13:2, 3). The parents were to be careful that their son drank no alcohol and that his hair was never cut (13:4, 5). In this encounter, the Angel of the Lord did not look like an ordinary man. Manoah's wife said, "His countenance was like the countenance of the Angel of God, very awesome" (13:6). Later, Manoah prayed that God would send the "Man of God" to instruct them further on rearing what must be a very special child (13:8). In answer to Manoah's prayer, the Angel of the Lord did return. Despite the angel's awesome appearance, Manoah was not sure of his identity. When Manoah offered a burnt offering to the Lord, as he was instructed, "the Angel of the LORD ascended in the flame of the altar!" (13:20). Manoah was terrified by this supernatural event and said "we shall surely die" (13:22). This time reassurance came from his wife, who sensibly pointed out that if the Lord had intended to kill them, He wouldn't have accepted their offering or revealed the future to them (13:23).

4. *1 Chronicles 21*. God sent a plague that killed many in Israel (21:14). King David saw the "angel of the LORD standing between earth and heaven, having in his hand a drawn sword stretched out over Jerusalem." David and the elders with him "fell on their faces" at the sight (21:16). The angel did not speak to David directly. Instead, the angel spoke to the prophet Gad and told him that David was to "erect an altar to the LORD on the threshing floor of Ornan the Jebusite," the future site of Solomon's temple (21:18). The angel was also seen by Ornan and his four sons, who hid in fear. In this encounter, the angel is visible and is clearly a supernatural being who inspires terror. David did as Gad, speaking in God's

name, told him. God stopped the plague, and David offered sacrifices (21:15b, 26, 27).

5. *1 Kings 19*. Elijah the prophet stood alone against King Ahab's and Queen Jezebel's vigorous efforts to supplant the worship of Yahweh with the worship of the pagan deity Baal. In a contest with 400 prophets of Baal, Elijah won the support of the people and convinced them that the Lord is God (18:5–40). When Queen Jezebel threatened to have Elijah killed, he was suddenly terrified and fled (19:1–3). Elijah collapsed, exhausted and in despair, and "an angel touched him" and provided him with food and water (19:4, 5). After Elijah slept awhile, the "Angel of the LORD came back a second time" and fed him once again. Elijah traveled for 40 days and 40 nights on the strength that food provided (19:6–8). There is no indication in the text about the angel's form or how Elijah perceived him. The impression we have of Elijah is that he was almost too exhausted to notice! After this event, however, the Lord Himself spoke with Elijah without mediation through an angel.

6. *2 Kings 1*. Elijah was strengthened and returned to his ministry. When King Ahaziah, the son of Ahab and Jezebel, was injured, he sent messengers to a pagan deity to ask if he would recover (1:2). The Angel of the Lord spoke to Elijah and told him to intercept Ahaziah's messengers and rebuke the king for looking to a pagan god and to inform Ahaziah: "You shall not come down from the bed to which you have gone up, but you shall surely die" (1:4). Rather than repent, the king sent soldiers to bring Elijah to him (1:9). The first group of 50 soldiers was consumed by fire from heaven, as was a second group (1:10–13). A third group of soldiers was spared when their captain begged Elijah for their lives. At this point, the Angel of the Lord again spoke to Elijah, telling him not to be afraid of the king and to go and repeat the message in person. Elijah did so. The prophet was unhurt, and "Ahaziah died according to the word of the LORD which Elijah had spoken" (1:17). In this encounter, it appears that Elijah heard and recognized the voice of the Angel of the Lord, but did not see him in visible form.

ANGEL ENCOUNTERS IN THE MAJOR PROPHETS   (Isaiah—Daniel)

Both Isaiah (6:1–13) and Ezekiel (1:1–28; 9:3—11:23) saw angels, but neither prophet interacted with the angels in a manner similar to what we have seen in the angel encounters examined so far. However, the book of Daniel reports several angel encounters.

1. Daniel 3. The kingdom of Judah was invaded by Babylon, and the enemy ruler, King Nebuchadnezzar, deported upper-class families and educated their sons for government service. Shadrach, Meshach, Abed-Nego, and Daniel were trained for posts in Babylon's bureaucracy.

When Nebuchadnezzar commanded his officials to worship a statue he erected, Shadrach, Meshach, and Abed-Nego refused (3:8–18). Nebuchadnezzar ridiculed the idea that any god could deliver them from the death penalty he had imposed, and they were thrown into a fiery furnace (3:21). There, they were seen walking with a fourth figure, whom Nebuchadnezzar himself saw and identified as a "son of God," that is, a supernatural being (see p. 143). When the three men came safely out of the flames, Nebuchadnezzar realized that God had sent an angel to save them (3:28) and made a decree that no one was to speak "anything amiss against the God of Shadrach, Meshach, and Abed-Nego" (3:29). This angel encounter not only resulted in the deliverance of the three faithful Jews, but played a part in the conversion of Babylon's ruler (see Dan. 4:28–37).

An angel joined Shadrach, Meshach, and Abed-Nego in the furnace.

2. Daniel 6. Daniel held high positions in the administrations of the Babylonian Empire and the Persian Empire which replaced it. Other high officials resented Daniel and feared his integrity. They tricked the Persian king, Darius, into making a law which mandated that for 30 days no one could pray to, or make a request of, anyone other than the king (6:4–9). Daniel continued to pray daily by his open window; he was accused, and the king reluctantly ordered him to be thrown into a den of hungry lions (6:10–15). Darius, who respected and liked Daniel, expressed his hope to Daniel: "Your God, whom you serve continually, He will deliver you" (6:16). The next morning, Daniel emerged alive and gave this report: "My God sent His angel and shut the lions' mouths, so that they have not hurt me" (6:22). We are not told how Daniel recognized the angel who delivered him or what that angel looked like, but apparently Daniel saw and recognized his deliverer.

3. Daniel 8. During the Persian period, Daniel had a vision in which a series of animals represented succeeding kingdoms (8:1–12). Daniel then heard the voices of "holy ones"—angels—talking about his vision. While Daniel puzzled over the meaning of the vision, a being "having the appearance of a man" (8:15), identified as "Gabriel" (8:16), approached him. Daniel was "afraid" and fell down before him. Daniel said, "I was in a deep sleep with my face to the ground," but the angel "touched me, and stood me upright" (8:18). The angel then explained the vision. Afterward, Daniel fainted and "was sick for days" (8:27).

4. Daniel 9. Daniel had read the prophecy of Jeremiah which predicted a return of the Jews to their homeland after 70 years of captivity in Babylon (see Jer. 25:11). That discovery moved Daniel to fast, to pray, to confess Israel's sins, and to ask God to forgive His people and to fulfill the prophecy (9:3–19). While Daniel prayed, "the man Gabriel, whom I had seen in the vision at the beginning" (9:21; see Dan. 8:16f), came to him. Gabriel explained more about God's plan for Israel's future and gave Daniel a specific timetable for future events (9:24–27).

5. Daniel 10. Two years after the previous angel encounter (Dan. 9), Daniel set aside three weeks for fasting and prayer (10:1–3). On the twenty-fourth day, "a certain man" appeared (10:5). The figure is obviously supernatural: "His body was like beryl, his face like the appearance of lightning, his eyes like torches of fire" (10:6). The angel explained that he had been sent to answer Daniel's prayer. Daniel turned his "face toward the ground" and "became weak and unable to speak" (10:15–17). Several times in this passage, the angel is described as "one having the likeness of the sons of men" (10:16, 18). Although he glowed with a supernatural radiance, the angel was unmistakably humanoid. The angel then gave a lengthy and graphic description of events to take place at history's end (Dan. 11, 12).

ANGEL VISITATIONS IN THE MINOR PROPHETS (Hosea— Malachi)

The "minor" prophets spoke God's words to His people. Only in Zechariah is an angel encounter described.

1. Zechariah. Throughout the first chapters of his book, Zechariah speaks with an angel he designated as "the Angel of the LORD" (1:11, 12), but whom he more frequently referred to as "the angel who talked with me" (1:9, 14, 19; 2:3; 4:1, 4, 5; 5:5, 10; 6:4, 5). The phrase "who talked with me" emphasizes the angel's role as the interpreter of a series of visions given to Zechariah. In one vision (Zech. 3), Zechariah saw the Angel of the Lord and Satan debating over the high priest, Joshua. The high priest was cleansed, and the Angel of the Lord identified Joshua as a "sign" of the coming Messiah. Joshua's cleansing foreshadows the day when God will cleanse and purify His people. Although this angel plays a prominent role in the book of Zechariah, he is never described.

ANGEL ENCOUNTERS IN THE GOSPELS   (Matthew—John)

The Gospels report a flurry of angel encounters during Jesus' life. Those angel appearances cluster around the events of Jesus' birth, passion, and resurrection—critical events in the life of Christ.

1. Luke 1. The priest, Zacharias, was offering incense in the temple when an angel appeared. Although the angel is not described, he is instantly recognized as a supernatural being. Zacharias "was troubled, and fear fell upon him" (1:12). The angel announced that Zacharias and his childless wife would soon have a son, who was to be named John. Zacharias expressed doubt (1:18). The angel identified himself as Gabriel, one "who stands in the presence of God, and was sent to speak to you and bring you these glad tidings" (1:19). Gabriel also announced that because Zacharias did not believe his words, Zacharias would be mute until the child was born.

2. Luke 1. Six months later, Gabriel appeared to a young, unmarried woman—a virgin named Mary. Mary was apparently unafraid at Gabriel's appearance, but was troubled by his greeting her as a "highly favored one" who is "blessed . . . among women" (1:28, 29). The angel announced (1:31–34) that Mary would conceive and have a child, who was to be named Jesus, and that her child would be "the Son of the Highest" and would fulfill the Old Testament's prophecies of the coming Messiah (Anointed One, Deliverer). Mary's response was one of faith and submission: "Behold the maidservant of the Lord! Let it be to me according to your word" (1:38). What a contrast between the simple faith of this young girl and the doubt that filled the heart of Zacharias, an experienced priest dedicated to a lifetime of service to the Lord!

3. Matthew 1. Joseph was "betrothed" to Mary when he learned that Mary was pregnant (1:18). Joseph quietly considered canceling the two-stage Jewish marriage contract, which legally committed Joseph and Mary to each other and would then be fulfilled when they began to live together (1:19). An angel visited Joseph in a dream and told him, "Do not be afraid to take to you Mary your wife, for that which is conceived in her is of the Holy Spirit" (1:20). No description of the angel is given; rather, the focus is on his message.

4. Luke 2. Shepherds in the fields near Bethlehem experienced an angel encounter on the night Jesus was born. "And behold, an angel of the Lord stood before them, and the glory of the Lord shone around them, and they were greatly afraid" (2:9). Here, the angel appeared as a supernatural being and caused great fear. The angel reassured the shepherds and told them where to find the Christ-child (2:11, 12). Suddenly a "multitude of the heavenly host" (angels) appeared, praising God (2:13). After the angels departed, the shepherds hurried to find the Christ-child and to tell of their encounter with the angel (2:15–18).

5. Matthew 2. After Christ was born, King Herod threatened His life. An angel appeared

❖

to Joseph in a dream and instructed him to flee to Egypt. Again no description of the angel is given, and the emphasis is on his message.

6. Matthew 2. After the death of Herod, an angel again appeared to Joseph in a dream and instructed him to return to Judea. Matthew tells us that Joseph was "warned by God in a dream" to go to Nazareth in Galilee rather than to return to Judea (2:22). No description of an angel is given in these dream encounters.

7. Matthew 4. Jesus fasted for 40 days and nights and was then tempted by Satan. After the third temptation, Matthew tells us that "behold, angels came and ministered to Him" (4:11). No description of the angels is given.

8. Luke 22. Jesus, under extreme stress, prayed in the Garden of Gethsemane the night before His trial and crucifixion. During this time of prayer, Jesus was in such "agony" that "His sweat became like great drops of blood falling down to the ground" (22:44). In Jesus' moment of duress, "an angel appeared to Him from heaven, strengthening Him" (22:43).

9. Matthew 28; Luke 24; John 20. Jesus had been crucified and was buried. Early Sunday morning, several women went to the site of His burial. These three Gospels describe what the women saw at the tomb that first Easter morning.

Matthew 28. Two women named Mary came to see Jesus' tomb. There they found an angel whose "countenance was like lightning, and his clothing as white as snow" (28:3). Earlier, he had come and rolled away the great stone that sealed the tomb. The guards were so terrified they "shook for fear" and fainted (28:4). The angel reassured the fearful women and told them that Jesus had risen from the dead (28:5, 6).

Luke 24. Later, a group of women from Galilee visited the tomb and discovered that it was empty. Two angels "in shining garments" then stood beside them (24:4). The supernatural aspect of the angels filled the women with fear, and they "bowed their faces to the earth" (24:5). These angels also announced that Jesus "is risen" (24:6), and the women hurried to tell the disciples.

John 20. Mary Magdalene returned alone to the tomb and stood outside it weeping. When she looked into the tomb, she saw "two angels in white sitting . . . where the body of Jesus had lain" (20:12). Immediately afterward, Mary saw a figure she assumed to be the gardener. He spoke to her, and through her tears Mary suddenly recognized the risen Christ (20:14–17).

ANGEL ENCOUNTERS IN THE BOOK OF ACTS

The book of Acts tells the story of the emergence and spread of the early church during a period of some 30 years duration after Jesus' resurrection. Several angel encounters occur in Acts.

1. Acts 1. During the 40 days after His resurrection, Jesus frequently spoke with His disciples. After He gave them final instructions, Jesus ascended into heaven. As the disciples stood watching, "two men stood by them in white apparel" (1:10). These angels assured the disciples that Jesus would return "in like manner as you saw Him go into heaven" (1:11). The reference to "white apparel" indicates that the "men" were supernatural angels in their radiant form.

2. Acts 8. Philip, one of the deacons and evangelists in the early church, was "preaching Christ" in Samaria (8:4) when an angel of the Lord spoke to him (8:26). This angel, who is not described, was a messenger who sent Philip to a roadside miles away. There Philip met a "eunuch" of the Ethiopian queen and won him to Christ.

The term "eunuch" originally was a designation for a man who had been castrated. Eastern monarchs assumed that such men, who did not have to provide for children, would be less likely to steal from them or plot against them; therefore, rulers frequently filled important government posts with eunuchs. The term lost its original meaning over time, and it came to be used as a title for one who held high office, whether the official was castrated or not. The fact that this eunuch went "to Jerusalem to worship" (8:27) is evidence that he had not been castrated, since no person with such a defect was allowed to worship at the temple (see Deut. 23:1). Thus, the "Ethiopian eunuch" was a high government official who supervised the Queen of Ethiopia's treasury (8:27). The angel directed Philip to meet him and that led to his conversion.

3. Acts 10. A Roman centurion named Cornelius "saw clearly in a vision an angel of God" (10:3). The Roman is identified as "one who feared God," a term applied to someone who believed in Israel's God but had not converted to Judaism, which required circumcision, ritual baptism, and a commitment to adopt the Jewish lifestyle as defined by the Law. Apparently, the angel in the vision appeared in his radiant, supernatural form, for the text says that when Cornelius "observed him, he was afraid" (10:4). Later, Cornelius described the angel as "a man . . . in bright clothing" (10:30). The angel assured Cornelius that God had heard his prayers and told him to send for the apostle Peter. Cornelius did so, and when Peter arrived Cornelius became the first Gentile to accept the risen Christ as Savior.

4. Acts 12. King Herod Agrippa I had killed the apostle James and had imprisoned Peter. Peter was chained and under close guard when "an angel of the Lord stood by him, and a light [from the angel?] shone in the prison" (12:7). The chains fell from Peter's feet, and the angel led him out of the prison, the iron gate opening "of its own accord" (12:10). During these events Peter thought he was having a vision. Only when the angel was gone and Peter found himself in the streets of the city did he realize that the angel really had been there (12:11).

5. Acts 27. Paul was on a ship heading toward Rome when a storm drove it far off course and threatened the life of everyone on

board. After many days at sea, when all the passengers and crew despaired of surviving, Paul urged everyone to eat and reported that he had been visited by "an angel of the God to whom I belong and whom I serve" (27:23). The angel told Paul God's plan for his future and promised him the lives of all on board (27:24). We are told nothing about the angel's appearance or Paul's initial reaction. We are, however, given insight into Paul's confidence in the message: "I believe God that it will be just as it was told me" (27:25). It was, and all aboard survived.

ANGEL ENCOUNTERS IN THE EPISTLES (Romans—Jude)

There are many references to angels in the New Testament letters. However, there are no stories of personal encounters with angels.

ANGEL ENCOUNTERS IN THE BOOK OF REVELATION

The book of Revelation contains the great vision of God's ultimate triumph over evil given to the apostle John. God's angels are actively involved in the events described. The vision is seen from a heavenly, rather than an earthly, point of view. The activities of the angels observed by John are discussed in chapter 17.

A REVIEW OF ANGEL ENCOUNTERS IN THE BIBLE

The chart which summarizes angel encounters recorded in Scripture readily suggests several points.

CHARACTERISTICS OF BIBLICAL ANGEL ENCOUNTERS

- Angels who appear to human beings either as ordinary men or as radiant beings are always referred to as "men" when their form is described. While Isaiah and Ezekiel described unusual winged angels, there are no other mentions of winged beings in reports of angel encounters. When angels appear as ordinary men, they may not be recognized as angels right away.

Angel Encounters at a Glance

Passage	Angel(s) appear(s) to	Appearance	Context	Purpose	Initial response	Outcome
Gen. 16	Hagar	A man	Life	Promise, guide		Obedience
Gen. 18	Abraham	Men	Life	Promise, inform	Faith	Prayer
Gen. 19	Lot	Men	Life	Deliver	Hesitance	Life saved
Gen. 21	Hagar	Voice	Life	Deliver		Life saved
Gen. 22	Abraham	Voice	Dream	Test	Faith	Faith shown
Gen. 28	Jacob	Radiant beings	Dream	Promise	Fear	Commitment
Gen. 31	Jacob	Voice	Dream	Promise, direct		Obedience
Gen. 32	Jacob	Radiant beings	Life	Reassure		
Ex. 3	Moses	Burning bush	Life	Call to mission	Reluctance	Obedience
Num. 22	Balaam	Radiant being	Life	Warn	Promise	Betrayal
Judg. 2	Israel	Radiant being	Life	Warn	Weeping	Obedience
Judg. 6	Gideon	Man	Life	Call to mission	Skepticism, fear	Obedience
Judg. 13	Manoah's wife	Radiant being	Life	Direct	Terror	Prayer, obedience
1 Chron. 21	Gad, David	Radiant being	Life	Punish	Fear	Obedience
1 Kings 19	Elijah		Life	Strengthen		
2 Kings 1	Elijah	Voice	Life	Call to mission		Obedience
Dan. 3	Nebuchad-nezzer	Radiant being	Life	Deliver three men	Astonishment	Honored the Lord
Dan. 6	Daniel		Life	Deliver Daniel		Daniel saved
Dan. 8	Daniel	Radiant being	Vision	Explain vision	Fear, collapse	Vision clarified
Dan. 9	Daniel	Man "Gabriel"	Life	Inform of future		Wrote the prophecy

Angel Encounters at a Glance (*continued*)

Passage	Angel(s) appear(s) to	Appearance	Context	Purpose	Initial response	Outcome
Dan. 10	Daniel	Radiant being	Life, Vision	Inform of future	Weakness	Wrote the prophecy
Zech.	Zechariah		Vision	Interpret		Wrote the prophecy
Luke 1	Zacharias	Radiant being	Life	Promise, instruct	Fear, disbelief	Faith, obedience
Luke 1	Mary	Man "Gabriel"	Life	Promise		Faith, submission
Matt. 1	Joseph		Dream	Instruct		Obedience
Luke 2	Shepherds	Radiant being(s)	Life	Announce birth	Fear	Go to see Jesus
Matt. 2	Joseph		Dream	Warn		Obedience
Matt. 4	Jesus		Life	Minister		
Luke 22	Jesus		Life	Strengthen		Continue to pray
Matt. 28, Luke 24, John 20	Women	Radiant beings	Life	Announce Jesus is raised	Fear	Faith
Acts 1	Many	Radiant beings	Life	Promise		
Acts 8	Philip	Voice	Life	Call to mission		Obedience
Acts 10	Cornelius	Radiant being	Life	Promise, instruct	Fear	Obedience
Acts 12	Peter	Radiant being	Life	Release from prison		Freed
Acts 27	Paul		Life	Encourage		Faith

- Angels appear to people when they are asleep and when they are awake. Typically, angels appear unexpectedly, when a person is doing something ordinary.
- The most common purposes of angel encounters are: to communicate a message (of promise, instruction, direction, warning, reassurance); to call a person to a special mission; or to rescue people from some great danger. Frequently, the angelic messages are predictions of events to happen in the near future, and these predictions invariably come true.
- When an angel appears as a radiant being, the most common initial reaction is astonishment, awe, fear, or terror.
- Angel encounters have an impact on the lives of those who experience them. However, Balaam, an unbeliever, showed no change in his basic attitude. An angel encounter will not create faith in the Lord where none exists. Some believers were rescued from imminent death; nearly all demonstrated a deeper faith and commitment to the Lord; and those who were called to a mission found the strength to carry it to completion.

CRITERIA FOR DISCERNING AN ANGEL ENCOUNTER

Based upon our study of angel encounters in Scripture, we can expect a true angel encounter to have at least these characteristics:

- The angel will seem to be an ordinary man or a recognizably supernatural being.
- The angel will either deliver a message from God, call us to a special mission, or rescue us from an imminent danger.

- The angelic messenger might tell us something about our future—and if it is a true encounter, the prediction will always come true.
- Our initial reaction to an angel encounter may well be one of astonishment and fear.
- An angel encounter will not cause us to focus our thoughts on angels, but to deepen our faith and commitment to the Lord—the One who sent the angels.
- A true angel encounter will also lead us to greater obedience to the Lord and His word.

CONCLUSIONS ABOUT ANGEL ENCOUNTERS TODAY

Our survey of angel encounters recorded in Scripture is suggestive in other ways. The fact is that few angel encounters are recorded in the Bible, and those seem to be concentrated in certain periods of sacred history. It seems unlikely that the typical modern believer can expect an angel visit.

The Bible tells the story of select individuals who play a significant role in the unfolding of God's plan in history. We know little or nothing of ordinary men and women of faith, who lived their lives with no one present to record their experiences. It would be foolish indeed to assume that God's angels, who are the guardians of all His people, never visited any of the millions of people who lived during biblical times but about whom we know nothing today.

In light of the many reports of angel encounters made by believers in our day, we need to keep an open mind, for a God who is both loving and sovereign can send His angels to us whenever He wills.

CHAPTER 5

ANGELS GUIDE AND PROTECT:

GOING BEFORE AND BEHIND GOD'S PEOPLE

Exodus 14; additional Old & New Testament passages

Generations of Jewish children have recited this ancient Hebrew prayer at bedtime:

In the name of the Lord, God of Israel! May Michael be at my right hand and Gabriel at my left, before me Uriel and behind me Raphael, and above my head—the Divine Presence of God.

The expectation reflected in this prayer for children is rooted in Israel's history and reflected in a statement made in Psalm 34:7: "The angel of the LORD encamps all around those who fear Him, / And delivers them" NKJV. This verse is an affirmation, not a promise; it is a statement of fact, not something we need to pray for. The Lord's angel *does* encamp all around those who fear Him, and the angel of the Lord does deliver.

The historic root of this statement is found in Exodus 14, which tells the dramatic story of Israel's rescue from an Egyptian army in pursuit. The involvement of angels in those events is clearly stated in Exodus 14:19: "And the Angel of God, who went before the camp of Israel, moved and went behind them, and the pillar of cloud went from before them and

stood behind them." With an angel before and behind them, providing both guidance and protection, God's people had nothing to fear.

ANGELS AT THE RED SEA
(Exodus 14)

At last the people of Israel, enslaved for so long in Egypt, were freed! Pharaoh himself, stunned by the plagues that both devastated his land and caused the death of his oldest son, urged the Israelites to get out (Ex. 12:29–33). The Israelites quickly assembled at Succoth and then camped at the edge of the wilderness in Etham.

There were two routes that the Israelites could have taken out of Egypt. One route, later known as "the way [road, highway] of the land of the Philistines," lay along the Mediterranean coast, but it was fortified by the Egyptians. God knew His people were not yet mentally or spiritually prepared for warfare (Ex. 13:17), so God chose a second route, one which led them into the wilderness itself. After some time, God told Moses to make camp "before Pi Hahiroth, between Migdol and the sea, opposite Baal Zephon" (14:2).

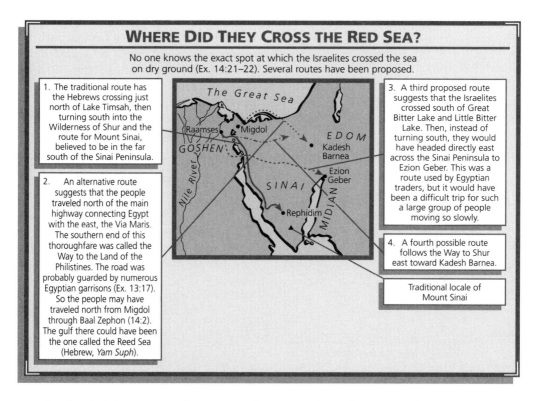

WHERE DID THEY CROSS THE RED SEA?

No one knows the exact spot at which the Israelites crossed the sea
on dry ground (Ex. 14:21–22). Several routes have been proposed.

1. The traditional route has the Hebrews crossing just north of Lake Timsah, then turning south into the Wilderness of Shur and the route for Mount Sinai, believed to be in the far south of the Sinai Peninsula.

2. An alternative route suggests that the people traveled north of the main highway connecting Egypt with the east, the Via Maris. The southern end of this thoroughfare was called the Way to the Land of the Philistines. The road was probably guarded by numerous Egyptian garrisons (Ex. 13:17). So the people may have traveled north from Migdol through Baal Zephon (14:2). The gulf there could have been the one called the Reed Sea (Hebrew, *Yam Suph*).

3. A third proposed route suggests that the Israelites crossed south of Great Bitter Lake and Little Bitter Lake. Then, instead of turning south, they would have headed directly east across the Sinai Peninsula to Ezion Geber. This was a route used by Egyptian traders, but it would have been a difficult trip for such a large group of people moving so slowly.

4. A fourth possible route follows the Way to Shur east toward Kadesh Barnea.

Traditional locale of Mount Sinai

The fact that the text gives four points of reference is significant. Although we don't know the exact locations today, the names are important. Pi Hahiroth means the "mouth [?] of Hirot," a river or canal. Migdol was a name given to several towns fortified by the Egyptians. Baal Zephon is thought to be located in the region of Lake Sirbonis. The point of these references, however, is to make it clear that Israel, camped "by the sea"—literally, "on the edge of the sea"—was trapped! There was no way that Israel could turn if the Egyptians pursued!

One last detail sets the scene for our examination of the angel's intervention. The "sea" in question is not the "Red Sea" of traditional translations. The Hebrew words *yom suph* mean "reed sea"—a "sea where papyrus reeds grow." There can be no doubt that the reference is to either the Bitter Lakes to the south of the Sinai Peninsula, or Lake Timsah in the center of the Sinai Peninsula. Again, however, the point is the same: The people of God were camped in a location that left them

trapped. So the matter of how Israel was released from the trap is preceded by the question of how they became trapped in the first place!

GOD GUIDES HIS PEOPLE INTO DANGER *(Exodus 13:18–22)*

The pillar of cloud (Exodus 13:21). When the Israelites left Egypt, they were guided by a cloudy, fiery pillar. During the day the cloud aspect was visible; during the night the fires roiling within it glowed in the darkness. The Bible says that the pillar was to "lead the way," with its different aspects allowing the Israelites to travel by day and by night.

The angel involvement (Exodus 14:19). While Exodus 13:21 tells us that "the LORD went before them" in the pillar "to lead the way," an angel was clearly involved with this phenomenon. It was the "Angel of God, who went before the camp of Israel" and who "moved and went behind them." The angel's change of

The Israelites' reaction (Exodus 14:10–12). The text makes it clear that God, through the agency of His angel, purposely placed the Israelites in this vulnerable position. God led His people into danger. Israel's angel-guide led them into a trap.

There are times when we must wonder if our guardian angel has taken a day off, times when we find ourselves trapped, or even injured—and we wonder: How, if God is really with us, could such a thing happen? In such times we should remember how the Israelites felt when they realized the position they were in: They panicked; they wished they had never been freed; and they complained that "it would have been better for us to serve the Egyptians than that we should die in the wilderness" (14:12). The Israelites assumed that God had led them into trouble to harm them!

It's not unusual to question God's concern for us when something terrible happens. But when tragedies occur, we need to remember that God has a good purpose in mind, just as He did for the fearful Israelites.

GOD'S PURPOSES IN LEADING ISRAEL INTO A TRAP
(Exodus 14:3–9)

Before the Egyptian army appeared, the Lord told Moses what He intended to do: "I will harden Pharaoh's heart, so that he will pursue them; and I will gain honor over Pharaoh and over all his army, that the Egyptians may know that I am the LORD" (Ex. 14:4).

Pharaoh's hardened heart (Exodus 14:4). This expression, repeated in several Exodus texts, has troubled many readers. They assume it means that God forced Pharaoh to make choices for which he was then punished. The text does say, here and elsewhere (Ex. 4:21; 7:3), that God hardened Pharaoh's heart, but it also says that Pharaoh hardened his own heart (Ex. 8:32; 9:34–35).

The important question to ask is, How did God harden Pharaoh's heart? God did not

A cloudy, fiery pillar led the Israelites.

❖

position is reflected in the movement of the cloudy pillar: When the angel moved, "the pillar of cloud went from before them and stood behind them" (14:19). The Angel of God was the Lord's agent who directed the Israelites in the path they were to take.

Do angels lead us into danger? It's clear from the text that God's angel led the Israelites to the edge of the sea, where they were to camp. It's also clear that this was a trap. Israel's way was blocked by the sea in front, the Hirot river (or canal) on one side, and Migdol, one of Egypt's fortified towns, on the other side.

The Israelites' location was significant for another reason. When Pharaoh received intelligence of where his ex-slaves were camped, he immediately assumed that "they [were] bewildered by the land; the wilderness has closed them in" (Ex. 14:3). That was clearly one of the factors which led Pharaoh to assemble an army to recover his slaves. Pharaoh concluded that the Israelites were trapped, that they had nowhere to go. He could simply marshal his army to scoop them up!

change any natural tendencies of Pharaoh's thoughts, emotions, or will—nor did God force Pharaoh to act against his will. What God did was to reveal Himself to Pharaoh—in Moses' words and in subsequent acts of power. When the elders of Israel were given a similar self-revelation by God, they believed (Ex. 4:30, 31). When God revealed Himself to Pharaoh, he hardened his heart.

When God reveals Himself to any person, that person will either respond with growing faith, and his or her heart will soften toward God, or that person will respond with disbelief, and his or her heart will harden toward the Lord. Each individual, like Pharaoh, is fully responsible for his or her own response to the Lord.

In this case, God saw to it that Pharaoh received word of the Israelites' plight. Pharaoh's response was to harden his heart, which committed him to pursue the Israelites in an attempt to recover the slaves that God had so recently freed. Pharaoh had not yet learned to respect the God of the Hebrews—but he was about to.

God's purposes (Exodus 14:4, 31). The Lord told Moses His purpose for the Egyptians: "I will gain honor over Pharaoh and over all his army, that the Egyptians may know that I am the LORD." The Egyptians still were not convinced that Israel's God must be respected. The coming events would erase all doubts. God also had a purpose for His own people. God led Israel into the trap *so that He might deliver them!* After God acted to deliver Israel, the Bible says that "the people feared [respected] the LORD, and believed the LORD and His servant Moses" (14:31).

If we were never in danger, we would never have the opportunity to *see* God act for us. If we were never frightened, we would never have the opportunity to trust God in extreme situations. When God delivers His people from troubles, it is a way that He witnesses about Himself to the world, and it is a way that He strengthens the faith of His people.

GOD'S VICTORY OVER THE EGYPTIANS *(Exodus 14:5–30)*

Egypt's army pursued (Exodus 14:5–9). When Pharaoh realized that the Israelites were in a trap, he assembled an army of chariots and rushed to recapture his slaves. Egyptian war chariots were lightweight and could be carried easily by a single individual. They were intended to provide quick transportation for an archer, who could attack or pursue an enemy from the swiftly moving platform. Pharaoh's army of chariots quickly came to the place where the Israelites were camped.

Moses encouraged Israel (Exodus 14:13, 14). When the Israelites saw Pharaoh's army, they panicked and "were very afraid" (Ex. 14:10). Moses encouraged them not to fear, but to "stand still, and see the salvation of the LORD" (14:13); he promised that "the LORD will fight for you, and you shall hold your peace" (14:14).

The words "stand still" are instructive. When we become fearful we tend to act unwisely. Panic urges us to do something, anything! Often, the best thing we can do is to "stand still" until the Lord shows us the salvation He surely will provide. That is what He did for Moses when He promised to divide the sea so Israel could pass through safely (Ex. 14:15, 16). Since we too have God as our protector, we can rest assured that He will "fight for us" while we continue to trust in Him; and while we wait on Him, He will show us what to do next.

The angel acted (Exodus 14:19, 20). At this point, the angel who had led Israel moved from the front to the back of the camp, taking up a position between Israel and the Egyptians. The cloudy, fiery pillar went with the angel. Strikingly, the cloud facing toward the Egyptians blocked out light, and so the Egyptians could not find a way to attack Israel. However, the cloud facing toward Israel showed its fiery aspect and gave the Israelites the light they needed to follow the path that opened through the sea.

God opened the sea for Israel (*Exodus 14:21, 22*). Two miracles occurred here. First, God sent a wind that swept the waters back and formed walls on the right and on the left. This opened a way for the Israelites to escape the trap—they went forward through the sea. Second, the Israelites passed on "dry land"—there weren't even any muddy sandals! God showed a wonderful attention to details!

God closed the sea on the Egyptians (*Exodus 14:23–29*). When morning came, the Egyptian army pursued the Israelites on the corridor of dry land. As soon as Pharaoh's forces were fully committed, the seabed became muck again, which dismounted the chariot wheels "so that they drove them with difficulty" (14:25a). The Egyptians realized that the Lord was now actively involved and tried desperately to turn back (14:25b), but it was too late. The Lord told Moses to stretch his hand out over the sea. The waters flowed back, and "the sea returned to its full depth" (14:27). Not a single Egyptian soldier escaped (14:28).

The angel who went before the Israelites and led them into apparent disaster, and who had then gone behind them to protect them from the pursuing army, had done his work. The Lord, in one of His most memorable acts of all, saved His people again. No wonder the children of Israel, when they saw the bodies of the Egyptian soldiers washed up on the shore (14:30), sang and danced and praised God:

> I will sing to the LORD,
> For He has triumphed gloriously!
> The horse and its rider
> He has thrown into the sea!
> The LORD is my strength and song,
> And He has become my salvation.
>
> *Exodus 15:1, 2a*

IN LIFE AND IN DEATH

The story of Israel's crossing of the Reed Sea, and particularly the reference in Exodus 14:19 to the angel "who went before the camp of Israel" and then "moved and went behind them," makes it very clear: God's angels are involved in leading His people (going before), and in protecting them from enemies (going behind to stand between the forces of Egypt and the people of Israel). We will soon examine both of those ministries of angels throughout the Scriptures, but first we will consider the biblical evidence which suggests that angels not only guide us during our lifetime, but also "go before" us when we die.

Many contemporary angel stories suggest that this is a reality. Take, for instance, a story in Ann Spangler's book, *An Angel a Day* (1994, p. 156), about a child named Catherine, who was dying of leukemia. Catherine's parents had been raised in Christian homes, but had long since abandoned their faith and their families. When Catherine was ten, she became so weak she couldn't leave her bed. Joann Kruse told Spangler the story:

> While my aunt and uncle were keeping vigil one afternoon at her bedside, she shocked them by suddenly sitting straight up and pointing. "Can't you see the angels? They're all around us!" she said excitedly.
> Uncle Ray asked her what the angels were doing.
> "They're laughing and one of them is stretching out his arms and asking me if I would like to go with them," the little girl replied.
> "Would you like to go?" my uncle asked.
> "If it's all right with you and Mom," she replied.

The parents nodded their assent. Catherine reached out both arms to the invisible angels, and she was gone.

HOW WE ARE TO VIEW DEATH

Stories like Catherine's not only reassure, but also capture the wonderful reality of which the laughing angels remind us. The material realm in which we live is not all there is; there is also a spiritual realm beyond or beside it. This spiritual realm is not only the home of God and angels, but it is the true home of believers as well. Physical death is simply a crossing over to another realm, a realm which is far better.

The unbeliever's grim view of death. Human beings throughout the ages have maintained the desperate hope that they will continue to exist after death. Plutarch wrote, "For my part, I will never let go of the continuance of the soul." This hope was desperate indeed and weighted down by a terrible uncertainty. The Roman poet Catullus begged for his love's kisses because an endless night lay just ahead.

> Lesbia mine, let's live and love!
> Give no doit for tattle of
> Crabbed old censorius men;
> Suns may set and rise again,
> But when our short day takes flight
> Sleep we must one endless night.

Eat, the poet suggests, drink and be merry, for tomorrow we die.

It is perhaps even more poignant to read the reflections of a person whose loved one has just died. Tacitus finished his tribute to Agricola in this way:

If there be any habitation for the spirits of the just; if, as wise men will have it, the soul that is great perishes not with the body, may you rest in peace.

Tacitus' haunting and uncertain "if" is followed by the only certainty that he knows.

Whatever we have loved in Agricola, whatever we have admired, abides and will abide, in the hearts of men, in the procession of the ages, in the records of history. Many of the ancients has Forgetfulness engulfed as though neither fame nor name was theirs; Agricola, whose story here is told, will outlive death, to be our children's heritage.

What a poor substitute fame is for personal immortality!

The believer's view of immortality (1 Corinthians 15:54, 55, 57). The uncertainty of the pagans of biblical times provides a stark contrast to the absolute sense of triumph reflected in Paul's great chapter on personal resurrection in his first letter to the Corinthians. Paul claimed that Christ rose bodily from the dead, the final proof that this destiny also awaits all who are His. Paul writes:

So when this corruptible has put on incorruption, and this mortal has put on immortality, then shall be brought to pass the saying that is written: "Death is swallowed up in victory."

> "O Death, where is your sting?
> O Hades, where is your victory?"
> . . . .

But thanks be to God, who gives us the victory through our Lord Jesus Christ.

1 Corinthians 15:54, 55, 57 (NIV)

There is no uncertainty here!

Even so, death remains an enemy which no one is eager to face. Our faith can be as strong as Paul's, and yet uncertainties and fears are only natural as we approach our last moment. It is then that we experience the last, and perhaps most special, of the guiding ministries of angels, for Catherine's experience, and the experience of others, suggests that angels are with us in the moment of our death, ready to welcome us with shouts of joy and to guide us into our new life in eternity.

BIBLICAL EVIDENCE OF ANGEL GUIDANCE AT DEATH

THE DEATH OF ELIJAH
(2 Kings 2:11, 12)

The setting (2 Kings 2:4–10). The prophet Elijah spent his life struggling against the efforts of Israel's rulers to replace the worship of the Lord with the worship of the pagan deity Baal. Soon Elijah would be replaced by Elisha, who had been his companion in his later years. The Lord revealed to both of them that He planned to "take" Elijah; He even specified the day. Elijah wanted to go on alone, but Elisha would not leave him. What Elisha wanted was a "double portion" of Elijah's spirit when the aged prophet passed over to the spiritual realm.

The phrase "double portion" refers to inheritance laws in Israel. The older son, who inherited the father's place as head of the family, was to receive a double portion of the family wealth (see Deut. 21:17).

Elisha wanted to inherit Elijah's role as God's chief prophet in Israel.

Elijah could not make that decision, so he told Elisha that if he should see what happened when Elijah was taken from him, then God would have granted his request.

Elisha saw angels (2 Kings 2:11). When the moment arrived for Elijah to go to heaven, Elisha saw what happened. What he saw is described in 2 Kings 2:11: "Suddenly a chariot of fire appeared with horses of fire, and separated the two of them; and Elijah went up by a whirlwind [tornado] into heaven."

There can be no doubt that Elisha's vision of a chariot of fire was a vision of angels.

Second Kings 6 tells the familiar story of a Syrian raid into Israel to capture Elisha. The enemy force surrounded the town where Elisha and his servant slept. The next morning the servant saw the Syrian force and ran to his master. In answer to Elisha's prayer, the servant's eyes were opened "and behold, the mountain was full of horses and chariots of fire all around them" (6:17). God's angels were "encamped around" his prophet, protecting him from the enemy.

When we compare these two stories, it is obvious that Elisha undoubtedly saw angels in their radiant form—not necessarily in the form of horses or chariots, but riding horses or chariots in the ether. Elijah was clearly taken up to heaven by angels, who bore him to the Lord.

❖

THE DEATH OF LAZARUS
(Luke 16:19–25)

Jesus' story of the rich man and Lazarus is not intended to be read as a parable. When He told parables, Christ typically introduced them with the phrase "the kingdom of heaven is like. . . ." Additionally, in no parable does Jesus identify a person by name or speak of an individual as if he or she was a real person. What we find in Luke 16 is best taken as Jesus' description of real people and of real events.

The rich man (Luke 16:19–21, 31). We know several things about the rich man in this story. He was very wealthy, he did not "hear [respond to] Moses and the prophets," as was evident in his treatment of the beggar who lay in the street outside his home. The rich man did not show mercy and generosity to the poor, as Scripture required (Deut. 15:2–12; see Job 29:11–17); rather he begrudged the beggar, who desired "the crumbs which fell" from the rich man's table.

The beggar (Luke 16:20, 21). The beggar, Lazarus, had a hard life, but he was a man of faith. When he died, he "was carried by the angels to Abraham's bosom." The phrase "Abraham's bosom" was used in the first century as a name for the place where believers went after death—"Paradise" (see Luke 23:43)—because Abraham, sacred history's model of faith and personal relationship with God, must be in a place of blessing. The name is accurate here, for Abraham himself comforted Lazarus (16:23, 25), who was delivered to him by angels (16:22).

BIBLE BACKGROUND
THE EGYPTIAN VIEW OF PARADISE

The ancient Egyptians had a strange view of Paradise. If a person could pass all the tests posed by the gods after death, then that person was welcomed into the domains of Osiris. However, one was expected to earn one's keep—one couldn't just sit around enjoying heaven. Every morning the roll was called and people had to plow the fields of Osiris or perform any other assigned duty.

The Egyptian solution was inventive; it involved a sculpted figurine, called *weshebti,* which means "answerer." When the roll was called each morning, the figurine would answer for a person and do his or her work, while that person did what he or she liked! Some Egyptian tombs contained chests in which there were 365 of these carved figures! Here are the instructions of the scribe Neb-Seny to his *weshebti* (quoted by Joseph Kaster, *The Wisdom of Ancient Egypt,* 1968, p. 142):

> O this weshebti of the scribe Neb-Seny, the son of the scribe Tchena, True of Voice, and of the lady of the house of Mut-Rest, True of Voice; if I be called, or if I be assigned to do any work whatsoever of the labors which are to be done in the Other World—for indeed an obstacle is presented therein—by a man in his turn, let the assignment fall upon you instead of upon me always, in the matter of sowing the fields, of filling the water courses with water, and of bringing the sands of the east to the west. "Here am I!" you shall say!

What a strange welcome the Egyptians expected to receive from their gods—far different from the one we know we will receive from the Lord. We will be welcomed by joyful angels and know the blessings of our Lord, not sent out to toil.

The angels (Luke 16:22). The picture of angels carrying Lazarus to Abraham's bosom is a lovely image to carry with us as we approach death. We do not die alone; we are surrounded by laughing angels, whose final act of guidance is to take our hand and carry us to the Lord.

ANGELS LEAD AND GUIDE

The Hebrew word for angel, *mal'ak,* means "messenger" or "representative." Hebrews 1:14 calls angels "ministering spirits sent forth to minister for those who will inherit salvation." One way in which the angel who "went before" the Israelites in the Exodus ministered to God's chosen people was by guiding them on their journey. Each day the angel, visible in the cloudy and fiery pillar, went before them and showed them the way God wanted them to go.

EXAMPLES OF ANGEL GUIDANCE IN SCRIPTURE

Many incidents reported in Scripture make it clear that throughout sacred history angels have played a continuing role in guiding God's people.

Angels guided Hagar *(Genesis 16:9).* When Abraham and Sarah failed to produce the child God had promised them (Gen. 15:4, 5), Sarah urged Abraham to make her Egyptian slave, Hagar, pregnant (see p. 23). According to the law and custom of that day, a child produced by Abraham and a surrogate wife would be considered to belong to Sarah. Abraham did as Sarah urged, but the result was disastrous. Hagar was filled with contempt for her mistress, and Sarah persecuted Hagar unmercifully (16:2–6). Finally, the desperate Hagar ran away, but she had no place to go and had no resources. It was at this point that the Angel of the Lord appeared to Hagar and told her, "Return to your mistress, and submit yourself under her hand" (16:9). These words of guidance were followed immediately by a promise: God had a future for Hagar's son, whom Abraham named Ishmael (16:15).

Angels guided Abraham's servant *(Genesis 24:7).* Later, Abraham and Sarah did have the son God promised to them. When their son, Isaac, matured, Abraham was unwilling for him to marry a Canaanite. So Abraham sent a servant to his home country to take a wife for Isaac from among his family (24:3–4). The servant was worried that he would not be able to fulfill the commission; he wondered if a woman would be willing to make the long journey to wed a man she had never seen. Abraham answered, "The LORD God of heaven . . . will send His angel before you, and you shall take a wife for my son from there" (24:7).

The story of how the servant arrived in Abraham's home country and prayed that the right young woman would come to the city well to offer him and his camels water is one of the most romantic stories in Scripture. The servant's prayer was answered, and the beautiful Rebekah (24:16) *was* willing to return to Canaan with him. The servant told Rebekah's family of the promised angel guidance (24:40), but he was careful to credit God for his success: "And I bowed my head and worshiped the LORD, and blessed the LORD God of my master Abraham, who had led me in the way" (24:48).

Angels guided Israel throughout the Exodus *(Exodus 23:20; 32:34; Judges 2:1).* At the beginning of this chapter we saw how God's angel went before the Israelites in a pillar of cloud and fire to guide them. Throughout the Exodus that angel continued to guide Israel's steps, from their departure from Egypt to their entrance into Canaan. Exodus 23:20 says, "Behold, I send an Angel before you to keep you in the way and to bring you into the place which I have prepared." Later, God told Moses, "Now therefore, go, lead the people to the place of which I have spoken to you. Behold, My Angel will go before you" (Ex. 32:34). After the Israelites had conquered Canaan, the Angel of the Lord spoke to the nation and said, "I led you up from Egypt and brought you to the land of which I swore to your fathers" (Judg. 2:1). God's angel stayed with the people of Israel and provided the daily guidance they needed to "keep them in the way"—that is, on the right path.

God's angel guided the parents of Samson *(Judges 13:8, 9).* God told a childless couple that they would have a son, and He gave instructions about how they were to raise the boy. The father, Manoah, then "prayed to the LORD and said, 'O my LORD, please let the Man of God whom You sent come to us again and teach us what we shall do for the child who will be born' " (13:8). The text tells us that God listened "and the Angel of God came" (13:9).

Not every claim of angel guidance is true (1 Kings 13:18). After the death of King Solomon, the kingdom that he and his father, David, had ruled was divided into northern and southern sections. The ruler of the northern kingdom, Jeroboam I, was afraid that if his people went to the Jerusalem temple to worship, their participation in the common Hebrew faith and language would ultimately lead to political reunification. In order to avert this, Jeroboam established a counterfeit religious system that resembled the worship established in God's Law, but which in fact seriously corrupted it.

When Jeroboam was about to dedicate one of the substitute worship centers he had established, God sent a young prophet from the south to announce God's condemnation of the king and his actions (1 Kings 13:1–10). When news of that reached "an old prophet" who lived in the north, he met the young prophet and urged him to stay with him. However, the young man was told by the Lord not to eat or drink while in the north (1 Kings 13:11–17).

The old prophet then told him, "I too am a prophet as you are, and an angel spoke to me by the word of the LORD, saying, 'Bring him back with you to your house, that he may eat bread and drink water' " (13:18). But the old prophet lied—an angel had not spoken to him! Because he disobeyed God, the young prophet was killed by a lion upon leaving the old prophet's home.

Not every report of an angel encounter is true, so we are not to accept uncritically every tale. We can't explain the motives of those who make up angel stories. Certainly, any report which contradicts the word of God in any way is to be rejected and ignored. As Paul wrote to the Galatians, "But even if we, or an angel from heaven, preach any other gospel to you than what we have preached to you [which *is* in harmony with the Old and New Testaments], let him be accursed" (Gal. 1:8).

A "lying spirit" may provide false guidance (1 Kings 22:22). The kings of the southern and northern Hebrew kingdoms united to fight the Syrians. Prior to the battle, King Ahab, one of the most wicked of the northern kingdom's rulers, sought guidance from his prophets—prophets who were part of the counterfeit religion which Jeroboam I had set up decades earlier.

The Lord permitted a "lying spirit" to deceive Ahab's prophets, who predicted a victory for the Hebrew kings, when in fact Ahab was to be killed and the Hebrews defeated in the coming battle. Because God does not lie, He revealed what was really going to happen to Micaiah, one of His prophets. However, Ahab chose to believe the false prediction of victory and went to his death.

This story reminds us that in addition to God's angels, there are evil angels as well. Not every supernatural word of guidance is from the Lord—an issue we'll explore further in Chapters 7 and 12.

God's angel guided Elijah (2 Kings 1:15). Elijah earned the wrath of King Ahaziah by predicting his imminent death. When the king sent soldiers to bring Elijah to him, the prophet was frightened (2 Kings 1:2–9). The angel of the Lord told Elijah, "Go down with him; do not be afraid of him" (1:15). The prophet did as he was told by the angel, and he confronted the king. Elijah was protected, but the king died.

An angel guided Joseph to wed Mary (Matthew 1:20). When Joseph learned that Mary was pregnant, he considered quietly breaking the marriage contract that bound Mary to him before their wedding. "An angel of the Lord appeared to him in a dream" and told Joseph not to be afraid of marrying her. Joseph followed the angel's guidance and became the "stepfather" of Jesus.

An angel advised Joseph when to leave Bethlehem and when to go to Nazareth (Matthew 2:13, 19). After Jesus was born, His life was threatened by Herod. An angel appeared to Joseph in a dream and told him to flee to Egypt. Later, when Herod was dead, the angel again appeared to Joseph in a dream and told him to bring his family to Nazareth.

An angel guided Philip to Gaza *(Acts 8:26).* While Philip was ministering in a great revival in Samaria, "an angel of the Lord spoke to Philip, saying, 'Arise and go toward the south along the road which goes down from Jerusalem to Gaza' " (8:26). There Philip met an Ethiopian official, whom he led to Christ.

God's angel guided Cornelius to send for Peter *(Acts 10:3; 11:13).* Cornelius was a Roman centurion who expressed faith in Israel's God. While he was praying one day, he "saw clearly in a vision an angel of God" (10:3). The angel identified the place where Peter was staying (in Joppa) and told Cornelius to send men to bring Peter to his house. Cornelius followed the angel's guidance; after Peter arrived, Cornelius and his household became the first Gentiles converted to Christianity.

CHARACTERISTICS OF ANGEL GUIDANCE

A review of these incidents brings to light several characteristics of angel guidance.

* Guidance was most frequently provided for individuals or couples when:
—someone did not know what to do (Hagar; Samson's parents);
—someone was about to make an understandable, but wrong, decision (Joseph);
—someone was unaware that he or she needed to do something else (Philip).
* The angel guidance was usually explicit and clear; but, as was the case with Abraham's servant, guiding angels may not appear visibly to those they lead.
* Reports of angel guidance might be lies; supernatural guidance might not actually come from one of God's angels.

OTHER MEANS OF DIVINE GUIDANCE

Despite the occurrence of angelic guidance in Scripture, it would be wrong to conclude that the only means God uses to guide believers are angels. The Bible presents at least five other means of divine guidance that are more common than guidance by angels.

The Lord provides personal guidance. Many passages of Scripture report that the Lord spoke directly to various individuals. We're not told the nature or form of this direct revelation, but we are often told that "the Lord said" something to someone or "spoke to" a particular individual. Even in the accounts where angels are mentioned, direct communication by God is often highlighted. For instance, the Angel of the Lord called to Abraham from heaven and told him not to sacrifice Isaac (Gen. 22:11); but as the story continues, we're told that God Himself called to Abraham and said, "Take now your son . . . and offer him there as a burnt offering" (Gen. 22:2). On this occasion—and many more—God provides direct guidance to His people without using the agency of angels.

God's Word provides general guidance *(Psalm 119).* From time immemorial, God's people have respected Scripture as His living word and have looked to it for guidance. Psalm 119 celebrates the guidance available to believers through God's Word. David, the psalmist, cries:

> Your word is a lamp to my feet
> And a light to my path.
>
> *(Psalm 119:105)*

The lamps of biblical times cast a dim light. Travelers carried them at night, not to see what lay in the distance, but to see where to make their next step. David's imagery reminds us that Scripture is rich in truths and principles that show us how to take the next steps in our life journey safely and in God's will.

Urim and Thummim provided special guidance for Israel *(Leviticus 8:8; 1 Samuel 22:6–11; 28:6).* Israel's high priest wore a pocketed "ephod," a cloth piece, over his chest. The Urim and Thummim—most likely stones bearing the words "yes," "no," and "unanswered"—were placed in the pockets (Lev. 8:8). When a person wanted to ask God a question about what he or she should do, that person went to the priest to "inquire of the Lord." The priest reached into the ephod and drew out a stone. God guided the priest's hand so that the correct engraved stone was selected, and thus the answer given on the stone was from the Lord.

David had taken refuge from Saul in a small city. When he heard that Saul was approaching with an army, David called a priest named Abiathar to inquire of the Lord in order to discover whether the people of the city would surrender him if Saul came. The answer was "They will deliver you"—that is, "Yes." So David quickly left the city.

Israel was later attacked by the Philistines, and Saul was terrified. The king had abandoned the Lord long ago, but now he sought His guidance. The text says, "But the LORD did not answer him, either by dreams or by Urim or by the prophets" (28:6). The priest drew out the stone, but the blank one was drawn time after time.

God's prophets provided national and personal guidance *(Deuteronomy 18).* The Canaanites were deeply aware of a need for supernatural guidance, and they relied on a variety of occult practices to obtain it (listed in Deut. 18:10–12). God called these practices "abominations" and forbade His people to use them. However, there were times when Scripture was not enough to show the choice that should be made in a particular situation. God's solution to that problem was the prophets, who served as God's spokesmen throughout Israel's history in the promised land. The Lord communicated His message to the prophets, and the prophets provided the necessary guidance to His people (18:18).

God's Holy Spirit guides us today *(Matthew 4:1).* Matthew tells us that Jesus "was led up by the Spirit into the wilderness." After Jesus' resurrection, inner guidance by the Holy Spirit became the primary means by which God leads His people. Romans 8:14, a passage which carefully explains the ministries of the Holy Spirit to believers today, states that being "led by the Spirit of God" is a mark of our personal relationship with Him.

In an important passage, Paul writes that "if you are led by the Spirit, you are not under the law" (Gal. 5:18). What Paul means is this: Unlike ancient Israel, we are not to look first to external standards for guidance about what is the right thing to do; rather, we are to look first to the Holy Spirit, who will prompt us from within. If we have doubts or uncertainty, we can, of course, look to the Scriptures to make sure that what we sense to be the right direction is in full harmony with God's word.

While angel guidance clearly occurs in Scripture, we need to remember that it is not the first, second, or even third most common means by which God has led His people in the past. While God is completely free to send angels to us with the same kinds of guidance reported in Scripture, today we have the Holy Spirit within, present with us, and we can expect Him to lead us.

ANGELS GUARD AND PROTECT

A delightful story is told by Ann Shields about a trip she took on a dangerous road in a winter storm. She prayed, "Father, send your angels to guide me." As she turned the key in the ignition, she sensed that two angels were seated on the front fenders of her car. Although she couldn't see them, she pictured them clearly—huge, young, powerful—talking and joking as her Ford Fiesta made its four-hour journey over the treacherous mountain roads (see Ann Spangler, *An Angel a Day,* 1994, p. 19).

There may well have been angels protecting Ann as she drove, but there's no way for us to know for certain. However, we can know for certain that one kind of mission on which God sends His angels is the mission of protection. We know this to be true because there are so many stories of angel protection found in the Scriptures.

ANGELORE

JOHN CALVIN ON ANGELS

In his famous *Institutes* (Book 1), John Calvin affirmed:

The point on which the Scriptures specially insist is that which tends to our most comfort, and to the confirmation of our faith, namely, that angels are ministers and dispensers of the divine bounty towards us. Accordingly, we are told how they watch for our safety, how they undertake our defense, direct our path, and take heed that no evil befall us. There are whole passages which relate, in the first instance, to Christ, the Head of the Church, and after Him to all believers. "He shall give his angels charge over thee, to keep thee in all thy ways. And they shall bear thee up in their hands, lest thou dash thy foot against a stone." Again, "The angel of the Lord encampeth round about them that fear him, and delivereth them." By these passages the Lord shows that the protection of those whom he had undertaken to defend he has delegated to his angels.

VERSES THAT AFFIRM ANGEL PROTECTION

Several verses teach that believers can expect angelic protection. David recalled a time when he fled to Philistia and was forced to feign madness in order to save his life. In Psalm 34, he drew a principle from that experience, one which is true for all believers. He writes:

This poor man cried out, and the
   LORD heard him,
And saved him out of all his
   troubles.

David drew this truth from God's answer to his prayer:

The angel of the LORD encamps
   all around those who fear Him,
And delivers them.

Psalm 34:6, 7

In the very next Psalm, David spoke of his enemies. He asks for—and expects—God's intervention.

Let those be put to shame and
   brought to dishonor
Who seek after my life;
Let those be turned back and
   brought to confusion
Who plot my hurt.
Let them be like chaff before the
   wind,
And let the angel of the LORD
   chase them.

Psalm 35:4, 5

Another Psalm supplies words that are applied to Christ in the New Testament; but these words also extend to cover all God's people.

Because you have made the LORD,
   who is my refuge,
Even the Most High, your
   dwelling place,
No evil shall befall you,
Nor shall any plague come near
   your dwelling;
For He shall give His angels
   charge over you,
To keep you in all your ways.

Psalm 91:9–11

Another powerful expression of angel protection can be found in Isaiah 69. The prophet reviewed God's faithfulness to Israel and wrote:

I will mention the
   lovingkindness of the LORD
And the praises of the LORD,
According to all that the LORD has
   bestowed on us,
And the great goodness toward
   the house of Israel,
Which He has bestowed on them
   according to His mercies,

According to the multitude of His
  lovingkindnesses.
For He said, "Surely they are My
  people,
Children who will not lie."
So He became their Savior.
In all their affliction He was
  afflicted,
And the Angel of His Presence
  saved them;
In His love and in His pity He
  redeemed them;
And He bore them and carried them
All the days of old.

Isaiah 63:7–9

The Bible does not simply affirm angelic protection; many reports of angelic activity demonstrate that frequently their mission is to protect.

BIBLE REPORTS OF ANGEL PROTECTION

God's angels protected Lot (*Genesis 19*). When Sodom was about to be destroyed, the two angels charged with carrying out its destruction rescued Abraham's nephew, Lot. They warned him first (19:12, 13); when Lot hesitated, the angels brought Lot's family "outside" Sodom (19:17). After Lot had safely arrived in a nearby town, "the LORD rained brimstone and fire on Sodom and Gomorrah" (19:24).

God's angels delivered Hagar and Ishmael (*Genesis 21*). When Ishmael was a teenager, he and his mother were sent from Abraham's tents. They wandered in the desert until their water was gone (21:10–15). When they were at the point of death, the angel of God called to Hagar and told her not to fear (21:17–18). God then opened her eyes so she could see a nearby well of water (21:19).

God's angel protected Jacob from Laban (*Genesis 31*). Jacob worked for his uncle Laban for 20 years. Laban constantly cheated Jacob by changing his wages and defrauding him. When it was time for Jacob to return to his home in Canaan, the Lord told him what to do to gain his fair share of Laban's herds and cattle (31:11–13). In this instance, there was no life-threatening danger. God's guardianship extended to protecting Jacob from unfair treatment and a threat to his economic well-being.

God protected Jacob all his life (*Genesis 48:16*). When Jacob (now renamed "Israel") neared the end of his life, he blessed his son, Joseph, and spoke of "the Angel who has redeemed me from all evil." Here, "evil" (Heb. *ra'*) is used in the sense of harmful or painful consequences. In his youth, Jacob cheated his brother Esau and was forced to flee for his life. God had protected Jacob, and by the time he returned 20 years later, God had changed Esau's attitude toward him.

On another occasion, two of Jacob's sons tricked and then killed the men of a small town (Gen. 34). The two brothers took revenge because the son of the town's leader had raped their sister, Dinah. Jacob immediately saw the implications of his sons' act. Not only was it wrong, but the murders exposed Jacob's family to danger from others living in the area. God's angel protected the family, and no harm came to them.

Later, Jacob's sons sold their brother, Joseph, into slavery in Egypt and told their father that he had been killed by wild animals. Years later, Joseph rose to a high position in Egypt and saved his entire family in a time of desperate famine. Jacob lived to see his son exalted and to know his son's children.

No wonder Jacob looked back over his long life and credited God's angel with protecting him from so many evils that might have overtaken him. God's protection of His own by means of guardian angels involves far more than we imagine.

God's angel protected Israel from an Egyptian army (*Exodus 14:19*). As we saw at the beginning of this chapter, God's angel interposed himself between an Egyptian army and the people of Israel, allowing them to pass safely through the Reed Sea.

God's angel brought Israel from slavery to the edge of the promised land (Numbers 20:16). Moses, in a request to the king of Edom for safe passage along a major trade route that passed through his land, acknowledges the role God's angel played in bringing Israel out of Egypt. Moses gives credit to God, who "sent the Angel" to deliver His people, for everything—from sending the plagues that struck Egypt and forced Pharaoh to free his slaves, to rescuing them from the pursuing Egyptian army, to providing them with food and water in the wilderness.

God's angel brought Israel to the promised land (Judges 2:1). After the Israelites completed their invasion of Canaan and the tribes were settled in their own lands, the Angel of the Lord reminded the Israelites: "I led you up from Egypt and brought you to the land of which I swore to your fathers. . . ." The Angel of the Lord fought for the Israelites in their struggles to overcome their Canaanite enemies and gave them the victory.

God's angel protected Jerusalem from an invading army (2 Kings 19:35). When the Assyrian army invaded Judah and crushed the fortified cities that protected her borders, the Assyrian ruler expected to take Jerusalem easily. King Hezekiah of Judah prayed for divine help, and the Lord responded. God sent an angel, who killed 185,000 Assyrian soldiers of all ranks. The Assyrian king was forced to return home, and Jerusalem was saved.

An angel protected Shadrach, Meshach, and Abed-Nego from death in a fiery furnace (Daniel 3). When these three Jews, who served in the Babylonian bureaucracy, refused to bow down to an idol erected by King Nebuchadnezzar, the king had them thrown into a raging fire. An angel appeared and kept them safe in the flames (3:25). (See p. 143 for an explanation of "sons of God.")

An angel protected Daniel from hungry lions (Daniel 6). When King Darius was forced to have Daniel cast into a den of hungry lions, God's angel "shut the lions' mouths," and they did not hurt him (6:22).

An angel protected Jesus from Herod's plot (Matthew 2:13). King Herod searched for the newborn "king of the Jews" in order to kill Him. An angel warned Joseph to flee to Egypt to protect the child, Jesus, and Mary.

Angels could have protected Jesus from those who crucified Him (Matthew 26:53). When Jesus was taken by a mob at night, Peter tried to protect Him. Christ told Peter to put away his sword and pointed out that He could pray to His Father, and He would provide Him with "more than twelve legions of angels" (26:53).

We sometimes wonder why, if angels really do protect us, accidents or tragedies happen to us. To answer that question we need to recall this incident and realize that Jesus specifically chose to forego angel protection. Christ chose instead a path that represented the will of God for Him—a path that led to His agonizing death on the cross. Only after His resurrection did that path lead Him to glory.

❖

Peter looked back on Jesus' death and reminds us that Christ "suffered once for sins, the just for [instead of] the unjust" (1 Peter 3:18). The men who plotted Jesus' death, who lied and victimized Jesus in an illegal trial, lived on. The Savior, the truly just Man, died. However, Peter goes on in the same verse to remind us that His death had a wonderful result. Christ died "that He might bring us to God."

Peter's point is that the suffering of God's own is never purposeless. When we do good and suffer for it, God has some overarching purpose in mind for us and for others, as was the case with Jesus' suffering and death.

God's guardian angels do not take days off, but sometimes they will stand back if what is to happen to us is best, if it is in accord with the will of our loving God.

God's angel delivered the apostles from prison (*Acts 5*). Hundreds of people in Jerusalem responded to the gospel, and that infuriated the Jewish leaders. Finally, they "laid their hands on the apostles and put them in the common prison" (5:18). That night an angel opened the prison doors and sent the apostles back to the temple to preach (5:19, 20).

God's angel delivered Peter from Agrippa (*Acts 12*). Herod Agrippa I, the grandson of Herod the Great (of the Christmas story), actively curried favor with his Jewish subjects. He executed James, the brother of John, and planned to kill Peter after some religious holidays were over (12:1–3). Peter was imprisoned under heavy guard, chained between two soldiers (Acts 12:4–6). An angel of the Lord appeared in the prison, released Peter, and brought him outside.

IMPLICATIONS OF THE GUARDIAN ANGEL STORIES

These stories from the Bible provide insight about what it means to have a guardian angel to protect us. We can see the breadth of such angel ministries in the chart below.

When angels acted to protect the Israelites, their mission was to deliver God's people from the threat posed by enemy nations. The types of protection angels provide for individuals seem to be wider in scope, ranging from removing Lot from danger, to warning Jacob of impending danger, to guaranteeing Jacob's financial well-being, and to guarding Jacob against the likely conse-

Guardian Angels

Passage	Person	Angel protection involved
Gen. 19	Lot	Removed Lot and his family from Sodom before its destruction.
Gen. 21	Hagar, Ishmael	Saved Hagar and Ishmael from death by revealing an unseen source of water.
Gen. 31	Jacob	Protected Jacob from unfair treatment; guaranteed his economic well-being.
Gen. 48	Jacob	Protected Jacob from the consequences of his (and others') foolish/wrong actions.
Ex. 14	Israelites	Protected the Israelites from the Egyptian army.
Ex. 20	Israelites	Brought Israel safely out of Egypt to the borders of Canaan.
Judg. 2:1	Israelites	Gave Israel victory in the conquest of Canaan.
2 Kings 19:35	Jerusalem	Protected Jerusalem from an invading Assyrian army.
Dan. 3	Shadrach, Meshach, Abed-Nego	Saved all three from the flames of a raging furnace.
Dan. 6	Daniel	Delivered Daniel from harm in a pit filled with hungry lions.
Matt. 2:13	Jesus	Warned Joseph to take his family to Egypt.
Matt. 26:53	Jesus	Angels failed to protect Jesus from crucifixion because it was God's will for Him.
Acts 5	Apostles	Delivered them from prison so they could continue sharing the gospel
Acts 12	Peter	Delivered him from Agrippa's death sentence by releasing him from prison.

quences of unwise, or even sinful, acts. Truly, our guardian angels are more involved in our lives than we imagine.

SUMMARY

God's guardian angels are active both in guiding and protecting believers. They go before us and behind us as well. When we come face to face with our frailties, we have an even greater sense of our need for the ministry of guardian angels. When we don't know what to do and appeal to God for direction, angels are one possible source of guidance. As we live our lives, God's guardian angels look out for our well-being in more ways than we might have supposed. As in days of old, God's angels protect us from dangers seen and unseen as we travel along life's way.

CHAPTER 6

ANGELS AND GOD'S LAW:

AGENTS FOR JUSTICE AND PUNISHMENT

Deuteronomy 32; additional Old & New Testament passages

The ideals of knighthood were well established in the fourteenth century. True nobility demanded a commitment to justice as a remedy for evil times, a remedy needed for the well-being of both church and kingdom. In medieval thought, the ideal of knighthood can be traced back to angels. The biography of Boucicaut, who was one of the purest representatives of the medieval ideal, proclaims that the archangel Michael's feat of arms in chasing Satan from heaven was "the first deed of knighthood and chivalrous prowess that was ever achieved." Thus, the medieval knight who rescued maidens in distress and fought evil to ensure social tranquillity was on the side of angels!

The medieval ideal of the chivalrous knight has helped shape the modern image of the guardian angel. There is, however, an unexpected downside to the image of angels as guardians. We think of angels as guardians who are committed to helping God's people, but what are the implications of viewing angels as fierce guardians of God's Law?

ANGELS AND GOD'S LAW

There can be no doubt that God's giving of His Law on Mount Sinai was a momentous occasion, significant for angels and for human beings as well. Angels were involved in the events that took place on Mount Sinai, and angels have played a role in administering the Law that was given there.

ANGELS WERE INVOLVED IN THE GIVING OF THE LAW AT MOUNT SINAI

Hosts of angels were present at Mount Sinai (Deuteronomy 33:2; Psalm 68:15–16). The Old Testament makes it clear that angels were present when the Lord gave Israel the Ten Commandments, the Mosaic Law. Deuteronomy 33:2–4 (NKJV) says:

MOUNT SINAI
Where God gave Moses the Law.

Dead Sea

Wilderness of Zin

GOSHEN

Wilderness of Shur

Kadesh Barnea

SINAI

Wilderness of Paran

Ezion Geber

Wilderness of Sin

Rephidim
Jebel Serbal ▲▲ Jebel Musa
Jebel Katerina

0 25 50 75
Miles

N

The LORD came from Sinai,
And dawned on them from Seir;
He shone forth from Mount Paran,
And He came with ten thousands
    of [holy ones*];
From His right hand
Came a fiery law for them.
Yes, he loves the people;
All His [holy ones*] are in Your
    hand;
They sit down at Your feet;
Everyone receives Your words.
Moses commanded a law for us,
A heritage for the congregation
    of Jacob.

The same thought is expressed in Psalm
68:16, 17:

Why do you fume with envy, you
    mountains of many peaks?
This is the mountain which God
    desires to dwell in;
Yes, the LORD will dwell in it
    forever.
The chariots** of God are twenty
    thousand,
Even thousands of thousands;
The Lord is among them as in
    Sinai, in the Holy Place.

These passages indicate that the Lord
gathered myriads of angels around Him at
Mount Sinai when He gave His Law to Israel.
For some reason, it was important that the angels witness this pivotal point in sacred history.

Angels participated in the giving of God's Law
(Acts 7). Acts 7 records the defense that
Stephen the Martyr made before the high
priest and governing council in Jerusalem after
he was accused of blasphemy. In his defense
speech, Stephen gave a review of sacred history
which contains several references to the relationship between angels and God's Law.

* The NKJV has interpreted the Hebrew "holy ones" as
"saints" in this passage, but the reference is to angels.
** God's "chariots" refers to His heavenly armies here and
in other passages, such as 2 Kings 2:11 and 6:17.

A medieval-style rending of God giving the Law at
Sinai.

❖

This is that Moses who said to the children of Israel, "The Lord your God will raise up for you a
Prophet like me from your brethren. Him you shall
hear." This is he who was in the congregation in the
wilderness with the Angel who spoke to him on
Mount Sinai, and with our fathers, the one who received the living oracles to give to us. . . . You stiff-
necked and uncircumcised in heart and ears! You
always resist the Holy Spirit; as your fathers did, so
do you. Which of the prophets did your fathers not
persecute? And they killed those who foretold the
coming of the Just One, of whom you now have
become the betrayers and murderers, who have received the law by the direction of angels and have
not kept it.

Acts 7:37, 38, 51–53

According to this passage, an angel— perhaps
the Angel of the Lord— spoke with Moses on
Sinai; indeed, Moses received the Law "by the
direction of angels." However, this is only one
aspect of the relationship between angels and
God's Law.

Angels administer the Law given on Sinai
(Galatians 3:19; Hebrews 2:2). Andrew Band-

stra (*Angels*, 1984, p. 96) suggests that Acts 7:53 might be translated:

"you who received the law by direction of angels," in the sense of being transmitted "by God's directing angels."

In either translation the angels' involvement in the law-giving is mentioned to add power to the law, to underscore the fact that it must be taken with utmost seriousness. Angels, as ministers of law-giving, are not to be taken lightly; or to put it the other way, the law, as ministered by angels, is not to be taken lightly.

What purpose does this Law, whose significance is underlined by the involvement of angels, serve? The Bible says:

It was added because of transgressions, till the Seed [Christ] should come to whom the promise was made; and it was appointed through angels by the hand of a mediator.

Galatians 3:19

The last phrase, "appointed through angels by the hand of a mediator," seems obscure, and it has been misinterpreted. This phrase is not one of four separate observations on the Law simply tacked on to the thought expressed in the first part of the verse. The verse begins with a rhetorical question, "What purpose then does the law serve?" The answer is given in the next phrase, "It was added because of transgressions." That answer is then modified by two phrases which express different thoughts. As to time, the Law was intended to function only until "the Seed [Christ] should come." As to cause, the Law was put into effect to aid the angels who were appointed to mediate it.

Still, what is the meaning of the phrase "because of transgressions" in Paul's answer to the question, Why the Law? From what Paul goes on to say in Galatians 3:21–25, it is best to think of the meaning as "to expose transgressions!" If we take that as the meaning of the phrase "because of transgressions" the verse will teach that "to expose transgressions . . . the law was put into effect by angels."

Thus, putting the Law into effect does not refer to *giving it,* but to *administering it!*

Another Bible passage links angels with the giving of God's Law and specifies this role. In the first chapter of Hebrews, the writer argues that Christ is clearly superior to the angels. This was an important point in ministering to Hebrew Christians, for the Jewish people were awed by the link between angels and the Law Moses gave them. The sacred nature of the Law was underlined by the fact that angels—those awesome creatures, so much greater in power than human beings—were involved in its giving at Sinai.

Why, then, the emphasis on Christ's superiority to angels? Because Christians taught that Christ brought a new revelation which not only fulfilled, but also superseded the Old Testament revelation. It followed, then, that if the person associated with establishing the new revelation was greater than the angels associated with the older revelation, then the new revelation must be superior to the old. The writer of Hebrews makes an additional point:

Therefore we must give the more earnest heed [*to the revelation introduced by Jesus*] . . . For if the word spoken through angels proved steadfast, and every transgression and disobedience received a just reward, how shall we escape if we neglect so great a salvation, which at the first began to be spoken by the Lord . . .? Hebrews 2:1–3

The Law introduced on Sinai was *binding.* It not only exposed transgression (Gal. 3:19), *but it also exposed the sinner to judgment!* The angels who gathered around to observe the events at Sinai, the angels who served God there in communicating the Law to Moses, those same angels also served to administer justice to those who broke the Law!

That is why the medieval association of Michael with chivalry is both appropriate and ironic at the same time. The true knight was so committed to justice that he was *obligated* to punish the wicked. In medieval times the role of angels as guardians was emphasized, but the institution of knighthood, which looked to Michael as its model, suggested an entirely different aspect of angelic activity. Angels, as agents who enforced God's Law, would be a terror to lawbreakers!

ANGELS AS GOD'S AGENTS OF JUSTICE

THE OLD TESTAMENT PORTRAYS ANGELS AS AGENTS OF DIVINE JUDGMENT *(Psalm 35, 78)*

In Psalm 35 David pleads with the Lord to fight against those who fight against him (35:1). Since David was God's anointed ruler, rebellion against David was rebellion against the Lord's express will. David had a right to expect divine intervention, and he pleads for angelic intervention on the side of justice.

> Let them be like chaff before the
>   wind,
> And let the angel of the LORD
>   chase them.
> Let their way be dark and
>   slippery,
> And let the angel of the LORD
>   pursue them.

> *Psalm 35:5, 6*

In another psalm Asaph looks back on God's deliverance of His people from Egypt, and he attributes the plagues that struck Egypt in judgment to the activity of angels.

> When He worked His signs in
>   Egypt,
> And His wonders in the field of
>   Zoan;
> Turned their rivers into blood,
> And their streams, that they could
>   not drink.
> He sent swarms of flies among
>   them, which devoured them,
> And frogs, which destroyed
>   them.
> He also gave their crops to the
>   caterpillar,

> And their labor to the locust.
> He destroyed their vines with hail,
> And their sycamore trees with
>   frost.
> He also gave up their cattle to the
>   hail,
> And their flocks to fiery
>   lightning.
> He cast on them the fierceness of
>   His anger,
> Wrath, indignation, and trouble,
> By sending angels of destruction
>   among them.
> He made a path for His anger;
> He did not spare their soul from
>   death,
> But gave their life over to the
>   plague,
> And destroyed all the firstborn of
>   Egypt.

> *Psalm 78:43–51*

The Lord sent the plagues and disasters upon Egypt, but "destroying angels" carried out His judgments.

ANGELS HAVE PUNISHED OTHER SINS IN THE PAST

In chapter 3 we examined the role of "law and order" angels in the administration of justice in God's moral universe. We saw that God was deeply concerned with righteousness even before the Law was given, and that God sent His angels to punish cultures and individuals when sin had totally corrupted them. The chart below summarizes the incidents in which angels served as God's agents for the punishment of sin treated in chapter 3.

THE NEW TESTAMENT PORTRAYS ANGELS AS AGENTS OF DIVINE JUDGMENT TO COME *(Luke 12; Matthew 13, 25; 2 Thessalonians 1; Revelation 8)*

The New Testament provides additional information about angels as agents of divine

Angels as Agents of Divine Punishment: Summary

Passages	Who is judged	Nature of the sin	The punishment
Gen. 19	Sodom, cities of the plain	Culture corrupt, as shown by homosexual rape	The cities were destroyed by fire
Ex. 1, 7—11	People of Egypt	Prolonged enslavement of Israelites	Egypt was devastated by plagues; eldest sons killed
Num. 11	Unbelieving Israelites	Refused to trust God who had freed His people and shown His presence to them	Many died in "great plague"
Ex. 23, 33; Gen. 15:13–16; Deut. 9:3	Peoples of Canaan	The culture was religiously and morally corrupt; threatened the purity of Israel's faith	Culture wiped out or people driven from Canaan
1 Sam. 24; 1 Chron. 21	Citizens of Israel	Shift from relying on God to relying on military might	70,000 killed in a plague before David confessed and sacrificed
2 Kings 19; 2 Chron. 32	King and army	Assyrians massacre Jews, intend to take Jews from the promised land	185,000 of the Assyrian army killed by an angel
Matt. 13:41, 42; 2 Thess. 1:7–9	Unbelievers on earth at Jesus' return	Sin as great as in Noah's day; persecution of believers	Angels execute God's vengeance (see chapter 17)
Acts 12	Herod Agrippa	He executed John and threatened the church; accepted worship as god	Angel struck him with fatal infection of roundworms

judgment. In this role angels are closely associated with the second coming of Christ.

Angels will bring devastating judgments on earth prior to the second coming *(Revelation 8; 2 Thessalonians 1:7–9).* The book of Revelation contains vivid images of the final battle between God and evil. Some interpret Revelation as a vision in which the events symbolize God's acts throughout history, while others interpret it as a prophetic preview of what will happen as history draws to God's intended close. Regardless of which interpretation one chooses, it is clear that in the book of Revelation angels are the main agents in executing divine judgment. For example, Revelation 8 depicts an angel throwing fire on the earth, which results in "noises, thunderings, lightnings, and an earthquake" (8:5). Other angels sound trumpets, and afterwards hail and fire destroy a third of the trees and all of the grass on earth (8:7). As the chapter continues, subsequent trumpet blasts by the angels bring forth greater and greater judgments.

The same expectation is present in the second letter to the Thessalonians. Paul writes that "the Lord Jesus is revealed from heaven with His mighty angels, in flaming fire taking vengeance on those who do not know God" (2 Thess. 1:7, 8).

Angels will separate the wicked from the just *(Matthew 13:24–30, 38–49).* Jesus told a parable about a man whose enemy planted weeds in his wheat field. When his servants asked if they should pull out the weeds, which in first growth looked much like young wheat plants, the owner told them to wait. The danger was too great that they might pull out the wheat by mistake. The owner told his servants to gather the weeds and burn them at harvest time.

In His interpretation of this parable, Jesus explained that the field represents the world; the wheat represents "sons of the kingdom"; the weeds, "sons of the wicked one"; and the servants, angels. He said further:

The Son of Man [Jesus Himself] will send out His angels, and they will gather out of His kingdom all

things that offend, and those who practice lawlessness, and will cast them into the furnace of fire. There will be wailing and gnashing of teeth. . . . So it will be at the end of the age. The angels will come forth, separate the wicked from among the just, and cast them into the furnace of fire.

Matthew 13:41, 42, 49, 50

Angels will participate in the denunciation of the wicked *(Matthew 25:31; Luke 12:8, 9)*. Two passages suggest that angels will be involved in the determination of human guilt. Matthew 25:31 tells us: "When the Son of Man [a term Jesus used when speaking of Himself] comes in His glory, and all the holy angels with Him, then He will sit on the throne of His glory." It is clear from the context that this is a judge's throne, for "all the nations will be gathered before Him, and He will separate them one from another" (Matt. 25:32).When we add to this a passage from Luke, we see a fascinating implication. In Luke 12:8, 9 Jesus taught:

"Also I say to you, whoever confesses Me before men, him the Son of Man also will confess before the angels of God. But he who denies Me before men will be denied before the angels of God."

The word "confess" (in Greek *homologeo*) is used in its basic sense of "to acknowledge." Jesus was saying that everyone who acknowledges Jesus before other people will be acknowledged by Jesus before the angels as His own when time for final judgment comes.

Why should we need to have Jesus acknowledge us *before angels?* The best answer to that question is that when Jesus comes— "and all the holy angels with Him"—to sit on His throne, the angels, who have been silent observers of our actions, will bear witness to what we have done and in this will become our accusers! They will come with Jesus not simply to observe His judgment, but to participate in the judgment of human beings. How tragic it will be at that time if Jesus is not able to stand beside us and acknowledge us as His own! How tragic if we have no relationship with the Savior, nothing to shelter us from the punishment our sins have earned us.

This leads us to one of the most surprising verses in Scripture. We can only understand that verse if we grasp certain truths about the Law mediated by angels on Sinai long ago, the same Law they administer today under God's direction.

THE MEANING OF THE MOSAIC LAW

Today many people completely misunderstand the function of biblical Law. Some see the Law as a standard that tells how one can please God and earn salvation. The assumption here is that if a person tends more toward keeping God's moral law than against keeping it, then God will judge their deeds favorably and welcome them into heaven. But God's Law has never had anything to do with personal salvation.

THE PRIORITY OF THE ABRAHAMIC COVENANT

Whenever we think about personal relationship with God, it's always important to remember that the covenant God established with Abraham has priority over the Law. That covenant, as we saw in chapter 2, was God's pure expression of the promises that He guar-

anteed He would fulfill. God said to Abraham, "I will . . . ," and with those words He fully committed Himself to do what He promised (Gen. 12).

The promises in the Abrahamic Covenant were "I will" promises (Genesis 12:1–3, 7). To provide assurance that He meant what He said, the Lord "signed and sealed" His commitment by performing a ritual used in cultures of that time to solemnly seal contracts. There were several ways for parties to "cut covenant" (a phrase analogous to our "sign the legal paper"). A covenant could be cut by erecting a pillar, or by sprinkling salt, as a symbol of an agreement. However, the most binding of ancient commitments was the "covenant of blood." To make a covenant of blood, animals were cut in half and then the persons making the contract passed between the halves, probably to symbolize that they swore by their own lives to do what they had promised.

Genesis 15 records the covenant of blood between God and Abraham. Before the covenant was formalized, however, Abraham fell into a deep sleep and the Lord *alone,* appearing as smoking oven and burning torch, passed between the halves of the animals. God committed Himself to keep His promises—regardless of what Abraham might do! The only One bound to keep the covenant God made with Abraham was the Lord Himself. No action of Abraham's could void the relationship with God established by the Abrahamic covenant.

The covenant relationship was entered into by faith (Genesis 15:6). What, then, was Abraham's part in this relationship initiated by God? The answer is found in Genesis 15:4–6. God told Abraham—now an old man whose wife was long past the age of childbearing—that a child from his own body would be his heir, and that his descendants would be as numerous as the stars of heaven. "And he believed in the LORD, and He accounted it to him for righteousness" (15:6).

All Abraham, a sinner like every other human being, *could do* was to believe God's promise. He couldn't wipe out his past and make himself righteous; he couldn't live the rest of his life in perfect harmony with God's will. So God *gave* the believing Abraham a righteousness which he had not earned, which he could not earn. Faith, and faith alone, established Abraham's saving relationship with the Lord.

The Abrahamic covenant was never changed or altered (*Galatians 3:17*). In Galatians, the apostle Paul points out that the Law, "which was [added] four hundred and thirty years later, cannot annul the covenant that was confirmed before by God in Christ" (3:17). Whatever the institution of the Law at Sinai accomplished, it in no way changed God's commitment to the promises He made to Abraham, and it in no way changed the fact that salvation—that is, being adjudged "righteous" in God's sight—is accomplished through faith and faith alone.

The Abrahamic covenant sets the pattern for all biblical covenants in one important respect. Each biblical covenant is in essence *God's statement of what He will surely do.* Each biblical covenant expresses a divine commitment to a course of action that has an impact on human beings!

THE NATURE OF THE LAW COVENANT   (*Exodus 19—23*)

The Law covenant was a treaty between God and Israel. Scholars of the Ancient Near East have long been aware that the Law covenant, as expressed in Exodus 19 and repeated in expanded form in the book of Deuteronomy, adheres to the form of an ancient "suzerainty covenant." Such a covenant was a treaty between a ruler and his people. Today we might call that type of covenant a "national constitution."

A suzerainty treaty contained the following features, which can be identified in Exodus. A suzerainty treaty had:

- a preamble which identified the ruler and gave his titles (see 19:1);

- a historical prologue which told what the ruler had done for his people (see 19:4, 5);
- stipulations which stated what the ruler expected from his people (see 20:2–17);
- a statement of blessings and curses which would apply if the people met (blessings) or failed to meet (curses) ruler's expectations (see 20:23–33); and
- an oath of acceptance to be spoken by the ruler's subjects (see 24:1–8).

A suzerainty covenant was executed between a ruler and *a people who were already his own.* The Law given at Sinai was never intended to *create* the people of God, rather it was intended to *guide* a people who were already God's own.

Biblical covenants state what God most surely will do. As is the case with other biblical covenants, the Law is *not* conditional. In the Ten Commandments God spelled out His minimum requirements for His people if they were to live in fellowship with Him. After the commandments were given, the Law covenant then spells out what God would do if His people live as He expected them to live (the blessings) and what God would do if His people failed to live as He expected them to live (the curses).

The clearest expression of those blessings and cursings is found in Deuteronomy 28. We need to read these statements of blessings and cursings as God's firm "I wills." The blessings and the cursings represent commitments God made to Israel: Keep the Law, and be blessed; or violate the Law, and be punished. Again we see that the Law never had anything to do with establishing a relationship with God. Any human being's relationship with God is, and always has been, established by faith, and faith alone.

What the Law did for God's people was to set two pathways before them. If the Israelites followed the path of obedience, God would surely bless them. If the Israelites followed the path of disobedience, God would judge their sins and punish them (the meaning of "curse"). It is clear from the history of God's people as recorded in the Bible that even the curses were blessings in disguise, for when Israel was punished for her sins, the nation often turned back to the Lord.

Angels carried out punishments imposed in accord with Moses' Law. God's angels, themselves holy and upright, are committed to the Law which God gave to His people. Hebrews 2:2 refers to the Law as a "word spoken through angels" through which "every transgression and disobedience received a just reward." The angels assembled to observe the Law being given at Sinai. They served as mediators of that covenant.

As we have seen, angels have also served as agents of "law and order" to punish individuals, and the nation of Israel itself, when the Law was transgressed. When Israel obeyed the Law, God blessed His people with peace, health, and prosperity (see Deut. 28:1–14). When a given generation disobeyed the Law, particularly when they turned to pagan deities, God brought national disasters, ranging from droughts and swarms of locusts to plagues and oppression by foreign nations (see Deut. 28:15–68). From what we have seen in this chapter and in chapter 3, there is every reason to believe that the punishment for transgression of God's Law was carried out by His "destroying angels" (Ps. 78:49).

ARE ANGELS A THREAT TO BELIEVERS TODAY?

There is a truly puzzling verse about angels in the New Testament. In Romans 8 Paul spoke about the full confidence believers can have in the salvation won for us by Jesus. The verse reads:

For I am persuaded that neither death nor life, nor angels nor principalities nor powers, nor things present nor things to come, nor height nor depth, nor any other created thing, shall be able to separate us from the love of God which is in Christ Jesus our Lord.

Romans 8:38, 39

These are familiar verses, and we often read them without paying careful attention. When we read them closely, something strange confronts us: *Angels are listed among the threats to our relationship with God!*

Now, why would Paul include *angels* among the threats which he is persuaded are unable to separate us from the love of God in Christ? The answer becomes clear given what we've discovered about angels in this chapter.

ANGELS ARE COMMITTED TO GOD'S LAW AND CHARGED WITH PUNISHING VIOLATIONS

As we saw earlier, God gathered His angels to Mount Sinai to witness and to participate in the giving of His Law to Moses. Angels have also been assigned the task of punishing violations of a universal moral code as well as violations of the written Law.

Angels are committed to punishing "every transgression" (*Hebrews 2:2*). Apparently angels take their law and order ministry very seriously, for Hebrews 2:2 says specifically that "*every* transgression and disobedience received a just reward" (emphasis added).

It is important for us to realize that angels are *holy* beings. The basic idea underlying the Old Testament concept of holiness is that anything "holy" is set apart from that which is common and moved to the sphere of the sacred. God's "holy ones" are thus angelic beings totally committed to the Lord and set apart for His service. There is also a moral dimension to holiness, which can be defined simply: A morally holy being is "committed to what is right as right is defined by God."

God's holy angels are committed to what is right, as right is defined by God. It is no wonder, then, that God gathered the angels around Him at Sinai, for the Law is God's specific definition of what is right for humankind, and especially for His own people. Angels, as holy ones, are fully committed to this standard of right and wrong. When angels, beings who are committed to God's standards as expressed in the Law, see any lawless act, they feel an obligation to punish it.

THE LAW MAKES ALL HUMANS SINNERS, FOR NONE HAVE KEPT THE LAW

The New Testament is careful to point out that we human beings must find our relationship with God through faith. One important reason for that is because we can never be good enough to win a relationship with Him by keeping the Law. Paul wrote that "whatever the law says, it says to those who are under the law, that every mouth may be stopped, and all the world may become guilty before God" (Rom. 3:19). Paul did not see the Law as a ladder which enables us to climb up to God. Paul saw the Law as a mirror. If we are honest as we look in the mirror of the Law, we will recognize ourselves as sinners and accept the fact that we are guilty of sin before God. Only when we see ourselves as guilty sinners in the mirror of Law are we likely to look away from self-effort and find our way to personal relationship with God through faith.

Paul identified several weaknesses of the Law that disqualify it as a way of salvation. The Law is not related to life, but to death and judgment. We do not receive spiritual life through the Law (Gal. 3:1–5). Old Testament saints were not made righteous through the Law (Gal. 3:6–9). The Old Testament itself testifies to the contrast between promise and works (Gal. 3:10–14). Scripture makes it clear that the Law, added 430 years after God's promise to Abraham, cannot void the covenant promise. Life comes through faith, not Law.

Paul argued that the Law has always had a severely limited role in God's plan. It was always intended to be temporary (Gal. 3:19, 20). The Law never could make a person spiritually alive (Gal. 3:21, 22). And the Law actually pointed toward faith and away from itself (Gal. 3:23, 24). While the Law governed the way Old Testament believers were to live their lives and while it established blessings for obedience and punishments for disobedience, the Law was never a factor that determined any person's salvation.

Yet Law does reveal God's character, and it defines God's minimum standards for humankind. Therefore, the Law makes all humans guilty before God, because "all have sinned and fall short of the glory of God" (Rom. 3:23).

ANGELS HAVE ALWAYS BEEN A THREAT TO SINNERS

It is in this regard, then, that Paul mentioned angels as a potential threat to believers. Angels, committed to the Law and committed to punish transgressions of the Law, can't help but point out our sins and call for our punishment! If God listened to angels, we would all be condemned! Yes, angels are holy, but angels are not perfect.

GOD'S PERFECTION IS DISPLAYED IN THE MERCY HE CHOOSES TO SHOW DESPITE OUR SINS   *(Psalm 103)*

One of the most wonderful themes in Scripture is powerfully developed in Psalm 103. This Psalm reminds us that God "made known His ways to Moses" in giving the Law, but it also points out something special about the way the Lord reacts to our transgressions.

The LORD is merciful and
   gracious,
Slow to anger, and abounding in
   mercy.
He will not always strive with us,
Nor will He keep His anger
   forever.
He has not dealt with us according
   to our sins,
Nor punished us according to our
   iniquities.
For as the heavens are high above
   the earth,
So great is His mercy toward
   those that fear Him;
As far as the east is from the west,

So far has He removed our
  transgressions from us.
As a father pities his children,
So the LORD pities those who fear
  Him.
For He knows our frame;
He remembers that we are dust.

Psalm 103:8–14

One thing which sets God apart from all His
creatures is His capacity to be totally just and
totally merciful at the same time. God alone is
perfect in love and in holiness.

And so it is that Paul promised us that
not even the holy angels, committed to what
is right as defined by God, can separate us
from the love of God in Christ Jesus. If we acknowledge Christ before others here, He will
acknowledge us before the holy angels; and
we will be safe, enveloped by a love so great
that the Son of God took the punishment we
deserve so that we might experience only the
mercy of God.

THE CASE OF MANASSEH, KING OF ISRAEL

The story of Manasseh is told in 2 Kings
21:1–18 and in 2 Chronicles 33:1–20. Both
passages describe the wickedness of this evil
king, who ruled Judah for fifty-five years. Second Kings says that Manasseh seduced the people of Judah to do "more evil than the nations
whom the LORD had destroyed before the children of Israel" (2 Kings 21:9). Second Chronicles tells us that Manasseh built altars to the
Baals, burned his own sons as sacrifices, and encouraged occult practices. He even erected an
idol in God's temple (2 Chron. 33:3–7). Second
Kings adds that "Manasseh shed very much innocent blood, till he had filled Jerusalem from
one end to another, besides his sin by which he
made Judah sin" (2 Kings 21:16). In short,
Manasseh was truly wicked and completely evil.

God's response was in accord with the
Law covenant. Because the king and his people had done evil, the Lord brought "calamity
upon Jerusalem" (2 Kings 21:12–14). The

king of Assyria invaded the land and devastated Judah. Manasseh was taken captive
"with hooks, bound . . . with bronze fetters,
and carried" off to Babylon (2 Chron. 33:11).
No doubt God's angels were involved in administering Manasseh's punishment for his
gross violations of God's Law. However, the
story of Manasseh doesn't end here. The
chronicler reports:

Now when he [Manasseh] was in affliction, he implored the LORD his God, and humbled himself
greatly before the God of his fathers, and prayed to
Him; and He received his entreaty, heard his supplication, and brought him back to Jerusalem into
his kingdom. Then Manasseh knew that the LORD
was God.

2 Chronicles 33:12, 13

A Jewish document dating from the first
century B.C. contains the legend that the angels resisted God's decision to show mercy to
Manasseh. They felt that in this case mercy
was inconsistent with justice. The wicked
king, who did not repent until he was punished, and near the end of a totally wicked life
at that, simply did not deserve to be forgiven
and restored.

While this legend goes beyond the story
of Manasseh as recorded in the Bible, it does illustrate the theme that angels are committed to
justice. It also helps us understand why Paul is
careful to include angels as one of the threats
which, he assures us, will never separate us
from God's love in Christ (Romans 8:38, 39).

But the story of Manasseh told in 2 Chronicles 33 does more. It displays not only the
mercy of God, but also the power of God's forgiveness. After Manasseh returned to his
throne:

He took away the foreign gods and the idol from
the house of the LORD, and all the altars that he had
built in the mount of the house of the LORD and in
Jerusalem; and he cast them out of the city. He also
repaired the altar of the LORD, sacrificed peace offerings and thank offerings on it, and commanded
Judah to serve the LORD God of Israel.

2 Chronicles 33:15, 16

Manasseh purifying God's temple.

God's forgiveness did what justice can never do: It transformed a sinner into a saint, an evil man into a man dedicated to good. The story of Manasseh displayed again the grace of a God who invites everyone who will to accept His forgiveness and, as new men and women, step confidently into the circle of His love.

DEMONS IN THE OLD TESTAMENT:

FALLEN ANGELS?

Leviticus 17; additional Old Testament passages

Every morning millions of Americans open the newspaper to check their horoscope. Because so many do so in my area, the *Tampa Tribune* includes "Astrology" with "Comics," "Editorials," and "Television" in the twelve-item index on the front page. My horoscope for the day I wrote this chapter, was this: "Many persons seem intent on taking for granted that you have decided questions relating to marriage"—pretty bland stuff, ambiguous enough to fit almost anyone. But horoscopes really aren't bland at all; in fact, their roots precede Old Testament times and go back to demons.

There certainly is far more about angels in the Old Testament than there is about demons. Yet the foundation of our understanding of the demons and evil spirits we meet in the New Testament lies in the Old Testament. The same can be said about our understanding of the true nature of the occult.

REFERENCES TO DEMONS IN THE OLD TESTAMENT

THE OLD TESTAMENT LINKS DEMONS TO PAGAN WORSHIP
(Leviticus 17:1–7)

Old Testament Law includes far more than just the Ten Commandments. The Mosaic Law governed the whole life of God's people: It spoke to issues of birth and death; it provided guidelines on what to eat and what to wear; it established patterns of work and rest; it defined sin and provided the means for forgiveness; and it identified acceptable worship and sacrifice. Leviticus 17 specifies the one location at which God's people were to offer Him sacrifices.

Sacrifices were to be offered only on the altar at the door of the tabernacle. The tabernacle was the portable worship center God told the Israelites to construct while they were still at Sinai (Ex. 25—27). An altar was placed just inside the single gateway that opened into the tabernacle court, and it was here that sacrifices were to be made. The permanent temple erected later in Jerusalem featured the same design. Leviticus 17:1–7 insists that *only* at this location were God's people to worship by offering sacrifices and explains why:

And the LORD spoke to Moses, saying, "Speak to Aaron, to his sons, and to all the children of

Israel, and say to them, 'This is the thing which the LORD has commanded, saying:

'Whatever man of the house of Israel who kills an ox or goat in the camp, or who kills it outside the camp, and does not bring it to the door of the tabernacle of meeting to offer an offering to the LORD before the tabernacle of the LORD, the guilt of bloodshed shall be imputed to that man. He has shed blood; and that man shall be cut off from among his people, *to the end that the children of Israel may bring their sacrifices which they offer in the open field, that they may bring them to the LORD at the door of the tabernacle of meeting,* to the priest, and offer them as peace offerings to the LORD. And the priest shall sprinkle the blood on the altar to the LORD at the door of the tabernacle of meeting, and burn the fat for a sweet aroma to the LORD.

'*They shall no more offer their sacrifices to demons,* after whom they have played the harlot. This shall be a statute forever for them throughout their generations.' "

Leviticus 17:1–7 (NKJV; emphasis added)

Sacrifices offered to pagan deities were offered to demons. Leviticus 17:7 makes a clear statement about the pagan religions of the ancient world. Real spiritual beings were behind the gods and goddesses the pagans invented, but the spiritual beings the pagans worshiped were not angels—they were demons.

This verse indicates that in the past the Hebrew people had worshiped pagan deities in Egypt. The sacrifices they offered then were made to demons, not to God. The popular notion that adherents of all religions worship the one true God certainly was not true in biblical times! Nor is it in ours.

Other Old Testament passages refer to demons in the context of worship. The word "demon" occurs in English translations of the Old Testament only four times. In each case it occurs with reference to the practice of pagan religion.

Deuteronomy 32 is a song Moses composed to instruct Israel about its relationship with the God who redeemed them and gave them His Law. Verse 17 pictures Israel abandoning the true God to worship pagan deities:

> They sacrificed to demons, not to
>   God,
> To gods they did not know,
> To new gods, new arrivals
> That your fathers did not fear.

Again we see that the sacrifices made to other gods were in fact offered to the demons who stood behind them.

Second Chronicles 11 relates what happened when Jeroboam I led a rebellion against Solomon's son, Rehoboam. That event led to the division of the unified Hebrew kingdom into two countries, Israel in the north, and Judah in the south. In order to avert the possibility of a reunion based on a common language and religion, Jeroboam set up a counterfeit religious system which was similar to the system God had ordained through Moses—but it was distinctly different. This counterfeit religion had established worship centers, supposedly for the worship of Yahweh, at Bethel and Dan. At each of these centers, Jeroboam erected statues of bull calves upon which the invisible deity was imagined to stand. Second Chronicles 11:15 says of this: "Then he appointed for himself priests for the high places, for the demons, and the calf idols which he had made." This passage also links demons and false worship practices.

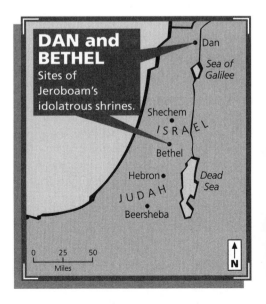

DAN and BETHEL
Sites of Jeroboam's idolatrous shrines.
Dan
Sea of Galilee
Shechem
ISRAEL
Bethel
Hebron
Dead Sea
JUDAH
Beersheba
0   25   50
Miles
N

Psalm 106 contains the fourth reference to "demons" in English versions of the Old Testament. This psalm reviews history and focuses on the response of God's people to the Lord. The psalmist draws attention to Israel's failure to destroy the Canaanites or to drive them from the land, and he then spells out the consequences.

They did not destroy the peoples,
Concerning whom the LORD had
    commanded them,
But they mingled with the
    Gentiles
And learned their works;
They served their idols,
Which became a snare to them.
They even *sacrificed their sons*
And their daughters to demons,
And shed innocent blood,
The blood of their sons and
    daughters,

Calf idols.

Whom *they sacrificed to the idols*
    of Canaan;
And the land was polluted with
    blood.

Psalm 106:34–38 (emphasis added)

It's clear that the Old Testament equates sacrificing to idols with sacrificing to demons. Behind the religions of the pagans lie real spiritual beings—demons.

ANGELORE
TERTULLIAN ON IMPURE SPIRIT BEINGS

These impure spirits, therefore—the demons—as is shown by the Magi, by the philosophers, and by Plato, consecrated under statues and images, lurk there, and by their afflatus attain the authority as of a present deity; while in the meantime they are breathed into the prophets, while they dwell in the shrines, while sometimes they animate the fibers of the entrails, control the flights of birds, direct the lots, are the cause of oracles involved in many falsehoods. . . . Thus they weigh men downwards from heaven, and call them away from the true God to material things; they disturb the life, render all men unquiet; creeping also secretly into human bodies, with subtlety, as being spirits, they feign diseases, alarm the minds, wrench about the limbs; that they may constrain men to worship them.

Tertullian

OTHER HEBREW TERMS THAT REFER TO DEMONS

Several Hebrew words have been taken to refer to demons in specific contexts.

Shedhim, which has the basic meaning of "rulers" or "lords," is the word translated "demons" in Deuteronomy 32:17 and Psalm 106:37 (both quoted above). In both texts idols are presented as the visible symbols of demons.

Sa'ir, which has the basic meaning of "goat," is the word used in Leviticus 17:7 and 2 Chronicles 11:15. The reference provides a striking parallel to the "goat satyr" which depicted hostile supernatural beings in Greek mythology. The word is probably used in the same sense in Isaiah 13:21 ("wild goats [demons] will caper there") and in Isaiah 34:14 ("And the wild goat [demon] shall bleat to its companion; / Also the night creature shall rest there").

'Elilim identifies pagan gods in Psalm 96:5, which should read "For all the gods of the peoples are demons."

Gad and *Meni* are found in Isaiah 65:11, where they are correctly transliterated and capitalized as proper names. They refer to two demon-gods of Babylon, "Fortune" and "Destiny."

Qeter in Psalm 91:6 is most likely a reference to the demon-god "Destruction."

'Elohim, usually translated God, is also used infrequently in the sense of "supernatural being" (see p. 146). In 1 Samuel 28:13 the witch of Endor reports, "I saw a spirit (*'elohim*) ascending out of the earth." The relationship of spiritism with demons, which we will look at later in this chapter, suggests that at first the witch mistook the shade of Samuel for a demon. The term certainly means "demons" in Isaiah 8:19, which should read: "And when they say to you, 'Seek those who are mediums and wizards, who whisper and mutter,' should a people seek demons? Should they seek the dead on behalf of the living?"

This brief survey makes it very clear that there are more references to demons in the Old Testament than a quick review of an English concordance would indicate. Strikingly, the previous references to demons are consistently linked either with false religion and idolatry or with the occult!

DEMONS IN THE ANCIENT NEAR EAST

The Bible's story reflects a society which in many ways was similar to, and yet in many ways was different from, other ancient Near Eastern cultures. One of the most notable differences is reflected in the relative silence of the Old Testament on demons, for demons were much on the mind of the peoples of Mesopotamia (the region from which Abraham came) and of the peoples in the nations bordering Israel.

THE DEVILS AND DEMONS OF MESOPOTAMIA

In his book *Devils and Evil Spirits of Babylonia* (1903, p. 65), R. Campbell Thompson describes the firm belief of Eastern races in the existence of evil spirits, ghosts, and similar beings. The Sumerian language, like the Assyrian and Babylonian languages derived from it, had numerous words for the various spirits and demons that were thought to infest the land. Thompson writes:

The primitive Sumerians recognized three distinct classes of evil spirit, all ready to torment the hapless wanderer. First came the disembodied human soul which could find no rest, and so wandered up and down the face of the earth; secondly, the gruesome spirits which were half human and half demon; and thirdly, the fiends and devils who were of the same nature as the gods, who rode on the noxious winds, or brought storms and pestilence. Each of these three kinds was divided into classes according to the several characteristics of the evil spirits which composed them, and the six chief of these are enumerated in the constantly recurring line UTUKKU LIMNU ALULIMNU EKIMMU LIMNU GALLU LIMNU ILU LIMNU RABISU LIMNU, "Evil spirit, evil Demon, evil Ghost, evil Devil, evil God, evil Fiend." But this by no means includes all the powers of evil, for this list is frequently amplified by the additions LABARTU LABASU AHHAZU LILU LILITU ARDAT LILI, all various forms of malignant spirits.

There is nothing comparable to this in Scripture, where the focus is clearly on the Lord as the one and only Sovereign of the universe, whose commitment to Israel frees His obedient people from subjection to malignant powers.

DEFENSES AGAINST THE DEMONS OF MESOPOTAMIA

Avoidance as a defense. The ancients had little defense against these demonic powers. Rabbinic Judaism, which emerged about the second century B.C., did incorporate a fear of demons, as is reflected in a number of rabbinic rulings. Those rulings deemed avoidance as the best defense: At all costs avoid demons, since their main function was to do harm to life and limb. Thus, the rabbis ruled that: a person who fears an evil spirit is allowed to extinguish the Sabbath lamp; because of demons a person should not enter ruins; and on account of the demon Agrath bath Machlath a person should never go out at night alone.

Exorcism as a defense. While avoidance was the primary defense against demons suggested by the rabbis, the peoples of Mesopotamia and Canaan relied on charms and magic incantations. One such incantation, translated from Utukki Limnuti Tablet V, Plate XIV, reads:

Seven evil demons of oppression,
Seven in heaven and seven on earth.
Evil Spirit, evil Demon, evil Ghost,
Evil Devil, evil God, evil Fiend.
By Heaven be thou exorcised! By
    Earth be thou exorcised!
By Bel, Lord of the World, mayest
    thou be exorcised,
By Beltis, Lady of the World, mayest
    thou be exorcised!
By Ishtar, Mistress of the World,
Who enlighteneth the night, mayest
    thou be exorcised!
Until thou art removed, until thou
    departest
From the body of the man, the son
    of his god,
Thou shalt have no food to eat,
Thou shalt have no water to drink.

CONTACT WITH THE GODS OF THE ANCIENT WORLD

While the ancients feared the supernatural world of demons, they also relied on their gods and goddesses—identified as demons in Scripture—for guidance. In a study of the Mari Tablets in the *Biblical Archaeologist* ("Prophecy in the Mari Letters," Vol. 31, 1968, pp. 101–124), Herbert Huffmon of Drew University distinguishes three kinds of "contact persons" through whom messages from the spirit world might be delivered.

Contact persons through whom the gods spoke to humans. One class of contact person was called *apilu,* "one who gives answers." Although this name implies that people would ask questions of the *apilu* and so solicit the god's advice, the Mari documents make it clear that many messages were not requested by those who received them.

Another class of contact person was called *assinuu.* This term apparently refers to a person who had a specific role in a deity's cult. *Assinuu* has generally been taken to refer to a male cult prostitute, possibly a eunuch.

A third class of contact person was called *muhhu,* meaning "ecstatic" or "madman." While this class of contact person had a lower status than the other two, his or her message was considered authentic, and official *muhhu* were part of a god's cult. At the same time, ordinary persons from any class of society might have an ecstatic trance and convey a message from the spirit world.

Evil demons and pagan gods are one and the same. In the Ancient Near East, then, demons were recognized and feared. What was not recognized was the fact that the gods and goddesses upon whom humans depended for protection from demons were themselves demons! Demons used the fear of demons to drive men and women to worship the demons themselves! Messages from the spirit world were used by the demons to further bind their worshipers to them. Yet any benefit an individual might derive from the demon-god he or she worshiped was insignificant in view of the fact that such worship blinded a person's eyes to the one true God, who alone truly loves humankind.

❖

ANGELORE

MESSAGES FROM THE SPIRIT WORLD

The following items from the Mari Tablets (1700 B.C.) contain messages from the spirit world.

From an apilu
When I offered a sacrifice to the god Dagan for the life of my lord, the apilu of Dagan of the city of Tuttul got up and spoke as follows, saying, "O Babylon, what are you trying to do? I will gather you up in a net. The house of the Seven Allies and all their property I will put into Zimri-lim's hand."

From an assinuu
Ili-haznaya, the assinuu of the goddess Annuntium . . . "That man is plotting many things against this land, but he will not succeed. My lord will see what the god will do to that man. You will overcome him and you will step on him. His time is near; he will not live long."

❖

An idol of a Mari goddess.

From a muhhu
The lady Qamatum from Dagan of Terqa has come and has spoken as follows, saying, "The peace terms of the man of Eshnunna are treacherous. 'Beneath the straw water flows.' In the net with which he collects I will gather him. His city I will destroy and his possessions . . . I will utterly ruin." This is what she said. Now take care of yourself. Without a (favorable) extispicy do not enter within the city."

It is easy to see why such messages of warning and advice were valued by rulers and individuals, and also how they would further bind a people to the idols of demons they worshiped.

❖

DEMONS IN THE HELLENISTIC WORLD

The Old Testament grew out of the Hebrew people's experience of God in the culture of the Ancient Near East. By the first century A.D. the culture of the Roman world was shaped by Hellenistic (Greek) thought. During the period that demons so dominated the thoughts of the peoples who lived in Mesopotamia, distinct beliefs about demons also developed in the West.

THE DEVELOPMENT OF THE MEANING OF "DEMON" IN HELLENISTIC THOUGHT

The *Theological Dictionary of the New Testament (TDNT)* carefully traces the development of the word *daimōn*, "demon" (Vol. 2, p. 1ff).

The original meaning of "demon." Originally "demon" was a term used to denote "gods." Specifically, however, it was applied to lesser deities and was usually used whenever any unknown supernatural factor was at work. Because these supernatural forces originally had an essential moral orientation, the moral orientation was indicated by coining the terms *eudaimōn* (good or beneficial demon) and *kakadaimōn* (bad or evil demon). Although in philosophy *"demon"* was a reference to abstract divine power, that was not the meaning it took on in popular religion.

The developed meaning of "demon" in popular religion. While the early philosophers had in mind an abstract force when they used the term *"demon,"* another form of the word, *daimōnēs,* was introduced to identify personal, intermediary divine beings. Views on these personal beings were shaped by popular thought and experience. As evidence mounted that such spiritual beings actually did exist, three doctrines formed around them. First, as rulers of human destiny demons were specifically connected with misfortune and distress. All demons were essentially bad or evil demons. Second, evil demons, located close to earth, were understood to be able to possess humans. Often, the extraordinary was attributed to indwelling demons. And third, the belief that demons could be manipulated or exorcised by the use of magic and incantations was increasingly accepted.

Central beliefs about demons in the West. The *TDNT* summarizes beliefs about demons in the Hellenistic world in this way:

In sum, we may say that in popular Greek belief the *daimōn* is a being, often thought of as a spirit of the dead, endowed with supernatural powers, capricious and incalculable, present in unusual places at particular times and at work in terrifying events in nature and human life, but placated, controlled or at least held off by magical means" (II:8).

ANGELORE

*MAGIC AGAINST DEMONS
IN THE GREEK WORLD*

The following quote from the Paris Magical Papyrus dates from about A.D. 300 and reflects Hellenistic presuppositions about the reality of the world of demons.

> For those possessed by daemons, an approved charm by Pibecis.
> Take oil made from unripe olives, together with the plant mastigia and lotus pith, and boil it with marjoram (very colorless), saying: "Yoel, Ossaarthiomi, Emori, Theochipsoith,

Sithemeoch, Sothe, Joe, Mimipsothiooph, Phersothi, Aeeioyo, Joe, Eochariphtha: come out of such and such a one." But write this phylactery upon a little sheet of tin: "Jaeo, Abraothioch, Phtha, Mesentiniao, Pheoch, Jaeo, Charsoc," and hand it round the sufferer: it is of every demon a thing to be trembled at which he fears. Standing opposite, adjure him. . . . Tannetis: let thy angel descend, the implacable one, and let him draw into captivity the daemon as he flieth around this creature.

THE ORIGIN AND NATURE OF DEMONS

It's clear from our brief survey of demons in the Old Testament, the Ancient Near East, and the West, that belief in evil supernatural beings was nearly universal in biblical times. In the East and the West, demons were regarded as hostile to human beings and as the cause of pain and suffering. Much of the religious energy of the people was spent in an attempt either to avoid these evil supernatural beings, or to manipulate or hold them off by magic.

The Old Testament, however, shows a marked *unconcern* with demons, except when they are associated with pagan deities and worship. As long as Israel was faithful to the Lord, God's people had nothing to fear from evil spirits.

While nearly every culture in the ancient world shared the belief that demons existed and were to be feared, there was little agreement about who or what demons were.

SPECULATION ABOUT THE ORIGIN OF EVIL SPIRITS IN THE EAST AND THE WEST

The previous discussion of demons and evil spirits included reference to theories about the origin of demons held by the pagan peoples whom the demons plagued. The Sumerians assumed that some evil spirits were disembodied humans, others were half-human and half-divine; they also believed that another class of demons—fiends and devils—were pure supernatural beings like the gods.

In the Greek world, many people assumed that demons were the spirits of the malevolent dead, particularly the disinherited or those who met with a violent death. Those spirits, however, had clearly taken on an aspect of the divine, and there was no clear differentiation between the nature of the gods and that of the demons.

PSEUDO-BIBLICAL THEORIES ABOUT THE ORIGIN OF DEMONS

Jews and Christian believers have also struggled with questions about the identity of demons. Two theories have been advanced and both can be called "pseudo-biblical theories" because the Scriptural support for both theories is extremely weak.

Demons as spirits of a pre-Adamic race. According to this theory, demons are the spirits of a race of mortals created by God before the creation of Adam and Eve. This theory is built on the notion that there is a gap between Genesis 1:1 ("God created the heavens and the earth") and 1:2 ("the earth was without form, and void").

The argument runs that God would not create a formless universe, so what verse 2 describes is the reshaping of a ruined universe rather than part of the original creation. Why would a universe fall into ruin? The cause must be sin. It follows that there must have been beings in the original creation who sinned and caused its ruin.

Thus, this theory holds that demons might be the spirits of sinners who died when the first creation was judged and ruined. Adherents of this theory point to demon possession as evidence. If demon-spirits are so eager to possess bodies, then, those spirits must have previously existed in bodies. This theory has no real biblical support, and few today would argue in its favor.

Demons are the offspring of fallen angels and human beings (Genesis 6:1–4). This theory was advanced by many early church fathers and is maintained by many today. Genesis reports that after the Fall, when humanity began to multiply, "the sons of God saw the daughters of men, that they were beautiful; and they took wives for themselves of all whom they chose" (6:2). The text then states that:

There were giants [nephilim] on the earth in those days, and also afterward, when the sons of God came in to the daughters of men and they bore children to them. Those were the mighty men who were of old, men of renown.

Genesis 6:4

Proponents of this theory point out that "sons of God" is a phrase used at times in the Old Testament to identify angels. The "sons of God" in this text, then, are fallen angels, and those angels impregnated human women. The nephilim, translated "giants" here, were neither human nor spirit beings, but halflings who were destroyed in the Flood. The undying spirits of these halflings are the demons who continue to plague humanity. Proponents of this theory cite as corroborating evidence the many stories in mythology of pagan gods in human form who impregnated humans and thereby produced offspring who became the supernaturally powerful heroes of legend.

Others strongly disagree with that scenario, arguing that "sons of God" refers to believers in the line of Seth, Adam's son (Gen. 5:3), while "sons of men" refers to the line of Cain (Gen. 4), a line which abandoned the Lord early. Thus, what the passage describes is the gradual deterioration of the race as evil influences overcame good. There is no evidence that when dark angels take on human form they are able to impregnate human women.

Even if the phrase "sons of God" is used here with reference to fallen angels, there is no indication anywhere in the Bible that their offspring became the demons who plagued the ancient world and who are active in our world today.

A SUBSTANTIAL SCRIPTURAL THEORY ON THE ORIGIN OF DEMONS: THEY ARE FALLEN ANGELS

Direct evidence from Scripture. The phrase "substantial Scriptural theory" was coined by Fred Dickason in his book, *Angels, Elect and Fallen.* The belief that the demons of Scripture and of pagan experience are fallen angels is a substantial theory because it is strongly supported by the Scriptures. Dickason's points can be summarized briefly:

- Parallel expressions seem to identify fallen angels with demons: for example, "the devil and his angels" (Matt. 25:41); "the dragon and his angels" (Rev. 12:7); "by Beelzebub [a name of Satan], the ruler [literally, "first"] of the demons (Matt. 12:24).
- There is a similar essence of being. Angels are designated as "spirits" (Ps. 104:4; Heb. 1:14), as are demons (Matt. 8:16; Luke 10:17, 20).
- There is a similarity in activities. Demons seek to enter and control individuals (Matt. 17:14–18; Luke 11:14, 15); the angel Satan does also (Luke 22:3; John 13:2). Evil angels join Satan in warring against God and man (Rev. 9:13–15; 12:7–17), and so do demons (Mark 9:17–26; Rev. 9:1–11).

Additional evidence from Scripture. The Bible makes it clear that Satan is followed by a host of angels who give allegiance to him rather than to the Lord. The obscure reference to Satan in Revelation 12:3, 4—where he is pictured as a "great, fiery red dragon" drawing to earth "a third of the stars of heaven"—is taken by many to indicate that about a third of the angels God created followed Satan in his rebellion. Those angels share Satan's attitude toward human beings and fight Satan's battles against the Lord. The following verses indicate the relationship between Satan and the fallen angels, and thus support the belief that the fallen angels are demons.

Now when the Pharisees heard it they said, "This fellow does not cast out demons except by Beelzebub, the ruler [literally, "first"] of the demons." But Jesus knew their thoughts, and said to them: "Every kingdom divided against itself is brought to desolation, and every city or house divided against itself will not stand. If Satan casts out Satan, he is divided against himself. How then will his kingdom stand? And if I cast out demons by Beelzebub, by whom do your sons cast them out?"

Matthew 12:24–27a

Then He will also say to those on the left hand, "Depart from Me, you cursed, into the everlasting fire prepared for the devil and his angels."

Matthew 25:41

And war broke out in heaven: Michael and his angels fought with the dragon; and the dragon and his angels fought, but they did not prevail, nor was a place found for them in heaven any longer. So the great dragon was cast out, that serpent of old, called the Devil and Satan, who deceives the whole world; he was cast to the earth, and his angels were cast out with him.

Revelation 12:7–9

Indirect evidence from Scripture: demon nature. Additional evidence supporting the belief that demons are fallen angels comes from New Testament passages which make it obvious that demons exhibit qualities also attributed to angels. This can be demonstrated in a single passage, which we will explore in detail in chapter 13.

- Demons, like angels, are referred to with personal pronouns. Luke 8:28 reads, "When he saw Jesus, he cried out, fell down before Him, and with a loud voice said, 'What have I to do with You, Jesus, Son of the Most High God? I beg you, do not torment me!'"
- Demons, like angels, have personal names. Luke 8:30 reads, "Jesus asked him, saying, 'What is your name?' And he said, 'Legion.'"

- Demons, like angels, can speak and can communicate with us. Luke 8:31 says, "So they [the demons] begged Him [Jesus] that He would not command them to go out into the abyss."
- Demons, like angels, have intelligence. Luke 8:28 (quoted above) shows that demons recognized Jesus and understood the implications of confronting Him.
- Demons, like angels, have emotions. Again, Luke 8:28 depicts the demons' fear, anxiety, and torment as a result of Christ's presence.

Given all of the above, it seems clear that the Scriptures identify demons with the fallen angels who followed Satan and who remain committed to Satan's agenda of resistance to the rule of God.

An apparent contradiction. One objection to the identification of demons as fallen angels deserves attention. Revelation 12:7–9 describes war in heaven and says that Satan and "his angels" were cast out of heaven "to the earth." This is also expressed in Isaiah 14:12, which says of Satan, "How you are fallen from heaven." But 2 Peter 2:4 says, "God did not spare the angels who sinned, but cast them down to hell and delivered them into chains of darkness to be reserved for judgment." Jude, in support of Peter, seems to make the same point in verse 6: "And the angels who did not keep their proper domain, but left their own abode, He has reserved in everlasting chains under darkness for the judgment of the great day."

If we take 2 Peter 2:4 and Jude 6 as the definitive verses, it would seem that fallen angels are already imprisoned. Thus, fallen angels could not possibly be the demons of pagan cultures and of the Old and New Testaments.

When attempting to resolve any supposed contradiction in Scripture, it's important to take a rigorous approach. First, we identify the contradiction. In this case, the supposed contradiction is "the Bible equates demons with fallen angels" versus "the Bible indicates fallen angels are currently held in chains."

Second, we establish which position is *most likely* to be correct, based on a preponderance of biblical evidence. In this case, the preponderance of evidence indicates that demons are to be identified as Satan's fallen angels.

Third, we examine the contradiction to see how it can be resolved while *maintaining the integrity of Scripture*. It is never acceptable to those with a high view of Scripture's inspiration and reliability to dismiss contradictory evidence as "a mistake" or "an error in the Bible." In this case, there is a relatively simple way to resolve the supposed contradiction. Note that neither Peter nor Jude require us to believe that *all* fallen angels are currently chained; on the other hand, both Peter and Jude clearly require us to believe that at least some fallen angels are currently imprisoned. At this point, we ask if there is any independent evidence for the idea that some, but not all, fallen angels or demons are "in chains of darkness."

When we research this issue, we discover that the theory that demons are fallen angels is actually *strengthened* by the passages in Peter and Jude! Revelation 9:1–11 describes a release of locust-like demons from a "bottomless pit" to torment human beings. The passage concludes: "And they had as king over them the angel of the bottomless pit, whose name in Hebrew is Abaddon" (Rev. 9:11). Apparently, some demons and angels alike are *temporarily chained,* or rather "reserved in everlasting chains" (Jude 6). This fits with the passage in Luke we looked at above, for the legion of demons possessing the man Jesus was about to heal begged Him not to "command them to go out into the abyss" (Luke 8:31). We can compare this with Revelation 20:1–3, where we read of an angel who throws Satan into "the bottomless pit" and binds him "for a thousand years." Later the same chapter in Revelation describes Satan's release after the thousand years are past.

Clearly, Scripture does describe at least one place of temporary imprisonment from which the demons of Revelation 9 and Satan, a fallen angel, are released. So a place of temporary imprisonment where active demons and fallen angels are both confined is mentioned in Scripture.

There is much we don't know about this issue. We are not told when fallen angels were or will be chained until judgment day. The time frame simply is not mentioned in the relevant passages. We're not told when the temporarily imprisoned angel and demons were or will be released. Also, references relating these events to each other are often lacking. Yet, the fact that both fallen angels and demons are mentioned in the context of confinement *supports* the identification of demons with fallen angels; and the fact that some demons begged Jesus not to confine them supports the conviction that not *all* fallen angels or demons are confined today. Given these facts, we can confidently say that 2 Peter 2:4 and Jude 6 *do not* teach that *all* fallen angels are currently in chains. Since all fallen angels are not in chains, no contradiction exists between these passages and the belief that demons are fallen angels.

DEMONS AND THE OCCULT IN THE OLD TESTAMENT

To this point, we've seen that in biblical times citizens of both the East and the West were convinced of the existence of demons and their malevolent influence. They tried desperately to protect themselves—to ward off or manipulate demons by magical means—and they relied on their gods and goddesses for help against the demons. The Old Testament does not reflect the same level of concern with demons as was exhibited in other cultures, but it does recognize the existence of demons. In fact, the Old Testament clearly identifies pagan religions as demon inspired, and it warns against sacrifices made to idols—which in reality were sacrifices made to demons. The religious practices of pagans are also demon driven. This is especially true in the occult practices intimately related to pagan faith.

THE OLD TESTAMENT REQUIRES GOD'S PEOPLE TO STAY AWAY FROM ALL OCCULT PRACTICES
(Deuteronomy 18)

The critical passage in the Old Testament which treats the occult is Deuteronomy 18, a

When Jesus cast demons out of individuals, He demonstrated His power over such spirits.

chapter which deals with priests and prophets, the two central offices in Israel's religion. The context is important, for it indicates that occult practices had religious significance in the religions of Canaan. The section on the occult reads:

When you come into the land which the LORD your God is giving you, you shall not learn to follow the abominations of those nations. There shall not be found among you anyone who makes his son or his daughter pass through the fire, or one who practices witchcraft, or a soothsayer, or one who interprets omens, or a sorcerer, or one who conjures spells, or a medium, or a spiritist, or one who calls up the dead. For all who do these things are an abomination to the LORD, and because of these abominations the LORD your God drives them out from before you. You shall be blameless before the LORD your God. For these nations which you will dispossess listened to soothsayers and diviners; but as for you, the LORD your God has not appointed such for you. "The LORD your God will raise up for you a Prophet like me from your midst, from your brethren. Him you shall hear."

Deuteronomy 18:9–15

The occult practices and practitioners mentioned here served a common function: Each was intended to access supernatural sources of information.

In the earlier discussion of pagan contact with the gods as described in the Mari tablets, we saw that information was communicated from the spirit world to worshipers, through *apilu, assinuu,* and *muhhu.* We also saw why such information was valued—for the same reason pagans felt a need for supernatural information and guidance through the occult practices described in Deuteronomy 18: The world was too dangerous and ambiguous a place for mere human beings to live without aid from the spirit world. However, the spirit world of the pagans was infested with demons, some of which masqueraded as deities. The occult practices of the Canaanites put practitioners in contact with the *wrong kind of spirits!* God was intent on protecting His people from this danger.

DEFINITIONS OF THE OCCULT PRACTICES IDENTIFIED IN THE SCRIPTURES

The word "occult" comes from a Latin term which means "hidden, secret, dark, mysterious, or concealed." Occult practices attempt to uncover that which is hidden from human beings, who are limited to reason and observation by accessing the supernatural. The following chart shows how several English versions of the Bible translate the words used to identify occult practices.

Biblical scholars generally treat each of the terms listed above together under the heading of "divination." The *Zondervan Pictorial Encyclopedia of the Bible* (Vol. 2, p. 146) defines divination as

"the practice of consulting beings (divine, human, or departed) or things (by observing objects and actions) in the attempt to gain information about the future and such other matters as are removed from normal knowledge."

The fact that occult terms are often found together in Bible verses shows the overlap and interrelationship of these practices; for example, "witchcraft" is mentioned with "soothsaying" in four passages (Deut. 18:10; 2 Kings 17:17; 21:6; 2 Chron. 33:6). It is also significant that four of the six references to "witchcraft" also mention worship of idols in the same verse (1 Sam. 15:23; 2 Kings 17:17; 21:6; 2 Chron. 33:6). But what do "witchcraft" and the other occult practices listed here involve?

Witchcraft. The Hebrew term *kashap* means to practice or use witchcraft. The term "practice black magic" (in the new GOD'S WORD translation) is a good modern synonym. The practice seems to involve the use of magic to compel a god or demon to do one's bidding by the use of spells or incantations.

Soothsaying (divination). The Hebrew word is *qāsam,* which means to discover information by various occult means. A number of those means are specified in the Old Testament. Ezekiel 21:21 mentions throwing sticks or ar-

Translations of Old Testament Terms for Occult Practices

NKJV	God's Word	CEV	Tanakh	NIV
Witchcraft	practice black magic	witchcraft	augur	witchcraft
Fortune teller	fortune teller	tells fortunes	soothsayer	soothsayer
Interpret omens			diviner	interprets omens
Sorcerer	sorcerer	practice magic	sorcerer	sorcerer
Conjures spells	casts spells	casts spells	casts spells	casts spells
Medium	asks ghosts for help	talks with the dead	consults ghosts	medium
Spiritist	asks spirits for help		consults familiar spirits	spiritist
Calls up the dead	consults the dead		inquires of the dead	consults the dead

rows and examining the entrails of animals. Ezekiel 21:21, 1 Kings 23:24, and Zechariah 10:2 speak of the use of images (*teraphim*) in divination. One common means of soothsaying was to consult the stars, which is referred to in Isaiah 47:13 and Jeremiah 10:2 (like modern astrology).

Sorcery. The Hebrew word '*anan* is translated "to practice witchcraft" in Deuteronomy 18, but it is rendered into English in a variety of ways in other translations: to practice magic, to practice sorcery, to divine, and to tell fortunes. That shows the uncertainty of the word's actual meaning. Some suggest that "'*anan*" is an onomatopoeic word, which represents the sound made by one practicing the dark art. There is no doubt that it is a form of magic—seeking to gain information about, or to control to some extent, the future by recourse to dark powers.

Casting spells. The Hebrew word *habar* means to tie or untie a magic knot. The idea here is to cast a spell that binds a person by magic.

Interpreting omens. The Hebrew word is *nahash* (divination), whose root is closely linked with the word for snake. Some suggest that the practitioner hissed like a snake when engaged in this dark art.

Medium. A *yidd'oni* is a wizard who has a familiar spirit with whom he or she consults.

Two passages in the Old Testament define this individual's activity. Leviticus 20:27 speaks of "a man or a woman who is a medium, or who has familiar spirits." Deuteronomy 18:11 places the medium in company with the "spiritist, or one who calls up the dead."

The most famous story in the Bible about a medium is found in 1 Samuel 28 and repeated in 1 Chronicles 10. First Chronicles 10:13 says: "So Saul died for his unfaithfulness which he had committed against the LORD, because he did not keep the word of the LORD, and also because he consulted a medium *for guidance*" (emphasis added).

As the full story is told in 1 Samuel, a desperate Saul must meet an overwhelming Philistine army. Afraid and uncertain, Saul asked God for information, but the Lord refused to speak to him. Saul then found a medium (the "witch of Endor"), who had a relationship with a demon (a "familiar spirit"). When she called on the demon to appear, to her amazement Samuel's shade appeared instead. Samuel told Saul that he and his sons would fall in the coming battle and that Israel would be defeated.

The point of this story for us is that there were persons called "mediums" or "spiritists" who had contact with the spiritual realm through a demon confidant, to whom they could address questions. It would seem that this was true of these mediums, spiritists, and those who call up the dead in Deuteronomy 18.

The spirit of Samuel appeared to Saul at Endor.

Scripture is very clear about the conduct of believers with regard to mediums: "Give no regard to mediums and familiar spirits; do not seek after them, to be defiled by them: I am the LORD your God" (Lev. 19:31). In fact, according to the Law: "A man or a woman who is a medium, or who has familiar spirits, shall surely be put to death; they shall stone them with stones" (Lev. 20:27). Demons were too great a threat to permit any Israelite to develop a relationship with them that might corrupt the nation's relationship with God, on which the people's well-being depended.

ILLUSTRATIONS OF THE REALITY OF OCCULT POWERS AND INTIMATIONS OF THE FORCES BEHIND THEM

Although many today tend to dismiss stories of the occult as primitive superstition, this is unwise. Demons are real, and, like angels, they can span the gap between the spiritual and material realms and affect our world. One explanation of the grip pagan religions have on their adherents lies in the fact that there are real beings with unusual powers behind the deities the pagans worship.

Biblical illustrations of occult activity. An incident that happened when the gospel came to Samaria illustrates the reality of the occult and the impact of occult powers upon inhabitants of the ancient world. The story is found in Acts 8:

But there was a certain man called Simon, who previously practiced sorcery in the city and astonished the people of Samaria, claiming that he was someone great, to whom they all gave heed, from the least to the greatest, saying, "This man is the great power of God." And they heeded him because he had astonished them with his sorceries for a long time.

Acts 8:9–11

It is clear in this text that the people among whom Simon lived were convinced that he had occult powers, which he attributed to God. Something supernatural was taking place. Philip the Evangelist performed miracles that amazed even Simon. So Simon, eager to have such powers himself, offered money to Peter and John. Simon apparently assumed that the apostles used magic and that the secrets of controlling the Holy Spirit could be passed on like a magic formula.

Another similar incident is reported in Acts. On his first missionary journey, Paul confronted a sorcerer named Bar-Jesus. The story is told in Acts 13:

Now when they had gone through the island to Paphos, they found a certain sorcerer, a false prophet, a Jew whose name was Bar-Jesus, who was with the proconsul, Sergius Paulus, an intelligent man. This man called for Barnabas and Saul and sought to hear the word of God.

But Elymas the sorcerer (for so his name is translated) withstood them, seeking to turn the proconsul away from the faith. Then Saul, who also is called Paul, filled with the Holy Spirit, looked intently at him and said, "O full of all deceit and all fraud, you son of the devil, you enemy of all righteousness, will you not cease perverting the straight ways of the Lord?"

Acts 13:6–10

Here Paul links the false prophet and sorcerer with the prince of demons, the devil.

Yet another incident in Acts firmly establishes the link between demons and the occult practices forbidden in Deuteronomy 18.

Now it happened, as we went to prayer, that a certain slave girl possessed with a spirit of divination met us, who brought her masters much profit by fortune-telling. This girl followed Paul and us, and cried out, saying, "These men are the servants of the Most High God, who proclaim to us the way of salvation." And this she did for many days. But Paul, greatly annoyed, turned and said to the spirit,

"I command you in the name of Jesus Christ to come out of her." And he came out that very hour. But when her masters saw that their hope of profit was gone, they seized Paul and Silas and dragged them into the marketplace to the authorities.

Acts 16:16–18

An evil spirit possessed the girl and enabled her to tell fortunes. The occult, in both the Old and New Testaments, is clearly associated with "evil spirits," a biblical synonym for "demons."

DEMONS AND THE OCCULT IN OUR WORLD TODAY

There is no reason to assume that the ministries of the angels we read about in Scripture have been put on hold for today. God still sends His angels to guard us.

Similarly, there is no reason to assume that the malevolent activities of the demons we read about in Scripture have been eradicated today. Demons still conspire with Satan to thwart God's plans and to corrupt and torment human beings. If this is so, we need to consider carefully the relationship between contemporary occult practices and demons.

Sean Sellers, on death row for the murder of his parents, tells of his involvement with Satanism and the occult in his book *Web of Darkness* (1990, pp. 90–91). These are some of his comments on the "harmless" Ouija board:

The danger of the Ouija board is that it provides—like all oracle-consulting tools—a focus point for the spiritual dark side to enter a person's life. A method called *Progressive Entrapment* is used by the spirit entities spoken to, in order to consume the will of the person who is contacting them. Progressive Entrapment is a slow process through which evil forces change and inhabit a human being.

Progressive entrapment begins with a subtle desire to use the board more and more. The more the Ouija board is used, the more results are gleaned from it. That subtle desire may slowly turn into an obsession until the Ouija-invoked entities actually control the person. As the powers of these entities become stronger, personality disorders may develop and the user's mind becomes distorted, especially concerning concepts of right and wrong. In time, the user will depend completely on the Ouija for every decision he or she makes and will be totally obedient to the board's instructions. . . .

When I was a satanist the Ouija was used frequently as a way to introduce individuals into the occult. We knew the Ouija was accepted by most people as being harmless, and once we got a person playing, it was only a matter of time before they would agree to join us in a satanic ritual.

There is no doubt that today, as in biblical times, many who claim to have occult powers are charlatans, preying on the naive for money; but there also is reason to believe that occult practices remain linked with the demonic. Certainly the strong admonition in Deuteronomy 18 against *any* involvement with the occult gives believers today every reason to stay away from all such practices.

OCCULT PRACTICES TODAY AND WHAT THEY PROMISE

If we make a list of modern occult practices and provide simple dictionary definitions, we note that they promise the same

kind of information as did the practices forbidden in Scripture. Common occult practices today include: astrology; palmistry; tarot (card laying); Ouija boards; crystal balls; consulting psychics, witchcraft, and spiritists who claim to have a "spirit guide" who brings them into contact with the dead. Contemporary definitions of these practices are taken from the *American Heritage Illustrated Encyclopedic Dictionary.*

Astrology. "The study of the positions and aspects of heavenly bodies with a view to assessing or predicting their supposed influence on human characteristics and the course of human affairs." The results of such studies are cast as horoscopes, which claim to forecast a person's future based on a diagram of the stars and planets at a given moment. Horoscopes are used to guide daily and significant decisions. A person who uses horoscopes to guide decisions relies on the stars, rather than the Lord, rather than his or her own judgment.

Palmistry. "The practice or art of telling fortunes from the lines, marks, and patterns on the palms of the hands." Those who seriously consult palmists are seeking advice from a source beyond their own faculties of judgment; thus, they may come to rely on the palm reader to make critical decisions.

Tarot (card laying). "Any of a set of 22 playing cards consisting of a joker plus 21 cards depicting vices, virtues, and elemental forces, used in fortune telling." The client seeks information outside the realm of normal sources to be used for guidance in making decisions. As a person comes to depend on tarot more and more for decision making, he or she not only becomes vulnerable to manipulation by charlatans, but may also become vulnerable to the demonic forces that use the cards as an avenue to influence or enter a person's life.

Ouija board. "A trademark for a board with alphabet and other symbols on it and a planchette that is thought, when touched with the fingers, especially by several people, to move in such a way as to spell out spiritualistic and telepathic messages on the board." As we saw earlier, people who use Ouija boards assume contact with the spirit world; such people are therefore more vulnerable to demonic beings than those who make use of other occult practices.

Crystal balls. Crystal balls are used in "crystal gazing," which is "a foretelling or attempt to foretell the future by or as if by seeing future events in a crystal ball."

Psychics. A psychic is a person who is supposedly sensitive "to extraordinary, especially extrasensory and nonphysical, mental processes or forces, such as extrasensory perception and telepathy." Today psychics advertise aggressively on television and can be accessed by placing calls to 900 numbers. We can assume that most psychics are charlatans, but once again the person who consults a psychic becomes open to influences from outside the natural world and may become vulnerable to demons, who use belief in psychic powers to access the person who relies on them.

Witchcraft. Witchcraft is "the practice of black magic or sorcery." Traditionally, the witch is believed to have contact with the devil. Witches work or cast spells that influence the lives of others. Females who practice the craft are called witches; males, warlocks. Witches often make a distinction between black and white witchcraft, depending upon whether the intent is to harm or to help. The distinction is a false one, however, in that both white and black witches make the same assumptions about the nature of their powers. Witchcraft, like Ouija, provides a more direct access to the spirit world, and it is more closely associated with Satanism and demons than some other occult practices today.

Spiritists and spiritualists. The two terms are synonymous in that "each assumes one can communicate with the dead, usually through a medium." Spiritists usually *are* mediums, who claim to bring the living into contact with the dead in séances or private consultations. Again, many spiritists are charlatans. However, the consultation of mediums, well established since before biblical times, is another of those occult practices which bring a person into direct, immediate contact with the demonic.

SCRIPTURE'S ANSWER TO THE OCCULT IN THE PAST AND IN THE PRESENT

There is no question that seeking guidance or information from occult sources is strictly forbidden to people who have a personal relationship with God. According to Deuteronomy 18, such practices are an "abomination"—an extremely strong term—even when practiced by unbelievers. Demons are under the judgment of God. They are evil beings who can only corrupt individuals and cultures. Any contact with demons is loathsome.

Yet Deuteronomy 18 implicitly acknowledges the fact that believers at times do need information not available to them through natural means. Thus, the same passage that forbids inquiring of the occult and says, "God has not appointed such for you," goes on to promise Israel, "The LORD your God will raise up for you a Prophet like me from your midst, from your brethren" (Deut. 18:14, 15).

There were times when Israel needed a direct word from God to know what to do. There were times when the laws and general principles embedded in Scripture were not enough for Israel to decide what course to take. For such times God promised to provide the needed guidance Himself, through prophets He would send to His people. There was no need for Israel to turn to the occult. Israel could, and must, rely on the Lord.

The same is true for us today. God has given us minds to think and Scriptures to read. We are to use our minds to evaluate courses of action, and we are to search the Scriptures to find principles to aid in decision making. Still, there will be times when we are unsure about what to do. At those times, when we cast about for help, we are *not to turn to the occult.* God has not "appointed such" for us, either. Rather, like Israel, we are to look to God and to rely on Him to provide the special guidance we need.

In Old Testament times prophets provided special guidance for God's people. In our time, with Christ risen and the Holy Spirit given, it is the Spirit who communicates God's will to our hearts and who guides us from within. We saw earlier (p. 90) Paul's teaching that "if you are led by the Spirit, you are not under the law" (Gal. 5:18). What Paul means is that we, unlike ancient Israel, are not to look first to external standards to guide us to do what is right, but we are to look first to the Holy Spirit, who will prompt us from within as we rely on Him.

What about angel guidance? Angel guidance is an option in Scripture, and thus for today, but it was not the most frequent means, or even the second or third most frequent means, that God used to lead His people in the past. While God is completely free to send angels to us today, we have the Holy Spirit already present with us; and usually we are to expect the Spirit to guide us as we make a commitment to avoid the occult and to rely fully on the Lord.

CHAPTER 8

SATAN, GOD, AND EVIL:

WHEN BAD THINGS HAPPEN

Job; additional Old & New Testament passages

A popular book in the 1980s, *When Bad Things Happen to Good People,* raised a question often posed to students in philosophy of religion courses. The question is a problem usually stated in the form of a syllogism:

> God is Good and All-powerful.
> Bad things happen.
> Therefore, God is not both Good
>   and All-powerful.

This type of reasoning is troubling, for the facts that evil exists and that bad things do happen to good people simply do not fit with our basic beliefs about the goodness and sovereignty of God.

This apparent contradiction has disturbed many throughout the ages. A traditional Jewish view holds that a person who performed certain ritual laws meticulously would be protected from the accusations of Satan, and thus preserved from trouble. So Rabbi Zeira complained, "I fulfilled these laws, yet I was caught in a royal labor-draft and forced to carry myrtle branches to the palace" (Yoma 67b, Sifra on Lev. 18:4). We can understand the rabbi's feelings. He did his part, but God let something bad happen to him anyway.

THE SOLUTION OF DUALISM

DUALISM PROPOSES TWO GODS, ONE GOOD AND ONE EVIL, AND THUS AVOIDS IMPUTING EVIL TO THE LORD

One approach to resolving the problem of evil was advocated by a prophet who appeared in ancient Persia (modern Iran) about 1400–1200 B.C. While some scholars argue that the prophet Zoroaster was a monotheist, others claim that he was a dualist; that is, he taught that there were two primordial uncreated Spirits—a Good Spirit (corresponding to God) and an Evil Spirit (corresponding to Satan)—rather than a single uncreated Spirit.

A text in the sacred book of the Zoroastrian faith, the *Avesta,* affirms however that there are two such spirits—twins (Yasna 30:3). The personal name Zoroaster gave to the Good Spirit was Ahura Mazda. His descriptive name was Spenta Mainyu, Good Spirit. This spirit was wholly good and the source of all that is good in the universe.

Aligned with him in his sphere were light, fire, summer, water, fertile land, health, growth, and domestic animals. The name of the other spirit was Angra Mainyu, Fiendish Spirit. Aligned with this Evil Spirit were darkness, night, winter, drought, infertile land, vermin, sickness, and death. Because the two spirits were twins, neither was able to triumph over the other unaided. Human beings tip the scales by their moral choice of good or evil.

Dualistic systems such as classical Zoroastrianism have a distinctive answer to the problem posed in the syllogism above. Dualists assert that God really is completely good, and they blame everything bad on the evil twin. The advantage of this view is that it never imputes evil to God Himself; the disadvantage is that it robs God of His uniqueness and His sole sovereignty over the universe. Further, dualism makes the twin god, Satan, far more powerful and far more frightful than he really is.

HOW FRIGHTFUL IS SATAN AS AN ADVERSARY OF GOD AND HIS FOLLOWERS?

Dualism tends to cast Satan as an awesome being, equal in power to his twin—the good god. Faithful Jews and Christians have at times fallen into the trap of making Satan more frightful than he really is. The Talmud numbers Satan's force of evil angels at 7,405,926 strong, divided into 72 companies. During the Renaissance there was an intense fascination with the diabolic; by the fourteenth century churchmen figured that some 301,655,722 supernatural beings hung just beyond the edge of our universe, and that 133,306,668 of them were demons ruled by Satan.

By that time the conception of Satan and his role in the universe had also changed. In *The Life of Anthony*, a book written by Athanasius, the Bishop of Alexandria, in A.D. 360, the evil one is depicted as meeting with Anthony one night to register a complaint.

Someone knocked at the door of my cell, and opening it I saw a person of great size and tallness.

Satan visits Anthony.

I inquired, "Who are you? and he replied, "Satan." When I asked, "Why are you here," he answered, "Why do monks and other Christians blame me so undeservedly? Why do they curse me every hour?" And I answered, "Why do you trouble them?" He replied, "I don't trouble them, for I am become weak: they trouble themselves. Haven't they read that 'the swords of the enemy are finished and the cities destroyed for him?' I no longer have a weapon or a city. The Christians are spread everywhere, and even the desert is now filled with monks. Let them take care of themselves and cease cursing me." I marveled at God's grace and said to Satan, "Although you are a liar and never speak the truth, you have spoken the truth here, albeit against your will. For the coming of Christ has weakened you, and He has cast you down and stripped you."

Athanasius reminds his readers that Christ has triumphed over the devil, and that Satan is a *defeated* enemy. Rather than blame Satan for our trials and temptations, we need to look within to our own sinful nature.

Over the centuries, this perspective was lost and Satan's awful being and awesome powers were emphasized, as can be seen in a tale about an Irish knight named Tundale written by a monk in A.D. 1149. This tale captured the imagination of the people of the Middle Ages, and it was translated into no less than 15 different languages. According to the story, Tundale, well on the way to hell, experienced a transforming vision. Tundale collapsed and lay in a coma for three days, during which time his soul was given a tour of heaven and hell by his guardian angel. Here is the monk's account of a scene Tundale is supposed to have witnessed in hell:

Drawing near, Tundale's soul saw the depths of hell, and he would not be able to repeat in any way how many, how great and what inexpressible torments he saw there if he had a hundred heads and in each head a hundred tongues. I do not think it would be useful to omit the few details he did bring back to us.

He saw the Prince of Shadows, the enemy of humanity, the Devil, whose size overshadowed every kind of beast that Tundale saw before. Tundale was not able to compare the size of the body to anything, nor would we dare to presume to say what we did not draw from his mouth, but such a story as we did hear we ought not to omit.

This beast was very black, like a raven, with a body of human shape from its feet to its head. He dispersed before, and he devoured those who fell into his mouth with the smoke and sulfur. But whoever fled from his hand he struck down with his tail, and the miserable beast, always striking hard, was struck hard, and the burning tormentor was tormented in the punishment with the souls.

Seeing this Tundale's soul said to the angel of the Lord, "My Lord, what is this monster's name?" Answering, the angel said, "This beast whom you see is called Lucifer, and he is the prince of the creatures of God who took part in the pleasures of paradise. He was so perfect [that is, powerful] that he would throw heaven and earth and even hell into total disorder."

Such tales, transformed into graphic images by artists intent on creating a fear of Satan and his demons, promoted the popular notion that Satan was a being with overwhelming powers.

The gradual transformation of the Christian view of Satan from a significant, but defeated foe into an implacable, monstrous, and dominant enemy attributed a significance to Satan that is not warranted by Scripture. It also shifted the responsibility for any evil that befalls a believer to Satan. In addition, it clouded the question of the nature of the relationship between God, Satan, and evil. Yet that issue is one we must face.

ANGELORE

CALVIN ON GOD, SATAN, AND EVIL

With regard to the strife and war which Satan is said to wage with God, it must be understood with this qualification, that Satan cannot possibly do anything against the will and consent of God. For we read in the history of Job, that Satan appears in the presence of God to receive his commands, and dares not proceed to execute any enterprise until he is authorized. In the same way, when Ahab was to be deceived, he undertook to be a lying spirit in the mouth of all the prophets; and on being commissioned by the Lord, proceeded to do so. For this reason, also, the spirit which tormented Saul is said to be an evil spirit from the Lord, because he was, as it were, the scourge by which the misdeeds of the wicked king were punished. . . .

It is evident, therefore, that Satan is under the power of God, and is so ruled by his authority, that he must yield obedience to it. Moreover, though we say that Satan resists God, and does works at variance with His works, we at the same time maintain that this contrariety and opposition depend on the permission of God. I now speak not of Satan's will and endeavor, but only of the result. . . . He eagerly, and of set purpose, opposes God, aiming at those things which he deems most contrary to the will of God. But as God holds him bound and fettered by the curb of his power, he executes those things only for which permission has been given him, and thus, however unwillingly, obeys his Creator, being forced, whenever he is required, to do him service (*Institutes*, Book 1).

If John Calvin is right in his *Institutes* when he argues that God is totally sovereign and that Satan can only do what God wills, are we driven to the conclusion that God is the source of evil, as well as the source of good in our universe? How can a truly and completely good God have any dealings with evil at all, except to punish it? We can best answer these questions by looking at specific cases in Scripture that treat the issue raised.

THE CASE OF JOB   *(Job 1—2)*

JOB IS PORTRAYED AS AN EXCEPTIONALLY GOOD PERSON
(Job 1:1, 8)

The book of Job directly explores the question of bad things happening to good people by telling the story of an exceptionally good man. We learn immediately that Job "was blameless and upright, and one who feared God and shunned evil" (Job 1:1 NKJV). This assessment of Job was repeated by God Himself (Job 1:8). This commendation does not imply that Job was sinless, but it does imply that Job trusted God and tried honestly to please Him. Job himself described the way he had lived (chapter 31)—one of the most com-

pelling descriptions of the moral life to be found in Scripture.

The point of the evaluations of Job is to make it clear that he does not represent "everyman." Job is a unique individual, outstanding in his generation for his piety and his commitment to what is right. God Himself said of Job, "there is none like him on the earth" (Job 1:8). This serves to focus our attention even more closely on the issue with which we are concerned in this chapter. With Job it is not a question of why bad things happen to an ordinarily good person, it is a question of why bad things happen to an *exceptionally* good person.

THE BOOK OF JOB TAKES US "BEHIND THE SCENES" TO OBSERVE DIALOGUES BETWEEN GOD AND SATAN
(Job 1:6–12; 2:1–6)

The first dialogue (Job 1:6–12). The first dialogue between God and Satan concerning Job is related this way:

Now there was a day when the sons of God came to present themselves before the LORD, and

Satan and other angels come before the Lord.

Satan also came among them. And the LORD said to Satan, "From where do you come?"

So Satan answered the LORD and said, "From going to and fro on the earth, and from walking back and forth on it."

Then the LORD said to Satan, "Have you considered My servant Job, that there is none like him on the earth, a blameless and upright man, one who fears God and shuns evil?"

So Satan answered the LORD and said, "Does Job fear God for nothing? Have You not made a hedge around him, around his household, and around all that he has on every side? You have blessed the work of his hands, and his possessions have increased in the land. But now, stretch out Your hand and touch all that he has, and he will surely curse You to Your face!"

And the LORD said to Satan, "Behold, all that he has is in your power; only do not lay a hand on his person."

So Satan went out from the presence of the LORD.

Job 1:6–12

Immediately after this conversation between the Lord and Satan, Sabean raiders took Job's cattle and killed his herders; fire fell from heaven and consumed his sheep; bands of Chaldeans raided his camel herds and took them away; and a tornado struck the house where Job's children were eating and killed them all.

There was no doubt in Job's mind that for some reason God had caused every disaster, but Job's reaction was to mourn—and worship, saying, "The LORD gave, and the LORD has taken away; Blessed be the name of the LORD" (Job 1:21).

The relationship between God and Satan.

This passage depicts Satan's coming before the Lord with other angels ("sons of God"). We are not told specifically that this gathering took place in heaven, although most commentators assume it did. Nor are we told that Satan normally participated in such gatherings. In fact, the preposition *"among"* is often used to refer to an intruder. So it may be that Satan alone had no right to be in this company of

holy angels, and thus he was singled out by the Lord for questioning.

In any case, the passage clearly depicts Satan as one who "presented himself" before God. Satan is not an equal to God, but a subordinate. As the situation develops, it is increasingly clear that the Lord is in control. It is the Lord who set boundaries around Job which Satan could not cross; and it is the Lord who gave permission before Satan could touch Job.

Satan's sphere of activity.

In answer to the Lord's question concerning where Satan had been, Satan gave an indefinite answer. He had been roving the earth, "walking back and forth on it" (Job 1:7). The image is one of restless wandering, and it suggests what other passages also indicate—that Satan had been forced out of heaven and was now limited to operating on the earth. Once again we get the impression of a being with severely limited powers. Satan may be a terror on earth, but he is an outcast in heaven.

The challenge initiated.

It is significant that the Lord was the one who singled out Job and drew Satan's attention to Job's blameless life. Satan apparently did not have any plan to threaten this servant of the Lord. The Lord set up the conflict which was about to take place, with Job as its focal point.

Satan's reaction.

Satan is a skeptic who does not believe in either God's unselfish generosity, or a pure love for God divorced from self-interest. So Satan's reaction is predictable. He knew of Job, but he also knew that faith had paid off for this servant of the Lord. God had even put a hedge around Job so that Satan had been unable to trouble him (Job 1:10). With a sneer Satan asked, "Does Job fear God for nothing?"

The taunt suggests that God had bribed Job and made life too easy for him. Job's response to God was not pure love at all; it was a payoff for benefits provided. Satan was so sure that was the case that he challenged God: "But now, stretch out Your hand and touch all that he has, and he will surely curse You to Your face!" (Job 1:11).

In this we again see the limitations under which Satan labors. Satan cannot break through the hedge of protection God places around His own. Satan could not even touch Job's possessions, but had to ask God to do the harm he intended.

A JEWISH RESPONSE TO THE PROBLEM OF EVIL

Many Jewish sages were deeply disturbed by the problem of evil. In particular, they rejected the notion that an evil Satan could act contrary to God's will. One solution was to postulate a sympathetic Satan. In the Babylonian Talmud the testing of Job was explained as Satan's shock that God might even suggest that Job was as righteous as Abraham. Satan proposed the testing of Job in order to uphold the reputation of Abraham! One teacher says explicitly, "Satan acted from the highest motives. When he saw God inclined to favor Job, he said: Heaven forfend that the piety of Abraham be forgotten." The Talmud adds this story. When Rabbi Aha ben Jacob repeated this interpretation in a sermon at Paphunia, Satan came and kissed his feet in gratitude!

Another story casts Satan as the righteous spirit of strict justice. Satan kept accusing Israel of real sins and preventing God from freeing the people from bondage in Egypt. So God pointed Job out to Satan to distract him. While Satan was busy trying to reveal Job's supposed flaws, God set Israel free. In this way the Lord got around Satan's legitimate accusations to deliver the Jewish people whom He favored. (See Bernard J. Banberger, *Fallen Angels,* 1952, p. 97.)

Satan as God's instrument. God Himself would not do the injustice to Job that Satan suggested. Instead, the Lord gave Satan permission to do as he wished. So the Lord said, "Behold, all that he has is in your power; only do not lay a hand on his person" (Job 1:12). Again, however, we see that Satan could act against Job only when God expressly permitted him to do so.

God's is the ultimate responsibility. When the disasters caused by Satan struck Job in a single day, Job did not blame the Sabeans or the Chaldeans; he did not blame Satan, or search for some other secondary cause he could charge with responsibility. Instead, Job traced the supernatural juxtaposition of events directly to the Lord, and said, "The LORD gave, and the LORD has taken away." He then concluded, "Blessed be the name of the LORD" (Job 1:21).

Even though what Job experienced as evil had been done by God, Job neither cursed the Lord, nor charged Him with wrongdoing. To Job, God was sovereign. The tragedies that struck him could not be accidents, yet God could not be accused of doing wrong. Satan, who had promised to make Job curse God to His face, had failed completely.

The second dialogue *(Job 2:1–7).* The contest was not over. God and Satan have another dialogue:

Again there was a day when the sons of God came to present themselves before the LORD, and Satan came also among them to present himself before the LORD. And the LORD said to Satan, "From where do you come?"

Satan answered the LORD and said, "From going to and fro on the earth, and from walking back and forth on it."

Then the LORD said to Satan, "Have you considered My servant Job, that there is none like him on the earth, a blameless and upright man who fears God and shuns evil? And still he holds fast to his integrity, although you incited Me against him, to destroy him without a cause."

So Satan answered the LORD and said, "Skin for skin! Yes, all that a man has he will give for his life. But stretch out Your hand now, and touch his bone and his flesh, and he will surely curse You to Your face!"

And the LORD said to Satan, "Behold, he is in your hand, but spare his life."

So Satan went out from the presence of the LORD, and struck Job with painful boils from the sole of his foot to the crown of his head.

Job 2:1–7

More evidence of Satan's subordinate role. These verses repeat verbatim many of the phrases found in the first dialogue. God again pointed Job out, and Satan again challenged God's characterization of Job as a blameless and upright person. But Satan could do nothing more against Job unless and until God permitted it. There is one, and only one, sovereign here.

Satan's argument. Earlier, Satan assumed that if all that Job held dear was taken away, he would curse the Lord. Now Satan argued that Job must be a much worse person than even he had imagined! Job seemed untouched by tragedy and loss. The only reason Satan could come up with was that Job was so completely self-centered that anything which did not touch him *directly* simply was not important to him. "Touch his bone and his flesh" Satan challenged, and the results would be different—then "he will surely curse You to Your face" (Job 2:5).

God permitted Satan to harm Job's person. Once again God permitted Satan to harm Job. While Job 2 mentions boils that covered Job's body, other references to his suffering are found in the book. The boils drew Job's strength and caused skin infections (Job 30:28) and peeling (Job 30:30). He became emaciated (Job 19:20) and had a high fever (Job 30:30b). Job experienced depression (Job 7:16; 30:15), uncontrollable weeping (Job 16:16a), and sleeplessness (Job 7:4). His vision failed (Job 16:16b), and his teeth rotted (Job 19:20). Clearly, Satan's torment led to hideous deformity and the most intense physical and mental suffering.

Job's response to his suffering (Job 2:9, 10). As Job's condition worsened, even his wife begged him to "curse God and die." Job refused, and responded instead, "Shall we indeed accept good from God, and shall we not accept adversity?" (Job 2:10).

Satan again failed to sense the depth of Job's faith in the Lord, and Satan now retired in defeat. He had failed completely to make Job curse God to His face.

THE RELATIONSHIP OF GOD, SATAN, AND EVIL IN THE STORY OF JOB

God had His own good purpose for permitting Job's suffering (Job 42:5, 6, 12–17). As we read Job 1—2, our impression might be that neither Satan nor God was concerned at all with Job's well-being. Job seems to have been treated like a chess piece on some cosmic game board in an unequal contest between a sovereign God and His frustrated enemy, Satan.

Satan retires in chapter 2 and is not mentioned again in the entire book, but the story of Job continues for an additional 40 chapters! Job's sufferings continued for weeks, during which time Job and three friends explore their limited understanding of God, sin, and evil.

The book ends with two striking revelations. God spoke to Job, and Job said, "I have heard of You by the hearing of the ear, / But now my eye sees You. / Therefore I abhor myself, / And repent in dust and ashes" (Job 42:5, 6). It is clear that Job's experience of suffering led to a more accurate understanding of himself and of God. However blameless and upright Job might have been, he now realized that he could not depend in the slightest on his human goodness, and so he repented. However accurate Job's sense of God's identity was before, Job now understood so much more about the Lord that he could only compare his previous understanding to hearsay (hearing with the ear), and his present insight to direct personal experience (seeing with the eye).

What is significant here is that while Satan may have been *using* Job in his struggle to show up the Lord, God had a very different—

and, in fact, loving—purpose in mind in permitting Satan to harm Job. The Lord intended to draw Job closer to Him through the experience.

The second revelation in Job 42 is of God's grace, for the Lord restored all that Job had lost twofold (Job 42:12–17). Remarking on this, James reminds us to be patient and to persevere when we suffer: "You have heard of the perseverance of Job and seen the end intended by the Lord—that the Lord is very compassionate and merciful" (James 5:11). Yes, God was ultimately responsible for Job's suffering, but from the beginning God intended Job's pain to result in good.

Implications of the story of Job. We can draw certain conclusions about God, Satan, and evil from the story of Job:

- God is in sovereign control of His creation.
- Satan is a created being whose freedom of action is limited by God's will.
- God guards and protects His own from Satan and the evil Satan would do to them if he could.
- God may at times permit Satan to harass or harm His own, but not with the intent to do them harm.
- Satan's motive in harming a believer is evil: Satan wants to do harm to God's own as a way of getting at the Lord.
- God's motive in letting Satan harm a believer is never evil: God only permits harm or suffering in order to bring glory to Himself and to enrich the life of the believer so tested.

THE CASE OF THE LYING SPIRIT
(1 Kings 22)

The problem that confronts us in 1 Kings 22 is slightly different from the one we encountered in Job. In Job the question was, Does God do evil? The answer was no—even when God permitted Satan to do evil, God transformed that evil into something good. In 1 Kings 22 the question is, Does God use evil

spirits to accomplish His good purposes? Or we might ask, Is it right to use evil means to reach a good end?

AHAB'S PROPHETS PREDICT A VICTORY   *(1 Kings 22:1–12)*

Ahab was king of Israel (the Northern Kingdom), and he was one of the most corrupt and wicked of all its rulers. Jehoshaphat was king of Judah (the Southern Kingdom), and he was a godly ruler. Jehoshaphat allied himself with Ahab to battle the Syrians, but he must have had some doubts because before going off to do battle, Jehoshaphat asked Ahab to "inquire of the Lord" about the undertaking.

Ahab called some four hundred prophets together, and they all reassured the kings. The

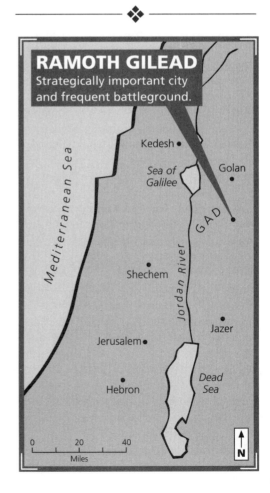

RAMOTH GILEAD
Strategically important city and frequent battleground.

Kedesh

Sea of Galilee

Golan

Mediterranean Sea

GAD

Shechem

Jordan River

Jazer

Jerusalem

Dead Sea

Hebron

0   20   40
Miles

N

prophets urged them to go up to Ramoth Gilead and fight, promising that "the LORD will deliver it into the hand of the king" (22:6). Still, Jehoshaphat remained uncomfortable because Ahab's prophets were adherents of the counterfeit religion that the kings of the Northern Kingdom had maintained ever since Israel was divided. So Jehoshaphat asked, "Is there not still a prophet of the LORD here, that we may inquire of Him?" (22:7).

Ahab admitted that there was one prophet of the Lord in the area, Micaiah the son of Imlah. To pacify Jehoshaphat, Ahab sent for Micaiah, even though, in his words, "I hate him, because he does not prophesy good concerning me, but evil" (22:8).

MICAIAH PREDICTS DEFEAT FOR THE COALITION AND DEATH FOR AHAB   (1 Kings 22:13–18)

When Micaiah was located and asked about the venture, he answered sarcastically:

Micaiah brought Ahab a true word from God.

"Go and prosper, for the LORD will deliver it into the hand of the king!" (22:15). Micaiah's sarcastic tone was so blatant that Ahab rebuked the prophet and asked for the authentic message. Micaiah announced that the combined Hebrew forces would be scattered, and that the king would be killed (22:17).

MICAIAH EXPLAINS THE DECEPTIVE MESSAGE OF AHAB'S PROPHETS   (1 Kings 22:19–23)

Micaiah then told of a vision in which "all the host of heaven" appeared before the Lord, who was seated on His throne. The Lord raised the question, "Who will persuade Ahab to go up, that he may fall at Ramoth Gilead?" (22:20). Various members of the host offered suggestions, but the Lord accepted the services of a volunteer who said, "I will go out and be a lying spirit in the mouth of all his prophets" (22:22).

The prophets of Ahab were clearly aware that a supernatural source had given them their message, and so they were angered by Micaiah's words (22:24). However, Micaiah alone had been permitted to see behind the scenes and to know what was really happening. He explained, "The LORD has put a lying spirit in the mouth of all these prophets of yours, and the LORD has declared disaster against you" (22:23).

THE MORAL PROBLEM RAISED BY THE "LYING SPIRIT"

This story has been singled out because it is said to raise one of the most significant of the supposed moral contradictions to the Judeo-Christian concept of God found in Scripture. How can a God who commands His people not to bear false witness (Ex. 20:16), who condemns sinful men and Satan as liars (John 8:44; 1 Tim. 1:10), and who tells His people to put away lying and to "speak truth" (Eph. 4:25), possibly justify sending a "lying spirit" to accomplish His purposes?

MICAIAH'S PRESENCE PROVIDES AN ANSWER

We saw in the story of Job that Satan himself could not act apart from the permissive will of God. Here we see God give permission to a "lying spirit," surely not one of His holy angels, to go and deceive Ahab's prophets and the king. The lying spirit was acting in harmony with his own moral bent, and the Lord permitted him to do so.

The rest of the story reveals that *God did not let even Ahab remain deceived!* Instead, God let Ahab and his prophets know the source of the prophecy that would have led this king to disaster. The "lying spirit" was permitted to tell his lie, but God made sure that Ahab knew the truth! Therefore, God can hardly be charged with using the lie to accomplish His purpose of punishing Ahab and ending his life.

AHAB AND HIS PROPHETS CHOSE TO BELIEVE THE LIE (1 Kings 22:23–36)

When Micaiah revealed the truth, Ahab's prophets were angry with him. One of them even struck Micaiah in the face (22:24). King Ahab ordered that Micaiah be imprisoned and fed only bread and water until he returned victorious (22:27). But Micaiah had spoken the truth, and Ahab was killed in the battle with the Syrians (22:30–37). When given the choice between believing God's truth or an evil spirit's lie, the king and his prophets chose to believe the lie.

IMPLICATIONS OF THE STORY OF THE LYING SPIRIT

We can draw the following principles from the story in 1 Kings 22:

- Evil spirits, like Satan himself, can act only with God's permission. God did not send the lying spirit to Ahab's prophets, but He did permit it to go.
- God did not rely on the lie to lead Ahab into a trap. In fact, God made sure that Ahab knew the truth through Micaiah.

- Ahab and his prophets chose to believe the lie, despite the fact that God made sure they knew the truth.
- God does not lie to accomplish His purposes; indeed, He counters Satan's lies with a revelation of His truth. The tragedy is that, like Ahab, sinful human beings tend to believe the lie rather than the truth.

THE CASE OF OTHER EVIL SPIRITS SUPPOSEDLY USED BY GOD

In a previous quote from Calvin's *Institutes,* the great theologian referred to Saul's deep depression as something caused by "an evil spirit from the Lord." Calvin was referring to the story in 1 Samuel in which a "distressing spirit from God" is said to have come "upon Saul" (16:14–16, 23; 18:10; 19:9).

The question is whether the text refers to a demonic being or to something else. For instance, in Psalm 51:10 David asks God to "renew a steadfast spirit within me," and in verse 17 he speaks of a "broken spirit." Proverbs 11:13 mentions a "faithful spirit," while in Proverbs 16:18, 19 there is mention of both a "haughty spirit" and a "humble spirit." Other similar phrases in the Old Testament include a "broken spirit"; a "calm spirit"; and a "perverse spirit," which the Lord is said to have mingled in Egypt (Isa. 19:14). Surely no one would argue that these are references to either demons or angels. What are they then? These phrases are simply ways of describing mental or moral states.

What about the "distressing spirit" that troubled King Saul? While Calvin and others have taken the phrase as a reference to a demon, it is much better, and more in keeping with Hebrew idiom, to take those references to the "distressing spirit" as a description of Saul's mental state.

Saul became more and more depressed and irritable as he lost contact with God. These moods were lightened when David played his harp; Saul would be refreshed and the "distressing spirit would depart from him."

These moods were "from the Lord" in that they were direct consequences of Saul's disobedience to God and of God's judgment of Saul (1 Sam. 13:1–15; 15:1–35). These passages simply do not suggest that God sent an evil spirit to torment the troubled king.

THE CASE OF KING DAVID'S SIN
(2 Samuel 24; 1 Chronicles 21)

THE SIN IS SAID TO BE INCITED BY BOTH GOD AND SATAN!

Both of these passages tell the story of a particular incident in David's life. The king decided to take a census and learn how many of his subjects were available for military service. The king's act was apparently a reflection of Israel's reliance on military power instead of God, and both the king and the nation were subsequently punished.

However, the special aspect of these parallel passages is centered in just a few verses. Second Samuel 24:1 says: "Again the anger of the LORD was aroused against Israel, and He moved David against them to say, 'Go, number Israel and Judah.'" The parallel passage in 1 Chronicles 21:1 reads: "Now Satan stood up against Israel, and moved David to number Israel."

Yet later in each passage David himself confessed, "I have sinned greatly, because I have done this thing" (1 Chron. 21:8; 1 Sam. 24:10).

OBSERVATIONS ON THE TEXTS

There are several interesting features worth noting in these texts. First, while God is said to have incited David to number Israel, the Israelites clearly had done some unnamed thing that aroused His anger and merited punishment. God's motive was a righteous one.

Second, while Satan is also said to have incited David to number Israel, no reason for his action is given. Satan is naturally hostile to God and His people, and he needs no more reason than that to act against them. More sig-

nificantly, there is no hint here that the Lord arranged for Satan to do the inciting. Satan was apparently acting on his own, but he necessarily needed permission from the Lord.

Third, David takes full and total responsibility for his actions. He does not try to shift the blame for what he did to Satan or to the Lord. As far as David was concerned, whether or not to take the census was completely up to him, and he made his decision freely without any coercion from an outside source, supernatural or otherwise.

THE HEBREW CONCEPT OF RESPONSIBILITY

In contemporary society the custom is to blame one's evil acts on others. A man who beats his wife to death is likely to complain that it was her fault; she did things that made him mad. The killer's lawyer is likely to blame his client's parents for abusing him as a child; or the lawyer might argue that his client's failure to get an education beyond sixth grade doomed him to be the kind of person he is.

This kind of thinking is foreign to the Old Testament. Each actor was fully responsibility for his or her own actions. Was God responsible for inciting David to number Israel? Yes, God is responsible for everything that *He* does. Did God *make* David sin? No, David was fully responsible for his own choice. Was Satan responsible for inciting David to number Israel? Yes, Satan is fully responsible for everything that *he* does. Did Satan *make* David sin? No, David was fully responsible for his own choice. We can chart this concept of responsibility as follows:

Who's Responsible? God, David, and Satan

Actor	Responsible for	Not responsible for
God	inciting David	Satan inciting David; David's census
Satan	inciting David	David's census
David	David's census	

Scripture provides no basis for any moral being to shift responsibility for his or her actions to any other being. In practice, neither God nor the devil can "make us" do anything. A moral being makes each choice freely; and a moral being is responsible only for what he or she does.

THE CASE OF PAUL'S THORN IN THE FLESH   *(2 Corinthians 12:1–9)*

We need to examine one more case in Scripture before we try to state what the Bible teaches about the relationship between God, Satan, and evil.

THE OCCASION LEADING TO PAUL'S THORN *(2 Corinthians 12:1–7a)*

The apostle Paul was given a revelation which he could not share. He was "caught up into Paradise and heard inexpressible words" (2 Cor. 12:4). Even Paul was in danger of being "exalted above measure by the abundance of the revelations" (2 Cor. 12:7a).

THE SOURCE OF THE THORN IN THE FLESH   *(2 Corinthians 12:7b)*

Paul relates that a "thorn in the flesh" was given to him, and he identified the thorn as a "messenger of Satan [sent] to buffet me." The Greek phrase translated "messenger of Satan" is *angelos satana,* and Paul intends for us to understand it to mean an "angel of Satan." It is far better to take this meaning and assume that a demon was in fact the cause of Paul's thorn. The thorn is generally understood to be a physical illness, one which has been variously identified as: a form of ophthalmia, which weakened Paul's eyes and ruined his looks; as epilepsy; as a recurring malarial fever or even a kidney stone! In any case, it is clear from the text that the "thorn" had a demonic source, and the demon's intent was to "buffet" the apostle.

PAUL'S RESPONSE TO HIS THORN   *(2 Corinthians 12:8)*

Paul, who himself had healed and exorcised demons in others (cf. Acts 19:11),

Paul prayed for relief from his "thorn."

turned to God in prayer. Paul prayed three times (the aorist tense of the Greek verb makes it clear that these seasons of prayer were now ended), but Paul received no relief. Instead, God gave Paul insight into how his sufferings would benefit him and his mission.

GOD'S PURPOSES IN PERMITTING SATAN'S ANGEL TO TORMENT THE APOSTLE PAUL *(2 Corinthians 12:9)*

God's response to Paul's prayers was no, but God explained to His servant why the torment was permitted to continue. "My grace is sufficient for you," the Lord told Paul, "for My strength is made perfect in weakness." God would use Satan's angel to buffet Paul and thereby keep him in a state where he was forced to rely fully on the Lord. In this state, Paul would be a more open channel through which the power of Christ could be expressed. Paul concludes, "Therefore I take pleasure in infirmities, in reproaches, in needs, in persecutions, in distresses, for Christ's sake. For when I am weak, then I am strong" (2 Cor. 12:10).

THE RELATIONSHIP BETWEEN GOD, SATAN, AND EVIL IN 2 CORINTHIANS 12

It's clear in this passage that what Paul experienced as a physical disability was an evil: It harmed Paul and caused him pain, and it was caused by one of Satan's angels. The phrase "to buffet me" indicates the demon's intent. Satan's motive was to do Paul harm, and perhaps to make Paul physically repulsive so as to alienate potential hearers of the gospel. So Paul makes a direct connection between Satan, his angel (demon), and evil—the same connection that is made when Satan is called "the evil one" (John 17:15; 1 John 5:18).

At the same time, it is clear that God permitted Satan's angel to buffet Paul, and that He even refused to answer Paul's repeated prayer for relief. However, the passage also indicates that God permitted the demon to continue buffeting Paul for a most positive purpose. Satan and his demon intended to do Paul harm, but God used what Satan and his demon did for good. The illness kept Paul from pride (2 Cor. 12:7), and it also taught Paul that he was strongest spiritually when he was weakest physically, unable to rely on his own abilities. In this case, Paul was forced to rely completely on God, and Paul made the important discovery that God's strength is made perfect in human weakness.

God did not do the evil to Paul. He permitted Satan to do the evil—and then God transformed the harm Satan intended into good.

SCRIPTURE'S SOLUTION TO THE PROBLEM OF GOD, SATAN, AND EVIL

Many people have been troubled by the existence of evil in a world supposedly ruled by a sovereign and supreme God. Some have tried to resolve the problem by proposing that God is limited. He does not like evil, but there is little He can do about it. This approach leads to a radical change in one's view of God, and it distorts Scripture's portrait of a sovereign, all-powerful God and leaves Him weak and ineffective.

Others have tried to resolve the problem of evil by attributing far more power and authority to Satan than he actually possesses. Dualistic religions have avoided potential charges of evil to their god by inventing an evil twin who can be blamed for everything harmful. Even Christians have at times exaggerated Satan's power to the extent that he has seemed almost as powerful as the Lord.

Scripture takes a very different approach to the problem posed by evil. It maintains the utter sovereignty of the Lord and puts Satan in proper perspective—a created being who is, compared to the Lord, limited and impotent. As we saw in chapter 1, evil originated in Satan's heart and will. Evil spread in heaven as Satan recruited angels to follow him rather than God, and evil infected our world when Satan deceived Eve and she and Adam sinned.

Ever since his fall Satan has been intent on thwarting God's plans and purposes, and he is equally intent on keeping human beings from discovering God's forgiving grace. The passages we have looked at in this chapter make it clear that God does allow Satan to do his evil work, for Satan could not act without God's permission.

Two additional truths are disclosed in the passages we have studied. First, God Himself does not do evil, nor is He responsible for it. The one who does evil is solely and completely responsible for his own actions. Second, God is so great that He is able to bring good from the evil done by Satan, demons, or human beings.

What Satan intends to result in harm, God transforms so that the actual results, even though they may involve temporary pain and suffering, are good. Satan caused Job to suffer. God used Job's pain to bring His servant even closer to Himself. One of Satan's demons, a lying spirit, put a false message in the mind of Ahab's prophets, but God sent Micaiah to reveal the truth. Ahab's choice of the lie over the truth displayed how right God was to end the wicked king's life.

David took a military census in Israel. Satan incited David to do this in an effort to turn the Lord against His anointed king. God incited David in order to use the incident as a basis for judging sin among His people, for bringing David to confession and worship, and for purifying the nation. Still, David was fully responsible for numbering Israel.

Satan sent an angel to buffet Paul with a deforming physical illness in order to limit his ability to reach people for Christ. God used the experience to teach Paul to rely completely on Him, making Paul an even more effective witness to all.

God is so great that He can and does work through Satan's evil acts to bring about a result that is good. It's no wonder that Paul wrote in Romans 8:28: "All things work together for good to those who love God, to those who are the called according to His purpose." Paul was not suggesting that all things that happen to us *are* good, for Paul, among all men, knew that life has its share of tragedies and pain as well as joys. What Paul claimed is just what we've seen in this chapter: that God is at work in everything that happens to us, and that He works so wonderfully that even our pains produce in us that which is good. In Romans 8:29 Paul defined the overarching good that God is committed to do in our lives: "For whom He foreknew, He also predestined to be conformed to the image of His Son."

Satan may attack us, his demons may do us injury, but through it all God is at work to reshape us into the beautiful image of His Son.

CHAPTER 9

MYRIADS OF ANGELS:

CATEGORIES, ROLES, AND RESPONSIBILITIES

Genesis—Zechariah

The twelfth and thirteenth centuries of our era witnessed the outbreak of "Angel Fever." Angels were thought to be involved in governing everything, from the seven known planets to the hours of the day and night. Although Scripture names only two angels, Michael and Gabriel, names were invented for other members of the angelic host who were thought to rule earthly events. According to Francis Barrett (*The Magnus,* 1801, p. 136), for example, the angelic rulers of the 12 hours of Thursday night are:

Night Hours	Angels Ruling Thursday
1	Gabriel
2	Cassiel
3	Sachiel
4	Samael
5	Michael
6	Anael
7	Raphael
8	Gabriel
9	Cassiel
10	Sachiel
11	Samael
12	Michael

ANGELORE

FROM THE BOOK OF JUBILEES

The pseudepigraphical book of *Jubilees* gives these names for eleven fallen angels who were supposed to have had sex with human women in Genesis 6. Each was supposed to have taught human beings some art or skill that corrupted our race.

Armaros	taught resolving enchantments.
Araqiel	taught the signs of the earth.
Azazel	taught how to make swords and create cosmetics for beautifying women.
Baraqijal	taught astrology.
Ezequeel	taught the knowledge of clouds.
Gadreel	taught men to make war.
Kokabel	taught the science of the constellations.
Penemune	taught writing.
Sariel	taught the course of the moon.
Semjaza	taught enchantments.
Shamshiel	taught the signs of the sun.

The game of naming angels is an ancient one. Many names for angels are found in Jewish religious writings of the first two centuries before Christ, including the Apocrypha. In fact, *A Dictionary of Angels* (1994) contains 331 pages of angels identified and named in sources from Christian, Jewish, and other traditions—names arranged in order from A (*A'albiel,* an angel in the service of the archangel Michael) to Z (*Zuriel,* who rules the sign of Libra in the zodiac and "cures stupidity in man"). Obviously, all of that goes far beyond Scripture's revelation of the unseen realm.

However, the Bible's treatment of angels is more complex and extensive than might appear to be the case at first glance. If we were to consult a concordance and look up every mention of "angel" in the Old Testament, we would miss many references to those special beings, who are God's ministers to us today. In this chapter we'll examine briefly every passage in the Old Testament that mentions angels by any name and then summarize what each passage teaches us about those wonderful beings.

EVERY REFERENCE TO GOD'S ANGELS IN THE PENTATEUCH

More passages in the Pentateuch refer to angels than in any other section of the Old Tes-

tament. In the Pentateuch angels are referred to as: *cherubim* (Gen. 3:24); possibly *sons of God* (Gen. 6:2); *men* (Gen. 18:2, 16); *stars* (Deut. 4:19); *host of heaven* (Deut. 17:3); and *holy ones* (Deut. 33:2, 3); and, of course, *angels.*

A CHERUBIM ON GUARD IN EDEN   (Genesis 3:24)

When God sent Adam and Eve from the Garden of Eden, "He placed cherubim at the east of the garden of Eden, and a flaming sword which turned every way, to guard the way to the tree of life" (3:24; NKJV). The cherubim are a special class of angelic beings associated with God's presence and with His holiness. Many Jewish and Christian commentators alike assume that the angelic guard was set so that Adam could not eat of the Tree of Life on the way out of the garden, or return to Eden later. In agreement with this interpretation, the Sage Rashi views the cherubim as destroying angels.

A better interpretation, however, is to view the cherubim as guarding the *way back* to the Tree of Life. This interpretation finds support in the fact that God commanded Moses to shape two golden figures of cherubim to

Two cherubim adorned the lid of the ark of the covenant.

lean over the cover of the ark of covenant. This cover was Israel's "mercy seat" (Ex. 25:17, 18), the place where God met with Israel and where sacrificial blood was sprinkled once a year on the Day of Atonement, symbolizing the reconciliation of Israel with God. The cherubim stationed at Eden symbolize God's commitment to keeping the way to eternal life open for human beings through faith in history's ultimate sacrificial Lamb, Jesus Christ.

SONS OF GOD AND HUMAN WOMEN *(Genesis 6:1, 2)*

Now it came to pass, when men began to multiply on the face of the earth, and daughters were born to them, that the sons of God saw the daughters of men, that they were beautiful; and they took wives for themselves of all whom they chose.

There can be no doubt that the phrase "sons of God" (*bene 'elohim*) does at times refer to angels (Job 1:6; 2:1; Ps. 29:1; 89:6). The Hebrew phrase translated "sons of" does not indicate biological relationship, but rather membership in a group or class. The essential meaning of "sons of God" is to identify angels as *supernatural beings*.

Whether or not the phrase *sons of God* in Genesis 6 refers to (fallen) angels is hotly de-

bated. Many commentators insist that the class to which "sons of God" refers here is that of godly men from the line of Seth (Gen. 5:3), while "daughters of men" refers to descendants of the wicked Cain (Gen. 4:1–17). The only time a phrase similar to "sons of God" is used of human beings is to identify those who have a covenant relationship with God (Deut. 14:1; 32:5; Ps. 73:15; Hos. 1:10). Even here (Gen. 6:2) the Hebrew is slightly different.

The arguments for and against "sons of God" referring to angels in Genesis 6:1, 3 are summarized in the chart below.

THE ANGEL OF THE LORD SENT HAGAR BACK TO SARAH *(Genesis 16:7–14)*

Hagar, the slave of Sarah, was pregnant with Abraham's son. Persecuted by her jealous mistress, Hagar fled toward Egypt. The Angel of the Lord appeared and told Hagar to return to Abraham's tents and submit to Sarah. The Angel of the Lord also told Hagar to name her unborn child Ishmael and promised, "I will multiply your descendants greatly."

This is the first recorded:

- appearance of the Angel of the Lord in Scripture;

Who Are the "Sons of God" in Genesis 6?

"The Sons of God" Are Human Beings	"The Sons of God" Are Fallen Angels
(1) "Sons of God" refers to men elsewhere (Deut. 14:1; Isa. 43:6; Hos. 1:10; 11:1).	(1) The exact phrase is used only of angels outside of Genesis.
(2) Angels are sexless (Matt. 20:22).	(2) The Matt. 20 text simply says angels do not procreate; it does not rule out gender when they take human form.
(3) The context (Gen. 4) refers to the lines of Seth (Gen. 4:16–24) and of Cain (Gen. 4:25—5:32).	(3) The context emphasizes the unusual nature of the relationship which produced "giants" (Gen. 6:1–4).
(4) The whole notion of fallen angels and humans having sex is grotesque.	(4) Pagan literature often refers to Titans and other offspring of deities and humans. Genesis 6 indicates the roots of this tradition.
	(5) Second Peter 2:4, 5 and Jude 6, 7 compare the sin of a group of angels now bound with the sexual perversion of Sodom and Gomorrah (i.e., unnatural sex) and closely connects the sin with the time of the Flood.

- appearance of a good angel;
- encounter of a human being with a good angel;
- example of angelic guidance, comfort, and promise;
- prophecy made by an angel, a strong element in many angel encounters.

ANGELORE

THE ANGEL OF THE LORD

The Angel of the Lord is Scripture's "Mystery Angel." While several passages seem to make a distinction between this angel and the Lord, other passages clearly identify the angel with the Lord Himself (see Gen. 16:3; Judg. 6:12, 14). Exodus 3 and 4 are particularly significant, for the Angel of the Lord called to Moses from the burning bush, identified Himself as the God of Abraham, Isaac, and Jacob, and revealed His personal name—YAHWEH, "I AM," meaning "the One Who Is Always Present." It seems that during the Old Testament era the Lord Himself at times appeared to human beings cloaked as an angel.

In the New Testament, Jesus identified Himself as the I AM of the Old Testament (John 8:58), and thus many Bible scholars regard appearances of the Angel of the Lord as preincarnation appearances of Christ Himself. If this is the case, we can see a foreshadowing of the ministries of Jesus to His people—such as guidance, comfort, and promise—in the various ministries of the Angel of the Lord. For a complete treatment of the Angel of the Lord, see chapter 2.

ANGELS APPEARED AS ORDINARY MEN TO ABRAHAM
(Genesis 18)

The Angel of the Lord and two other angels visited Abraham's camp and received the hospitality given to strangers in the ancient Near East. This incident is the basis for the exhortation to Christians to offer hospitality to strangers, for in so doing "some have unwittingly entertained angels" (Heb. 13:2). Abraham's visitors appeared to be ordinary men, but one was subsequently revealed to be the Lord (Gen. 18:13). The Lord promised that Sarah would bear a son in about a year. God went on to tell Abraham that He had also come to investigate the "very great" sin of Sodom and Gomorrah. Abraham pleaded with the Lord to spare the city if even ten righteous people could be found in it.

This angel encounter is the first in Scripture to indicate that:

- angels may appear cloaked as ordinary human beings;
- when angels appear as ordinary human beings they come as men rather than women (there is no mention in Scripture of an angel appearing as a woman);
- angel encounters may involve what seems to be normal conversation between persons.

ANGELS INVESTIGATED SODOM'S SINS AND EXECUTED GOD'S JUDGMENT   (Genesis 19)

Two of the angels who visited Abraham (Gen. 18) continued on to Sodom and Gomorrah, where they were offered hospitality by Abraham's nephew, Lot. The whole male population of Sodom turned out, intent on the homosexual rape of the angel visitors. The angels blinded the eyes of the men of Sodom so that they could not find the door of Lot's home, and the angels supernaturally removed Lot and his family from Sodom. The reaction of the men of Sodom demonstrated the total moral corruption of the five cities of the plain, and the angels carried out God's judgment as He rained fire and brimstone on the cities.

This is the first indication in Scripture that:

- angels may investigate human sin in person by becoming the target of sinful intentions and acts;
- angels can affect the ability of human beings to perceive with their senses;
- angels can supernaturally transport individuals from place to place;
- angels are involved in carrying out God's judgment on human sin.

THE ANGEL OF THE LORD SAVED HAGAR AND HER TEENAGE SON *(Genesis 21:15–21)*

Hagar and Ishmael were about to die of thirst in the wilderness after being expelled from Abraham's tents. The Angel of the Lord spoke to Hagar and showed her a nearby well of water.

THE ANGEL OF THE LORD KEPT ABRAHAM FROM SACRIFICING ISAAC   *(Genesis 22:1–19)*

God told Abraham to offer his son, Isaac, as a sacrifice on Mount Moriah. Abraham immediately set out with his son for the distant height. Abraham was confident that God would keep His word to him (that is, the offspring God promised earlier will come through Isaac): "in Isaac will your seed be called" (Gen. 21:10). Abraham believed that if it were necessary God would bring Isaac back from the dead (see Heb. 11:19). As Abraham was about to plunge the knife into his bound son, the Angel of the Lord stopped him. The angel, speaking as God, then reconfirmed His earlier

❖

Hagar and Ishmael.

promises to Abraham, who had demonstrated his absolute reliance on God's word.

The passage clearly identifies the Angel of the Lord as the Lord Himself (see 22:5, 6).

ABRAHAM WAS SURE THAT AN ANGEL WOULD GUIDE THE SERVANT HE SENT TO FIND A BRIDE FOR ISAAC   *(Genesis 24)*

A servant set out on a journey to find a bride for Isaac from among Abraham's relatives in Haran. Abraham promised his servant: "The God of Heaven . . . will send His angel before you" (24:7). When the servant arrived, he prayed that the girl God had chosen would meet him at the town well and offer to water his camels. His prayer was answered. Later, the servant explained to the girl's relatives that Abraham had promised: "The LORD . . . will send His angel with you and prosper your way" (24:40).

This is the first indication in Scripture that angels:

- prepare persons and circumstances beforehand;
- "accompany" human beings unseen;
- are involved in answering prayers.

JACOB SAW ANGELS CROSSING A RAMP BETWEEN THE SPIRITUAL AND MATERIAL REALMS *(Genesis 28:12)*

In a dream Jacob, the son of Isaac, saw a "ladder" (ramp, stairway, or bridge) "set up on the earth, and its top reached to heaven; and there the angels of God were ascending and descending on it." The Hebrew phrase "set earthward" clearly indicates that the ladder or ramp originated in heaven. Immediately, the focus of Jacob's dream shifted to the Lord, who stood above the ladder and spoke directly to Jacob (28:13–22).

The vision of the ladder is significant in several ways:

- Its anchor in "heaven" identifies the natural abode of angels as the spiritual realm rather than material.

- The traffic over this bridge between realms indicates that many of God's angels are constantly passing between the two realms to carry out the missions on which God sends them.
- The phrase "the angels of God" suggests that many more angels are involved in a particular mission than earlier texts indicate. In previous passages the greatest number of angels identified is three (Gen. 18).

THE ANGEL OF THE LORD SHOWED JACOB HOW TO RECOVER THE WEALTH HIS UNCLE LABAN HAD CHEATED HIM OUT OF   *(Genesis 31:11)*

Jacob, Abraham's grandson, was sent to find a bride from among his father's relatives. In Haran he worked for his uncle, Laban, and married two of his daughters. During the years of service Laban constantly changed Jacob's wages and cheated him. The Angel of the Lord appeared and instructed Jacob how to regain the wealth that was rightfully his.

This is the first incident in Scripture of angel involvement:

- in the fiscal affairs of human beings;
- in giving guidance that leads to prosperity.

ANGELS MET JACOB AS HE RETURNED TO CANAAN *(Genesis 31:1)*

Jacob's parents urged him to leave Canaan because they were concerned that his brother, Esau, whom Jacob had cheated out of his inheritance, would kill him. The official reason given to Jacob, that he should find a bride, was an excuse. Now, 20 years later, Jacob was returning with a large family, large flocks and herds, and great wealth. Jacob remembered his guilt and his brother's anger, and he was terrified of how Esau would react. On the way back, "the angels of God met him. When Jacob saw them, he said: 'This is God's camp' " (Gen. 32:1, 2). The phrase "the angels of

God," as well as Jacob's reference to a "camp," indicate a large number of angels. Jacob made camp at that place, most likely because he felt secure in the presence of God's angels. The name Jacob gave the locality, Mahanaim (Gen. 32:2), means "double camp." The angels and Jacob's family were there together. The phrase "Jacob saw them" suggests that the others in Jacob's party were not aware of the supernatural beings camped with them.

This is the first indication in Scripture that:

- Angels can be seen by one person and not seen by others present.
- Many angels may be assigned to guard and protect an individual or party. Jewish midrash says that there were 60 myriads (or 600,000) of angels at the camp! The timing of the appearance, as Jacob entered "hostile territory," was God's gracious way of assuring Jacob that He was with him and would surely protect him.

A "MAN" MET JACOB AND WRESTLED WITH HIM *(Genesis 32:24–32)*

Jacob sent his family across a brook, out of Mahanaim and the safety of the camping angels, and he alone remained behind. Jacob wrestled with "a Man" until daybreak. The "Man" changed Jacob's name to Israel—literally, "Prince with God"—and blessed him. Jacob was moved to exclaim: "I have seen God face to face, and my life is preserved" (32:30). The capitalization of "Man" in the NKJV indicates that the translators assume the mysterious person was the Lord in His cloak as the Angel of the Lord. He is identified as an angel in Hosea 12:4.

Some Jewish commentators, troubled by this interpretation, have suggested that the text describes Jacob being ambushed by the "angel of Esau," that is, the dark angel associated with Jacob's "evil" brother. The wrestling match was thus a type of classic struggle between good (Jacob) and evil (Esau's angelic "twin"). Jacob's remark about seeing God's face referred to his earlier encounter at Bethel

Jacob wrestled all night with an angel.

(Gen. 28:13–16), and the valiant Jacob gave credit to God for preserving him from the attack of the evil angel. This interpretation is strained, no doubt in part to support the view of Jews (Jacob) and Gentiles ("Esau's angel") expressed in rabbinic writings.

The traditional Christian interpretation identifies the "Man" as the Angel of the Lord. The physical struggle is viewed as a reflection of Jacob's very real inner struggle to trust God as he returned to face Esau. The stalemate suggests that Jacob's faith had matured to a point where he was now ready to rely on the Lord. Jacob's name was then changed to Israel. There is another indication in the text that Jacob experienced an inner transformation. Earlier, Jacob sent his wives and children ahead, over the stream that bordered Canaan, and he remained behind alone (Gen. 32:22, 23). Imme-

diately after his struggle with the Angel of the Lord, Jacob looked up and saw Esau coming (Gen. 33:1). Jacob then organized his family and "he crossed over before them" to meet his brother. Seeing God face to face truly effects an inner transformation in any human being.

This is the first indication in Scripture that the Angel of the Lord works within the human heart to transform human beings.

JACOB RECALLED THE ANGEL WHO REDEEMED HIM FROM ALL EVIL (Genesis 48:16)

Jacob was near death when he blessed Joseph's sons and his brothers (Gen. 48:15—49:28). In his blessing Jacob called upon "the Angel who has redeemed me from all evil." The NIV translates this as "the angel who has

delivered me from all harm." The NKJV translation is to be preferred for two reasons. First,
"redeemed" is a strong word that refers to rescue from trouble which one brings upon oneself. Second, "evil" is far more than harm: It
includes the consequences which sin would
normally bring into one's life.

Jacob did not live a sinless life. His original
name, Jacob, means "deceiver," and truly Jacob
did trick and lie to obtain the covenant
promises he valued so highly. The consequence
that flowed from his actions was the intense
hostility aroused in his brother, Esau, which
forced Jacob to flee from his home. Yet God
protected Jacob, gave him a family, provided
him with wealth in the land to which he fled
penniless, and worked in Esau's heart so that
Esau would welcome him when he returned 20
years later. God's angel protected Jacob from the
consequences of his evil actions, as well as from
the evil others intended to do to him. What a
demonstration of God's grace this was! And
how fervently Jacob sought a similar blessing
from God for Joseph's children (Gen. 48:16)!

This is the first indication in Scripture
that the Angel of the Lord dispenses redeeming grace.

THE ANGEL OF THE LORD APPEARED TO MOSES IN A BURNING BUSH   (Exodus 3)

The age of the patriarchs was now some
four hundred years past. The Angel of the
Lord spoke to Moses, a Hebrew brought up as
Egyptian royalty, but who was in exile as a
shepherd in the Sinai desert for 40 years. After
"the Angel of the Lord appeared to" Moses
(3:2), "God called to" Moses (3:4), and said, "I
am the God of your father—the God of Abraham, the God of Isaac, and the God of Jacob"
(3:6). In His dialogue with Moses, the Lord
provides specific information about what will
happen in the future (Ex. 3:18–22), which illustrates the prophetic element characteristic
of many angel encounters.

Exodus 3 is a pivotal passage in the Old
Testament, for in it God not only commissioned Moses to deliver Israel from Egypt,

where they have been enslaved for generations, but God also revealed His personal
name, Yahweh, "the Lord." That name affirms
God's constant presence with His people as
history's I AM, and that name provides the
foundation for Jesus' claim (John 8:38) to be
the God of the Old Testament incarnate.

This is the first time in the Old Testament
that the Angel of the Lord, or any angel, has:

- commissioned a human being for a special mission;
- appeared in nonhuman form, here as a
"flame of fire from the midst of a bush."
Other biblical passages will emphasize
the fire-like appearance of angels in their
natural state.

A "DESTROYER" ANGEL STRUCK DEAD THE FIRSTBORN IN THE LAND OF EGYPT AND PASSED OVER THE HOMES OF THE ISRAELITES   (Exodus 12:23)

Moses told the elders of Israel how the
people of God should prepare for the final

The "destroyer" angel.

plague to be wrought against the Egyptians by God, and why.

"For the LORD will pass through to strike the Egyptians; and when He sees the blood on the lintel and on the two doorposts [of Israelite homes], the LORD will pass over the door and not allow the destroyer to come into your houses to strike you."

"The destroyer" is an angel, a view supported by the reference in Psalm 78:49 to "angels of destruction." An important point is made here in Exodus: the first part of the verse says that "the LORD will pass through to strike the Egyptians"; the second part of the verse intimates that the actual striking was to be done by "the destroyer." In incidents where the Lord seems to be identified with an angel (other than the Angel of the Lord) on a mission, the angel carrying out God's will is so closely identified with His purposes that Scripture speaks as if God Himself performs the act directly, rather than through His angel.

ANGELS ACCOMPANIED ISRAEL OUT OF EGYPT, GOING BEFORE TO LEAD AND GOING BEHIND TO PROTECT   (Exodus 14:19)

After the people of Israel left Egypt, they were led by a cloudy and fiery pillar, which showed one aspect during the day and another at night. Exodus 14:19 relates that "the Angel of God, who went before the camp of Israel, moved and went behind them; and the pillar of cloud went from before them and stood between them" and the Egyptian army.

This is the first time the Old Testament mentions an angel:

- who is a "national angel," an angel assigned to guide and protect Israel as a people, rather than an angel commissioned to guide and protect an individual or the head of a family group;
- who is directly associated with a visible phenomenon such as the cloudy and fiery pillar.

THE PROMISE OF AN ANGEL TO PROTECT THE ISRAELITES ON THE WAY TO CANAAN AND TO "GO BEFORE" THEM WHEN THEY INVADE THE LAND
(Exodus 23:20, 23)

God promised Israel angelic protection as the people journeyed from Sinai to Canaan, the land which He promised Abraham would be the possession of his descendants. In Exodus 23:20 God said, "Behold, I send an Angel before you to keep you in the way and bring you into the place which I have prepared." This is a promise of protection and guidance. In Exodus 23:23 God said, "For My Angel will go before you and bring you in to the Amorites . . . and I will cut them off." This is a promise that the angel will not only lead the Israelites but will also fight for them when the invasion takes place.

This is the first indication in Scripture that angels join in warfare on the side of God's people. In addition, the text suggests that "national angels" guide, protect, and provide support in the military conflicts of the nation Israel.

GOD'S ANGEL PUNISHED AND PROTECTED ISRAEL
(Exodus 32:34)

While Moses was on Mount Sinai receiving the Ten Commandments from the Lord, the Israelites pressured Aaron, Moses' brother, to make a golden calf for them to worship. God told Moses He would hold the guilty responsible (32:33), and then promised, "My Angel shall go before you. Nevertheless, in the day when I visit punishment, I will visit punishment upon them for their sin" (32:34). This passage emphasizes God's commitment to His covenant promises to Abraham, but makes it clear that the Lord distinguished between those descendants of Abraham who trusted and obeyed Him and those who did not.

GOD'S ANGEL WILL DRIVE OUT THE CANAANITES   (Exodus 33:2)

The promise reiterates the commitment made in Exodus 23:23. God said, "And I will send My Angel before you, and I will drive out the Canaanite." The image here is of angels serving in the first ranks coming in contact with an enemy force and driving them out.

This is the second reference in Scripture to angels engaging in warfare on the side of God's people.

MOSES' LETTER TO THE EDOMITES CREDITED GOD'S ANGEL WITH DELIVERING ISRAEL FROM EGYPT
(Numbers 20:16)

When the Israelites approached the borders of Moab, they requested safe passage through that land. In the letter Moses sent to the king of Moab he wrote, "When we cried out to the LORD, He heard our voice and sent the Angel and brought us up out of Egypt."

This is the first reference in the Bible to angels being sent in answer to prayer. It is significant that Moses credited the angel with bringing Israel "up out" of Egypt. The phrase implies that angels were directly involved in the plagues that struck Egypt (see Ex. 12:23, especially Ps. 78:43–49).

THE ANGEL OF THE LORD CONFRONTED THE PAGAN PROPHET BALAAM
(Numbers 22:22–35)

After Balak, king of Moab, tried to hire the pagan prophet Balaam to curse Israel, God warned Balaam in a dream not to go. Balaam went with Balak's representatives, and he was met on the way by the Angel of the Lord. The angel was immediately perceived by Balaam's donkey, but not by Balaam. The angel made himself visible to Balaam and warned him to speak only what God showed him. Balaam offered several sacrifices on Balak's behalf, but each time was forced to bless rather than curse Israel.

This is the only incident in Scripture which suggests that angels might be sensed by an animal even when they are not perceived by a human being. This incident also suggests

that angels can make themselves visible to humans in their natural spiritual form, and they are then immediately recognized as angels. The angel's conversation with Balaam, who spoke a language other than ancient Hebrew, reminds us that angels are able to communicate across cultures. Whether this is because they have learned human languages or because they communicate directly with humans, mind to mind, is unclear.

MOSES WARNED ISRAEL NOT TO WORSHIP ANGELS, WHICH HE IDENTIFIED WITH "STARS"
(Deuteronomy 4:19)

Moses said,

"And take heed, lest you lift your eyes to heaven, and when you see the sun, the moon, and the stars, all the host of heaven, you feel driven to worship them and serve them, which the LORD your God has given to all the peoples under the whole heaven as a heritage."

At face value, the reference is to visible heavenly bodies, not to angels. However, the drive to worship the host of heaven is reflected in pagan religions, and stars were frequently identified with gods or demonic beings.

ANGELORE
ANGELS REFERRED TO AS STARS

Job 38:7 speaks of the Creation as a time "When the morning stars sang together, / And all the sons of God shouted for joy." Hebrew poetry does not rely on rhyme but on parallelism—the repetition or development of ideas from phrase to phrase.

Job 38:7 is an example of synonymous parallelism; that is, the second phrase repeats the thought in the first phrase, using different words to express the same thought. Here the passage equates "the morning stars" with "the sons of God," which is a definite reference to angels.

Other verses which employ a similar metaphor for angels include Psalm 103:21, where angels are called "hosts"; Psalm 148:3, where angels are called "stars of light"; and Isaiah 14:13, which refers to angels as "stars of God." The same imagery is found in Daniel 8:10. On this basis, we need to carefully examine verses like Deuteronomy 4:19 to see if they contain a subtle reference to angelic beings. It seems likely that whenever stars or the "hosts of heaven" are linked with worship, there is an intentional reference to angels, faithful or fallen, as well as to the actual heavens.

MOSES WARNED ISRAEL NOT TO WORSHIP ANY OF THE "HOST OF HEAVEN" *(Deuteronomy 17:3)*

This verse is a parallel to Deuteronomy 4:19. Here, any Israelite "who has gone and served other gods and worshiped them, either the sun or moon or any of the host of heaven, which I have not commanded" (17:3) was condemned to death. Depending on the context, "host of heaven" refers either to stars or to angelic beings.

One of the most common descriptive names of God found in the Old Testament is "Lord of Hosts," which emphasizes His command of armies of angels in the spiritual realm, as well as His command of the stars in the material creation. Interestingly, the phrase "Lord of Hosts" occurs 245 times in Scripture: "God of Hosts," 40 times; "His Hosts," once. Each of the 19 occurrences of "host of heaven" in Scripture is with respect to the idolatrous worship of fallen angelic beings who stand behind the pagan deities.

MOSES STATED THAT GOD GATHERED MULTITUDES OF ANGELS AROUND HIM WHEN HE GAVE THE LAW AT SINAI *(Deuteronomy 33:2)*

The NKJV translates the Hebrew word *kadoshim* as "saints." The pure meaning of the word is "those set apart to God"—thus, "holy ones" or "saints." It is best to take *kadoshim* here as a reference to angels, for the text says "He [God] came with ten thousands of holy ones" (NIV). Those angelic hosts came with

God to be witnesses of the Law He gave to Israel through Moses. Both Acts 7:53 and Hebrews 2:2 specifically associate angels with the giving of the Law.

This is Scripture's first:

- specific reference to God's angels as set apart completely to Him, and thus "holy," in contrast to fallen angels who followed Satan;
- link between angels and the Mosaic Law.

EVERY REFERENCE TO GOD'S ANGELS IN THE HISTORICAL BOOKS

Angel activity in the Pentateuch is closely linked with God's actions on behalf of the Israelites. God made great covenant promises to Abraham, and He guarded Abraham's son and grandson. When Israel was enslaved in Egypt, angels were active in bringing plagues on their oppressors and in leading the people of God from Egypt to Canaan. Angels were also active in the giving of the Mosaic Law, which taught Israel about the nature of God and how the Israelites should live as a people dedicated to Him.

Most references to angel encounters in the Historical Books have to do with God's faithfulness in carrying out His commitment to Israel as stated in the Abrahamic covenant and God's faithfulness in keeping the word He gave to Israel as stated in the Mosaic Law.

THE ANGEL OF THE LORD REBUKED ISRAEL *(Judges 2:1–4)*

The Israelites conquered Canaan, but they failed, even after some years, to obey God and drive out all the pagan peoples in the promised land. The Angel of the Lord appeared and rebuked the Israelites for making treaties with some inhabitants and for failing to "tear down their altars." Because of the Israelites' disobedience, God told them His angel would no longer drive out the Canaanites. Instead, the pagan peoples who remained in the land would be a constant threat to the purity of Israel's faith. According to Judges, "So it was, when the Angel of the LORD spoke these words to all the children of Israel, that the people lifted up their voices and wept" (2:4).

This is the first time in Scripture that an angel:

- spoke directly to a multitude of people ("all the children of Israel");
- rebuked anyone for failing to obey God;
- announced specific consequences for disobeying the Lord. This passage also illustrates the prophetic dimension of the ministries of angels.

DEBORAH'S VICTORY SONG GAVE CREDIT TO ANGELS
(Judges 5:20)

As predicted by the angel in Judges 2, many Israelites turned from the Lord to worship the idols of their pagan neighbors. God permitted His people to be oppressed by a Canaanite king until they despaired and turned back to Him (Judg. 4:1, 2). The Israelites, led by Deborah, then defeated the Canaanites. Her song of celebration includes the poetic expression, "They fought from the heavens; / The stars from their courses fought against Sisera" (5:20). The mention of "stars" is most likely a reference to angels who joined the army of Israel in its battle against the enemy's chariot army (See Angelore, p. 144).

AN ANGEL CURSED MEROZ FOR FAILING TO JOIN THE BATTLE AGAINST THE CANAANITES
(Judges 5:23)

In the context of Deborah's victory song, composed after Israel's victory over the Canaanite king of Hazor, the angel's words, "Curse Meroz," were especially strong. Meroz was a town located either about seven miles from the site of the battle or about five miles from Hazor. The town was cursed for failing to supply men to fight in the battle. F. F. Bruce suggests that the town, like others in the area, was "under sacred obligation" to join in the armed struggle against Israel's oppressors.

This is the first instance of an angel uttering a binding curse (Heb. *'arar*) that served as an announcement of divine punishment.

THE ANGEL OF THE LORD CALLED AND COMMISSIONED GIDEON   *(Judges 6)*

The Israelites once again turned aside to worship idols, and as a result they were oppressed by Midianite raiders for seven years (6:1). The Angel of the Lord appeared to a young man from an insignificant Hebrew family and commissioned him to save Israel. The dialogue between Gideon and the Angel of the Lord is noteworthy because Gideon was openly skeptical about the Lord being with His people since the "age of miracles" seemed, in Gideon's estimation, to be long past. The Angel of the Lord must have appeared to Gideon as an ordinary man because Gideon asked for a "sign that it is You who talk with me" (6:17). Only after the sign is given does Gideon perceive that the man was the Angel of the Lord (6:22).

An angel commissioned Gideon.

Throughout the story, which covers three chapters in Judges, Gideon remained hesitant and unsure, yet he was committed to do as the Lord instructed him.

This is the second time in the Old Testament that the Angel of the Lord commissioned an individual for a special mission (Moses was the first). We note again that when an angel appears as an ordinary man, his true identity may remain unrecognized. Nothing about this angel—his dress, his speech patterns—seemed unusual to Gideon. Angels cloaked as human beings seem to fit naturally into the social and cultural context of the human beings to whom they appear.

AN ANGEL PREDICTED THE BIRTH OF SAMSON AND INSTRUCTED HIS PARENTS ABOUT HIS UPBRINGING (Judges 13)

Israel sinned again and was now dominated by the Philistines. The Angel of the Lord appeared to a childless woman, whose husband was of the tribe of Dan, and predicted that she would bear a son, whom she named Samson. The angel instructed her to bring Samson up according to a strict code of dedication to the Lord (as a *Nazirite*). The angel also predicted that "he shall begin to deliver Israel out of the hand of the Philistines" (13:5). The words "shall begin to" are significant, for Samson indeed killed many Philistines in his personal feud with Israel's enemy, he was the only leader of the era who did not succeed in throwing off the bonds of Israel's oppressor. This suggests that we should pay very close attention to every nuance of the words spoken by an angel.

On this occasion, the Angel of the Lord did not appear to be an ordinary human being, for his countenance (face, appearance) was "very awesome" (13:6). At the same time, the Angel of the Lord maintained a human guise, for Samson's parents realized that they had spoken with the Angel of the Lord only after He ascended in the smoke of the offering they made to the Lord (13:19–23).

An angel who appears cloaked as a man to human beings apparently may be perceived as either an ordinary man or as an exceptional human being. This story illustrates once more the prophetic role of angels in their encounters with humans. It would seem from the wife's words to her husband (13:6, 7) that the angel's message was self-authenticating; that is, the authority and integrity of the message delivered by the angel was immediately accepted by the wife, who recognized the speaker as a "man of God" even though she did not perceive him to be an angel.

While an angel's message may be self-authenticating, we need to note that the spiritual state of the recipient is important, also. Gideon, a young skeptic, had his doubts about God's presence with His people when the angel told him that he was to deliver Israel (6:12–15). When the angel Gabriel appeared to Zacharias and announced that he was to have a son (John the Baptist), Zacharias did not believe the message at first (Luke 1:11–20). An angel's message may be self-authenticating, but the spiritual state of the one to whom the message is addressed has an effect upon how it is received.

The ministries of angels illustrated in this passage are:

- prophetic—the angel announced ahead of time the birth of Samson and predicted that he would only partially fulfill a judge's mission;
- instructive and guiding—the angel told Samson's parents how to rear their child. It is also worth noting that this is the second time an angel was sent as an answer to prayer (see also Num. 20:16).

THE CHARACTER AND ABILITIES OF ANGELS AS REFLECTED IN SEVERAL SAYINGS RECORDED IN 1 AND 2 SAMUEL

Sayings addressed to King David reflect the Hebrew view of the character and abilities of angels at that time (about 1000 B.C.). Each saying attributes qualities to David or refers to qualities that he required in a given situation.

1 Samuel 29:9. "I know that you are as good in my sight as an angel of God." These are the words of Achish, king of the Philistine city of Gath. David and his followers fled there after being pursued by King Saul for years. Achish accepted David and his men as a mercenary force and gave them a small city. According to custom, David became a vassal of Achish; thus, his responsibility was to support Achish in the event of an attack. When war erupted between the Philistines and Israel, the king of Gath expected David to fight with the Philistines against Saul. The other Philistine rulers felt threatened by David's presence; they feared that David and his men would turn against them in the battle. Achish apologized to David and, in the verse quoted, expressed his confidence in David's integrity: He was sure that David would have faithfully supported the Philistines, even if that meant fighting against his own people. The quote suggests that even among pagan nations an "angel of God" had a reputation for speaking and acting with complete honesty and integrity.

2 Samuel 14:17. "For as the angel of God, so is my lord the king in discerning good and evil." David's son, Absalom, murdered his half brother and fled the kingdom. Three years later David, who had not acted to recover or punish his murderous son, missed Absalom terribly. General Joab, recognizing David's feelings, arranged for a woman to present David with a hypothetical case in which she pleaded for the life of her only remaining son, who also had killed his brother. David listened to the woman and promised her that her remaining son would not be executed.

The woman in return, challenged David to allow Absalom safe passage to return to Israel. Her words reflected the conviction that God's angels always do the right thing. The woman's words also implied that once David discerned the right thing to do about her imaginary son, he would allow Absalom to return home.

2 Samuel 14:20. "My lord is wise, according to the wisdom of the angel of God, to know everything that is in the earth." David recognized the part General Joab played in getting the woman to tell a story about her imaginary murderous son. The woman admitted that Joab told her what to say. The woman's words showed her admiration for David's discernment in perceiving Joab's role; she complimented David by attributing to him "the wisdom of the angel of God, to know everything that is in the earth." These words reflected an awareness that angels have sources of knowledge about affairs on earth unavailable to human beings. To the woman, David's insight about Joab's role seems to derive from just such supernatural knowledge.

2 Samuel 19:27. "My lord the king is like the angel of God. Therefore do what is good in your eyes." Mephibosheth, the son of Jonathan and grandson of Saul, spoke these words. For the sake of his dear friend Jonathan, David found the crippled youth and granted him all the family's land. When Absalom led a rebellion against David, Mephibosheth tried to come to David's aid. Mephibosheth's servant lied to David and claimed that his master was staying in Jerusalem, expecting to be made king. After David's victory, Mephibosheth explained what had really happened. Mephibosheth's words to David, reported in 2 Samuel 19:27, expressed his confidence in David's wisdom and fairness and also acknowledged his subordination to his king.

Each of these sayings exhibits a common view of certain traits of angels. God's angels are trustworthy, and their words are reliable. God's angels know the difference between right and wrong, and they always choose what is right. God's angels are wise; they possess insight into reality that is not available to ordinary human beings. God's angels are perceptive; they can discern when people are telling the truth and when they are lying. Angels are also fair; they choose to do what is right and appropriate to both the truthful and the liar.

The irony in these passages lies in the fact that in each instance David was *not like* the angels to whom he was compared. After David accepted Achish as his lord, he led his men against various pagan towns and then lied to Achish, saying that he had raided in Israel or Judah. David never intended to fight against Israel, the nation he expected to rule one day.

David did not do what was right in the case involving Absalom. David kept silent about his daughter's rape, which led to Absalom's murder of his half brother. David refused to condemn or forgive Absalom, which left Absalom in limbo.

David recognized the role Joab played in getting the woman to tell her story, but he did not perceive that the case the woman presented was significantly different from the one involving Absalom. David surely was not as wise as God's angels are in discerning reality.

Finally, David failed to realize that Mephibosheth was telling the truth and that Mephibosheth's servant had slandered him. What David did in dividing the lands between Mephibosheth and his servant was totally unfair: David punished a faithful friend and rewarded a lying slanderer.

It is certainly true that God's angels are trustworthy, they know and choose the right, they have great insight into human affairs, and they can accurately assess human behavior and character; but sadly not even the best of us come close to the angels in consistently exhibiting those qualities.

ANGELORE:

ANGEL ROLES IN MEDIEVAL JEWISH THOUGHT

Seraphim, the highest order, the six-winged ones, surround the throne of God, singing ceaselessly, "Holy, Holy, Holy." They are angels of love, light, and fire.

Cherubim are the guardians of the fixed stars, keepers of the celestial records, bestowers of knowledge. In the Talmud cherubim are equated with the order of wheels, also called ophanim. Chief rulers are Ophaniel, Rikbiel, Zophiel, and, before his fall, Satan.

Thrones bring God's justice to us. They are sometimes called *wheels* and in the Jewish Kabbalah, **chariots** or the **merkaba.** The occult book, the *Zohar,* ranks wheels above seraphim, but other sources place them on the same level as cherubim, the whole thing being confused. The ruling prince is Oriphiel or Zabkiel or Zaphiel.

Dominions or **dominations** regulate angelic duties. Through them the majesty of God is manifested. They hold an orb or scepter as an emblem of authority, and, in Hebraic lore, the chief of this order is named Hashael or Zadkiel.

Virtues work miracles on earth. They bestow grace and valor.

Powers stop the efforts of demons to overthrow the world—or they preside over demons, or perhaps (according to Saint Paul) they are themselves evil. Ertosi, Sammael, or Camael (depending on the source) is the chief of the Powers.

Principalities are protectors of religion. Nisroc, in Milton, is "of principalities the prime," and others, according to various sources, are named Requel, Anael, and Cerviel.

Archangels and **angels** are guardians of people and all physical things.

Sophy Burnham, *A Book of Angels* (1990).

CHERUBS ARE LINKED WITH GOD'S PUNISHMENT OF SIN
(2 Samuel 22:11)

This chapter in 2 Samuel contains a long psalm of praise to the Lord written by David after he was delivered from his enemy, Saul. The psalm opens with an expression of faith in God (22:2–4) and an admission that the fear of enemies drove David to the Lord (22:5–7). Next comes a lengthy and powerful description of God's awesome response to David's prayer. In that context, David provided a vivid picture of the Lord: "He rode upon a cherub, and flew; / And He was seen upon the wings of the wind." Cherubs (or cherubim) are a special class of angels associated with God's presence (See Angelore, p. 149). Here, David envisioned the Lord coming to be present for him, ready to crush his enemies.

AN ANGEL STRUCK ISRAEL WITH A PLAGUE UNTIL THE ANGEL OF THE LORD COMMANDED HIM TO STOP   (2 Samuel 24:16, 17; 1 Chronicles 21:12–30)

David sinned by taking a census of his nation's fighting men. The Lord told the prophet Gad that David must choose one of three punishments. David chose three days of "the sword of the Lord"—a plague to be administered by the Angel of the Lord through the agency of other angels (2 Sam. 24:16). Several features of this story are significant.

First, it is clear in this text, as well as in other texts involving angels in the Old Testament, that God's "good" angels *do* administer punishment. This is true despite a Jewish tradition which insists that God does not use His own angels, but relies on Satan's angels, to visit destruction. God does not apologize for administering justice directly or through His angels, whether His justice calls for the punishment of pagans (see Ex. 23:20; 32:3; 2 Kings 19:35) or the punishment of His own people, as is the case here.

Second, David saw the Angel of the Lord, but the Angel of the Lord communicated with David through the prophet Gad (1 Chron. 21:16, 18). We should not conclude from this that we must accept implicitly every report of an angel encounter or do what others say an angel has instructed. David clearly saw the Angel of the Lord; moreover, David knew Gad to be a confirmed prophet of the Lord. David's personal sighting of the angel, his personal knowledge of Gad's prophetic office, as well as the harmony of Gad's message and Scripture's teaching on sacrifice—all of these factors led David to accept Gad's report of what the angel commanded. Likewise, we need to have confirmation before we act on directions supposedly given by an angel to another person.

Third, the experience created a fear which deeply affected David (see 1 Chron. 21:30). From that time on, David sacrificed only on the hill where God commanded him that day to sacrifice, which was the future site of the Jerusalem temple. David no longer

sought God at the Tabernacle that was erected at Gibeon, "for he was afraid of the sword of the angel of the LORD."

David's reaction to the angel's appearance provides a striking contrast to that of Ornan, the owner of the height David purchased as a place of sacrifice. When the Angel of the Lord appeared to David, he was also visible to Israel's elders (1 Chron. 21:16) and to Ornan and his four sons, who were threshing wheat on the hill. The four sons fled, but Ornan just kept tossing the wheat stalks up in the air with his fork, letting the wind blow away the chaff and the grain fall at his feet. Perhaps the difference in reaction stemmed from the fact that David was aware of his guilt, whereas Ornan was aware of no unconfessed sins (or perhaps Ornan was simply one of those phlegmatic individuals whom no sight can unsettle).

AN OLD PROPHET LIED ABOUT AN ANGEL ENCOUNTER (1 Kings 13:18)

Jeroboam I led the ten northern tribes of Israel to rebel against Solomon's son, Rehoboam, and established a counterfeit religious system. Still, Jeroboam feared that if the northern tribes went to Jerusalem to worship, then they would, in time, reunite with the southern tribes. God sent a young prophet to announce His judgment on Jeroboam and the religious system he instituted. God also told the young prophet not to eat or drink while he was in the Northern Kingdom.

An old prophet from the north heard of the youthful prophet's visit and met him on his way home. The old prophet lied and said that an angel of the Lord told him to invite the young prophet home and feed him. The young prophet listened—and was later killed by a lion for his failure to obey God.

This story reminds us that each individual must recognize and respond to God's voice—whether communicated by angels or communicated in the written Word—for himself or herself. Reports of angel encounters are not necessarily to be greeted with skepticism, but when others relay a message containing God's will for us—from an alleged angel encounter or from any other source—that message is to be examined critically, especially when it contradicts what we know to be God's will for us.

ANGELS STRENGTHENED ELIJAH
(1 Kings 19:5–8)

An exhausted and frightened Elijah fled from Queen Jezebel after she threatened to kill him. When Elijah finally collapsed, he begged the Lord to let him die and then fell into a deep sleep. An angel touched Elijah, awoke him, and told him to eat and drink. Elijah fell asleep again until the angel returned, awoke him, and again had him eat.

The fact that the angel is said to have touched Elijah indicates that cloaked angels are not apparitions, but are real in form and substance. This is the first time in Scripture that an angel provided food ("a cake baked on coals") for an individual.

THE PROPHET MICAIAH SAW THE LORD ON HIS THRONE WITH "ALL THE HOST OF HEAVEN STANDING BY, ON HIS RIGHT HAND AND ON HIS LEFT" (1 Kings 22:19)

In his prophecy, Micaiah stated that he saw "all the host of heaven" standing by God's throne. The reference to the right hand and the left hand most likely was meant to indicate that Micaiah did indeed see "all the host of heaven," both the holy angels (on the right) and the fallen angels (on the left). Jesus used similar imagery in Matthew 25:32–46.

This is the first indication in the Old Testament that God is sovereign over both the elect and the fallen angels, despite the rebellion of Satan and the many angels who followed him. Even fallen angels are subject to God's will.

Later in this story a fallen angel, referred to as a "spirit," volunteers to lie to King Ahab's prophets about what will happen in the upcoming battle against the Syrians.

AN ANGEL SENT ELIJAH ON A MISSION TO KING AHAZIAH
(2 Kings 1:3)

The original text reads "But the angel of the LORD said to Elijah the Tishbite, 'Arise, go up to meet the messengers of the king of Samaria,' " and so on. Here, an angel served as a messenger to communicate God's instructions to Elijah. The underlying meaning of the Hebrew *mal'ak,* angel, is *"messenger"* or *"representative."* The mission of a human *mal'ak* was:

(1) to carry a message;
(2) to fulfill a specific or special commission; and so
(3) to represent the one who sent him.

The primary mission of angels is the same as is expressed by the choice of the word *mal'ak* to designate the beings from the spiritual realm who serve and represent God.

THE ANGEL OF THE LORD INSTRUCTED A FEARFUL ELIJAH TO MEET KING AHAZIAH FACE TO FACE (2 Kings 1:15)

King Ahaziah sent messengers to inquire of a pagan deity whether an injury he had sustained was fatal. The Angel of the Lord told Elijah to intercept Ahaziah's messengers and inform them that the king would indeed die. The king sent for Elijah, but Elijah, fearful that Ahaziah would have him executed, retreated to a hilltop. When Ahaziah sent soldiers to compel Elijah, the prophet called down fire from heaven. A third troop of soldiers approached Elijah, and the captain begged for his life and the lives of his men. The Angel of the Lord instructed Elijah to accompany the soldiers and told him to have no fear. Elijah did as he was instructed, and he boldly delivered God's message to the king's face.

The angel's message was a combination of instruction and reassurance. The God who sends us into danger remains with us to protect us when we obey.

ANGELS CAUGHT ELIJAH UP AND CARRIED HIM TO HEAVEN
(2 Kings 2:11, 12a)

The day Elijah finished his ministry, God revealed that it would be his last on earth. As Elijah headed into the tangled growth in the upper Jordan valley, Elisha followed—hoping to be commissioned as Elijah's successor. The text describes the situation:

Then it happened, as they continued on and talked, that suddenly a chariot of fire appeared with horses of fire, and separated the two of them, and Elijah went up by a whirlwind [tornado] into heaven. And Elisha saw it, and he cried out, "My father, my father, the chariot of Israel and its horsemen!"

Here, the prophet saw angels as—or riding in—a "chariot of fire." This is another indication that human beings perceive the "natural" form of angels as fire or light and the first time that angels are spoken of as "chariots" or "chariots of fire." This is also the first

Elijah being taken up.

indication in Scripture that angels may accompany human beings at death when they cross from the material realm to spiritual.

ANGELORE
ANGELS AS "CHARIOTS"

In the ancient world chariots and horses were powerful symbols of military might. Chariots were the "tanks" of the northern powers of the Ancient Near East, who often proved dominant in battle. The Old Testament's reference to angels as "horsemen" or "horses" associated with "chariots" or "chariots of fire" emphasizes the overwhelming power of angelic beings. References to angels as "chariots" occur in 2 Kings 2:11, 12; 6:16, 17; Psalm 68:17; and Zechariah 6. The phrase "of fire" describes the appearance of angels in their natural spiritual state, in contrast to their appearance when cloaked as men.

AN ARMY OF ANGELS PROTECTED ELIJAH FROM AN ENEMY MILITARY FORCE
(2 Kings 6:17)

The king of Syria learned that the prophet Elisha was responsible for telling the king of Israel about Syria's military plans. The Syrian ruler sent a raiding force into Israel to capture Elisha. The Syrian force surrounded the town where Elisha and his servant were sleeping. When the servant saw the enemy all around the city, he panicked. Elisha prayed for the Lord to open the eyes of his servant. The text says: "Then the LORD opened the eyes of the young man, and he saw. And behold, the mountain was full of horses and chariots of fire all around Elisha." A force of powerful angels stood between God's prophet and the enemy force.

This story reminds us that we do not need to see angels in order to be guarded by them. There are angels all around, protecting God's own from dangers they may not perceive and dangers they cannot imagine.

THE ANGEL OF THE LORD KILLED 185,000 ASSYRIAN SOLDIERS WHO THREATENED JERUSALEM   *(2 Kings 19:35; 2 Chronicles 32:21; Isaiah 37:36)*

An Assyrian army battered down the fortified cities on the borders of Judah and threatened a defenseless Jerusalem. When an Assyrian officer demanded surrender and ridiculed the Lord, King Hezekiah of Judah brought the matter to the Lord in prayer. The Lord, through the prophet Isaiah, assured Hezekiah that not a single arrow would fly over the walls of Jerusalem. The text says:

"And it came to pass on a certain night that the angel of the LORD went out, and killed in the camp of the Assyrians one hundred and eighty–five thousand; and when people arose early in the morning, there were the corpses—all dead."

With such a large percentage of his soldiers dead, the king of Assyria, Sennacherib, returned to his capital at Nineveh.

This story, in which angels intervened in answer to prayer, is so significant that it is repeated three times in the Old Testament. In this story, we see that angels:

- visit divine judgment on nations as well as individuals;
- fight on the side of God's people;
- may be sent in answer to prayer;
- defend the honor and glory of God.

AN ANGEL STRUCK ISRAEL WITH A PLAGUE UNTIL THE ANGEL OF THE LORD COMMANDED HIM TO STOP   *(1 Chronicles 21:12–30)*

See the discussion of the parallel passage, 2 Samuel 24:16, 17, on p. 41.

THE ANGEL OF THE LORD KILLED 185,000 ASSYRIAN SOLDIERS WHO THREATENED JERUSALEM   *(2 Chronicles 32:21)*

See the discussion of the parallel passage, 2 Kings 19:35, on p. 41.

EVERY REFERENCE TO GOD'S ANGELS IN THE POETIC BOOKS

References to angels are found in two of the five books of Old Testament poetry, Job and Psalms. Angels are not mentioned in Proverbs, Ecclesiastes, or the Song of Solomon.

ANGELS REPORT TO THE LORD *(Job 1:6; 2:1)*

"Now there was a day when the sons of God came to present themselves before the LORD, and Satan also came among them." The location of this gathering was not given, but most commentators assume that the assembly took place in heaven. The phrase "sons of God" refers to angels and may include fallen angels and holy angels as well. The phrase "Satan also came among them" indicates to some that Satan was not normally found in this company; others point to the same phrase as evidence of Satan's unwilling subjection to the sovereign will of God. The story of Ahab and the lying spirit (1 Kings 22) clearly indicates that both fallen angels and holy angels are subject to God's will.

ANGELORE

IN WHAT SENSE ARE ANGELS "SONS OF GOD"?

The context of several passages which speak of "the sons of God" makes it very clear that the reference is to angels. Some interpreters have understood the phrase as emphasizing the direct creation of angels by God. However, the phrase "sons of" is an idiomatic expression denoting membership in a class or group. Thus, identifying someone as one of the "sons of the prophets" is equivalent to saying that the person *is* a prophet. Here, the Hebrew phrase is *bene 'elohim,* translated "sons of God," and it clearly identifies the beings in view as members of the class of *'elohim, gods*—that is, *supernatural beings.*

Therefore, "sons of God" portrays angels as supernatural beings with exceptional powers, and that sets them apart from humanity. Satan and fallen angels belong in this class because *"sons of God"* does not refer to an angel's holiness or relationship with the Lord, but to an angel's essential nature as a supernatural being. This understanding tends to support the idea that Genesis 6:1–3 refers to fallen angels rather than humans.

JOB VIEWED ANGELS AS LESS THAN PERFECT   *(Job 4:18)*

Most English translations render Job 4:18b in this way: "He charges His angels with error." Job's friend, Eliphaz, was struggling with the idea of human righteousness and was troubled by the fact that Job was unwilling to admit that his problems were caused by his sins. Surely no mere mortal could ever claim to be pure before God (4:17–19)! In his argument, Eliphaz suggested that God even charges His angels with error. The word translated "error" is *taholah,* found only here in the Old Testament. It is from the root *t-h-h,* which suggests confusion or chaos. The best rendering of Job 4:18b seems to be: "He charges His angels with moral and spiritual confusion"—that is to say, even angels, apart from God's guiding hand, become confused about issues of right and wrong. How, then, can mere mortals claim to be righteous before God?

ELIPHAZ CHALLENGED JOB TO FIND AN ANGEL WHO WOULD SUPPORT HIS CLAIMS *(Job 5:1)*

Eliphaz stated his challenge: "Call out now; / Is there anyone who will answer you?/ And to which of the holy ones will you turn?" The book of Job is thought to have roots in patriarchal times before the Scriptures were written, a time when special revelation from God came through dreams, seers, and angel visitations (see Heb. 1:1). Here, Eliphaz challenged Job to cite some angelic revelation to support his position, and Eliphaz was confident that Job could not do so.

ELIPHAZ ASSERTED THAT GOD PLACES NO CONFIDENCE IN HIS HOLY ONES   *(Job 15:15)*

Eliphaz, a friend of Job's, is the speaker here (as in 4:18 and 5:1). Eliphaz looked to dreams, visions, and angels as the source of traditional knowledge about God. Against Job's claim to be pure, Eliphaz repeated his earlier argument and insisted that "if God puts no trust in His holy ones," then "how much less man, who is abominable and filthy" (NIV). The point is that even good angels, no matter how wonderful they may be, fall short of God's absolute purity and righteousness.

GOD SPOKE OF CREATION AND THE ANGELS WHO WITNESSED IT   *(Job 38:7)*

God finally responded to Job's demand that he be given a chance to speak to the Lord Himself, but God did not explain the reason for Job's suffering. Instead, God displayed His own greatness by describing the beginning when He "laid the foundations of the earth" (Job 38:4)—a time "When the morning stars sang together, / And all the sons of God shouted for joy" (38:7).

This passage provides clear indication that God populated the spiritual realm with angels before the material realm was created.

DAVID CELEBRATED GOD'S CREATION OF HUMAN BEINGS AS "A LITTLE LOWER THAN THE ANGELS"   *(Psalm 8:5)*

The Hebrew text of Psalm 8:5 reads *'elohim* where we read, in most English translations "angels"; and so the KJV renders the verse "a little lower than God." However, the author of Hebrews wrote, "You have made him a little lower than the angels" (Heb. 2:7), and thereby made it clear that *'elohim* is synonymous with "angels" in this context. The psalm suggests the following hierarchy of beings:

- God, who is sovereign and supreme;
- Angels, who are supernatural beings;

- Humans, who are both material and spiritual beings; and
- All other living creatures, which exist in only the material realm, and which are under the dominion of human beings.

ANGELORE

IN WHAT SENSE ARE ANGELS "GODS"?

The Hebrew word *'elohim* is commonly rendered "God" or "gods" in our English translations of the Bible. In the ancient world *'el* was the generic name for a deity; and the plural *'elohim*, often called the "plural of majesty," was the general name of Israel's God, as well as of the gods of pagan peoples.

However, *'elohim* is sometimes found in passages, such as in Psalm 8, where it is clear that God is neither the subject nor the object. In those passages—as in the phrase "sons of God," which indicates membership in a class of beings—*'elohim* is best rendered *"supernatural being"* or *"supernatural beings,"* that is, angels.

CHERUBS ARE LINKED WITH GOD'S PUNISHMENT OF SINS
(Psalm 18:10)

See the discussion of 2 Samuel 22:11 on p. 139, where this psalm is reproduced in its entirety.

ANGELS ARE REFERRED TO AS "MIGHTY ONES"   *(Psalm 29:1)*

The psalmist called on angels to give the Lord the glory due His name. The Hebrew phrase translated "mighty ones" is *bene elim*, "sons of the mighty"—that is, those who belong to the class of mighty beings. This designation emphasizes the vastly superior powers of angels.

THE ANGEL OF THE LORD PROTECTS AND DELIVERS
(Psalm 34:7)

This psalm, like many others, expresses the faith of the psalmist, who affirms reliable truths. Psalm 34 celebrates what God did for his people: "The angel of the LORD encamps all around those who fear Him, / And delivers them" (v. 7). The conviction expressed here grew out of the experience of God's people. The truth of this affirmation of faith has already been worked out in history past and surely will hold true for the future.

DAVID CALLED ON GOD TO LET THE ANGEL OF THE LORD PURSUE HIS ENEMIES
(Psalm 35:5, 6)

These verses read:

> Let them be like chaff before the
>   wind,
> And let the angel of the LORD chase
>   them.
> Let their way be dark and slippery,
> And let the angel of the LORD pursue
>   them.

David justified his cry to the Lord stating: "For without cause they have hidden their net for me in a pit, / Which they have dug without cause for my life" (35:7). It is not wrong for one to call on God to act against one's enemies, for He has often intervened on His people's behalf in history.

GOD'S ARMY OF ANGELS IS GREAT AND POWERFUL
(Psalm 68:17)

The psalmist spoke of God's army of angels using the imagery of chariots to indicate power. He claims: "The chariots of God are twenty thousand, / Even thousands of thousands."

IN CONTEMPLATING GOD'S COVENANT WITH DAVID, ETHAN REFERRED TO ANGELS AS "HOLY ONES" AND "SONS OF THE MIGHTY"   *(Psalm 89:5–7)*

We often say that "a person is known by the company he keeps." Here the psalmist meditates on God, who is far greater than the awesome company around Him, a company intent on exalting Him as far greater than they.

> And the heavens will praise Your
>   wonders, O LORD;
> Your faithfulness also in the
>   assembly of the [holy ones].*
> For who in the heavens can be
>   compared to the LORD?
> God is greatly to be feared in the
>   assembly of the [holy ones],*
> And to be held in reverence by all
>   those around Him.

* The NKJV has interpreted the Hebrew "holy ones" as "saints" in this passage, but the reference is to angels.

ANGELS WILL SUPPORT AND PROTECT THE COMING MESSIAH   (Psalm 91:11, 12)

This messianic psalm promises God's protection for His Anointed One:

> For He shall give His angels
>   charge over you,
> To keep you in all your ways,
> In their hands they shall bear you
>   up,
> Lest you dash your foot against
>   a stone.

Satan quoted these verses in an effort to tempt Christ to leap from the pinnacle of the temple and thus prove that He was under God's special care (Matt. 4:6). This psalm has long been recognized as messianic; it predicts the confidence that Christ would have in the Father during His days on earth. There is also a direct message application for every believer: God has also set His love on us and sends His angels to minister to us (see Heb. 1:14).

ANGELS ARE SUBJECT TO GOD AND DO HIS WILL (Psalm 103:19–21)

These verses are among the strongest affirmations in Scripture of the mission for which angels were created. They also express powerfully the centrality and sovereignty of God.

> The LORD has established His
>   throne in heaven,
> And His kingdom rules over all.
> Bless the LORD, you His angels,
> Who excel in strength, who
>   do His word,
> Heeding the voice of His word.
> Bless the LORD, all you His
>   hosts,
> You ministers of His, who do His
>   pleasure.

ANGELS ARE SPIRITS WHOSE NATURAL FORM IS LIKE FIRE OR FLAME   (Psalm 104:4)

Psalm 104 was written to praise God as Creator and says of His creation of angels, "Who makes His angels spirits, / His ministers a flame of fire."
This psalm indicates that:

* Angels are beings who by nature belong to the spiritual realm.
* The natural form of angels is flame-like.

ANGELS ARE CALLED TO PRAISE GOD WITH THE REST OF HIS CREATION   (Psalm 148:1–4)

This psalm, addressed to the spiritual realm and its inhabitants, opens with a call to praise the Lord. In the first four verses, angels are referred to as angels, hosts, and "stars of light." The psalm reads:

> Praise the LORD from the heavens;
> Praise Him in the heights!
> Praise Him, all His angels;
> Praise Him, all His hosts!
> Praise Him, sun and moon;
> Praise Him, all you stars of light!
> Praise Him, you heavens of heavens,
> And all you waters above the
>   heavens.

EVERY REFERENCE TO GOD'S ANGELS IN THE PROPHETS

The Prophetic Books are the writings of the prophets, dating from the time of the divided kingdom in the eighth century B.C., through the period of the exile of Jews to Babylon and the return of a small group to Israel in the fifth century B.C., to the time of the last prophet in the Old Testament, Malachi, who lived in the late fifth century B.C. Not every prophet mentions angels, but these supernatural beings figure prominently in Ezekiel, Daniel, and Zechariah. Angels are also mentioned in Isaiah and Hosea.

SERAPHIM FLEW ABOVE GOD'S THRONE   (Isaiah 6:2, 6)

Isaiah's account of his commission as a prophet is unique, for he alone describes six-winged angels who hovered over God's throne and praised Him with the cry, "Holy, holy, holy is the Lord of hosts" (6:2,3). Isaiah identified those angels as seraphim, which means "burning ones." Seraphim—despite their wings—

❖

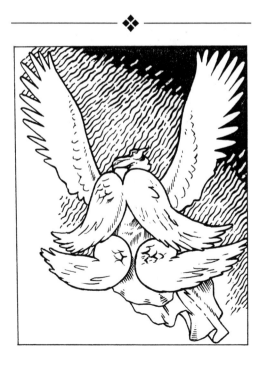

apparently have human features, for the text speaks of their faces, feet, and hands. The name "burning ones" has been taken to indicate a burning devotion to the Lord; but in light of other passages which indicate that the natural form of angels is fiery, the name more likely indicates that seraphim burn with flame of greater intensity, reflecting their closeness to the throne of God.

In his vision Isaiah saw the Lord, was overcome by a sense of his own sinfulness, and was cleansed by a burning coal carried from heaven's altar by a seraphim (6:6). Once cleansed, Isaiah responded when God called for a volunteer to perform a mission.

The position of the seraphim, their cry ("Holy, holy, holy . . ."), and their mission here (to cleanse Isaiah)—all suggest a close association with the holiness and the glory of God. This is the first indication in Scripture that

- angels have wings;
- angels fly; and
- angels participate in cleansing—purging!—the sins of human beings.

HOLY ANGELS WILL PUNISH BABYLON   (Isaiah 13:3)

In his announcement of God's judgment on Babylon, Isaiah quoted the Lord as saying: "I have commanded My [holy ones]; / I have also called my Mighty ones for My anger—/ Those who rejoice in My exaltation." Angels are described here as rejoicing in God's judgment on Babylon, which will result in His exaltation. The angels were called "holy ones" and "mighty ones" in view of the mission of judgment on which God sent them.

LUCIFER (SATAN) PLANNED TO BECOME THE MOST EXALTED OF ANGELIC BEINGS   (Isaiah 14:13)

Isaiah 14:12–14 takes us into the mind of the angel Lucifer by describing his motives for rebellion against God, which introduced evil into the created universe. Satan's "I will" statements betray his desire for an existence independent of God's will and reveal that he was totally self-centered. In one such statement Satan declared, "I will exalt my throne above the stars of God"—that is "the angels of God." Satan intended to rule the angelic hosts whom God created to be agents of His will.

THE ANGEL OF THE LORD KILLED 185,000 ASSYRIAN SOLDIERS WHO THREATENED JERUSALEM   (Isaiah 37:36)

See the comments on the parallel passage, 2 King 19:35, p. 78.

ISAIAH PROMISED THAT THE ANGEL WHO CARRIED ISRAEL IN THE PAST WILL AGAIN ADMINISTER THE LORD'S LOVE AND PITY   (Isaiah 63:9)

Isaiah's prophecies mixed predictions of coming judgment on Israel with promises of ultimate redemption and blessing. Here, Isaiah spoke of the "Angel of [God's] Presence" (almost surely the Angel of the Lord) to remind Israel of how God had expressed His love for Israel through angelic intervention. This verse, which contains the only reference to an "Angel of His [God's] Presence," emphasizes the fact that God suffered with His people when they were afflicted and then acted to deliver them.

> In all their affliction He was afflicted,
> And the Angel of His Presence
>   saved them;
> In His Love and in His pity He
>   redeemed them;
> And He bore them and carried them
> All the days of old.

ANGELIC "LIVING CREATURES" ACCOMPANIED GOD'S THRONE IN EZEKIEL'S VISION
(Ezekiel 1; 3:13)

Ezekiel gave an extensive and detailed description of four "living creatures" (Heb. hayuth, "living beings") which he saw in a vision. Those angelic beings escorted God's throne (1:26–28) as it approached the prophet like some fiercely burning tornado (1:4).

The living creatures Ezekiel saw had human features—"the likeness of a man" (1:5)—but they were strikingly different from humans. Each had four faces—one like a human being, one like a lion, one like an ox, and one like an eagle (1:10). Some interpreters suggest that these faces represented four classes of beings in the material world: humanity, wild animals, domesticated animals, and birds.

Each living creature also had wings (possibly a pair of wings?) on each of its four sides. "The hands of a man" were under each wing (1.8). When the angels moved, their wings were extended, and "whenever they stood, they let down their wings" (1:25). Their legs were unjointed, and their feet "like the soles of calves' feet" (1:7). Each living creature had something like a gigantic double wheel associated with him (1:15, 16). Those wheels were "full of eyes," and each wheel faced a different direction (1:17, 18).

The aspect of these living creatures emphasized most was their fiery appearance. They came in a "great cloud with raging fire engulfing itself; and brightness was all around it and radiating out of its midst like the color of amber, out of the midst of the fire" (1:4). "They sparkled like the color of burnished bronze" (1:7), and "their appearance was like burning coals of fire, like the appearance of torches going back and forth among the living creatures. The fire was bright, and out of the fire went lightning" (1:13). When the living creatures moved, they were "in appearance like a flash of lightning" (1:14).

These living creatures are different from the living beings (Gk. zōa) of Revelation 4:6–9. The living creatures are identified as cherubim in Ezekiel 10:15, a distinct class of powerful angels who served as escorts of the Lord and His throne. It is significant that they were like other angels in their fiery appearance, which seems to be distinctive of angels in their natural, rather than their uncloaked, state. It is also significant that these truly unique angels also have "the likeness of a" human.

The awesome appearance of these angels created the context for Ezekiel's vision of God and his commission to be God's prophet (Ezek. 1—3).

ANGELS AND CHERUBIM ARE FEATURED IN EZEKIEL'S VISION OF GOD'S ABANDONMENT OF THE JERUSALEM TEMPLE
(Ezekiel 9:1; 10:1–20; 11:22)

When Solomon dedicated the Jerusalem temple the "glory of the Lord" filled it, and the temple became the symbolic focus of God's presence with His people on earth. Through the centuries God's people worshiped Him at the temple, and they turned toward the temple when they prayed. When foreign nations attacked, the Jews took comfort in the fact that God was present in His temple, guaranteeing the ultimate security and national integrity of the Jewish state.

In Ezekiel's time Babylonian rulers launched several campaigns against Judea, and took many Jews as captives to Babylon. Ezekiel himself was one of those captives. Despite their powerlessness, the people remaining in Judea assumed their nation would survive, for God would never permit the temple in which He dwelled to be taken or destroyed.

Three critical chapters in Ezekiel (9—11) are devoted to the prophet's vision. An angel, who is introduced as "a likeness, like the appearance of fire" (8:2), took Ezekiel and transported him from Babylon to Judea. The context suggests that this "likeness" is in fact the Angel of the Lord (see 9:8). In Judea, Ezekiel is shown the Jewish people and their religious leaders engaged in various forms of pagan worship, even worshiping the sun in the temple itself (8:16).

Ezekiel's angel guide then called for six angels (designated "men") to mark the foreheads of the worshipers for death, and com-

manded those angels to "defile the temple, and fill the courts with the slain" (9:7).

Chapters 10 and 11 introduce cherubim, whose descriptions seem to match those of the "living creatures" in Ezekiel 1; indeed, the "living creatures" are identified as cherubim in Ezekiel 10:15. These beings accompanied the "glory of God"—a term symbolizing God's visible presence—as it slowly rose from its place between two golden models of cherubim in the Holy of Holies and paused over the threshold of the temple (10:4). The "glory of God" then moved on to stand momentarily at the door of the east gate of the temple (10:19), and it finally left the city of Jerusalem entirely (11:22, 23).

Ezekiel's vision must have stunned the other exiles because the last hope for their homeland rested on God's living presence in the temple. The glory of the Lord withdrew because of the people's abominable sins, and the temple on which they relied was now nothing more than a heap of empty stones.

In Ezekiel 9—11 the primary role of the cherubim was to escort the "glory of the Lord." Also, according to Ezekiel 10:6, 7, one of the cherubim took some of the "fire that was among the cherubim" and delivered it to an angel who was to scatter it on Jerusalem as a symbol of divine judgment (10:2).

ANGELORE
WHAT ARE CHERUBIM?

Cherubs, or cherubim, are a special class or order of angels. Satan himself belonged to this order before his fall (Ezek. 28:14). The first reference to cherubim in the Bible is found in Genesis 3:24. Golden models of cherubim were placed on the cover of the ark of the covenant, which was located in the Holy of Holies in the tabernacle and later in the Jerusalem temple. The "glory of God," symbolizing God's visible presence with His people, rested there. Hebrews 9:5 refers to those figures as "cherubim of glory" because of their intimate association with the divine presence. The models of cherubim were less complex than the real beings

Ezekiel saw in the visions recorded in chapters 1, 10, and 11 of his prophecy. The description of cherubim in Scripture is nothing at all like the mythological winged sphinx of Assyria, commonly identified with cherubim by some archaeologists.

The fact that cherubim were never referred to as angels (ma'lakim) is likely due to the fact that cherubim did not serve God as messengers. Instead, cherubim were intimately associated with God's presence and His visible glory. They escorted the Lord wherever He went, and the coals of fire among which they live (Ezek. 10:6) represented His purity. In these ways they proclaimed God's presence and His holiness.

The placement of two golden models of cherubim on the cover of the ark of the covenant is especially significant. Not only did God's presence rest there, but also the blood of the sacrifice offered on the Day of Atonement to cleanse Israelites from all their sins (Lev. 16:30) was sprinkled between the cherubim on the ark's cover. Thus, cherubim also symbolize God's grace; they remind us that our God is awesome and holy, yet full of grace in that He forgives all our sins.

SATAN WAS A CHERUBIM PRIOR TO HIS FALL   (Ezekiel 28:14, 17)

Ezekiel provides insight about the origin of sin and Satan. Ezekiel 28:14–19 describes Satan's fall (see also Isaiah 14), and relates that he was once "the seal of perfection" (28:12), the "anointed cherub who covers" (28:14). Satan was also addressed as "O covering cherub" (28:16) before being cast out of heaven as a consequence of his pride (28:17–19).

AN ANGEL DELIVERED THREE FAITHFUL HEBREW MEN (Daniel 3:25, 28)

King Nebuchadnezzar erected an idol and commanded every official in his land to worship it. Three Jewish officials refused and were thrown into an overheated furnace. The three men were not destroyed; rather, they were seen walking in the flames with a fourth figure described by the king as "like the Son of God" (3:25). That figure has sometimes been

identified as Jesus Himself, but almost certainly without warrant. As explained earlier, the Hebrew phrase bene'elohim means "a member of the class of supernatural beings," and thus refers to an angel. The phrase bene'elohim should not be translated "Son of God."

This interpretation is confirmed by what Nebuchadnezzar later said to the three men who stepped from the furnace:

"Blessed be [your] God, who sent His Angel and delivered His servants who trusted in Him, and they have frustrated the king's word, and yielded their bodies, that they should not serve nor worship any god except their own God!"

Daniel 3:28

Many believe that this vivid witness to the power and faithfulness of God, along with Daniel's ministry, led to Nebuchadnezzar's conversion (see 4:34–37).

ANGELS WATCHED NEBUCHADNEZZAR AND STRUCK HIM WITH MADNESS WHEN HE SINNED (Daniel 4:13, 17, 33)

Nebuchadnezzar had a vision warning him that he would fall victim to madness unless he reformed. Daniel interpreted the vision and underscored the warning. Nevertheless, within a year the king's overweening pride triggered the predicted curse (4:28–31). In time, the madness was withdrawn and Nebuchadnezzar was restored to the throne, completely convinced of God's sovereignty and committed to honoring the Lord.

One angel in the king's dream, who administered the punishment, was called "a watcher, a holy one" (4:13). As the dream ended, the king heard the watcher cry aloud:

"This decision is by the decree of
   the watchers,
And the sentence by the word of
   the holy ones,

In order that the living may know
That the Most High rules in the
kingdom of men. . . ."

Daniel 4:17

The final reference to these angels ("a watcher, a holy one") is found in Daniel's explanation of the dream (4:23).

The term "holy ones" (Hebrew *kadoshim*) is placed in apposition to "watchers." "Holy ones" is an established name for angels, and it is attached here so that the "watchers," a name found only in Daniel 4, will be clearly understood as a reference to angels.

The term "watcher," according to many interpreters, refers to a sort of angel supervisor, who not only closely observes events on earth, but who is also authorized to pass sentence on those who step beyond established limits. Because this term is used only here and in direct relation to King Nebuchadnezzar, some interpreters have argued that the mission of watcher angels is to influence the control of governments and their human rulers.

AN ANGEL DELIVERED DANIEL FROM HUNGRY LIONS
(Daniel 7:22)

Daniel was thrown into a lions' den for violating a command of King Darius, in whose administration Daniel served, but the king desperately hoped that God would somehow save Daniel's life. After a night in the lions' den, Daniel answered the call of the anxious king: "My God sent His angel and shut the lions' mouths, so that they have not hurt me." This is one of Scripture's most vivid stories of angelic protection from danger.

AN ANGEL INTERPRETED DANIEL'S VISION *(Daniel 7)*

The second half of the book of Daniel is filled with vivid reports of the visions God gave Daniel, visions that have to do with the near and distant future of Daniel's people. After having a vision of four wild beasts who struggle with and overcome each other in or-

der (7:1–14), Daniel comes to "one of those who stood by." This angel then identified the beasts as symbolic representations of four great powers destined to succeed one another in the future. Those predictions so clearly depict the Babylonian, Media-Persian, Greek, and Roman empires that some scholars, especially those who do not believe in prophecy, insist that the book of Daniel must have been written in the second century B.C. rather than the sixth century, where the book dates itself.

While "those who stood by" are never specifically identified as angels, it is clear from the context that they are indeed angels. That angels function as interpreters of visions is emphasized in the experiences of Daniel and also in the book of Zechariah.

THE ANGEL GABRIEL INTERPRETED ANOTHER OF DANIEL'S VISIONS *(Daniel 8)*

Daniel had another vision, this time involving a ram and a male goat engaged in a struggle with each other (8:1–12). Daniel heard "holy ones" (angels) speaking to each other. He sought the meaning of his vision, and suddenly "one having the appearance of a man" stood before him (8:15). This "man," identified as the angel Gabriel (8:16), explained the vision. The ram and the goat were specifically identified as Media-Persia and Greece. The angel's interpretation ended with the introduction of a king who, at history's end, would "even rise against the Prince of princes" (8:25).

This is the first time in Scripture that one of God's angels is referred to by name. The name "Gabriel" means "mighty one of God." In Daniel 9:21 he was called "the man Gabriel," indicating that he appeared in human form. Gabriel's appearance in human form was emphasized in Daniel 10:18, which describes him as "the one having the likeness of a man."

Gabriel appears in Scripture four times, twice in both Daniel (9:21; 10:18) and Luke (1:13–17, 19, 26, 31–35). In each of his appearances, Gabriel spoke of God's plans and purposes as they relate to the Messiah and His coming kingdom.

THE ANGEL GABRIEL APPEARED TO ANSWER DANIEL'S PRAYER FOR UNDERSTANDING
(Daniel 9)

Daniel read God's promise, as recorded in the book of Jeremiah, that Israel's captivity would last only some 70 years (9:2). That discovery moved Daniel to say a prayer of confession and praise, in which he made a fervent request for God to forgive His people and act now to keep His promise.

The angel Gabriel came in response to the prayer with special information about the future. In what is known as the "prophecy of 70 weeks" Gabriel provided more insight about Israel's future and God's plan to establish the promised kingdom of the Messiah. The prophecy stated that the Messiah would appear 483 years (70 "sevens," or 70 weeks of years) after the decree went out to rebuild the city of Jerusalem and its wall.

The dates of this prophecy have been carefully computed. The decree to rebuild Jerusalem was given in 458 B.C. The predicted 70 weeks (literally, 70 sevens) of years is divided into three groups. The first group of seven sevens (49 years) brings us to 409 B.C. and the rebuilding of Jerusalem's walls under Nehemiah. The second group of 62 sevens (434 years) brings us to A.D. 26. Depending upon the dating of Christ's birth, that would be the date of either Jesus' baptism by John or, more likely, the Triumphal Entry. The text in Daniel says that after the sixty-second week the Messiah would be "cut off" (die). Other events that follow His death, including the destruction of Jerusalem and its temple in A.D. 70, are described. A final seven-year period remains, the seventieth week, during which a number of events will take place, including the appearance of a "prince who is to come" who will make war on God and His people.

Gabriel, the angel whom Scripture associates with major revelations of God's plan for His future kingdom, is the source of this prophecy.

ONE OF GOD'S ANGELS WAS DELAYED BY A DARK ANGEL WHO TRIED TO PREVENT HIM FROM ANSWERING DANIEL'S PRAYER   (Daniel 10)

Daniel understood from Gabriel's prophecy that it would be a long time before God's kingdom takes its final shape on earth. Daniel was troubled about many unknown details, and so he determined to fast and pray for further insight (10:1–3). After three weeks an angel appeared. Daniel described the angel as "a certain man." This was, however, an unusual man, for "his body was like beryl, his face like the appearance of lightning, his eyes like torches of fire, his arms and feet like burnished bronze in color" (10:4). Daniel's visitor was an angel in his natural form—he had the likeness of a human, but was fiery and undoubtedly supernatural. That angel's extensive prophecy is reported in Daniel 11—12.

Daniel 10 is one of the most suggestive of all the passages in Scripture that speak of angels. When the angel reached Daniel, he reported that "the prince of the kingdom of Persia withstood me twenty-one days" until "Michael, one of the chief princes, came to help me" (10:13). The angel also told Daniel that when he completed his mission of revealing more to Daniel about history's end, he "must return to fight with the prince of Persia" (10:20).

Conclusions to be drawn from the angel's words include:

1. An invisible war is being fought in the spiritual realm between God's angels and Satan's angels.
2. Angels have different ranks or powers. The angel designated as "the prince of the kingdom of Persia" was powerful enough to keep the angel sent to speak to Daniel from completing his mission. When Michael, "one of the chief princes" among angels appeared, Satan's angel was forced to give way.

3. Angels appear to influence the course of events among nations and peoples. The "prince of the kingdom of Persia" was a dark angel or demon who attempted to direct the history of the nation in his charge.

4. The invisible war is being fought in both realms; while good and evil angels struggle with each other in the spiritual realm, they also seek to influence affairs on earth so as to gain strategic advantages for their leaders, God and Satan, respectively. This is also suggested in Colossians 1:13–15 and Ephesians 6:10–12.

5. Despite the warfare between good and evil angels, God remains in absolute control, and He can send angels to unveil what will happen in the future.

This chapter contains the first mention in Scripture of the only other named angel of God, Michael. The name "Michael" means "Who is like God?"—a name which reflects an attitude completely opposite that of Satan, who declared, "I will be like the Most High" (Isa. 14:14). Michael was associated with the welfare of Israel as their "prince" (Dan. 10:21). As other angels are assigned various nations by God or Satan, Michael is "the great prince who stands watch over the sons of" God's people (12:1).

Jude 9 refers to Michael as "the archangel"—that is, the "head" or "chief" angel. Strikingly, Jude reports that even Michael did not directly rebuke Satan; Michael showed respect for Satan's evil power, and so he relied on the Lord to deal with him. Still, in Revelation 12:7 Michael is envisioned as the commander of the army of angels who do battle with Satan and his forces.

ANGELORE

IN WHAT SENSE ARE ANGELS "MEN"?

In a number of Old Testament passages, angels are referred to as "men" (Gen. 18:2; Dan. 10:5) or as like one of the "sons of men" (Dan. 10:18). In each case, the description emphasizes the resemblance of angels to human beings.

This resemblance is obvious when an angel appears so completely cloaked as a human being that his true identity is known only later, as in Judges 6. Even when the angel appears as a truly unusual man, as in Judges 13, his identity may go unrecognized at first.

However, there is an abundance of evidence to indicate that even when an angel appears uncloaked—in his native fiery aspect—his form bears a striking resemblance to that of a human being. Even the angel whose face was like the appearance of lightning could only be described by Daniel as "a certain man" (Dan. 10:5, 6). While certain specialized angels, such as the seraphim and cherubim, have unique forms, the majority of angels, cloaked and uncloaked, have a form in the likeness of human beings.

Although passages that describe angels as a "man" are primarily making reference to their human shape, it is also true that no angel in Scripture appears as a woman. Although angels do not have gender (Matt. 22:20), they look distinctively masculine when they appear to human beings.

THE ANGEL MICHAEL IS SAID TO "STAND WATCH" OVER THE JEWISH PEOPLE   (Daniel 12:1)

See the comments on Daniel 10, p. 57.

HOSEA REFERRED TO THE "MAN" WHO STRUGGLED WITH JACOB AS "THE ANGEL"   (Hosea 12:4)

The prophet Hosea called on God's people to return to the Lord, and he reminded them of the high points and low points in sacred history.

ANGELS APPEAR FREQUENTLY IN THE BOOK OF ZECHARIAH

Most of the angels in the book of Zechariah were masculine in form and were referred to as men. Exceptions can be found in Zechariah 6, where angels were described as "chariots" and "spirits," and in Zechariah 14:5, where they were called "holy ones" (NIV).

The first six chapters of Zechariah contain a series of visions experienced by the prophet. Those visions were interpreted by one whom Ezekiel identified as "the angel who talked with me." This angel interpreter and Zechariah are the central figures in these chapters.

In his visions Zechariah saw angels perform various acts. One of the angels Zechariah saw was the Angel of the Lord (1:11, 12; 3:1–6). Zechariah's visions, like Daniel's, were of the future, but the focus was on the experience of God's people rather than on the history of Gentile world powers. The ultimate triumph of God as depicted in Zechariah's writings has led commentators to call him "the prophet of hope."

The final eight chapters of Zechariah contain prophecies God gave to him. In Zechariah 12:8 the Lord promised a restoration of the kingdom of David through the Messiah, and said, "In that day the LORD will defend the inhabitants of Jerusalem . . . and the house of David shall be like God, like the Angel of the Lord before them." In Zechariah 14 the prophet depicted a day when the nations gathered to fight against Jerusalem, and the Lord returned in person to fight against Israel's enemy: "Thus the LORD my God will come, / and all the [holy ones] with You" (14:5).

It is no wonder that to a people who for centuries were scattered throughout the ancient world, with no national homeland of their own, Zechariah and the angel who spoke to him were harbingers of hope.

CHAPTER 10

ANGELS IN JESUS' LIFE:

HOW THEY HELPED, AND WHAT HE SAID ABOUT THEM

Matthew—John

We're all familiar with Christmas hymns which highlight the role of angels at Jesus' birth. We sing them every year. "Angels from the Realms of Glory." "Angels We Have Heard on High." "Hark! the Herald Angels Sing."

But most of us are unaware of the significant role angels played during the rest of Christ's life on earth, and many of us do not know about Jesus' teachings on angels recorded in the Gospels. Indeed, most of us aren't aware of an important passage which highlights the essential relationship between Jesus Christ and all of God's angels.

ANGELS AND CHRIST'S INCARNATION

Jesus Christ was born in the little town of Bethlehem. For some 27 years he lived a quiet life in Nazareth, probably practicing the trade of his stepfather, Joseph. Then for three intense years the young carpenter presented Himself to the Jewish people as their Messiah, the Anointed One (Christ) promised by the prophets of the Old Testament. Although His claims were substantiated by many miracles, and although He assembled a committed group of followers, He was ultimately rejected. The religious-political leaders of His

people manipulated the Roman governor, and he condemned Jesus to the most painful death administered under Roman law—crucifixion. Nevertheless, three days after Jesus' burial, the tomb where His body was laid was found to be empty, and afterward many disciples saw the Lord, risen and alive. At each stage of Jesus' sojourn on earth, angels were involved.

ANGELS PREPARED HEARTS FOR JESUS' COMING

Angels prepared the way for the birth of Jesus and joyfully announced the moment of His arrival.

Gabriel announced the birth of Jesus' fore-runner *(Luke 1:5–25).* The priest Zacharias and his wife, Elizabeth, were a godly couple who had no children (1:6). Ordinary priests were divided into 24 teams or divisions, and each team ministered for two nonconsecutive weeks each year at the Jerusalem temple. The privilege of entering the temple to offer incense before the morning or evening sacrifice was decided by lot. Because there was a large number of priests in the first century, a priest might have one such opportunity during his life.

Gabriel met Zacharias in the temple to announce his coming son.

❖

On one particular day, the lot fell to Zacharias. Inside the temple, Zacharias was met by the angel Gabriel, who came with a message. "When Zacharias saw him, he was troubled, and fear fell upon him" (1:12; NKJV). This suggests that Gabriel appeared in his natural fiery form, rather than cloaked as a man.

Gabriel announced to Zacharias that he and Elizabeth would have a son, who was to be named John. Gabriel told Zacharias that his son "will turn many of the children of Israel to the Lord their God. He will also go before Him in the spirit and power of Elijah" (1:16, 17). These words are significant, for (1) they identify the One whom John will serve as a "forerunner." In modern terms, John was an "advance man," one who enters a community to prepare the way for the company or politician he represents. According to Luke 1:16, 17, John was to serve as "advance man" for the Lord God. This is just one of Scripture's clear indications that Jesus, who was born in Bethlehem, was God as well as man. (2) These verses also link John's ministry to an ancient prophecy about the Messiah which is recorded in Malachi, the last book of the Old Testament, written some four hundred years before Gabriel met Zacharias. That prophecy says:

Behold, I will send you Elijah the
    prophet
Before the coming of the great and
    dreadful day of the LORD.
And he will turn
The hearts of the fathers to their
    children,
And the hearts of the children to
    their fathers,
Lest I come and strike the earth with
    a curse.

Malachi 4:5, 6

By saying that John would come in the "spirit and power of Elijah," and by quoting from Malachi, Gabriel confirmed John's role in history in terms that Zacharias would surely understand.

Zacharias's response was one of doubt. "How shall I know this? For I am an old man, and my wife is well advanced in years" (1:18). Some interpreters suggest that there was little difference between Zacharias's reaction and that of Gideon, who asked God for signs that He would keep promises made by an angel (see Judg. 6:17, 36–40). However, Gabriel appeared to Zacharias uncloaked—there could be no question about his identity. Furthermore, the promise Gabriel made was linked to the prophecies contained in the Old Testament. There was not the slightest basis for questioning the identity of the messenger or the authenticity of his message. So Gabriel announced to Zacharias: "But behold, you will be mute and not able to speak until the day these things take place, because you did not believe my words" (1:20).

This is the first in a series of events involving angels at the time of Jesus' birth. We should pause here to recall earlier findings about angels.

- Angels in their natural uncloaked form cannot be mistaken for mere human beings.
- Messages delivered by God's angels are self-authenticating; that is, they *should* be believed and acted on. Still, the recipient's reaction may well be one of unbelief.
- Angels can affect human beings physically, a truth we'll see even more clearly as we examine the activity of demons in later chapters.

❖

Gabriel and Mary.

Gabriel announced the coming of Jesus to Mary *(Luke 1:26–38).* Six months after Elizabeth became pregnant, Gabriel appeared to a young virgin in Nazareth. Mary was probably in her middle teens at the time. There is no indication that Gabriel appeared in his natural form. The text simply says that Mary "was troubled" at the manner of Gabriel's greeting, not at his appearance (1:3). Gabriel told Mary, "And behold, you will conceive in your womb and bring forth a Son, and shall call His name JESUS" (1:31). Again, Gabriel described the role of the child to be born, summarizing in a few words major themes developed in the prophets concerning the promised Messiah.

He will be great, and will be called the Son of the Highest; and the Lord God will give Him the throne of His father David. And He will reign over the house of Jacob forever, and of His kingdom there will be no end.

Luke 1:32, 33

Mary, unlike Zacharias, did not doubt the angel's message, but she did wonder how she could become pregnant, in view of the fact that she had never had sex with a man (1:34). The angel answered her question by explaining that the Holy Spirit would impregnate her, so that the child to be born would be, literally, the "Son of God." Thus, it was Gabriel's privilege not only to announce Jesus' birth to Mary, but also to reveal the true nature of her child.

Mary's response is striking: "Behold the maidservant of the Lord! Let it be to me according to your word" (1:38). There was none of Zacharias's unbelief or Gideon's hesitation. There was no hint of worry about what her fiancé Joseph would do, or what her neighbors in the close-knit community would think or say. Whatever we may believe about Mary's role in contemporary Christianity, there can be no doubt that her simple faith and readiness to respond to the Lord's will sets an example for us all.

And there can be no doubt that the angel Gabriel played a significant role in preparing the world for the Savior's birth and in preparing us to understand who Jesus is.

Angels prepared Joseph to go through with his marriage to Mary *(Matthew 1:18–25).* When Joseph realized that Mary was pregnant, he intended to "put her away secretly." Jewish marriages of that time took place in two stages. A contract was executed by the parties, after which they were considered married. The actual wedding took place later. Thus, breaking the contract was equivalent to divorce ("put her away").

As Joseph considered a quiet divorce, "an angel of the Lord appeared to him in a dream" (1:20). The angel told him not to be afraid to take Mary as his wife, "for that which is conceived in her is of the Holy Spirit. And she will bring forth a Son, and you shall call his name Jesus, for He will save His people from their sins" (1:20, 21). It is apparent in Matthew 1:24 that the angelic message was a command to complete the marriage ceremony *at once.* This was a gracious provision to protect Mary's reputation, as well as that of her child. Once again, the angelic messenger left no uncertainty about either Jesus' nature as the Son of God, or the role He was to play in God's plan.

Matthew also linked the angel's message with Old Testament prophecy. Isaiah 7:14 predicted that a virgin would bear a son. Whereas the Hebrew word for "virgin" in Isaiah means "young woman" and was usually reserved for the unmarried, the Greek word used to translate it, *parthenos,* has the unmistakable meaning of "virgin."

Joseph "did as the angel of the Lord commanded him." He went through with the marriage ceremony, but he "did not know [have sex with] her till she had brought forth her firstborn Son. And he [Joseph] called His name JESUS." It was the father's privilege to name his son.

There are certain similarities in each of the three angelic visitations connected with the birth of Jesus. In each case the angel: (1) named the child to be born; (2) indicated what His mission would be; and (3) linked His mission with the fulfillment of Old Testament prophecy. It is interesting that although

Zacharias doubted the angel's message, neither Mary nor Joseph did. This is particularly significant in view of the fact that Gabriel appeared to Zacharias in his natural form, but Gabriel apparently came to Mary cloaked, and the angel who spoke to Joseph appeared to him in a dream. How much easier it would have been for Zacharias to believe, and yet he chose not to. So the angel visitations underscore a significant truth: Jesus was to be brought up by parents whose very lives breathed faith and trust in God. Mary and Joseph both exhibited a readiness to do God's will, whatever the cost.

ANGELORE

WHOM DID GABRIEL ANNOUNCE?

Gabriel and the angel who appeared to Joseph both emphasized the fact that the child to be born and named Jesus would be the Son of God. In the Church Council convened at Chalcedon in A.D. 451, the following definition of the person of Jesus Christ was formally adopted.

Therefore, following the holy fathers, we all with one accord teach men to acknowledge one and the same Son, our Lord Jesus Christ, at once complete in Godhead and complete in manhood, truly God and truly man, consisting also as a reasonable soul and body; of one substance (*homousias*) with the Father as regards His Godhead, and at the same time of one substance with us as regards His manhood, like us in all respects apart from sin; as regards his Godhead, begotten of the Father before the ages, but yet as regards to his manhood begotten, for us men and for our salvation, of Mary the Virgin, the God-bearer (*theotokos*); one and the same Christ, Son, Lord, Only-begotten, recognized in TWO NATURES, WITHOUT CONFUSION, WITHOUT CHANGE, WITHOUT DIVISION, WITHOUT SEPARATION; the distinction of natures being in no way annulled by the union, but rather the characteristics of each nature being preserved and coming together to form one person and substance (*hupostasis*), not as parted or separated into two persons, but one and the same Son and Only-begotten God the Word, Lord Jesus Christ; even as the prophets from earliest times spoke of Him, and our Lord Jesus Christ Himself taught us, and the creed of the Fathers has handed down to us.

Angels announced Jesus' entry into the world (Luke 2:8–15). On the night Jesus was born, an angel of the Lord appeared in his natural form to shepherds in the fields near Bethlehem. We can be certain about the angel's form because the text says that "the glory of the Lord shone around them"; the text also makes it clear that the shepherds "were greatly afraid" of the apparition (2:9). The angel reassured the shepherds and told them: "I bring you good tidings of great joy . . . for there is born to you this day in the city of David [literally, the "town of David"] a Savior, who is Christ the Lord" (2:11).

A multitude of the heavenly host then appeared, praising God. The exact meaning of the angels' shout of praise has been debated. The translation of the original KJV text was based on a Greek manuscript which contained the word *eudokia* (a nominative noun). This led the translators to render the verse in such a way that the angels announced "peace on earth to men of good will." Older Greek manuscripts were discovered later and those texts added an "s" to *eudokia,* changing it to *eudokias,* a genitive noun. This alters the meaning of the angels' praise to: "Glory to God in the highest, / And on earth peace to men *on whom His favor rests*" (2:14; NIV, emphasis added). Through Jesus, God's favor now rests on all of humankind, and everyone is invited to respond to the gospel message.

This meaning is beautifully illustrated in God's choice of the persons to whom the announcement was made—shepherds. We tend to think of these shepherds as brave and godly men, like the shepherd David. However, in the first century to call someone a "shepherd" was equivalent to calling someone a thieving vagabond. Shepherds were held in such contempt that their testimony, like that of tax collectors, would not be accepted in a rabbinic court! How appropriate, then, that the angels appeared to shepherds, first-century outcasts, to underscore the fact that Jesus came to be the Savior of all. Through Christ, God's favor truly does rest on *all* humankind.

ANGELORE

DO ANGELS SING?

One of our most familiar Christmas hymns says they do: "Hark! the Herald Angels Sing." But do angels really sing? Luke 2:13 portrays the host of angels who announced Jesus' birth "praising God and *saying.* . . ." There's no hint of "singing" in the text. In fact, the Bible never states that angels sing; indeed, when quoting the words of an angel, the Greek New Testament always uses the introductory word, "saying."

Of course, this isn't absolute proof that angels do not sing. Revelation speaks of angels who "sang a new song" and then introduces the words they sang with the word, "saying." It seems that the New Testament frequently uses the word "saying" in a fashion similar to the way we use quotation marks.

It is certainly clear in the Old Testament that praising God included singing (see Ps. 68:32; 138:1; 147:1). This evidence may not prove that angels sing, but it does seem likely that since heaven is filled with joy, angels must often break out in songs of praise.

ANGELS GUARDED JESUS DURING HIS EARLY YEARS

An angel warned Joseph to leave Bethlehem and take his family to Egypt *(Matthew*

2:13–15). Several Magi, a class of scholars ("wise men") in Persia, saw a star which they thought was the one identified in the prophecy of Numbers 24:17. The naïve "wise men" went to King Herod to ask about the birthplace of the "king of the Jews." Herod's scholars, citing Micah 5:2, identified Bethlehem as the city where the Christ would be born. Herod sent the wise men on their way and told them to return to him when they located the child. However, God warned the Magi in a dream to go home another way. No angels are mentioned here, but it is possible that an angel delivered this message to the wise men.

An angel did warn Joseph in a dream to leave Bethlehem and take his family to Egypt. No sooner had they left than Herod sent soldiers to murder every male child under two years of age in the district. Joseph undoubtedly used the Magi's gifts to finance the trip and the family's stay in Egypt.

An angel told Joseph when it was safe to return and where to settle *(Matthew 2:19–21).* After Herod died (in 4 B.C.), an angel told Joseph that it was safe to return and that he should settle in Nazareth of Galilee. Bethlehem, of course, was the hometown of Mary and Joseph. Why, then, did the angel specify Nazareth?

Archaeological research indicates that many inhabitants of the region around Bethlehem relocated to areas near Nazareth while Archalaus ruled Judea. (Archalaus, who succeeded his father, Herod, in Judea, was an ineffective ruler later deposed by the Romans.) Although it was a small town, Nazareth was located on a major road—near enough to the city of Sepphoris that Joseph could easily have found work. Thus, Jesus was brought up in a relatively cosmopolitan setting. The Judaism practiced in Galilee was of a simpler sort than the Judaism practiced in Judea. Thus, there was less pressure on the holy family to observe many of the rigorous practices imposed on the population in the Pharisaic strongholds of Judea. These, then, are some of the more

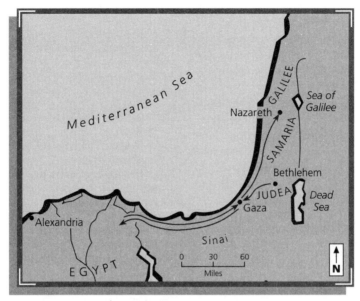

TO EGYPT AND BACK

obvious benefits to be derived from settling in the location specified by the angel who appeared to Joseph in a dream.

ANGELS OFFERED JESUS SUPPORT AT CRITICAL MOMENTS IN HIS LIFE ON EARTH

Angels ministered to Jesus after His temptation (Matthew 4:11). Jesus fasted for 40 days before His temptation by the devil. The forty-day fast obviously weakened Christ. Medical research indicates that a forty-day fast exhausts the body's reserves and that hunger pangs, absent after the first two or three days, return then. Christ met the devil's challenge but was exhausted afterward. Matthew 4:11 tells us that when the devil left Jesus, "angels came and ministered to Him." We are not told exactly what the angels did, but surely they supplied Jesus with food, just as an angel did for Elijah (1 Kings 19:5–7).

Angels ministered to Jesus in Gethsemane (Luke 22:43). Although each Gospel portrays Jesus as experiencing intense stress while He prayed in Gethsemane the night before His cru-

cifixion, Luke tells us that during the Savior's tortured prayers "an angel appeared to Him from heaven, strengthening Him" (22:43). Again, we do not know exactly what the angel

❖

Jesus' anguish in Gethsemane.

did to strengthen Jesus. What is significant in the two situations recorded in Matthew 4:11 and Luke 22:43 is that: (1) Jesus was utterly exhausted, and (2) angels were sent to minister to Him and strengthen Him. It is encouraging to realize that God is aware when our strength is exhausted and that He is eager to strengthen us too. God's promise to Israel applied to Jesus, and it applies to us as well: "Fear not, for I am with you; / Be not dismayed, for I am your God. / I will strengthen you, / Yes, I will help you, / I will uphold you with My righteous right hand" (Isa. 41:10).

ANGELS WERE INVOLVED IN EVENTS SURROUNDING JESUS' RESURRECTION

An angel rolled away the stone that sealed Jesus' tomb (*Matthew 28:1, 2*). Jesus' body was placed in the tomb of a rich man, Joseph from Arimathea. It was a typical cave-tomb, cut into the rocky face of a cliff. The tomb was sealed by rolling a rounded, heavy stone some twelve feet tall along a track cut into the rock. Some women set out for the tomb early Sunday morning, intending to wrap Jesus' body in spices placed between layers of linen, and they worried about how they would ever roll back the stone that sealed the tomb.

Matthew tells us that "an angel of the Lord descended from heaven, and came and rolled back the stone from the door" (28:2). This was associated with a "great earthquake" (28:2).

No angel was needed to unseal the tomb in order to release Jesus, for He was already risen and gone. The angel was sent for the followers of Jesus who would visit the tomb, find it empty, and be the first to hear of the resurrection.

❖

ANGELORE

ANGELS AND RESURRECTION MORN

The following chart of Sunday morning events highlights the involvement of angels in Jesus' resurrection.

Three women start for the tomb.	Luke 23:55—24:1
They find the stone rolled away, an act performed by an angel.	Luke 24:2–9 Matt. 28:2
Mary Magdalene leaves to tell the disciples.	John 20:1, 2
Mary, the mother of James, sees two angels.	Matt. 28:3–5
Peter and John arrive and look in the tomb.	John 20:3–9
Mary Magdalene returns and sees angels and Jesus.	John 20:10–18
Mary, the mother of James, returns with others.	Luke 24:1–4
These women see the angels.	Luke 24:5; Mark 16:5
The angel tells the women that Jesus is risen.	Matt. 28:6–8
As the women leave, they meet Jesus.	Matt. 28:9, 10

❖

Angels announced Jesus' resurrection the first Easter morning (*Matthew 28:3–5; Mark 16:5–7; Luke 24:4–8; John 20:11–16*). There is complete agreement among the Gospel accounts with regard to the angels and their mission to Jesus' followers.

The angels appeared in their natural form to at least two parties, and probably three. Matthew 28:3 says of the angel who appeared to Mary, the mother of James: "His countenance was like lightning, and his clothing as white as snow." That explains why the guards posted at the tomb by the chief priests fainted "and became as dead men" when they saw the angels. John 20:12 says Mary Magdalene saw "two angels in white" inside the tomb. While John does not describe the angels in detail, the phrase "in white" suggests that they were not dressed like ordinary men. It's likely that "white" here indicates brightness. The other two Gospels also place angels at Jesus' tomb. Mark 16:5 describes "a young man clothed in a long white robe," while Luke 24:4 describes "two men . . . in shining garments." Each passage agrees that the angels looked like men, but these were clearly unusual "shining" men, who were immediately recognized as angels.

In each report of an angel encounter at Jesus' tomb, the same basic message was shared. The angel who spoke with Mary, the mother of James, first said:

"I know you seek Jesus who was crucified. He is not here; for He is risen, as He said. Come, see the place where the Lord lay" (Matthew 28:5, 6).

The angel who spoke to three women first said:

"Do not be alarmed. You seek Jesus of Nazareth, who was crucified. He is risen! He is not here. See the place where they laid Him" (Mark 16:6).

A similar message is reported in Luke 24:5:

"Why do you seek the living among the dead? He is not here, but is risen! Remember how He spoke to you while He was still in Galilee."

The angels' mission was to interpret the empty tomb for Jesus' followers so they would not misunderstand its significance. The angels' message was intended to prepare them for actually meeting the risen Christ.

In the reports of the angels' words, there is another recurring theme. In Matthew 28:7:

"And go quickly and tell His disciples that He is risen from the dead, and indeed He is going before you into Galilee; there you will see Him. Behold, I have told you."

In Mark 16:7:

"But go, tell His disciples—and Peter—that He is going before you into Galilee; there you will see Him, as He said to you."

In the other two passages there is no mention of this angelic message, but Luke 24:9 says, "Then they returned from the tomb and told all these things to the eleven and to all the rest."

Angels had the privilege of being the first to announce Jesus' resurrection, but the mantle of being an evangelist—a bearer of good news—passed immediately from angels to human beings. In fact, women were the first evangelists, the first to tell anyone the stunning news that the Jesus who died on Calvary was alive—now and forevermore.

Angels rolled away the stone that blocked the entrance to the tomb so that witnesses could see that it truly was empty. Angels interpreted the meaning of the empty tomb to the women and invited them to examine the evidence of Jesus' resurrection. And angels sent those first witnesses to tell others. The one ministry that angels cannot perform today is sharing the gospel with human beings. That privilege is reserved for you and me.

ANGELS WERE PRESENT AT JESUS' ASCENSION AND PROMISED HE WOULD RETURN   (Acts 1:11)

Some 40 days after the Resurrection, a crowd of Jesus' followers gathered on Mount Olivet. There they saw Christ rise up into the air, until He was lost from view. Two angels "in white apparel" came and stood by them as they watched Him disappear. The angels' message is for us as much as it was for the first followers of Christ: "Men of Galilee, why do you stand gazing up into heaven? This same Jesus,

who was taken up from you into heaven, will so come in like manner as you saw Him go into heaven" (1:11).

Disciples of Christ are not to stand around, gazing up into heaven, waiting. We are to be involved in our world, building Christ's kingdom. When the day comes, Jesus will return "in like manner"—physically, visibly—from heaven. Then human history will have reached its intended end, and all the blessings promised by God, through angels and prophets, will be ours.

EVERY TEACHING OF JESUS ABOUT ANGELS

Each Gospel was carefully crafted to tell the story of Jesus from a particular point of view. If we're to see all the implications of Jesus' teachings on angels, we will need to set them in the context of the Gospel in which they are found.

Matthew wrote to show the Jewish people that Jesus fulfilled the Old Testament prophecies about the Messiah and to explain what happened to the kingdom the Messiah was destined to establish. In carrying out this task, Matthew included many of Jesus' teachings about angels, especially with regard to their involvement in His future return to earth.

Mark wrote to show the Romans that Jesus was a man of action and authority. Mark's Gospel contains fewer of Jesus' teachings on angels.

Luke wrote to show those with traditional Greek values that Jesus fulfilled their ideal of "excellence." Jesus was the perfect human being, who showed compassion for the helpless and a special concern for women and the poor. Strikingly, Luke's Gospel also contains many of Jesus' sayings and teachings about angels as they pertain to human beings.

John's Gospel, often called the "universal Gospel," emphasized to all humankind that Jesus was the Son of God. It contains none of Jesus' teachings about angels.

JESUS' TEACHINGS ABOUT GOD'S ANGELS IN THE GOSPEL OF MATTHEW

Jesus' teaching on angels in Matthew 13. Matthew 13 contains a series of parables known as "parables of the kingdom." The Jewish people of the first century expected Messiah to defeat the Romans, their Gentile oppressors, and to reestablish a dominant Jewish kingdom, with Jerusalem as the capital of the world, rather than Rome. Jesus' kingdom parables highlighted the difference between the secret spiritual kingdom He intended to establish then and the public, political kingdom God's Old Testament people expected (see the chart on page 165).

Jesus' kingdom parables do not deny the Old Testament vision, but they do point out that the public expression of Christ's rule lies in the future; and so it is that Jesus spoke of angels being involved at history's end. This is clearly illustrated in Jesus' interpretation of the parable of the wheat and tares:

[Jesus] answered and said to them: "He who sows the good seed is the Son of Man. The field is the world, the good seeds are the sons of the kingdom, but the tares are the sons of the wicked one. The enemy who sowed them is the devil, the harvest is the end of the age, and the reapers are the angels. Therefore as the tares are gathered and burned in the fire, so it will be at the end of this age. The Son of Man will send out His angels, and they will gather out of His kingdom all things that offend, and those who practice lawlessness. . . . So it will be at the end of the age. The angels will come forth, separate the wicked from among the just, and cast them into the furnace of fire. There will be wailing and gnashing of teeth.

Matthew 13:37–41, 49

Jesus' teaching on the role of angels at the end of history emphasized their "law and order" function (see chapter 3). Angels have served as God's agents of justice throughout history, and as history draws to a close, angels will gather "the wicked" for final punishment.

Jesus' Kingdom Parables: Matthew 13

The Parable	Expected Form of the Kingdom	Unexpected Characteristic
1. The Sower 13:3–9, 18–23	Messiah turns *Israel,* all *nations* to Himself.	*Individuals* respond to the Word differently.
2. Wheat and Tares 13:24–30, 37–43	The kingdom's righteous citizens *rule over* the world with the King.	The kingdom's citizens are *among* the people of the world and grow together until God's harvest time.
3. Mustard Seed 13:31, 32	The kingdom *begins* in *power and glory.*	The kingdom *begins in insignificance,* with its greatness coming as a surprise.
4. Leaven 13:33	Only the righteous *enter* the kingdom; others are *excluded.*	The kingdom is *implanted* in a sinner's heart and *grows* to fill the personality.
5. Hidden Treasure 13:44	The kingdom is *public* and for all.	The kingdom is *hidden* and for individual "purchase."
6. Priceless Pearl 13:45, 46	The kingdom *brings* all things that people value to them.	The kingdom demands we *abandon* all other values in favor of God's values.
7. Dragnet 13:47–50	The kingdom *begins* with the separation of the righteous and the unrighteous.	The kingdom *ends* with the separation of unrighteous from the righteous.

Jesus' teaching on angels in Matthew 16:27. Matthew 16 is the theological turning point of this Gospel. Until this point, Jesus directed His message about His messiahship and His kingdom to the Jewish people. Now, for the first time, Jesus began to speak of His coming death and to direct His message to the individuals who will choose to follow Him. In Matthew 16:24–28 Jesus called His followers to complete commitment. They could abandon their own worldly interests and follow Him, or they could choose to live for themselves. If they chose the latter, they would lose themselves* and never be what they could become by following Jesus. An individual can choose what might seem temporarily to be benefits, but doing so means that one will know poverty in God's future.

Jesus put this thought in context by reminding His disciples: "For the Son of Man will come in the glory of His Father with His angels, and then He will reward each according to his works" (16:27). Again, we see that Jesus' teaching on angels concerned the fu-

ture; but this time the focus was not on punishment, rather it was on the rewards awaiting those who commit to follow Him. Here, the angels disperse and enhance God's glory; and when they appear with Christ, they will inspire awe.

Jesus' teaching on angels in Matthew 18. This chapter records an incident in which Jesus called a child to Him, and then called on His disciples to be as responsive as the child was to His word. He also told them to guard the quality of "childlikeness" in each other. Jesus concluded, "Take heed that you do not despise one of these little ones, for I say to you that in heaven their angels always see the face of My Father who is in heaven" (18:10).

This passage has been taken as strong support for the concept that each believer has a guardian angel, and that this is particularly true for children. In essence, Jesus said that children are represented in heaven by members of God's heavenly host, that angels are especially close to God (they see God's face), and that angels are ready at any moment to respond should God send them to the aid of the children in their charge.

---

* In the idiom of the day, "soul" often served as a reflexive pronoun; that is, it means "the person himself" or "the person herself."

ANGELORE:

JOHN CALVIN ON GUARDIAN ANGELS

The point on which the Scriptures specially insist is that which tends most to our comfort, and to the confirmation of our faith, namely, that angels are the ministers and dispensers of the divine bounty towards us. Accordingly, we are told how they watch for our safety, how they undertake our defense, direct our path, and take heed that no evil befall us. There are whole passages which relate, in the first instance, to Christ, the Head of the Church, and after him to all believers. "He shall give his angels charge over thee, to keep thee in all thy ways. They shall bear thee up in their hands, lest thou dash thy foot against a stone." Again, "The angel of the Lord encampeth round about them that fear him, and delivereth them."

By these passages the Lord shows that the protection of those whom he has undertaken to defend he has delegated to his angels. . . . Whether each believer has a single angel assigned to him for his defense, I dare not positively affirm. When Christ says that the angels of children always behold the face of His Father, he insinuates that there are certain angels to whom their safety has been entrusted. But I know not if it can be inferred from this, that each believer has his own angel. This, indeed, I hold for certain, that each of us is cared for, not by one angel merely, but that all with one consent watch for our safety (*Institutes*, Book 1).

Jesus' teaching on angels in Matthew 22. Jesus was challenged by a group of religious leaders who rejected the supernatural, and thus denied the existence of angels or the possibility of resurrection. The Sadducees presented Christ with a case that they used against the Pharisees, a group of religious leaders who affirmed the supernatural.

Old Testament Law required a man to marry his dead brother's wife if she had no son. The first son from such a marriage would be considered the heir of the dead brother, and carry his name (Deut. 25:5, 6). The Sad-

ducees, using this requirement as a premise, concocted a hypothetical case in which a woman had married seven brothers, who died in succession, before her own death. With a smirk, the Sadducees asked Christ, "Therefore, in the resurrection, whose wife of the seven will she be?" This case puzzled the Pharisees and was an embarrassment to them, but Christ had a ready answer. He told his questioners that their error was rooted in their failure to know the Scriptures and the power of God. Jesus explained, "For in the resurrection they neither marry nor are given in marriage, but are like angels of God in heaven" (22:30).

This verse has often been misunderstood and misapplied, so we must carefully distinguish between what Jesus did and did not teach. First, Jesus taught that angels do not marry. This follows from the fact that the whole company of angels was created before our universe (see Job 38:7). Angels do not procreate, so the institution of marriage does not apply. We've also seen that in every one of their appearances angels are spoken of as "men." There is no indication in the Old Testament that angels are of two sexes. When He said that the saved in heaven are "like the angels," Christ meant like them *in this regard.* There will be no continuation of marriage or procreation in eternity. Life in heaven will not be like life on earth.

Sadly, Jesus' very specific teaching has often been understood to imply things that Christ Himself did not say.

1. Jesus did not teach that people become angels when they die. Angels and human beings are distinctively different orders of created beings.
2. Jesus did not teach that angels cloaked as humans cannot have intercourse with human women. He simply stated that there was no marriage in heaven.
3. Jesus did not teach that a person will have no intimate relationships with his or her spouse and other loved ones in heaven. The relationships we build now will be

deepened and strengthened in eternity as we come to know one another more perfectly and love one another more purely. What Jesus' words suggest is that in heaven sexual intercourse will no longer be needed to bond a couple in intimacy. We can expect something far better when we join the Lord in glory.

Jesus' teaching on angels in Matthew 24—25. Matthew's purpose in writing his Gospel was to show that Christ's mission was in harmony with that of the Old Testament Messiah and, by so doing, to lead his own people, the Jews, to faith in Christ. Therefore, Matthew constantly linked Old Testament prophecies to events in Christ's life in order to show how Christ fulfilled, or will fulfill, the prophets' vision of God's kingdom on earth.

In Matthew 24—25 Christ answered two questions raised by His disciples, who said, "Tell us, when will these things be? And what will be the sign of Your coming, and of the end of the age?" (24:3). Jesus answered the question about the sign of His coming in Matthew 24:30–46. His teaching on angels was embedded in an extended discussion of His return to earth.

"And He will send His angels with a great sound of a trumpet, and they will gather together His elect from the four winds, from one end of heaven to the other" (24:31).

"But of that day and hour no one knows, not even the angels of heaven, but My Father only" (24:36).

"When the Son of Man comes in His glory, and all the holy angels with Him, then He will sit on the throne of His glory" (25:31).

These three passages sum up the role of God's angels at Christ's return. Not even the angels know when Jesus will come back to establish His rule on earth, but before that event Christ will send His angels to gather together all those on earth who trust Him. Then Jesus will come personally, in glory, accompanied by *all* the holy angels. Christ will sit on His throne, as the prophets foretold, to rule in glory. The kingdom which began in weakness, with its king crucified and His subjects in hiding, will end with the glorious revelation of the power of God.

JESUS' TEACHINGS ABOUT GOD'S ANGELS IN THE GOSPEL OF MARK

Jesus' teaching on angels in Mark 8:38. Jesus warned everyone "in this adulterous and sinful generation" not to be ashamed of Him and His words. The word "shame" in this context means to fear the ridicule of others. It is important not only to do right, but also to take pride in the right action itself rather than depend on the approval of others. We are to be far more concerned about what the Lord thinks of us. Choosing the wrong lifestyle is important, for Jesus warned that the person who is ashamed of Jesus, "of him the Son of Man also will be ashamed when He comes in the glory of His Father with the holy angels."

Angels are watching all we do now. When Jesus returns, the choices we made will be on open display for the angels and everyone else to see.

Jesus' teaching on God's angels in Mark 12:25. Jesus said that when believers rise from the dead "they neither marry nor are given in marriage, but are like angels in heaven." See the discussion of Matthew 28:30, p. 166.

Jesus' teaching on God's angels in Mark 13:27, 32. Mark repeated two teachings that correspond to Matthew 24—25. "And then He will send His angels, and gather together His elect from the four winds, from the farthest part of earth to the farthest part of heaven" (Mark 13:27). And: "But of that day and hour no one knows, not even the angels in heaven" (Mark 13:32).

JESUS' TEACHINGS ABOUT GOD'S ANGELS IN THE GOSPEL OF LUKE

Jesus' teaching on angels in Luke 9:26. "For whoever is ashamed of Me and My words, of him the Son of Man will be ashamed when He comes in His own glory, and in His Father's, and of the holy angels." See the discussion of this teaching in Mark 8:38, p. 167.

Jesus' teaching on angels in Luke 12:8, 9.
Luke quoted Jesus as saying, "Whoever confesses Me before men, him the Son of Man also will confess before the angels of God. But he who denies Me before men will be denied before the angels of God."

This saying makes a different point than the parallel passage in Mark 8. The word rendered "confess" is *homologeō* and it is used here in its basic sense of "to acknowledge." The religious meaning of the term is defined in the Old Testament, as the *Expository Dictionary of Bible Words* (1985, p. 16) explains:

To acknowledge God means more than to recognize his power and presence. It implies a deep personal response. That response is one of moral commitment rather than simply intellectual assent. Thus, where God is not known (acknowledged) "there is no faithfulness, no love. . . . There is only cursing, lying and murder, stealing and adultery; they break all bounds, and bloodshed follows bloodshed" (Hos. 4:1–2). In contrast Jeremiah recalls the reign of a godly king with these words. " 'He did what was right and just, so all went well with him. He defended the cause of the poor and needy, and so all went well. Is that not what it means to know [*yada'*, acknowledge] me,' declares the Lord" (Jer. 22:15–16).

Acknowledging, or knowing, the Lord implies a deep personal commitment to God, expressed in moral and personal transformation. On the basis of God's self-revelation we make a commitment of ourselves to him, acknowledging him as Lord of our lives. Only this full commitment adequately expresses what the OT means in its call for us to acknowledge God (cf. Pr. 3:5–6).

Some commentators have suggested that Luke 12:9 depicts a scene in heaven which implies a courtroom setting in which Jesus plays the role of prosecutor and defense attorney, which was common in the Old Testament legal system. Those who made a personal commitment to the Lord which results in a godly lifestyle that can be seen by all will benefit from having Christ as their defense attorney. Those who made no such commitment, who in essence denied (rejected) Christ's claims, must face the accusations of the angels who have observed them all their lives and must then face Jesus Himself as prosecutor.

Jesus' teaching on angels in Luke 15:10.
"Likewise I say to you, there is joy in the presence of the angels of God over one sinner who repents." God's angels truly are involved in our lives and committed to God's plan. Angels witnessed Christ's coming, His life, His death, and His resurrection, and they understand that all this was for us. It is no wonder that angels—who, as individual beings, were endowed with emotions—rejoice when a single sinner turns to the Lord.

Jesus' teaching on angels in Luke 16:22. "So it was that the beggar died, and was carried by the angels to Abraham's bosom." We do not die alone. Angels joyfully await us on the other side, eager to carry us to the Lord.

Jesus' teaching on angels in Luke 20:36. Luke repeated Jesus' teaching that there is no marriage in the resurrection. However, Luke added a saying the other Gospel writers chose not to report: "nor can they die anymore, for they are equal to the angels and are sons of God, being sons of the resurrection."

In the Old Testament the phrase "sons of God" was used with regard to angels in order to indicate that they were members of a class of beings created directly by the Lord. There is neither birth nor death among angels. Here Jesus says of our resurrection that, like the angels, we will no longer be subject to death, for the believer, like the angels, is a child of God, a member of a group created by the work of the Holy Spirit. The book of Ephesians develops that thought when it says, "We are His workmanship, created in Christ Jesus for good works, which God prepared beforehand that we should walk in them" (Eph. 2:10).

Each of the Gospels, except John, records some of Jesus' teaching about angels. The Gospel of Matthew includes teachings which fit the theme of Christ as present and coming King. The Gospel of Mark contains teachings on angels that correspond to those in Matthew. Luke, however, added fresh material which emphasized the humanity, love, and compassion of our Lord.

JESUS' RELATIONSHIP TO GOD'S ANGELS

To this point we've learned that angels were active in Jesus' life on earth, and we have examined Jesus' teachings about angels as recorded in the Gospels. Although the Gospels seem to assume that Christ is superior to angels, the exact relationship between Jesus and angels has not yet been specified—but that relationship is spelled out in the book of Hebrews.

Hebrews was written by a Jewish-Christian, who had a specific purpose in mind—to convince wavering believers who were strongly attracted to Jewish ways that God's revelation in Christ was the fulfillment of, and thus was superior to, the Old Testament revelation. The belief that angels played a role in the giving of Moses' Law, which governed every aspect of Israel's way of life, was part of the Law's mystique which made it so attractive to the average Jew. So at the very beginning of the book of Hebrews, the writer took pains to demonstrate that Jesus is superior to God's angels in every way. As we trace the development of the writer's reasoning in Hebrews 1, we immediately see the distinctions made in Scripture between Jesus and God's angels.

Jesus is a unique individual (Hebrews 1:1–3). These three verses contain seven statements about Jesus:

1. Jesus is "heir of all things." In the first century, an "heir" retained all rights of "lawful possession." Jesus, as Son of God, holds rightful title to the universe and all it contains.
2. Jesus is the one "through whom also He [God] made the worlds" [tous aiōnas, literally means "the ages"]. Jesus is the master of history, who from the beginning has guided all things toward God's intended end.
3. Jesus is "the brightness of His [God's] glory." The phrase means that Jesus shines with God's own glory.
4. Jesus is the "express image of His [God's] person." The Greek word *character* was used to denote a press that stamped an image on a coin. Here, the phrase means that Jesus bears the stamp of God's essential nature.
5. Even now, Jesus is "upholding all things by the word of His power." The very existence of natural law depends on the active involvement of the Son of God.
6. Jesus "purged our sins." The awesome cosmic Being described by the writer has shown concern for *us* by personally cleansing us of our sins.
7. Jesus "sat down at the right hand of the Majesty on high." The phrase "sat down" symbolizes rest; "right hand" symbolizes the place of honor. Christ's redemptive work complete, He has been restored to His original glory.

Surely no angel is equal to Christ, and the writer proves that by drawing specific comparisons.

God never acknowledged angels as "My Son" (Hebrews 1:5–7). The writer quotes several Messianic texts from the Old Testament which identify the Messiah as God's Son. The phrase "when He again brings the firstborn into the world" has been distorted by cults intent on arguing that Christ is "a" god, but not "the" God. What they do not understand is the quasi-legal way "firstborn" was used in the biblical world—to establish the *status* of a son. Here, as firstborn (*prōtotokos*) Jesus has the status of heir to all the universe. The Old Testament speaks of angels as *worshiping* Christ, and it describes angels as "ministers of flame" under His control.

Scripture makes it clear that Christ is far greater than angels.

God never invited angels to rule His universe (Hebrews 1:8–14). The writer of Hebrews quotes the Old Testament again, this time the messianic psalms, to show that God called His

Son to the throne of the universe, which He created and which He will outlast. God never said to any angel: "Sit at My right hand" (that is, share My throne and rule). Instead, He called angels "ministering spirits" and sent them to minister to the human beings who will inherit salvation. Angels, despite their innate superiority to humans, are servants of believers, and thus lower than humans.

There is absolutely no way—neither with respect to identity, nor glory, nor status, nor role in God's universe—that angels can compare to Christ. The writer of Hebrews issues a warning.

Therefore we must give the more earnest heed to the things we have heard, lest we drift away. For if the word spoken through angels proved steadfast, and every transgression and disobedience received a just reward, how shall we escape if we neglect so great a salvation, which at the first began to be spoken by the Lord, and was confirmed to us by those who heard Him.

Hebrews 2:1–3

Since Christ is so much greater than angels, the revelation given in Christ must be far greater than the revelation given through angels—and it surely must not be neglected.

The writer of Hebrews reminds his readers that angels not only played a role in the transmission of the Law, but that they also have a law and order function as administrators of the Law. If every transgression of the angel-borne Law received a "just reward," how much more serious is it to "neglect so great a salvation" inherent in Christ?

Surely this is a question we need to ask today, when so many are caught up in another outbreak of "angel fever." We must never permit a fascination with angels to cause us to neglect Christ, who is far greater than angels. And we must never let those who espouse doctrines supposedly delivered by angels turn our hearts from a simple faith in the salvation provided so freely by the Son of God.

CHAPTER 11

GOD'S ANGELS IN ACTS AND IN THE EPISTLES:

CONTINUING THEIR MINISTRY

Acts—Jude

At the beginning of the book of Acts, Jesus returned to heaven. During the first few years after Christ's resurrection and ascension, angels appeared on numerous occasions to support Christ's followers as they met the challenge of spreading the gospel. The story of one such incident is found in Acts 12.

ANGEL ACTIVITY IS THE SAME IN THE OLD AND NEW TESTAMENTS
(Acts 12)

Herod Agrippa I was the grandson of Herod the Great (the Herod of the Christmas story). Agrippa, a childhood intimate of the emperor Claudius, was a personal friend of the imperial family in Rome. After the Romans made Herod Agrippa the client king of his grandfather's lands, he actively sought the support of his Jewish subjects. He played the part of an observant Jew, carefully observing all the rituals and following every rule. Herod Agrippa moved the seat of the province from Caesarea to Jerusalem, and he then began to rebuild Jerusalem's northern wall. In addition, Herod Agrippa was able to prevent the mad

emperor Caligula from erecting a statue of himself in the Jerusalem temple.

Those actions won him the people's affection. The Jewish mishna relates how this king of Edomite origin showed his respect for the Scriptures when he stood to read from Deuteronomy 17:14–20 at a celebration of the Feast of Tabernacles.

King Agrippa received it [the holy book] standing and read it standing, and for this the Sages praised him. And when he reached "Thou mayest not put a foreigner over thee which is not thy brother," his eyes flowed with tears; but they called out to him, "Our brother art thou! Our brother art thou! Our brother art thou!"

So it's not surprising that Herod would regard the suppression of Christians, a divisive faction in Jerusalem, as a wise policy. When Herod Agrippa executed the apostle James—who, along with his brother John, was one of Christ's earliest followers—the Jewish leaders were delighted. To please them even more, Herod Agrippa also seized Peter. Herod Agrippa was unable to bring Peter to trial and execution until after Passover, an important religious holiday. So he put Peter in a cell under heavy guard. Peter's execution would serve Herod Agrippa's political purposes well. Whether Peter had done anything to deserve death was irrelevant.

Peter was imprisoned in Antonia, the fortress just beyond the magnificent temple Herod the Great had spent thirty-eight years and untold millions enhancing. Normally, important prisoners kept under guard were chained to one soldier. The political significance that Agrippa attached to the execution of Peter is indicated by the fact that the apostle was "bound with two chains between two soldiers" (12:6, NKJV). In addition, guards were placed outside the locked cell door. Herod Agrippa's careful arrangements were useless, however, for "an angel of the Lord stood by him [Peter], and a light shone in the prison; and he struck Peter on the side and raised him up" (12:7).

Stories of angelic deliverance from prison were common biblical lore, so at first Peter assumed that he was dreaming. Peter saw the chains drop from his wrists. He saw the soldiers seated there, unmoving. Peter saw himself stoop to pick up the outer cloak he'd used as a blanket as he slept on the stone floor. Peter even tied on his sandals, wrapping the leather thongs carefully around each calf. Then Peter followed the angel out of the prison, past the great iron gate that swung open of its own accord, and out into the city. It wasn't until they had walked some distance from the fortress and the angel departed that Peter realized it wasn't a vision. The night before his scheduled execution, Peter was liberated by an angel!

While Peter was in prison, many Christians gathered to pray. Even as Peter was being led from the prison, Christians were praying in the home of Mary, the mother of John Mark (who later would write the second Gospel). It was to her house that Peter walked that night.

In first-century Jerusalem the wealthy lived in walled homes. Large gates were set in the outer wall and were opened only on special occasions. Smaller doors were built into the large gates. Peter knocked on the smaller "door of the gate" (12:13) when he arrived at Mary's house.

A girl named Rhoda was serving as doorkeeper, or porter, that night. It was her duty to respond to anyone who knocked. Rhoda recognized Peter's voice, but she was so excited that she neglected to open the door. Instead, she ran to tell the congregation inside the good news. The believers, certain she was wrong, tried to calm her, but she kept on insisting.

This incident is encouraging for those who have the notion that their prayers can be answered only if they have an unshakable faith. Here the church was, praying earnestly, yet certain that Peter couldn't possibly be outside the door. Surely, God couldn't have answered *their* prayer. But He did!

ANGELORE

"IT IS HIS ANGEL"

Rhoda recognized Peter's voice and, in her excitement, she ran to tell those inside Mary's house the good news. When they finally were convinced the girl had heard Peter's voice, they still could not believe that Peter was actually outside. Instead, they insisted, "It is his angel." What did they mean?

They did not mean to suggest it was Peter's ghost. In first-century Judaism, it was commonly believed that a guardian angel closely resembled the human being he guarded. Apparently, that resemblance extended to the angel's voice, as well as to his appearance.

This story doesn't end here, however. The divine intervention that won Peter's release also resulted in the execution of the guards. Even Herod Agrippa himself did not escape.

Josephus, the first-century Jewish historian, gave an account of Herod Agrippa's death in his *Antiquities* (XIX, viii.2, 343–50). His account is clearly independent of Luke's, but the two are similar in structure and share many details in common. Both make it clear that

Agrippa was stricken while the crowds praised him as a god.

Honoring rulers as deities was common in the Hellenistic world. An entry in a child's exercise book, quoted by A. D. Nock in *Conversion* (1933, p. 91), reads, "What is a god? That which is strong. What is a king? He who is equal to the divine." Sacrifices offered *for* a king's well-being often slipped over the already blurred line to become sacrifices made *to* the king. A first-century inscription honors King Antiochus I of Commagene as "The Great King Antiochus, the God, the Righteous One, the Manifest Deity."

In Judaism, however, the practice of honoring rulers as deities was viewed as a depraved form of blasphemy. When Herod Agrippa accepted the divine honors offered him, the book of Acts tells us: "Then immediately an angel of the Lord struck him, because he did not give glory to God. And he was eaten by worms and died" (Acts 12:23). The king was probably killed by intestinal roundworms, which grow to a length of ten to fourteen inches. Clusters of roundworms can obstruct the intestine, which causes severe pain.

Josephus provided a graphic description of Herod Agrippa's demise. He writes that Herod Agrippa was "overcome by more intense pain. . . . Exhausted after five straight days by the pain in the abdomen, he departed this life in the fifty-fourth year of his life and the seventh of his reign."

Two events, the release of Peter and the death of Herod Agrippa, were undoubtedly linked in the minds of first-century Christians. A pagan king who pretended to live as a pious Jew had threatened the existence of the early church. The angel who protected Peter from execution was also God's agent in carrying out the death sentence passed on the persecutor of the church. The conclusion was inescapable: Angels are the friends and protectors of God's own, but they are a terror to His enemies.

There is another inescapable conclusion to be drawn from this story. The angels of New Testament times had the same ministries as those of Old Testament times:

- Angels are God's agents who carry out His will.
- Angels guard and protect believers.
- Angels, like the one who delivered Daniel from the lions, still deliver believers threatened with death.
- Angels often come in answer to prayer.
- Angels are agents of God's justice, carrying out His sentence on those who go too far in their sin.

EVERY ANGEL ENCOUNTER IN THE BOOK OF ACTS

The book of Acts picks up the story of Jesus and His followers after His resurrection and provides reports of selected events that occurred over the next three decades. The author—Luke, who also wrote the third Gospel—recounts what happened first in Jerusalem, tells about the spread of the gospel from Palestine to nearby regions, and then traces the missionary activities of the apostle Paul and his companions as they carry the gospel to the major cities of the Roman Empire. Angels appear frequently throughout this period.

In fact, given that the story of Acts is compressed into a span of three decades, there are more accounts of angel intervention during this period than in any other period of biblical history, excluding the Exodus.

TWO ANGELS SPOKE TO THE APOSTLES AS THEY WATCHED JESUS ASCEND INTO HEAVEN (*Acts 1:10, 11*)

Some 40 days after Jesus' resurrection, He rose into heaven, an event witnessed by some 500 persons gathered on the Mount of Olives (see 1 Cor. 15:6). As the apostles watched Jesus rise higher and higher, until he disappeared from view, "two men stood by them in white apparel" (1:10). Angel appearances exhibit several common features, and a review of those features indicates that the "two men" were angels. First, angels, when they appear to human beings, are normally cloaked as men.

The biblical texts frequently describe them as men, specifically, as masculine human beings. Second, the Gospels especially describe angels who appear as men as being dressed in white. At times, an adjective is added to describe the angels' garments, such as "dazzling white" or "white as snow." There is a brightness about angels when they appear in their natural form—they appear human, but their aspect shines.

The two angels at the beginning of Acts had a message for Christ's followers: "Men of Galilee, why do you stand gazing up into heaven? This same Jesus, who was taken up from you into heaven, will so come in like manner as you saw Him go into heaven" (1:11). The Greek word *angelos,* like the Hebrew *mal'ak,* means "messenger" or "envoy." These two angels were carrying out the function implied by their name—they were delivering God's message to Jesus' followers.

Moments before Jesus ascended into heaven, the apostles asked Him if He was going to fulfill the prophets' dreams: "Lord, will You at this time restore the kingdom to Israel?" (1:6). Jesus told them that the "when" was something only God knows, something human beings are not to know. Instead, Jesus told them, they were to return to Jerusalem to await their empowerment by the Holy Spirit, and more: "You shall be witnesses to Me in Jerusalem, and in all Judea and Samaria, and to the end of the earth." The apostles watched as Jesus departed, and then the angels appeared. The angels told them not to stand gazing upward; the apostles were to do what Jesus told them to do. In God's own time, Christ will return—bodily, visibly, in the clouds— just as He left. In the meantime, the text implies, the apostles were to be about Jesus' business.

This message applies to us as well. We are not to be a people who simply stand around, gazing into heaven. The boundaries of our age begin with the departure of Jesus to heaven and end with His return. Between those boundaries, we, like the apostles, are to be Jesus' witnesses to the end of the earth.

AN ANGEL RELEASED THE APOSTLES FROM PRISON
(Acts 5:19)

On the Day of Pentecost, some 50 days after Jesus' death, the Holy Spirit filled Jesus' disciples and they began to preach. Peter's sermon on that occasion led to some 3,000 conversions (Acts 2). Quickly, fresh questions arose about Jesus. Could He have been the Messiah after all? When Peter and John healed a cripple at the temple gate and used the occasion to preach another powerful sermon (Acts 3), the leaders who had plotted Christ's death were greatly disturbed. They took Peter and John into custody and were shocked when the two apostles boldly witnessed to *them* (4:1–12).

Although the Jewish leaders threatened them, Jesus' followers kept preaching. The community of Christians lived such a loving lifestyle (4:32–37) that they won the approval of the whole population, and many more were converted to faith in Christ. When the apos-

Peter and John were released from prison by an angel.

tles began to perform many healing miracles, and people from cities around Jerusalem flocked to them, the officials panicked. They arrested the apostles and placed them "in the common prison" (5:18). Acts describes the next angel encounter this way:

But at night an angel of the Lord opened the prison doors and brought them out, and said, "Go, stand in the temple and speak to the people all the words of this life." And when they heard that, they entered the temple early in the morning and taught. But the high priest and those with him came and called the council together, with all the elders of the children of Israel, and sent to the prison to have them brought. But when the officers came and did not find them in prison, they returned and reported, saying, "Indeed we found the prison shut securely, and the guards standing outside before the doors; but when we opened them, we found no one inside!"

Acts 5:19–23

Rather than transport the apostles out of the prison, as the angels did for Lot and his family (Gen. 19), the angel opened the door, escorted them out, and then apparently closed the door and locked it, while remaining invisible and unnoticed by the guards posted there. Presumably, the angel also cast a cloak of invisibility around the apostles, for the guards failed to notice them as well.

One of the things we notice here, and in many other stories of angels in the Bible, is that angels are not just spirits or "ghostlike" beings. They can and do affect objects and people in the material world. Opening prison doors, material or spiritual, is something angels do well.

AN ANGEL SENT PHILIP ON A MISSION   (Acts 8:20)

At first the church was localized in Jerusalem, but the gospel message spread as visitors to Jerusalem went back to their homes in Judea. After a time, intense persecution occurred in Jerusalem, so intense that most of the believers were forced to leave the city. The believers scattered throughout Judea and into Samaria (8:1), but as they scattered, they went "preaching the word" (8:4). The Greek word translated "preaching" might be understood as "gossiping." Everywhere they went, the early Christians talked about Jesus.

It's not surprising that one of the early church's deacons, Philip, stimulated a great turning to the Lord in the city of Samaria, especially since his preaching was accompanied by healing miracles and exorcisms. While "revival" was at its peak,

an angel of the Lord spoke to Philip, saying, "Arise and go toward the south along the road which goes down from Jerusalem to Gaza." This is desert. So he arose and went.

Acts 8:26, 27

The angel did not explain the message. He simply told Philip where to go, and Philip went there. Philip's quick response is a tribute to his faith; it is also another indication of the self-authenticating nature of angelic messages. It may have made no sense to Philip to leave a "revival" and head into the desert, but he did not question; he simply followed the angel's instructions. To the eyes of faith, the truth is clear. To those who doubt, angelic messenger or no, truth is difficult ⌐ distinguish from falsehood.

The purpose of Philip's mission soon became clear. Philip met an official of the queen of Ethiopia. The text identifies him as a "eunuch." Earlier rulers employed men who were castrated in their youth as officials on the assumption that eunuchs, since they were without families or other sexual entanglements, would have less reason to betray them. In time, a person holding certain high offices was addressed by the title "eunuch," whether or not he was a eunuch physically. Since the official in Acts had come to Jerusalem to worship, and since true eunuchs were not permitted to attend services at the temple, he was most likely a whole man.

What is important here is that the eunuch was reading a prophecy about Christ from Isaiah 53, but he did not understand it. Philip explained the passage to him, the eunuch believed, and he was baptized. Philip had been taken away from a ministry to multitudes to reach a single individual.

We should never assume that only the Billy Grahams of history are important. Anyone who reaches a single individual with the gospel is responding to angels' words.

CORNELIUS WAS DIRECTED BY ANGELS TO SEND FOR PETER
(Acts 10)

Cornelius was a retired officer of the Roman army who had settled in Caesarea Mamartea, a city on the Mediterranean coast with a spectacular man-made harbor. It had been constructed by Herod the Great and was the seat of the Roman governor. Cornelius is described as a "devout man and one who feared God with all his household, who gave alms generously to the people, and prayed to God always" (10:2). The term "feared God" is a technical one. A person who believed in Israel's God but did not go through the ceremony of conversion or adopt the lifestyle given Israel in the Mosaic Law was called a "God-fearer," and there were many in the Roman world. The Old Testament's clear vision of the God of Creation, whose pure moral code defined right and wrong unambiguously, was attractive to many in the relativistic world of the first century.

Cornelius, then, was a Gentile who believed in the God of the Jews; his generosity and commitment to prayer demonstrated the sincerity of his faith. When an angel, visible in his natural form (see 10:30), appeared to Cornelius in a vision, this brave military man was afraid, and so the angel reassured him: "Your prayers and your alms have come up for a memorial before God." Then the angel instructed Cornelius: "Now send men to Joppa, and send for Simon whose surname is Peter. He is lodging with Simon, a tanner, whose house is by the sea. He will tell you what you must do" (10:4–6).

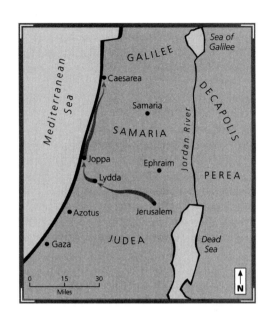

The angel left, and Cornelius immediately sent men to approach Peter. Meanwhile, Peter was prepared for their visit by a vision and told by the Holy Spirit to accompany the men sent by Cornelius.

In the first century no pious Jew who was dedicated to keeping Old Testament Law as interpreted by the rabbis would enter the house of a Gentile. Such an act was considered to so defile a person that he would be ritually "unclean" and unable to participate in worship until he had been ritually "cleansed." Had he not had the vision, Peter would never have gone to a Roman officer's house. The messengers told Peter that Cornelius had been "divinely instructed by a holy angel" to summon him (10:22), so this angel encounter was important. Later, when Peter gave his report about what had happened at Cornelius's home, he was careful to mention the angel who instructed Cornelius to call for him (11:13).

When Peter arrived he found Cornelius and a large group of his clients (that is, free men and slaves who owed Cornelius loyalty for a variety of reasons, commonly called his "household") waiting. Peter shared the gospel, and Cornelius, together with "all those who heard the word," believed (10:44).

Two things about this angel and his mission are of interest. First, the angel sent a person to share the gospel message, as was also the case with Philip in Acts 8. The angel did not speak about Jesus directly either to the Ethiopian eunuch or to Cornelius. Today the privilege of sharing the gospel is given only to human beings. Angels can direct us, observe what happens, and rejoice when others respond. However, angels do not serve God as bearers of the good news.

Second, the angel was involved in preparing someone to hear the gospel. The angel's appearance and his words—"he [Peter] will tell you what you must do"—certainly prepared Cornelius's heart. No wonder the Roman officer told Peter, "Now, therefore, we are all present before God, to hear all the things commanded you by God" (10:33).

The conversion of Cornelius and his household marked the first time that Gentiles became Christians, a true turning point in the life of the early church. Within a few decades the predominantly Jewish-Christian church would be opened up, and thousands upon thousands of non-Jews would flock to Christ and then establish Christian congregations throughout the Roman world.

PAUL WAS ENCOURAGED BY AN ANGEL DURING A STORM AT SEA (Acts 27:23)

The seed planted in Caesarea flowered years later. Under the impetus of the apostle Paul, who traveled throughout the Roman Empire preaching Christ and establishing churches, Cornelius was one of many thousands of Gentile Christians.

However, when Paul visited Jerusalem he was the subject of a riot. After his arrest, when it was clear that his case could not be resolved in Judea, Paul exercised his right as a Roman citizen to appeal to Caesar. Paul had a right to be tried in Rome in a capital matter, and his accusers had to travel there to bring their charges. So Paul and his guards set sail for Rome.

On the way to Rome, the ship Paul and his guards traveled on was struck by a fierce fall storm and driven before it. Despite throwing cargo overboard to lighten the ship and passing ropes under its keel to strengthen the hull, the ship seemed on the verge of sinking, and the crew and passengers despaired. Then Paul stood up and delivered an encouraging message.

An angel reassured Paul in the midst of a storm.

"And now I urge you to take heart, for there will be no loss of life among you, but only of the ship. For there stood by me this night an angel of the God to whom I belong and whom I serve. Saying, 'Do not be afraid, Paul; you must be brought before Caesar; and indeed God has granted you all those who sail with you.' Therefore take heart, men, for I believe God that it will be just as it was told me."

Acts 27:22–26

Several things about this story are significant. First, Paul identified the angel's message as God's message. The angel promised, and Paul believed God. The message of an authentic angel is a message from God.

Second, the angel's message was prophetic. The angel told Paul what would happen in the future. Few details were provided about what was to happen and how things would be worked out. We simply know that the ship would be lost, but that every person on it would live. Prophetic messages seldom explain how God will accomplish something, but they do tell what it is that God will do.

Finally, the message was one of encouragement. The angel came after the storm had whipped the ship for days. Messages from angels are often delivered at the time of our greatest need, after our faith has been exercised. However, whether or not you and I receive encouragement from an angel, we can find encouragement in this: We know the God of angels loves us, and angels, though invisible, are hovering around us.

ANGEL MINISTRIES IN THE NEW TESTAMENT ERA ARE THE SAME AS THOSE IN OLD TESTAMENT TIMES

When we compare the stories of angel encounters found in the Old Testament with those in the New Testament, we find striking and compelling similarities. In both Testaments:

- Angels guide and direct believers.
- Angels are depicted as guardians who protect believers from harm.

- Angels deliver God's messages, provide instruction, and predict the future.
- Angels are sent by God to humans to prepare hearts, to commission them for special ministries, and to encourage them.

Angels were active in the lives of believers in both the Old Testament and the New Testament. There is no reason to conclude that angels are less active in the lives of believers today. Throughout sacred history angels have been God's ministers, sent to serve those who are heirs of salvation, and the same is true today. Angels are all around us. We can rely on the God of angels each and every day.

EVERY TEACHING ON ANGELS IN THE EPISTLES

Although the letters written by the leaders of the apostolic church do not contain stories of angel encounters, we find many references to angels in them. There is much for us to learn from the teachings on angels found in the Epistles.

TEACHINGS ABOUT ANGELS IN THE EPISTLES OF PAUL

How could angels threaten our salvation? (Romans 8:38). It's peculiar to think that angels might threaten our salvation. Yet in this verse angels are third on a list of possible threats—death, life, angels and principalities and powers, things present, things future—that have the potential "to separate us from the love of God which is in Christ Jesus our Lord."

Paul, of course, might be referring here to the dark angels who follow Satan. Yet that seems unlikely, for he goes on to mention "principalities and powers," which the New Testament clearly identifies as dark angels.

A better explanation for why angels are on this list lies in their law and order ministry (see chapter 3). We observed earlier that angels are involved in investigating egregious sins and punishing them. Romans 8:38 reminds us about that ministry of angels; it also promises that not even our failures can shake God's love or separate us from it.

This interpretation fits completely the flow of the chapter. Paul directed his attention to the Cross and asked:

Who shall bring a charge against God's elect? It is God who justifies. Who is he who condemns? It is Christ who died, and furthermore is also risen, who is even at the right hand of God, who also makes intercession for us.

Romans 8:33, 34

No wonder Paul was so certain that nothing, nothing at all, "shall be able to separate us from the love of God which is in Christ Jesus our Lord" (8:39).

Are angels watching the way we live? *(1 Corinthians 4:9).* Many members of the church in Corinth were harshly critical of its founder, the apostle Paul. Paul responded to his critics by pointing out that even he was not qualified to judge himself. Paul's goal was to be faithful to God, not to please critics. In verse 9 Paul wrote, "I think that God has displayed us, the apostles, last, as men condemned to death; for we have been made a spectacle to the world, both to angels and to men."

Here, Paul drew an analogy to the gladiator games held in the Roman world. Gladiators were hired to fight each other, or wild animals, in order to create a spectacle for great crowds, such as the eighteen thousand who would gather in the amphitheater in Corinth. The person putting on the games would introduce the gladiators and then, "last of all," he would march in a criminal who was condemned to die that day and who was greeted by the jeers of the crowd.

Paul was saying that he saw himself not as a great leader who demands respect, but as one called by God to suffer for Christ and, in so doing, one who became a spectacle observed intently by both angels and humans. Angels and other people as well closely observe the lives we lead and our faithfulness to the Lord.

Will believers judge angels? *(1 Corinthians 6:3).* Paul criticized the church at Corinth for failure to discipline sin in the congregation, and he chastised individuals for taking disputes into secular courts. He pointed out that the believers themselves were surely qualified to judge such small matters and asked, "Do you not know that we shall judge angels?"

Paul was apparently suggesting that judging angels is something the church at Corinth should already know about, and that this knowledge should have led the congregation to deal with the "things pertaining to this life" among themselves. Since the church at Corinth was predominantly Gentile, perhaps Paul taught them about angels earlier. It is unlikely, as some suggest, that this verse reflects the Jewish belief that the righteous will judge the nations, expanded by Paul and applied to the fallen angels assigned to influence the leaders of those nations.

How does Israel's history relate to Christian experience? *(1 Corinthians 10:10).* Paul reviewed various judgments on Israel during the Exodus period (10:5–11). "Complaining" was one of the sins of the people, and those who complained "were destroyed by the destroyer," a reference to a destroying angel. In this description of the Exodus, the word for complaining, or murmuring, indicates bitter hostility toward God and contempt for His provision. Israel not only did what God expected, but also suffered the consequences of disobedience.

Do angels speak in tongues? *(1 Corinthians 13:1).* Here, Paul was not referring to the gift of tongues, but to fluency in languages. Angels seem to have the capacity to speak in any human language fluently, whether it be the Egyptian spoken by Hagar (Gen. 16), the Hebrew spoken by Gideon (Judg. 6), the Aramaic spoken by the virgin Mary (Luke 1), or the Greek spoken by Cornelius (Acts 10). It is also likely, as Paul seems to indicate, that angels have a language that they use among themselves.

Paul's point in this passage was this: No matter how talented or gifted a believer may be, no matter how committed or selfless, for a believer to be driven to do things by any motive other than love means that the believer cannot profit from his or her actions, no matter what they are. One may give generously, and what is given will surely benefit the recipients; but without love, a gift will do nothing to warm the heart or enrich the life of the giver.

Do angels care about the role of women in the church? *(1 Corinthians 11:10)*. The passage has long been debated and frequently misunderstood. In it, the apostle Paul affirmed the right of women to pray and prophesy in church meetings (1 Cor. 11:5), but he insisted that they do so with their heads covered. In a lengthy discussion, Paul argued his case from the order of creation (11:3–9), from the interdependence of the sexes (11:11, 12), and from cultural expectations of proper attire (11:13–15).

In the midst of these reasoned arguments, Paul wrote, "for this reason the woman ought to have *a symbol of* authority on her head, because of the angels" (11:10). It is important to note that the words "a symbol of" are italicized in the NKJV text, indicating that they do not appear in the original Greek text. Many have assumed that the woman's head covering is a symbol of *man's authority over her* and of woman's subordination to man. This interpretation, however, is highly doubtful. It is more likely that the head covering is a sign of a *woman's authority* to participate fully in the life of the church.

In these verses we see the overenthusiastic reaction of women who suddenly discovered that, in Christ, they were equal citizens of Christ's kingdom, equally gifted, and equally called to be kingdom builders. They overreacted, as did the women of the 1960s who signaled their equality with men by rejecting feminine clothing and manners. Some of the women at Corinth overreacted by abandoning the head covering which was then seen as fit-

ting for women. If, in Christ, they were now equal to men, they would adopt this feature of men's dress.

Paul, however, told them to keep wearing their head coverings. He pointed out that while equal, men and women are different. This difference is rooted in the creation order and demonstrated in the continuing interdependence of men and women, and it is *not* demeaning. What wearing the head covering when they pray or prophesy actually symbolizes is *their own authority* to participate in church meetings just as men do!

This was a stunning element in Christian worship. In Judaism women were separated from men in the synagogue, and a *minyan,* or quorum, of ten males was necessary to convene a worship service. In the pagan world, cults tended to serve men or women rather than both. In Rome the cult of the Great Mother was for women only. The eastern cult of Mithras was for military men. In the official cult of the Roman Empire, only men served in its priesthood or as augurs.

Then suddenly, Christianity invaded this divided world and invited Jew and Gentile, male and female, slave and free, to participate together as full and equal members of the unified body of Christ and as equal recipients of the Holy Spirit and His gifts (see Gal. 3:28). No wonder many women wanted to find ways to express their new freedom and status. Paul's instruction here, however, is a word of caution. "Women, never express your freedom in a way that implicitly denies your femininity. You are fully accepted as women. Do nothing to suggest that you can be acceptable only if you are like a man."

But why would Paul want women to wear head coverings as a symbol of their own authority "because of the angels"? The answer may lie in 1 Peter 1:12, which tells us that everything about the salvation we have is intensely interesting to angels. Even angels do not fully understand what God is doing through the church in human lives, and this they eagerly "desire to look into." When men and women worship together as equals, a unique dimension of our salvation is displayed, and angels stand in awe.

How important then to be careful always to display the uniqueness of the way that the gospel transforms every relationship and all that we do—especially in the church of God.

What does it mean to be "an angel of light?" (2 Corinthians 11:14). We will examine how this verse relates to Satan's activities in more detail later (see chapter 14). For the moment, it is sufficient to note that the phrase "angel of light" has a double meaning.

On the one hand, the phrase indicates the brightness or radiance that marks the aspect of angels when they appear in their natural form. Metaphorically, "light" has moral and spiritual connotations. Spiritual darkness is an evil power that holds people in its grip. On the other hand, the phrase identifies the source of an angel's light. Jesus is "the light of the world" (John 8:12), and believers are called "children of light" (Eph. 5:8). God's angels are radiant beings who, by nature, are members of the kingdom of light.

Do angels preach the gospel? (Galatians 1:8). The mission of sharing the gospel has been entrusted to human beings. Even the angel who appeared to the Roman centurion, Cornelius, did not share the gospel but told him to send for Peter and promised that Peter would tell him what he must do (Acts 10:3–6).

In this verse, Paul insisted: "But even if we, or an angel from heaven, preach any other gospel to you than what we have preached to you, let him be accursed." We should recall that in the first century many religions claimed that their teaching was based on revelations given by angels. Indeed, the Old Testament makes it clear that fallen angels—demons—were behind pagan religions. Paul was not suggesting that he or any angel from heaven *would* preach another gospel. Only an angel from hell would do so. Paul wanted to make it extremely clear that there *was* no other gospel and that the Galatians were to ac-

cept no modification of the gospel he preached to them.

How are angels related to the Mosaic Law? (Galatians 3:19). In this passage the apostle Paul specified the weaknesses of Mosaic Law and pointed out that it was impossible for the Law to give life. Paul anticipated the obvious question: "What purpose then does the Law serve?" His response? "It was added because of transgressions, till the Seed [Christ] should come to whom the promise was made; and it was appointed through angels by the hand of a mediator." We can better understand what Paul is saying if we diagram the verse as it appears in Greek—as one statement modified first by time and then by cause.

> Answer: It was added because of transgressions,
> Modification: until the Seed should come . . .
> Modification: since it was put into effect by angels through a mediator.

Paul's point concerning angels was one that the Old Testament also made. Angels served as ministers of God's justice, both in the giving of the Law and in the punishment of those who failed to keep it. God's Law, therefore, has to do with justice. However, Christ came bringing the mercy and forgiveness promised by God in the Abrahamic covenant. The Law—administered by angels—is not a matter of grace, but of works. The gospel—introduced by God's own Son—is a matter of grace apart from works. (For more on the ministry of angels' justice, see chapter 3.)

How are angelic hosts organized? (Galatians 6:12). Several verses in Scripture refer to Satan's angels by various names. One of the clearest references to dark angels is found in Ephesians 6:12, where Paul encouraged believers to put on "the whole armor of God" and explained why:

For we do not wrestle against flesh and blood, but against principalities, against powers, against the rulers of the darkness of this age, against spiritual hosts of wickedness in the heavenly places.

Other New Testament passages refer to dark supernatural beings—Satan's angels—and identify them as: thrones, dominions, principalities, and powers (see Rom. 8:28; Col. 1:16; 2:15; 1 Pet. 3:22). These evil angels, Paul claimed in Ephesians, are "the rulers of the darkness of this age" and "spiritual hosts of wickedness in the heavenly places."

In chapter 9, we observed that different classes of God's angels exist, such as angels, seraphim, and cherubim. We also noted that angels are referred to in a variety of ways—holy ones, sons of God, 'elohim (supernatural beings)—or are simply described as "men." When we add the testimony of Daniel 10, which spoke of both dark angels and good angels as "princes" with different ranks, whose assignment was to influence nations, the natural conclusion is that there is a hierarchy of supernatural beings who inhabit the spiritual world.

That idea has fascinated many through the centuries, and numerous attempts have been made to determine the hierarchy of angels. Most attempts have mixed Scripture's categories of good angels and evil angels. Although Satan *was* a cherub before his fall (Ex. 28), that was his *former* status. Thus, it seems better to assume that the angels who remained faithful to the Lord have their own hierarchy and that Satan's angels have a distinctive hierarchy of their own. Because the information we have is very limited, any proposed hierarchy of angelic beings is a guess at best.

The hierarchy presented here is based on (1) the relative brightness of God's angels and their closeness (proximity) to Him and (2) the sequence in which Satan's angels are mentioned in New Testament texts.

God's angels	Satan's angels
Seraphim	Thrones
Cherubim	Dominions
Archangels	Principalities
Angels	Powers

ANGELORE

ORDERS OF ANGELS IN THE HEAVENLY HIERARCHY

Here are three of the many rankings of angels found in Christian writings. Jewish and Islamic writings provide other rankings.

Ambrose	Gregory the Great	John of Damascus
1. Seraphim	1. Seraphim	1. Seraphim
2. Cherubim	2. Cherubim	2. Cherubim
3. Powers	3. Thrones	3. Thrones
4. Dominions	4. Dominions	4. Dominions
5. Thrones	5. Principalities	5. Powers
6. Archangels	6. Powers	6. Authorities
7. Angels	7. Virtues	7. Rulers
	8. Archangels	8. Archangels
	9. Angels	9. Angels

What should be our attitude toward angels? (*Colossians 2:18, 19*). It is well-established that during the first century angels were held in awe. In Colossians 2 Paul warned against the delight some took in "false humility and worship of angels." The word "false" does not appear in the original text. Paul was referring to ascetic practices—which involved fasting and sleep deprivation ("neglect of the body"; 2:23)—by means of which individuals sought to obtain special revelations from, or visions of, angels. Although the worship of angels was discouraged in traditional Judaism, many Jews of the Diaspora (Jews living in Gentile cities outside the homeland) did pray to angels and even used the names of angels in magical formulae.

According to Paul, all of that was inappropriate. We can respect angels and their powers, but we are to hold "fast to the Head [Christ], from whom all the body, nourished and knit together by joints and ligaments, grows with the increase that is from God" (2:19).

Will Jesus return alone? *(1 Thessalonians 3:13).* Paul prayed for the believers in the young church at Thessalonica that they might abound in love toward each other and that their hearts might be blameless "before our God and Father at the coming of our Lord Jesus Christ with all His saints."

Although the NKJV translates *hagioi* as "saints" here, it is best to understand *hagioi* as a reference to angels rather than believers. Angels are frequently called "holy ones" in the Old Testament, and the Gospels make it clear that when Christ returns He will be accompanied by all of God's angels (see Matt. 25:31).

What will God's angels do when Jesus returns? *(2 Thessalonians 1:7).* The church at Thessalonica experienced serious persecutions and troubles. Paul praised the believers for their continuing response to the gospel, and he reminded them that

"it is a righteous thing with God to repay with tribulation those who trouble you, and to give you who are troubled rest with us when the Lord Jesus is revealed from heaven with His mighty angels, in flaming fire taking vengeance on those who do not know God."

2 Thessalonians 1:6–8

God's angels do administer justice in this universe. When Christ returns, the angels will execute their law and order duties, and those who persecuted God's people will receive what their attitude and actions deserve.

Why was it important for Christ to be "seen by angels"? *(1 Timothy 3:16).* This verse records what was undoubtedly an early Christian confession of faith or hymn. Christians have always believed that in Christ:

- God was manifest in the flesh;
- Justified in the Spirit (that is, His claims were validated by His resurrection);
- Seen by angels;
- Preached among the Gentiles;

- Believed on in the world;
- Received into glory.

The phrase "seen by angels" reminds us that angels are not omnipotent. However, angels are vitally interested in everything that God does; they are eager to understand Him better and to glorify Him for His wisdom and all His other attributes.

Who are the best witnesses to the way we keep our commitments? *(1 Timothy 5:21).* Paul charged Timothy to exercise his ministry without partiality. Paul reminded Timothy that there are witnesses to the charge he received—"God and the Lord Jesus Christ and the elect angels." There is no chance that these witnesses will die or be unavailable to observe what Timothy does. God, Christ, and angels are therefore ideal witnesses, for they will always be there to confirm the commission given and to see how well it is carried out.

What is the relationship of angels to Jesus Christ? *(Hebrews 1).* See the discussion of this passage on p. 169.

What is the relationship of angels to human beings? *(Hebrews 2).* See the discussion of this passage on p. 50.

What do the angels who were active at Sinai have to do with the Christian revelation? *(Hebrews 12:22).* Hebrews was written to convince Jewish believers, who deeply appreciated their ancient faith, that Christianity is a fulfillment of the Old Testament revelation and superior to it. Psalm 68:17 spoke of the involvement of angels in the giving of the Law. By the first century, some rabbis suggested that there were thousands of angels at Sinai for every Israelite. Here, the writer of Hebrews compared the two revelations.

One revelation was given on an earthly mountain "that may be touched" (12:18), while the other revelation was given on a mountain in the "heavenly Jerusalem." Just as significant, while there were angels at Sinai, there is "an innumerable company of angels" in the heavenly Jerusalem (12:22). Surely,

The hospitality of Abraham.

❖

there are more angels in heaven than could have assembled at Sinai! And all of the angels in heaven are deeply involved in the revelation brought by God's Son.

What is one good reason for entertaining strangers? *(Hebrews 13:2).* The writer of Hebrews referred to an incident reported in Genesis 18, where Abraham showed hospitality to three men—who, he later learned, were angels. The writer of Hebrews suggested that it was a good thing for Christians to entertain strangers because one day a stranger might turn out to be an angel. This is one of the clearest indications in the New Testament that there are angels among us now, some of whom may come into our lives cloaked as humans.

❖

ANGELORE

DO ANGELS WALK AMONG US NOW?

Hebrews 13:2 clearly suggests that angels cloaked as men may walk among us today, just as they did among people of the Old Testament. Here are two stories retold from Tracy Mullins's book, *Breakfast with Angels* (1996). Read and judge for yourself.

Margaret was going to the dentist's office when two Doberman Pinschers charged out of their front yard and sandwiched her between them. No one driving by noticed the danger. Then, suddenly, a young man jumped out of a pickup truck, crossed through the traffic, and with a word and a gesture sent the dogs back into their yard. Then he walked back through traffic to the truck. Noticing that he had signaled a left turn into a parking lot, she hurried to thank him. They should have arrived simultaneously. But when she arrived, there was no young man. And no truck.

When a young naval officer traveling in the Alps with his family came to a six-foot gap in the road, he took the children ahead to the next town while his wife remained in the car. All their belongings were in that car. As night began to fall she remembered the words of Psalm 9:11–12. Suddenly she just blurted out, "Lord, send some of your angels. Please."

A moment later a truck appeared, out of which climbed six rough-looking men. Without saying a word they carried their truck over the washout, and then picked up her car—with her in it!—and set it on the other side of the gap. She drove into the village and found her family. Nobody in the village had any idea of who the men might be.

❖

What do angels have to learn? *(1 Peter 1:12).* At the beginning of this letter Peter wrote about the wonders of our salvation. He pointed out that the prophets who predicted Christ's coming, who searched the ancient prophecies to understand the meaning of "the sufferings of Christ and the glories that would follow," and who wanted to know when those things would occur—those prophets of old prophesied of a grace that was to come to those who followed Christ and believed in Him (1:10, 11). They did understand that the wonderful salvation God had in mind was not for their own times. Moreover, they were never able to grasp the implications of the salvation we now experience—"things which angels desire to look into" (1:12). How fascinating it is to realize that angels closely watch our lives to discover how the salvation we have been granted will find fresh expression in us!

To whom are all angels now subject? *(1 Peter 3:22).* After the Resurrection, Christ returned to heaven and to power. Peter's words remind us that now "angels and authorities and powers" have been made subject to Him. Even the evil powers who may cause us to "suffer for righteousness' sake" (3:14) are under the control of Christ. If we should suffer, it is because God has a purpose in mind, even as He had our salvation in mind when He permitted His Son to suffer rather than punish the unrighteous, who should have been crucified instead of Him.

Who were the "angels who sinned"? *(2 Peter 2:4; Jude 6, 7).* To answer this question, we must first look for clues provided in the surrounding context of this verse which reads: "For if God did not spare the angels who sinned, but cast them down to hell and delivered them into chains of darkness, to be reserved for judgment." Two clues are readily

apparent: First, the context locates this event in the time of Noah (2 Pet. 2:5); and second, the context links this event with the sexual perversion of Sodom and Gomorrah (2 Pet. 2:6, 7).

Another clue is provided in Jude 6, which reads: "And the angels who did not keep their proper domain, but left their own abode, He has reserved in everlasting chains under darkness for the judgment of the great day." This text links the transgression of "the angels who sinned" with that of the men of Sodom even more explicitly than does 2 Peter. The passage continues:

as Sodom and Gomorrah, and the cities around them in a similar manner to these, having given themselves over to sexual immorality and gone after strange flesh, are set forth as an example, suffering the vengeance of eternal fire.

Jude 7

These two verses (Jude 6, 7) seem to indicate that the sin of the angels who "did not keep their proper domain" was going after "strange [that is, forbidden] flesh."

These passages in 2 Peter and Jude provide what is undoubtedly the strongest sup-

Fallen angels in chains.

port for the theory that the "sons of God" in Genesis 6:1–3 were indeed angels who appeared in their cloaked form as humans and had sex with human women, which produced "nephilim." These angels, unlike other angels who rebelled with Satan, are now in chains awaiting judgment. The other dark angels, whom we know as demons, remain free for a time.

Do angels show respect for authority? *(2 Peter 2:11).* Peter described the characteristics of the false teachers who threatened the church from within. Among their unattractive qualities: they were "presumptuous, self-willed" and they were "not afraid to speak evil of dignitaries" (2:10). Peter pointed out that angels, "who are greater in power and might, do not bring a reviling accusation" before the Lord against "dignitaries" (a term which, in the first century, might apply to human rulers or to demons). Angels have qualities which we might do well to emulate.

Who are the angels in chains today? *(Jude 6).* See the comments on 2 Peter 2:4, p. 185.

SUMMARY

The book of Acts and the Epistles have much to tell us about angels. The angel encounters reported in Acts are extremely similar to those reported in the Old Testament. The Old and the New Testaments seem to agree that angels have certain characteristic features and specific functions and duties. Hence, we may conclude that angels have similar ministries today.

Although the Epistles do not record angel encounters, they do contain many references to angels that add important details and enhance our understanding of angels, both the good and the evil kind.

CHAPTER 12

ANGELS AT WORSHIP:

CEASELESS PRAISE AND SERVICE

Psalms; Revelation

The English scholar and saint, the Venerable Bede, never missed the gatherings for worship at his monastery. "I know," he said, "that angels come to the canonical hours and visit our monastic communities; what would they say if they did not find me there among my brethren?" We know from reading Scripture that angels worship God, but we may never have stopped to think this: Angels may assemble with us when we gather for worship.

Psalm 148 calls on all that exists to worship the Lord. That call is directed first to the heavens, where God is most intimately known:

Praise the LORD!
Praise the LORD from the heavens;
Praise Him in the heights!
Praise Him, all His angels;
Praise Him, all His hosts!
Praise Him, sun and moon;
Praise Him, all you stars of light!
Praise Him, you heavens of heavens,
And you waters above the heavens!

Psalm 148:1–4 (NKJV)

Why praise God?

Let them praise the name of the
LORD,
For He commanded and they were
created.
He also established them forever and
ever;
He made a decree which shall not
pass away.

Psalm 148:5, 6

All of creation—including "Both young men and maidens; / Old men and children" (Ps. 148:12)—are to praise God.

Let them praise the name of the
LORD,
For His name alone is exalted;
His glory is above the earth and
heaven.

Psalm 148:13

THE NATURE OF WORSHIP AND PRAISE

Before we look at passages depicting angels at worship, we need to define "worship" and "praise."

OLD TESTAMENT WORDS FOR "WORSHIP"

The word translated "worship" in the Old Testament is usually a form of the Hebrew word *sahah,* which means "to bow down," literally "to prostrate oneself out of respect." In Old Testament times people prostrated themselves before kings and others of high status as a sign of extreme respect. It would be far more appropriate for one to prostrate oneself before God out of respect for His supreme position in the universe. In a few instances, *'asab,* which means "to serve," is also translated as "worship."

NEW TESTAMENT WORDS FOR "WORSHIP"

Several Greek words are translated as "worship" in our English versions of the Bible. One of them, *latreuō,* which means "to serve," was used by the translators of the Old Testament into Greek (the Septuagint) to render the Hebrew *'asab.* In most cases where *latreuō* is used in the New Testament, it refers to some element of cultic worship at the tabernacle or temple. However, *latreuō* is also used three times with regard to Christian worship, once by Luke (Acts 24:14) and twice by Paul (Rom. 1:9; Phil. 3:3). In all three of these instances, *latreuō* refers to living a life of service to the Lord as an act of worship. *Sebomai* and its cognates are used occasionally in the sense of "worship," especially when the emphasis is on showing reverence.

The word used for worship most frequently in the New Testament is *proskyneō,* which means "to bow down" or "to prostrate oneself." This word is used of worship that is, or should be, directed only to God, it occurs some 60 times in the New Testament, 24 times in Revelation. Although worship is a matter of the heart which expresses an inner and personal relationship with God, worship can also be a public act which expresses the relationship of a group of humans or angels to God (see John 12:20; Acts 8:27; 24:11). In Revelation, worship (*proskyneō*) clearly involves praise and adoration.

OLD TESTAMENT WORDS FOR "PRAISE"

A number of Hebrew words are associated with the praise of God. Certain forms of *halal* mean "to acclaim," "to glory in," or "to boast of." The basic idea is one of finding deep satisfaction in exalting the qualities and acts of the one being praised.

Yadah and *todah* are translated "to praise," "to confess," and "to give thanks." These words focus on the act of acknowledging God's works and His character. Essentially, *yadah* is praise that focuses on God's goodness, a praise through which one is filled with the joy of knowing Him personally.

Zāmar means "to sing praise" or "to make music." While there is no positive evidence that angels sing, this term is found only in Bible poetry, and its use there strongly suggests that there are angelic, as well as earthly, choirs who praise God in song. *Zāmar* is found in contexts where the focus is on who God is and what He has done.

Certain forms of *sabah* mean "to praise" or "to commend." Adoring praise is directed to the Lord, as God is exalted for the mighty and wonderful works He has done. The psalmist expresses this well:

> Great is the LORD, and greatly to
>   be praised;
> And His greatness is unsearchable.
> One generation shall praise Your
>   works to another,
> And shall declare Your mighty acts.
> I will meditate on the
>   glorious splendor of
>   Your majesty,
> And on Your wondrous works.
> Men shall speak of the might
>   of Your awesome acts,
> And I will declare Your greatness.
> They shall utter the memory of
>   Your great goodness,
> And shall sing of Your
>   righteousness.
>
> *Psalm 145:3–7*

The *Expository Dictionary of Bible Words* (p. 494) identifies the common elements in Old Testament words for praise:

(1) Praise is addressed to God or his "name." God himself, his attributes, or his acts are the content of our thoughts, words, and songs. (2) Praise is linked with the believing community's joy in the person of God. Most praise in the OT is corporate, though an individual certainly could praise God in private. Most praise comes from those who are filled with a sense of joy in who God is and in how deeply he is committed to his people. (3) Praise exalts the Lord. It is in praise that the believer implicitly acknowledges creaturely dependence on God and explicitly acknowledges God's greatness and goodness.

NEW TESTAMENT WORDS FOR "PRAISE"

The essential nature of praise is established in the Old Testament, and no passage in the New Testament modifies its character. However, various Greek words are used to express the elements of praise.

Aineō, "to praise," is the word most commonly used in the Septuagint to translate Hebrew words for praise. In the New Testament, the object of *aineō* is God alone. *Epaineō* means "to commend" and carries with it the sense of praising. It is used in the context of commending people and praising the Lord. *Eulogeō* means "to bless" or "to speak well of." *Exomologeō* means "to confess" or "to acknowledge," and it is translated "praise" in Luke 10:21 and Matthew 11:25 (NIV). Several other words are also used to express the idea of praise, such as *hymneō*, "to sing a hymn," "to sing praises"; *psallō*, "to sing psalms"; and *megalynō*, "to magnify."

By far the most common word for praise in the New Testament is *doxazō*. *Doxazō* occurs 62 times; it means "to give glory to" or "to glorify," and it is often translated "to praise." At times, the noun *doxa* is used with the verb "to give" to mean "praise" ("to give glory").

The New Testament language of praise is as rich and varied as that of the Old Testament. The Bible teaches that we should never lose sight of the fact that it is God we praise and that we praise God by recounting His works and expressing delight in His qualities. As we praise the Lord, we exalt God far above anything in His creation.

ANGELS AT WORSHIP

The first books of the Bible never picture angels at worship. As salvation history unfolds in Scripture, we catch glimpses of angels worshiping, until in Revelation we encounter a heaven filled with angelic praise. An examination of how angels worship God will enable us to learn how we can better worship Him.

ANGELS AT WORSHIP IN THE PENTATEUCH

The Pentateuch contains many reports of angel encounters. Angels deliver, instruct, predict the future, investigate sin, promise, and provide protection. Angels judge the Egyptians, lead Israel out of servitude, and fight with the Israelites against the Canaanites. However, there is no portrait of angels at worship in the first five books of the Bible.

ANGELS AT WORSHIP IN THE HISTORICAL BOOKS

The Historical Books also tell many stories of angel encounters. Angels commission Gideon, instruct Samson's parents, strengthen Elijah, and later take him up to heaven. Angels stand between Elisha and a Syrian army, and deliver Jerusalem by striking dead 185,000 Assyrian soldiers. We see angels active in our world, but we are not taken into their world to see their relationship with God. There are no passages about angels at worship in the Historical Books of the Old Testament.

ANGELS AT WORSHIP IN THE POETIC BOOKS

When we come to the Books of Poetry there is a dramatic shift. Now and then these books provide glimpses of one of the most significant ministries of angels—the worship and praise of God. Here, for the first time, the curtain between the material and spiritual realms is drawn back slightly, and we are allowed to peer into a region that is almost beyond our capacity to imagine.

Angels praised God at the Creation (*Job 38:7*). In Job 38 God Himself spoke to Job from a whirlwind (tornado). He challenged Job, who demanded to see and speak with Him, by focusing Job's awareness on who He actually is. In the immediate context, God urged Job to consider the creation, and specifically to compare himself to the One who laid the foundations of the earth. God challenged Job to explain,

> Who determined its measurements?
> . . .
>
> To what were its foundations
>   fastened?
> Or who laid its cornerstone,
> When the morning stars sang
>   together,
> And all the sons of God shouted for
>   joy?
>
> *Job 38:5–7*

❖

Angels at the Creation.

In Hebrew poetry the arrangement of thoughts, rather than rhyming words, is central. Here, the parallelism between "morning stars" and "sons of God" makes it clear that God was referring to angels by each of these unique titles.

The scene pictured here is incredible. God alone created the material universe, but He was not unobserved. Before the Lord made our heavens and earth or shaped humanity from earth's dust, He peopled the spiritual realm with hosts of angels. At the moment of Creation the angels gathered around, an awed and awesome choir, watching God fling the stars across the heavens, peering intently as He created, and then carefully shaped, earth as a home for humankind.

The angels' response was to sing together and shout for joy. Yet they did not sing about the majesty of the universe or rejoice in the beauty of the earth. The angels' songs of praise and shouts of joy were for the Lord Himself, who displayed His wisdom and power in the creative act.

One of the first things we learn from angels about worship is that a focus on God and His acts fills the hearts of worshipers with joy. We worship God for who He is, but in the process of worship our own hearts are filled with song and delight. That truth is reflected in the Westminster Catechism's answer to the question, "What is the chief end of man?" The answer, taught here by angels and throughout the Scriptures is, "The chief end of man is to glorify God and to enjoy Him forever."

Angels worship God by serving Him (*Psalm 103:20*). The psalm begins with the psalmist's call to his own heart:

> Bless the LORD, O my soul;
> And all that is within me, bless
>   His holy name!
> Bless the LORD, O my soul,
> And forget not all His benefits.
>
> *Psalm 103:1, 2*

In the Old Testament, blessings were pronounced on subordinates by those in authority. How then can we "bless" the Lord? The general thought is that when believers recognize the Lord as gracious and faithful, to "bless" Him is to acknowledge His goodness with praise. Yet the example of angels went even further. Verses 20–22 of this psalm read:

Bless the LORD, you His angels,
Who excel in strength, who
do His Word,
Heeding the voice of His Word.
Bless the LORD, all you His
hosts,
You ministers of His, who do His
pleasure.
Bless the LORD, all His works,
In all places of His dominion.
Bless the LORD, O my soul!

Clearly, the angels blessed the Lord not only by praising Him, but also by doing His word, heeding the voice of His word, and doing His pleasure. This threefold emphasis on obediently responding to God's word and will sensitizes us to an essential element in worship. Worship is *an appropriate response to God's word whatever that word to us may be.*

Worship is not simply singing praises or participating in worship services. Angels bless the Lord by serving as His ministers, ever ready to do His pleasure. When the psalmist cried, "Bless the LORD, all His works," he called for universal submission to the will of God as an appropriate act of worship. When he concluded, "Bless the LORD, O my soul," the psalmist acknowledged the fact that he worshiped God most purely by an eager readiness to do His will. The same is true for us.

Angels praise God as the Creator (*Psalm 148*). The psalmist called on the heavens, the heights, all God's angels, and all His hosts, along with the material creation, to praise God as Creator. This psalm brings Creation into an even sharper focus. Angels and the material universe are to praise God as *their* Creator:

Let them praise the name of the
LORD,

For He commanded and they were
created.
He also established them forever and
ever;
He made a decree which shall not
pass away.

Psalm 148:5, 6

Like the angels, we can sing for joy as we see the wonderful work of God expressed in the world we inhabit. The more we learn about the stars that extend creation to unimaginable distances, and the more we learn about the makeup of living things, the more we stand back in utter awe at God's power and wisdom. The angels never forget that God is the source of their very being; He gave each of them life and personal identity.

This is another aspect of creation on which we need to meditate. We should let our meditations move us, just as the psalmist's moved him to praise God:

For You formed my inward parts;
You covered me in my mother's
womb.
I will praise You, for I am fearfully
and wonderfully made;
Marvelous are Your works,
And that my soul knows very well.
My frame was not hidden from You,
When I was made in secret,
And skillfully wrought in the
lowest parts of the earth.
Your eyes saw my substance,
being yet unformed.
And in Your book they all were
written,
The days fashioned for me,
When as yet there was none of
them.

Psalm 139:13–16

We can learn from the angels to worship God not simply as the Creator, but as our Creator—the One who gave us life and who guides us through life on into an eternity to be spent with Him.

ANGELS AT WORSHIP
IN THE PROPHETIC BOOKS

There are few references to angels in the writings of the Old Testament prophets. However, both Isaiah and Ezekiel do provide a glimpse of angels at worship in the presence of God.

Angels cry, "Holy, holy, holy" (Isaiah 6). In this chapter Isaiah reported a vision he had of the Lord seated on His throne in heaven's temple. There were seraphim hovering above the throne, crying to each other, "Holy, holy, holy is the LORD of hosts; / The whole earth is full of His glory!" (6:3).

The cry of the seraphim shook the heavenly temple where the Lord was seated, and this vision of the holy God shook Isaiah as well. Overwhelmed by a sense of his own sinfulness, Isaiah said, "Woe is me, for I am un-

done! / Because I am a man of unclean lips." Immediately, one of the seraphim carried a live coal from the temple's altar, touched it to Isaiah's lips, and said, "Behold, this has touched your lips; / Your iniquity is taken away, / and your sin purged" (6:7). Then Isaiah heard the voice of the Lord asking, "Whom shall I send, / And who will go for Us?" And Isaiah responded, "Here am I! Send me" (6:8).

This interaction—between Isaiah, the seraphim, and God—and the three shouts of "holy" are interrelated:

- God is holy, and in sensing this we see ourselves as sinners.
- God is holy, yet in His holiness He reaches out to cleanse us and forgive us.
- God is holy, and we who have had our iniquity taken away joyfully respond, "Here am I!"—ready to serve.

Isaiah was overwhelmed by his vision of God in heaven.

The ones who hear only the first "holy" are aware of their sin, but strangers to forgiveness. The ones who also hear the second "holy" are cleansed, but are all too often complacent. The ones who hear the angels' cry of "Holy, holy, holy," and echo it in their hearts, become forgiven sinners who commit themselves to do God's will. The angels who hover about God's throne praised Him as the thrice holy. The ones who see themselves as sinners, who come to Christ for salvation, and who go on to live for Him—only they *experience* the deepest meaning of the angel's cry.

Angels cry, "Blessed is the glory of the Lord" *(Ezekiel 3:12)*. Ezekiel saw a vision of the Lord accompanied by cherubim, which he wrote down in chapters 1—3 of his book. Toward the end of the vision Ezekiel said, "Then the Spirit lifted me up, and I heard behind me a great thunderous voice: 'Blessed is the glory of the LORD from His place!' "

There is some question as to whether the last part of verse 12 is a phrase shouted by an angel in praise of God or, as the CEV renders it, simply a statement: "And as the glory of the LORD started to leave, I heard a loud, thundering voice behind me." Another possibility, that it is an interjection by Ezekiel, is reflected in the NIV: "May the glory of the Lord be praised in his dwelling place." If we accept the NKJ version, what would an angel mean by shouting, "Blessed is the glory of the LORD"?

The *Expository Dictionary of Bible Words* (pp. 310–311) offers an explanation:

In the OT, the glory of God is intimately linked with the Lord's self-revelation. There is much imagery: a blazing splendor and flaming holiness mark his presence. But neither raw power nor burning holiness adequately expresses God. . . .

But "glory" implies more than a disclosure by God of who he is. It implies an invasion of the material universe, an expression of God's active presence among his people. Thus, the OT consistently links the term "glory" with the presence of God among Israel in tabernacle and temple (e.g., Ex. 29:43; Ezek. 43:4–5; Hag. 2:3). God's objective glory is revealed by his coming to be present with us, his people, and to show us himself by his actions in our world.

What is our response to be? We are to "ascribe to the LORD glory" (1 Chron. 16:10) and to "glory in his holy name" (1 Chron. 16:10). We are to worship him by recognizing his presence and praising him for those qualities that his actions for us unveil.

Thus the angel's shout—"Blessed is the glory of the Lord from His place"—is an expression of praise, rooted in the experience of being in God's presence and seeing God express Himself in our world "from His place."

The angel's voice teaches us to be ever aware that God is present with us now. We are to learn to discern Him in both the common and uncommon events of our day and to rejoice that God is willing to step from His place into ours, to accompany us on our way.

ANGELS AT WORSHIP IN THE GOSPELS

The Gospels contain only one passage in which the veil between the two realms is drawn back momentarily for us to see angels at worship. Even that passage at first seems to be an angel encounter rather than a glimpse into heaven.

Luke relates that on the night Christ was born, shepherds in the fields saw an angel, who brought them "good tidings of great joy."

And suddenly there was with the angel a multitude of the heavenly host, praising God and saying,

> "Glory to God in the highest,
> and on earth peace to men
> on whom His favor rests."
>
> *(Luke 2:13, 14; NIV)*

This passage seems out of place in a study of verses that portray angels worshiping God, but it is uniquely appropriate because, for the first time, God is now truly on earth, born in Bethlehem. How appropriate that the angels who sang praises at the Creation should now sing praises at the Incarnation! The superlative, "Glory to God in the *highest*" is also appropriate, for while God's wisdom and power are displayed in His creation, only the Incarnation expresses the fullness of His love and grace. This is the fitting fulfillment of the words first written in Psalm 97 and quoted in Hebrews 1:6: "But when He again brings the firstborn into the world, He says: 'Let all the angels of God worship Him.' "

ANGELS AT WORSHIP
IN THE EPISTLES

The Epistles contain many teachings about angels, but they do not describe angels at worship.

ANGELS AT WORSHIP
IN REVELATION

The book of Revelation is the record of an extended vision the apostle John had while he was in exile on the Island of Patmos near the end of the first century A.D. The first three chapters report what transpired as John stood on Patmos. The fourth chapter begins with an angel calling to John from heaven, "Come up here, and I will show you things which must take place afterward" (4:1). The rest of the vision is viewed from the standpoint of heaven, where John was shown what is to happen on the earth and saw what was happening in heaven. One of the things John saw was angels at worship.

Angels worshiped God for Himself and as Creator *(Revelation 4:8–11).* One of the first things John saw was God sitting on heaven's throne, surrounded by angels (identified as "living creatures").

The four living creatures . . . do not rest day or night, saying:

> "Holy, holy, holy,
> Lord God Almighty,
> Who was and is and is to come!"

Whenever the living creatures give glory and honor and thanks to Him who sits on the throne, who lives forever and ever, the twenty-four elders* fall down before Him who sits on the throne and worship Him who lives forever and ever, and cast their crowns before the throne, saying:

---

* The twenty-four elders are not identified here or elsewhere in Scripture. Some interpreters regard them as angels, others as representatives of Old and New Testament saints.

John saw heaven as a place of perpetual praise of God.

"You are worthy, O Lord!
To receive glory and honor and
  power;
For You created all things,
And by Your will they exist and were
  created."

Revelation 4:8–11

These angels teach us that it is appropriate to praise God continually, and that we should not only praise God for what He does, but for who He is by nature. God is the Holy One, the Almighty, who has always existed and will exist eternally. He is God, and there is no other being who can compare with Him. Although we may not imitate the constant cry of praise uttered by the angels, we can and should be constantly aware of who God is; and in that awareness we should rely on God completely, giving Him glory for all that He will accomplish through us.

The words of the twenty-four elders echo a theme we have encountered previously in the praises uttered by angels. God is worthy to receive glory and honor and power as Creator. In our day the meaning of the doctrine of creation is too often limited by debates over the seven "days" of Genesis 1 and by the assumption that "creationism" is "unscientific," that it is merely a matter of "faith." In fact, the truth that God created all things, and that all things and all creatures continue to be dependent on Him for their very existence, lies at the heart of Scripture's conception of God. While it is true to say that without God there would be no creation, it is also true to say that without a deep awareness that God is Creator there is no true vision of God. God's very identity and His power are expressed in the angels' praise of Him: "You created all things, / And by Your will they exist and were created" (4:11).

We learn from the angels to praise God as the Eternal and Almighty, and we learn to see His power expressed in Creation. The only appropriate response we can make to God's revelation of Himself is to worship Him, to praise Him, and to thank Him.

Angels praised Christ as the Redeemer of humankind (*Revelation 5:9*). As John observed events in heaven he saw "a Lamb as though it had been slain" (5:6). This is a clear reference to Christ, the Lamb of God, and His work of redemption (see John 1:29, 36). The four angels designated "living creatures" and the twenty-four elders all bowed down before the Lamb and worshiped Him with a "new song":

"You are worthy to take the scroll,
And to open its seals;
For You were slain,
And have redeemed us to God
  by Your blood
Out of every tribe and tongue and
  people and nation,
And have made us kings and priests
  to our God;
And we shall reign on the earth."

Then I looked, and I heard the voice of many angels around the throne, the living creatures, and the elders; and the number of them was ten thousand times ten thousand, and thousands of thousands, saying with a loud voice:

"Worthy is the Lamb who was slain
To receive power and riches and
  wisdom,
And strength and honor and glory
  and blessing!"

And every creature which is in heaven and on the earth and under the earth and such as are in the sea, and all that are in them, I heard saying:

"Blessing and honor and glory and
  power
Be to Him who sits on the throne,
And to the Lamb, forever and
  ever!"

Then the four living creatures said, "Amen!" And the twenty-four elders fell down and worshiped Him who lives forever and ever.

Revelation 5:8–14

In this passage the focus shifts from God the Father to Christ the Son. The angels and elders praised the Father for the creation (4:11), the "new song" sung by elders and angels praised the Son for the redemption of human beings. Redemption was won by the Lamb's blood and it drew human beings to God "out of every tribe and tongue and people and nation" (5:9). Not only that, the Son who redeemed us has purchased a future for us. He has "made us kings and priests to our God, / And we shall reign . . ." (5:10).

In this too we are taught to worship. We worship Christ as the Redeemer who transforms our destiny. We need to remember every moment that He is worthy to receive from His Father "power and riches and wisdom, / And strength and honor and glory and blessing"—and from us, worship and praise.

Angels praised God for the salvation displayed in believers (*Revelation 7:11*). As the vision progressed from stage to stage, John saw a multitude of people who were identified as those who lost their lives in "the great tribulation" because of their faith in Christ. They cry out, "Salvation belongs to our God who sits on the throne, and to the Lamb!" (7:10). At this:

All the angels . . . fell on their faces before the throne and worshiped God, saying:

> "Amen! Blessing and glory and
> wisdom,
> Thanksgiving and honor and
> power and might,
> Be to our God forever and ever.
> Amen."

Revelation 7:11, 12

The angels praised God as Creator and the Lamb as Redeemer. When they saw the saved gathered before His throne, they praised God not for what He had done for them, but for the revelation of Himself that was given in those who responded to the gospel message.

In one sense, our belief in Christ glorifies Him. In another sense, the tribulations suffered by believers glorifies Him. In our continuing commitment to a faith which promises so much for the future—but which at times seems to provide so little here and now—God

receives a portion of the glory and honor due Him.

Angels praised God for His just judgment of sinners (*Revelation 16:5–7*). In Revelation angels praised God for Himself and praised Him as Creator. They praised the Lamb as the Redeemer of humanity, and they praised Him as they saw His salvation transform the saved. While God poured out His wrath on an unbelieving world (16:1–5), an angel praised God for another aspect of His nature which is revealed only in judgment.

> "You are righteous, O Lord,
> The One who is and who was and
> who is to be,
> Because You have judged these things.
> For they have shed the blood
> of saints and prophets,
> And You have given them blood
> to drink,
> For it is their just due."

And I heard another [angel] from the altar saying, "Even so, Lord God Almighty, true and righteous are Your judgments."

Revelation 16:5–7

Revelation's round of four praises reviews central features of God's plan for the ages. God is praised for Himself and for His self-determined existence "forever and ever." God is praised as the Creator of the universe and of each individual. Christ is praised as the Redeemer, and He is praised for the work salvation does in the hearts of humans. Finally, God is praised as Victor over sin, who judges the ones who reject His grace and persist in doing evil.

Just as the angels praised God for Himself and for each element of His plan for the ages, so may we. Together with the apostle Paul and the angels we can lift our hearts and cry:

Oh, the depth of the riches both of the wisdom and knowledge of God! How unsearchable are His judgments and His ways past finding out! . . . For of Him and through Him and to Him are all things, to whom be glory forever. Amen.

Romans 11:33, 36

GOD'S ANGELS AS OBJECTS OF WORSHIP

In his *Institutes* (Book 1), John Calvin wrote that "the minds of many are so struck with the excellence of angelic natures, that they would think them insulted at being subjected to the authority of God, and so made subordinate." We saw in chapter 7 that fallen angels were—and continue to be—worshiped in the guise of pagan deities. We also saw that fallen angels use their supernatural abilities to bind pagans to their idolatry. Why would people be tempted to worship God's angels?

PEOPLE ARE TEMPTED TO WORSHIP ANGELS BECAUSE OF THE AWE EXPERIENCED DURING ANGEL ENCOUNTERS

If we recall the reaction of many individuals to whom angels appeared, we can perhaps understand the temptation to worship angels. A cursory review of the reactions to angels reminds us that when angels appear in their uncloaked form, they are truly impressive.

Daniel wrote about an angel visit: "So he came near where I stood, and when he came I was afraid and fell on my face" (8:17). Later, he described another angel encounter.

His body was like beryl, his face like the appearance of lightning, his eyes like torches of fire, his arms and feet like burnished bronze in color, and the sound of his words like the voice of a multitude. . . . [W]hen I saw this great vision, and no strength remained in me; for my vigor was turned to frailty in me, and I retained no strength.

Daniel 10:6, 8

The New Testament contains reports of similar reactions to angels. Matthew described a scene at Jesus' tomb this way. "His [the angel's] countenance was like lightning, and his clothing as white as snow. And the guards shook for fear of him, and became like dead men" (28:3, 4). Luke reported that believers reacted in a similar way. When they saw two men standing by them in shining garments, "they were afraid and bowed their faces to the earth" (Luke 24:5). The immediate reaction of the human participants in these angel encounters was for them to fall to the ground with their faces toward the earth—the classic position for worshipers in the ancient world. The most important passage on this theme is found in Revelation 22:

Now I, John, saw and heard these things. And when I heard and saw, I fell down to worship before the feet of the angel who showed me these things. Then he said to me, "See that you do not do that. For I am your fellow servant, and of your brethren the prophets, and of those who keep the words of this book. Worship God."

Revelation 22:8, 9

The awesome appearance of uncloaked angels has inspired fear in humans and has elicited an instinctive worshipful response from them. However, angels are simply our fellow creatures, fellow servants of the Lord. We are not to worship angels. We are to worship God.

PEOPLE UNDER THE INFLUENCE OF FALSE DOCTRINE ARE TEMPTED TO WORSHIP ANGELS

In the book of Colossians the apostle Paul warns his readers,

Let no one cheat you of your reward, taking delight in false humility and worship of angels, intruding into those things which he has not seen, vainly puffed up by his fleshly mind, and not holding fast to the Head.

Colossians 2:18, 19

Here, Paul was referring to a worship of angels not rooted in experience ("things which you have not seen"), but in doctrine. Commentators agree that Paul was writing about an early form of a major heresy call "Gnosticism."

What Gnostics believed about God. The Gnostics based their beliefs about God on the propositions "God is good" and "God is Spirit." They also were convinced that the material world was evil. This led the Gnostics to assume that the good God simply could not be personally involved in the material realm in any way. They explained the creation of the "evil" material realm with the supposition that there must be a chain of angelic beings who insulate God from contact with the material. The angels in the chain closest to God are most like Him, while the angels in the chain closest to the material are least like God.

What Gnostics believed about Jesus. The Gnostics were driven by their doctrine to one of two conclusions: Either Jesus was not really a human being, but merely appeared to be human; or Jesus was a real human being who, because He had a material nature, could not possibly be God. To many Gnostics, Jesus seemed little more than a "contact angel," who, because of His involvement in the material realm, must be inferior to angels (in the chain of angels) closer to God. Hence, it followed that the best way to approach God was not to worship Jesus, but to worship the angels who were "above" Jesus in this chain.

What Gnostics believed about salvation. Since the material world was by nature evil, it followed that the human body was evil too. To the Gnostics, the true person could be identified as the spark of the spirit which was imprisoned in the body. Salvation involved developing the inner, spiritual person. To some Gnostics, this called for a denial of bodily desires and pleasures (asceticism). To other Gnostics, it meant letting the body have its way, since what the evil body did could have no impact on the spiritual spark within (hedonism).

No matter which lifestyle a Gnostic might choose, it was clear that what Jesus had done on earth in His body had nothing to do with salvation at all. For nothing done in this evil earthly realm could affect the inner spiritual spark's relationship with a God who is Himself Spirit.

How the Bible contradicts Gnosticism. Throughout the Bible God is portrayed as Cre-

ator of a universe which, according to Genesis 1, is good. It is sin which has corrupted nature, not its material nature. Throughout Scripture God is portrayed as acting in our world and as being present with us. God is not insulated from His creation by any invented chain of angels.

Paul carefully made the point that "in Him [Christ] dwells all the fullness of the Godhead bodily" (Col. 2:9). Jesus was both fully human and fully God. Moreover, Jesus was Himself the Creator, "for by Him all things were created that are in heaven and that are on earth, both visible and invisible" (Col. 1:16). What Jesus did here on earth is the key to our salvation. It was only "in the body of His flesh through death" that we, who were once enemies "in [our] mind," have been reconciled to God (Col. 1:21, 22). Finally, the salvation that Christ brought makes a vital difference in the way we live our lives in this world. Faith is not merely a matter of the mind, but of bringing one's whole life into harmony with God's will (see Col. 3:1–17).

The Bible directly contradicts the teachings of Gnosticism on every essential point. Scripture demonstrates that Gnosticism's doctrine of the worship of angels as an adjunct to salvation is utterly false and wrong. It's no wonder then that Paul warned the Colossians—and us—against the worship of angels. According to Paul, we are to hold "fast to the Head, from whom all the body, nourished and knit together by joints and ligaments, grows with the increase that is from God" (Col. 2:19). Anything—even an unhealthy fascination with angels—that shifts our focus away from Jesus Christ and anything that diminishes our reliance on Him is destructive to spiritual growth.

GOD'S ANGELS MAY WORSHIP WITH US

Revelation provides a picture of humans and angels together worshiping God. Every angel and elder in heaven cried out in praise: "Worthy is the Lamb" (5:12). Then "every creature which is in heaven and on earth" says, "Blessing and honor and glory and power" be to the Lord. Later, a multitude of humans cried out: "Salvation belongs to our

---------------- ❖ ----------------

God" (7:10). After that, the angels and elders said, "Amen! Blessing and glory and wisdom, / Thanksgiving and honor and power and might, / Be to our God forever and ever" (7:12).

Angels and humans are created beings, and we are privileged to worship God together.

Do angels worship with us in our churches now? Two New Testament verses seem to suggest that they do. In 1 Corinthians 11, Paul urged women to dress appropriately when they gathered with men to worship "because of the angels" (11:10). First Peter speaks of the salvation described by the prophets and of our experience of the gospel—"things which angels desire to look into" (1:12).

Each passage suggests a fascinating possibility: When we gather for worship on Sunday mornings, angels are in our congregations. Angels listen intently to the sermon, they sing and pray with us, and they closely observe our ways and worship. What a wonderful possibility! When you sit by what you perceive to be an empty chair or a vacant spot in the pew, there might actually be an angel sitting right there beside you.

CHAPTER 13

JESUS AND SATAN AT WAR:

From Temptation to Triumph

Matthew—John; Epistles

After the birth of Jesus, there was relative quiet in the Holy Land. The Romans collected their taxes, the descendants of Herod played at politics, and ordinary Jews struggled to live under the oppressive burdens of the day. Everyone knew times were hard, but no one felt they were extraordinary.

Then, about 30 years after His birth, Jesus began His public ministry—and suddenly everything seemed to change. It wasn't just that the appearance of the young prophet aroused hopes that He might be the Messiah. What stunned the people of Galilee and of Judea was that Jesus was healing and casting out demons. In fact, Jesus encountered such a flurry of demonic activity that the religious leaders accused Him of being in league with Beelzebub, the prince of demons (Matt. 12:24; Mark 3:22).

Satan, the prince of demons, marshaled all his forces to oppose Jesus. In the next chapter we'll look at Jesus' confrontations with demons. In this chapter we'll concentrate our attention on the opening battle, when the invisible war between God and Satan visibly began to spill over into our world. We will also explore how Satan wages his war today.

THE OPENING BATTLE: THE TEMPTATION OF JESUS

The opening battle is described in Matthew (4:1–11) and Luke (4:1–13) and mentioned in Mark (1:12, 13). Jesus was baptized by John and identified by a voice from heaven as God's beloved Son. All three synoptic Gospels report that it was immediately after this that Jesus was led into the desert to be tempted by the devil. Luke's account reads:

Then Jesus, being filled with the Holy Spirit, returned from the Jordan and was led by the Spirit into the wilderness, being tempted for forty days by the devil. And in those days He ate nothing, and afterward, when they had ended, He was hungry.

And the devil said to Him, "If You are the Son of God, command this stone to become bread."

But Jesus answered him, saying, "It is written, 'Man shall not live by bread alone, but by every word of God.'"

Then the devil, taking Him up onto a high mountain, showed Him all the kingdoms of the world in a moment of time. And the devil said to Him, "All this authority I will give You, and their glory; for this has been delivered to me, and I give it to whomever I wish. Therefore, if You will worship before me, all will be Yours."

And Jesus answered and said to him, "Get behind Me, Satan! For it is written, 'You shall worship the LORD your God, and Him only you shall serve.'"

Then he brought Him to Jerusalem, set Him on the pinnacle of the temple, and said to Him, "If you are the Son of God, throw Yourself down from here. For it is written:

'He shall give His angels charge over you,
    To keep you,'

and,

'In their hands they shall bear you up,
    Lest you dash your foot against a stone.'"

And Jesus answered and said to him, "It has been said, 'You shall not tempt the LORD your God.'"

Now when the devil had ended every temptation, he departed from Him until an opportune time.

Luke 4:1–13 (NKJV)

PARALLELS BETWEEN THE TEMPTATION OF JESUS AND THE TEMPTATION OF EVE

We first met Satan in the guise of a serpent in the first book of the Bible (see chapter 1). From the remainder of Scripture we learn that Satan is a fallen angel. Created as a cherubim and named Lucifer (meaning "light bearer"), this angel desired to supplant his Creator as ruler of the universe. Satan also corrupted other angels, who chose to follow him in his rebellion against the Lord. Those rebel angels fell with their leader. Just as Lucifer was transformed by his sin into Satan, so the other angels who fell with him were transformed into demons.

Our study of demon activity in the Old Testament (chapter 7) showed that supernatural evil beings were behind pagan religions and idolatry, and that they operated through the occult practices associated with pagan religions. Later, we'll examine what the Gospels and the Epistles teach about demon activity in Jesus' time and in our own era (chapters 14 and 15). For the moment, however, our focus is on Satan, the Prince of Demons, whose carefully shaped words deceived Eve and led the first couple into sin—but whose words, just as carefully crafted, failed to deceive Jesus or distract Him from His commitment to do His Father's will. What are parallels between those two temptations?

Each temptation was addressed to innocents. When Satan confronted them, neither Adam nor Eve nor Jesus were burdened by a sinful nature. God created the first pair sinless and pronounced His creation "very good" (Gen. 1:31). Jesus' virgin birth meant that He too was untainted by a sinful nature, a nature which all of Adam's descendants inherited (see Rom. 5:14–21). Greydanus points out that since the Saviour conquered as an innocent, we have proof that humanity's original fall.

was not due to any defect or inadequate equipment of that nature (as God created it), but to the subject of that nature, to man himself, who led his nature wrongly. By the temptations of the Lord and His firmness against all temptation, even the severest, there had thus to be brought to light God's right, man's guilt, sin's culpability, Satan's criminality.

Each temptation was intended to corrupt the individual. Angels and human beings, creatures both, were created to find fulfillment in joyfully doing God's will. Satan's efforts in Eden and in the Judean wilderness were focused on leading the first pair and Jesus to violate the will of God. Adam and Eve surrendered to the temptation, with terrible consequences for them and for us. Jesus did not surrender to the temptation, but remained committed to the will of God. The wonderful consequence for us is that Jesus became the Saviour so desperately needed by sinful humans.

The Greek verb for "tempt" in the New Testament is *peirasmos*. A fascinating distinction in the way *peirazō* is used determines whether it is translated as "to tempt" or "to test." Used in a positive sense, *peirazō* means to test something with a view to demonstrating that it is genuine. The tree God placed in Eden (Gen. 2:16, 17), from which Adam and Eve were not to eat, wasn't placed there to trip up the first pair. The tree was planted to provide an opportunity for them to demonstrate their trust in, and commitment to, the Lord. The distinction between positive testing and negative temptation is not to be found in the Greek term, but in the intent of the one devising the test or the temptation.

When Satan tempts people, he does it to lure them to do evil. This is what is described in both Genesis and Luke. God never tempts anyone to do evil, and nothing can tempt God to do evil (James 1:13–15). God may test people, but He never tempts them. God's intent in permitting us to be tested is to strengthen our faith and to demonstrate its genuineness (1 Pet. 1:6, 7).

In each temptation Satan raised questions about the trustworthiness of God's word. Satan raised doubts in Eve by questioning God's motives—specifically by suggesting that a selfish motive lay behind His command (Gen. 3:4, 5). Satan subtly tried to get Jesus to question both His relationship with the Father and the path chosen for His life. Whereas Eve failed to rely on God's word when she was challenged by the serpent, Jesus responded to each of Satan's temptations by quoting—and then relying on—a word from God.

As we look more closely at each temptation, we'll discover the nature of Satan's approach to temptation, and we will learn more about how we can overcome any temptation which Satan presents to us.

THE FIRST TEMPTATION: IF YOU ARE THE SON OF GOD, TURN STONES INTO BREAD
(Luke 4:1–4)

It was strange. A few days earlier, God had announced from heaven, "You are My beloved Son; in You I am well pleased" (Luke 3:22). Then, as soon as Jesus left the region around the Jordan River, He "was led by the Spirit into the wilderness" (Luke 4:1). After 40 days of fasting in the wilderness, Satan approached Christ with the first temptation.

"When they ended, He was hungry" (Luke 4:2). Although Jesus was the Son of God, He was at the same time fully human. Throughout His incarnation Jesus chose to live under the rules that govern our own lives. The New Testament speaks of times when Jesus was exhausted (Mark 4:38; John 4:6), when He suffered thirst and hunger (Matt. 4:2; John. 4:7; 19:28), and when He was "sorrowful and deeply distressed" (Matt. 26:37). The full humanity of Jesus is underlined in the description of his fast.

Studies of fasting indicate that after the first two or three days hunger disappears. After the body's stored resources have been exhausted, typically in 35 to 40 days, hunger returns. The statement that Jesus was hungry at the end of a forty-day fast tells us that His physical resources had been exhausted. Jesus

"Command this stone to become bread."

was extremely weak physically, and hunger had returned. Jesus experienced exactly what any other human being would experience in the same situation.

"If You are the Son of God, command this stone to become bread" (Luke 4:3). Satan's statement seems strange. Satan surely knew that Jesus was the Son of God, and Jesus was fully aware of His own identity. Just days before, He heard the Father say from heaven: "You are My beloved Son; in You I am well pleased" (Luke 3:22).

To any student of Greek, Satan's message is clear. The Greek language has four classes of conditional ["if"] statements. A first-class conditional statement assumes the condition to be fulfilled; that is, a first-class conditional statement can be read as "since."

The same type of thing can be expressed in English. Suppose a businessperson is complaining about a salesperson. Each night he comes home with another story about his bumbling employee. Finally, this businessperson's wife can't stand it any longer and says, "Listen. If you're the boss, why don't you fire him?" The wife isn't expressing doubt that her husband is the boss. What she's saying is, "Since you're the boss, act like the boss and fire the fellow!"

This is the sense of Satan's words: "Since you're the Son of God, act like God and turn this stone into bread. Don't limit Yourself to acting in Your human nature. Choose to act as who You indeed are—God."

"Man shall not live by bread alone" (Luke 4:4). Jesus responded to this temptation by quoting Deuteronomy 8:3. Several things are significant about His response.

(1) *The first word.* The first word Jesus said was *anthropos,* a Greek word usually to be understood as "humankind" or "human being(s)." A very different Greek word, *anēr,* is used when the intent is to specify a male. Jesus' response to Satan indicated that He was committed to living His life on earth as a human being, sharing fully in the human condition without

using the perquisites of deity to alleviate any suffering.

(2) *The significance of Deuteronomy 8:3.* The verse Jesus quoted reads:

So He humbled you [Israel], allowed you to hunger, and fed you with manna which you did not know nor did your fathers know, that He might make you know that man shall not live by bread alone; but man lives by every word that proceeds from the mouth of the LORD.

The reference here is to the travels of the Israelites after they left Egypt and entered a desert where there were no natural sources of food. It's important to remember that God led the Israelites into the Sinai desert by means of a cloudy and fiery pillar. When the people became hungry, they forgot that it was God who had led them, and they grumbled and complained. However, God intended for them to be hungry so that He could provide them with manna, and so teach them to rely on His every word.

In the same way, the Spirit led Jesus into the Judean desert, and He hungered. God led Jesus, and Jesus' role as a human being was to keep trusting in God until God provided for His needs.

"But by every word of God" (Luke 4:4b). Two Greek terms can be translated as "word." *Logos* has a very broad meaning; in the New Testament, it frequently indicates the entire revelation of God. John referred to Christ as "the Word" in the first verses of his Gospel to show that Jesus is the One who reveals God to humanity. However, the term translated "word" here is *rhēma.* This term focuses attention on a specific word or discrete message. God led Israel into the wilderness by the cloudy and fiery pillar, His *rhēma* to them in that situation. Jesus was also led by the Spirit into the wilderness, and that was God's *rhēma* to Christ: a clear, specific, guiding word that called for obedience.

God's guiding word (*rhēma*) caused both Israel and Jesus to experience hunger. Whereas the Israelites' hunger was momentary,

God provided manna in place of bread during the wilderness years.

Jesus' hunger was intense and demanding, coming as it did after a 40-day fast. Yet, what a difference between their responses! Even God's supply of manna failed to teach Israel that they could rely fully on His word (*rhēma*). However, even God's failure to supply Jesus with food could not shake Christ's confidence in the Father, nor could it alter His commitment to the Father's last word (*rhēma*) to Him.

What Satan hoped to accomplish (*Hebrews 2:17*). The book of Hebrews devotes no less than five chapters to a discussion of Jesus' role as High Priest of what is called the "new covenant." The role of the high priest in Israel's religion was to represent the people before God. Once a year, on the Day of Atonement, the high priest entered the innermost sanctuary of the temple to make a sacrifice which covered all the sins of God's people (Lev. 16:30).

Those Old Testament sacrifices were a foreshadowing of the sacrifice that Jesus, as our High Priest, would one day make on Calvary—Himself—to win forgiveness for all. Hebrews points out that there were certain qualifications that must be met by one called to serve as high priest. Hebrews 5:1 says that the high priest

must be "taken from among men" (that is, be human). Hebrews 2:17 is even more specific. In order to offer Himself as a sacrifice for sins,

therefore, in all things He [Jesus] had to be made like His brethren, that He might be a merciful and faithful High Priest in things pertaining to God, to make propitiation for the sins of the people.

Jesus had to live a truly human life if He was to fulfill His destiny and win our salvation. If Satan had succeeded in tempting Christ to make stones into bread to satisfy His hunger, Jesus would not have been "made like His brethren" "in all things." Such was the hidden significance of what seemed, on the surface, to be such a small temptation to perform an apparently harmless act.

What we learn from the first temptation. There is much for us to learn from Jesus' first temptation. Here are a few lessons that will help us when we are tempted.

(1) *One avenue through which temptation comes is the physical.* We can easily identify grosser temptations: sexual sins, gluttony, the abuse of drugs or alcohol, and so on. However, subtler temptations are rooted in the fact that we must live in the material world.

When Earnie was invited to move from California to the Midwest to take a position with a company there, he felt it was what God wanted him to do. However, it was winter, and he had no winter clothing for his kids— and no money to buy any. Earnie almost rejected the offer, fearing that his children would freeze. Finally, he decided that since the Lord was leading, he must go despite his fears. When Earnie reached the Midwest, he and his family went to a church whose members heard of the family's predicament and outfitted the kids for winter with gifts of outgrown clothing.

As human beings we all have material needs that make us vulnerable. Satan often attacks us by pressuring us to put those needs first when we make a decision. We must learn to listen for a word (*rhēma*) from God and do as He directs.

(2) We are to hold fast to our word from God. Often there is no doubt about what is right. We know, for instance, that sex outside of a marriage between a man and a woman is never right. Many specific teachings in Scripture make this clear. Whatever our temptations or rationalizations, we are to hold fast to this word (*rhēma*) when tempted.

Those who live close to the Lord will often be aware of His leading apart from a clear, specific teaching in Scripture. Our conviction that a particular course of action is God's will may be based on a specific Bible verse or on a sense of the Holy Spirit's direction. In either case, we need to hold fast to that word (*rhēma*), even when things seem to go wrong.

(3) The real significance of a temptation is seldom obvious. The issue Satan raised in his first temptation of Jesus seems simple on the surface. "You're the Son of God. Why go hungry? Use your powers to turn this stone into bread." But the underlying issue was extremely subtle. If Jesus had done what Satan suggested, the act would have disqualified Him as High Priest and made His sacrifice on Calvary meaningless.

We can ponder whether or not Jesus, in His humanity, recognized the subtle trap Satan had set; but what we must learn is that no temptation is as simple as it may seem. Each failure to obey God's word (*rhēma*) to us reverberates through the years and affects our future in ways we cannot imagine. In the same way, each victory over temptation will resonate through our lives and open doors to possibilities we could not begin to gauge at the time. The only safe way to live our lives is to follow Jesus' example and hold fast to every word (*rhēma*) of God as He speaks it to us.

(4) Jesus' victory gives us confidence when we face temptation. Jesus chose to meet His temptations as a human being, without relying in any way on the prerogatives of deity. Because Jesus won His victories as a human, we know that we can have victory when we are tempted. Jesus sets the pattern for us: He shows us the significance of taking a stand on a *rhēma*, a particular word from God, and choosing to be obedient to it.

When we find ourselves tempted, too often we become aware of our weaknesses and simply give in. Jesus reminds us that even though we are weak, God has provided in His word (*rhēma*) the one resource we require. If we take a firm stand on that word, we will overcome temptation. So let's approach our temptations confidently, fully aware that while Satan may attempt to trip us up, God intends us to overcome temptation, and so demonstrate the reality and quality of our faith.

THE SECOND TEMPTATION: SATAN OFFERED JESUS ALL THE KINGDOMS OF THE WORLD AND THEIR GLORY   (Luke 4:5–8)

The Old Testament pictured the coming Messiah (a Hebrew word which is rendered "Christ" in Greek) as a future world ruler. The prophet Isaiah said this about the future Messiah:

Of the increase of His government
and peace

There will be no end,
Upon the throne of David and over
    His kingdom,
To order it and establish it with
    judgment and justice
From that time forward, even
    forever.

Isaiah 9:7

This Old Testament messianic theme was repeated over and over again. The image is sharp and clear. Jesus is destined to rule this world. It is against the background of such prophecies that Satan tried a different approach in a second temptation.

"Then the devil . . . showed Him all the kingdoms of the world in a moment of time" (Luke 4:5). The history of the world is filled with tales of empire building in which conquerors and potentates seek to construct monuments to themselves by extending their authority over more and more lands and peoples. The cost of empire building has always been paid in the sweat, the blood, and the suffering of ordinary people. The kingdoms of the world

❖

"All this authority I will give You."

Satan showed Jesus, their pomp stained with the tears of the multitudes, would hardly have been attractive to the Lord. What would have appealed to Jesus, however, is captured in the words of Isaiah quoted above: "Of the increase of His government and of peace there will be no end."

If Christ ruled the kingdoms of the world today, there would be no war, no hunger, no injustice, no crime; human society would, for the first time since the Fall, know peace—and that is a worthy goal. When Satan showed Jesus the kingdoms of the world and "their glory," Jesus' first reaction must have been to imagine what might be in place of what then was.

"All this authority I will give You" (Luke 4:6). Satan offered Christ the opportunity to rule the nations of the world *then* rather than in the future. There are two things to say about Satan's offer.

(1) Accepting rule then would have saved our world at least 2,000 years of strife. The promise of the endless rule of Christ has not yet been fulfilled. Satan, the "god of this age" (2 Cor. 4:4), still exercises his corrupting influence over nations and societies. It would seem, at first glance, that had Christ chosen to accept Satan's offer, something truly good would have resulted!

(2) Satan is a liar. Satan claimed that he could give Jesus "all this authority . . . for this has been delivered to me, and I give it to whomever I wish" (Luke 4:6). At best this is half-truth. Satan's power is limited to what God permits; Satan's power is also limited by the destiny which awaits him. There is nothing Satan can offer that is truly his to give; his gifts are always a mirage, flawed in some fundamental way—which, in the last analysis, makes them worthless.

Perhaps Satan could have given Jesus an earthly authority to maintain an enforced public peace. However, Satan could never have given Jesus the authority to transform human beings from within and thus to provide an inner peace which comes from growth in godliness. If Jesus had accepted Satan's offer, He would never have gone to the cross, and the transforming forgiveness His death provides would never have been available to human beings. We would have enjoyed "peace" during our brief years on earth, but we would die as unforgiven sinners. What on the surface might seem to be a good thing would, in the final analysis, have brought eternal disaster to humankind and would have thwarted God's plan to provide humanity with an eternal salvation.

"If You will worship before me, all will be Yours" (*Luke 4:7*). Satan was apparently willing to trade power for worship. Why? In chapter 1, we established the origin and nature of Satan's sin. We saw that Satan was determined to "exalt [his] throne above the stars of God" and "be like the Most High" (Isa. 14:13, 14). Satan wasn't satisfied to be a creature; he was jealous and desperately wanted the prerogatives that belonged only to the Creator.

Satan sought to satisfy this driving desire of his innermost being. If Jesus, God the Son, had worshiped Satan, Jesus would have, in essence, put Satan in the place occupied by His Father. Satan would have won! He actually would have supplanted God! Measured against the fulfillment of his corrupt desire, authority over the kingdoms of this world meant nothing to Satan, who cares not a bit for humankind.

"You shall worship the Lord your God, and Him only you shall serve" (*Luke 4:8*). Jesus quoted Deuteronomy 6:13, which is found in the context of a warning to Israel about the worship of idols and pagan deities. Again, Jesus turned to Scripture and found a specific word (*rhēma*) from God. On the basis of that word, He decisively rejected Satan's demand.

Jesus surely was not tempted to worship Satan, an unsavory figure at best. However, Jesus, being human, might well have been tempted by the prospect of doing "good" for others—by taking authority, He would save

humanity centuries of struggle and pain. Whether or not Jesus, at this point, saw clearly the pathway that would lead Him to the cross, whether or not He understood Satan's motives—all that is irrelevant. Jesus had a word from God, and on that word He chose to act.

What Satan hoped to accomplish. Again we're reminded that Satan is subtle. It is clear that Satan's driving motivation was to supplant God, whether in the universe or in the hearts of human beings. Just as in the first temptation, Satan's invitation to Jesus was a trap. If Jesus had succumbed to the temptation to assume power, His path would not have led Him to the cross, and then God's great plan of salvation—through which the Lord displays His love, His grace, and His righteousness—would have failed. First and foremost, Satan is an enemy of God, and he is hostile to the ones whom God loves.

What we learn from the second temptation. Once again we see the significance of taking a stand on a word (*rhēma*) from God, but there are additional lessons.

(1) We are not to let a "good" end divert us from God's will. Few believers today would be tempted if someone said, "Let's go out and rob a bank," or "Let's go buy cocaine and get high." But if someone should invite us to join a crusade to help the homeless or to provide Bibles for prisoners, we'd be more apt to listen. If someone showed us how a particular course of action could do great good for many people and, at the same time, triple our income, we'd probably be ready to consider it.

The problem is that we often find ourselves evaluating choices solely on the ends they seem likely to achieve and the apparent benefits for us. Satan's second attempt at tempting Jesus reminds us to seek God's will in making choices. In doing so, we must carefully consider the means to be used to reach any "good" end. We are to test both ends and means by God's will as it is revealed in Scripture or spoken to us by the Holy Spirit. When a word (*rhēma*) from God conflicts with either the means or the ends, we are to reject that choice as decisively as Jesus rejected Satan's offer.

(2) *We are to trust that God's will leads us to the greater good.* Jesus' rejection of the "good" of taking authority over the kingdoms of the world and establishing peace led to the greater good of our eternal salvation. The Bible reminds us that God is so wise that He can turn tragedy into triumph. Scripture says that "all things work together for good to those who love God, to those who are the called according to His purpose" (Rom. 8:28). The only thing we can do to *ensure* that good will follow from any choice we make is to obey the will of God as we understand it.

THE THIRD TEMPTATION: SATAN TEMPTED JESUS TO LEAP FROM THE PINNACLE OF THE TEMPLE (*Luke 4:9–12*)

The "pinnacle" of the temple has been identified as the corner of the building from which the priest blew the trumpet on sacred occasions. Alfred Edersheim (*The Life and Times of Jesus the Messiah*) describes the pinnacle as the southeastern angle of the temple cloisters, which reaches a height of four hundred and fifty feet on one side. Rabbinic tradition taught that the Messiah would announce His presence by appearing on the pinnacle of the temple, as is apparent in this comment on Isaiah 60:1:

Our Rabbis give this tradition: in the hour when King Messiah cometh, He standeth upon the roof of the sanctuary, and proclaims to Israel, saying, Ye poor (suffering), the time of your redemption draweth nigh. And if ye believe, rejoice in My Light, which is risen upon you. . . . In that hour will the Holy One, blessed be His Name, make the Light of the Messiah and of Israel to shine forth; and all shall come to the Light of the King Messiah and of Israel, as it is written.

Yalkut on Isaiah 60:1

How significant, then, that in the last temptation (as reported by Luke), Satan takes Jesus to the pinnacle of the temple and tells Him to leap. If Jesus were to do so, surely angels would catch Him before his foot struck the stones of the pavement, and everyone would realize that Isaiah's words, as understood by the rabbis, were fulfilled. How could Israel's leaders fail to acclaim Jesus as the Messiah King?

"[Satan] brought [Jesus] to Jerusalem, [and] set Him on the pinnacle of the temple" (Luke 4:9). Jerusalem was the religious and political center of the Jewish people. The leaders who could authoritatively acclaim Jesus as the Messiah King dwelt there, and their activities focused around the temple. In light of the rabbinic tradition quoted above, Satan seemed to be presenting Christ with a strategic opportunity to convince the leaders of His identity; yet Satan's next words show how subtle the Deceiver was (and is) in his temptations.

"If You are the Son of God, throw Yourself down from here" (Luke 4:9). Earlier we noted that Satan's statement, "if you are the Son of God," assumed the condition to be fulfilled. Satan was saying, "Since You are God's Son. . . ."

❖

"Throw Yourself down from here."

Here, the same statement, with a mixed conditional, introduces a shade of doubt. "If You are the Son of God—by the way, You really are, aren't You?—then throw Yourself down." How subtle was Satan's hint: "You really are, aren't You?" Yet how understandable it would have been for Jesus to doubt at this point.

Suppose you and I felt led by God to catch a plane to Florida, drive out into the Everglades, and stop. We did what we felt we were supposed to do, but after a day of waiting, nothing happened. No stranger came by for us to witness to, as Philip witnessed to the Ethiopian (Acts 8:26ff). We waited another day, then another. Finally, after 40 days, when we were utterly exhausted and at our weakest, a stranger showed up and began to pressure us to make choices we felt were wrong. If that happened to us, we surely would have begun to wonder long before the fortieth day whether our understanding that it was God's will for us to come to Florida was real, or just our imagination.

It would not be at all surprising if Jesus, who chose to meet His temptations as a man, did not also have moments of doubt. Did the Spirit really lead Him into the wilderness? Why was He supposed to be there, going without food for such a long time? Why would God put His "beloved Son" in such a situation? Even if no shadow of a doubt existed, Satan's question and his tone of voice were designed to provoke it. Satan even quoted Scripture to reinforce his point.

"For it is written" (Luke 4:10, 11). Satan quoted Psalm 91:11, 12 to remind Jesus that God was committed to protect the One He loved from all harm, even to the extent of sending angels to catch Him "lest [He] dash [His] foot against a stone."

On the surface, the third temptation appeared to be an enticement for Jesus to gain immediate acceptance as Israel's Messiah and not risk rejection. However, the temptation was, in fact, far different. Satan was reminding Jesus that He could settle any doubts about His relationship with God or God's commitment to Him by simply stepping off the pinnacle of the temple into thin air. God's Word, which Jesus Himself had quoted and acted on with confidence, promised that angels would catch Him before He suffered harm.

"You shall not tempt the LORD your God" (Luke 4:12). Once again Jesus returned to Deuteronomy (6:16) for a word (*rhēma*) of God on which to stand. The verse in Deuteronomy says, "You shall not tempt the LORD your God as you tempted Him at Massah." This is an intriguing reference to another incident in the history of Israel's wilderness years.

The original story is told in Exodus 17. The Israelites camped in Rephidim, but there was no water there. The people confronted Moses, complained, and demanded water to drink. Moses, frustrated at their reaction, asked, "Why do you tempt the LORD?" (Ex. 17:2). The nature of that "temptation" is explained in 17:7. The people demanded water and tempted God, saying, "Is the LORD among us or not?"

What a fascinating turn of events. Just a short time before, the Lord opened a way for Israel to pass through the Reed Sea. God provided the people with manna when they ran out of food. He led them every step of the way in the visible form of a cloudy and fiery pillar. Yet the people doubted God's presence and demanded that He provide water as proof that He was with them!

This incident, and the comment on it in Deuteronomy 6:16, came to Jesus' mind when Satan challenged Him to make God prove that He was God's "beloved Son" by leaping from the temple pinnacle. Jesus decisively chose to live, as we humans must, by faith rather than sight—without putting God to the test.

What Satan hoped to accomplish. Had Christ leapt from the temple pinnacle, it would have forced an immediate decision concerning His messiahship. Jesus' ministry involved far more than presenting Himself to Israel as Messiah. It would take Christ years of teaching and healing and casting out demons to form, in the minds of His followers, a fresh understanding of the God He revealed in word and deed. It would take Jesus years to train disciples and equip them for building the church He was to found. Moreover, Christ's presentation of Himself as a personal, not a political, Messiah would force Israel to choose whether to accept God's vision of His kingdom rather than their own.

For Jesus to have leapt from the temple would have undercut significant ministries that He could perform best only by coming to His people as someone poor and lowly, rather than as someone high and mighty. Even more significantly, failure to live by faith would have shown a lack of trust in God, a lack of trust which falls short of the mark God has set for human beings. Thus, had Jesus put God to the test and demanded proof that God was with Him, He would have sinned, and by sinning Jesus would have disqualified Himself as our Savior.

We're reminded again that Satan's temptations, however transparent they may seem on the surface, are in fact extremely subtle. We dare not treat Satan lightly; we dare not dismiss his efforts to trap us as crude and easily avoided. They most surely are not.

What we learn from the third temptation. The subtlety of Satan's strategies for temptation is impressive. Yet we learn from Jesus several important principles to help us overcome temptation.

(1) Satan cannot make us sin. Satan urged Jesus: "Throw Yourself down from here." The choice was up to Jesus, not to Satan. People who say, "The devil made me do it," miss the point of temptation entirely. People can encourage us to do wrong, but no one can *make us* choose to sin. Satan can entice and urge and try to deceive, but the choice of what to do is ours. It's important to remember that in this we have the power and authority, not Satan. The choice is ours, and ours alone.

(2) Satan can quote Scripture. The issue is not whether a particular teaching is in the Bible, the issue is whether or not that teaching applies. Satan reminded Jesus that God's angels would catch Him if He jumped off the temple pinnacle, and Satan was right! The issue, however, was whether or not Jesus *should* leap from that height, and that particular issue was not addressed in the verse Satan quoted.

Sometimes we may be confused by others who quote Scripture as they advise one course of action or another. Let's not be confused. What we need to do is to analyze carefully the issue confronting us and then seek the help of the Holy Spirit to guide us to the word (*rhēma*) of God that applies.

(3) We are vulnerable to temptation. Satan aimed each temptation of Christ at an area of human vulnerability.

Satan's first temptation was directed toward humanity's vulnerability as mortal beings living life in this world. The biblical principle that humans do not live by bread alone, but by every word (*rhēma*) of God, reminds us that God cares about our material well-being. Satan may whisper in our ear that we *need* this or that, but if we have confidence in God to provide for all our needs, when temptation comes we will listen to His word and do His will.

Satan's second temptation was directed toward humanity's vulnerability as moral beings who are attracted to what is good. All too often we are tempted to make choices based on the desired end, without carefully considering whether the means are in harmony with God's will. We are also vulnerable because, as we have seen in Satan's temptation of Jesus, a supposedly "good" end may in fact bring about disasters we did not anticipate. If we remember that God is good and that His will always promotes that which is best, we will listen for a word from God directing us in His way.

Satan's final temptation was directed toward humanity's vulnerability to spiritual doubt. We live in a relationship with a God who is unseen. In times of trouble, we often feel helpless and alone—which is precisely the moment when we may be tempted to devise some test to "prove" that God is with us. However, we have God's word that He will never leave us or forsake us (Heb. 13:5). Like Jesus, we are called to walk through dark times with faith, never letting the doubts raised by Satan shake our confidence in God.

SATAN AND OUR TEMPTATIONS

The Gospel accounts of the temptation of Jesus teach us much about Satan's strategies and about how to resist temptations. We often credit Satan with a more significant role in our temptations than he deserves. It's important to understand the nature of temptation if we are to withstand it and defeat it.

SATAN'S INVOLVEMENT IN OUR TEMPTATION IS LIMITED BY HIS NATURE

Satan is a created being; he is not like God, no matter how much he desires to be. This fact has several implications.

Satan cannot be present everywhere. Unlike God, who is present everywhere, Satan can only be in one place at a time. Thus, it is highly unlikely that we will be tempted by Satan personally during our lifetime. When Scripture refers to being tempted by Satan, as in 1 Corinthians 7:5, "Satan" is used in a representative way to include all his demonic followers. Even if we grant that Satan's followers might tempt us, our temptations typically come from an entirely different source.

Satan cannot make us give in to temptation. Satan and his demon followers are unable to make us act against our will. Human beings have the privilege of choice, which means that we are in control of our own lives and decisions. Whereas God could "make" us choose to act one way or another, He will not. Although Satan would make us choose to sin if he could, he cannot. When we are tempted,

we are free to decide how to act, and we are responsible for our choices.

THE SOURCE OF OUR TEMPTATIONS LIES WITHIN, NOT WITHOUT

Origen, writing about A.D. 250, described a common, but flawed, belief held by some Christians. Origen noted that the holy Scriptures teach that there are "certain invisible enemies who fight against us, and against whom it commands us to arm ourselves," but he contended that the "more simple among the believers" draw a false conclusion:

[They] are of the opinion that all the sins which men have committed are the persistent efforts of these opposing powers exerted in the minds of sinners, because in that invisible struggle these powers are found to be superior (to man). For if, for example, there were no devil, no single human being would go astray.

Origen rejected that view in light of "those sins which manifestly originate as a necessary consequence of our bodily constitution."

What Origen was referring to are teachings in Scripture, such as James 1:14 and 1 Corinthians 10:13. The former verse says: "But each one is tempted when he is drawn away by his own desires and enticed." The latter verse adds: "No temptation has overtaken you except such as is common to man." The normal pressures which stem from the human condition, and are thus "common to man," become temptations when we are "drawn away" by our own desires.

It's important to make a distinction between tests and temptations. God may use difficult circumstances as a test which gives us the opportunity to display our faith. Such tests are transformed into temptations when something within us pulls us away from God's will and entices us to sin. Our sinful nature—not God, not Satan, not circumstances—is what turns tests into temptations, and temptations into occasions to sin. When we seek the source of temptation, we are to look within ourselves, not outside ourselves.

THE NATURE OF TEMPTATION ANALYZED (James 1:12–18)

The passage on temptation in James helps us see the relationship between God and our temptations; it clearly shifts the burden of responsibility for temptation away from God to human beings.

Blessed is the man who endures temptation; for when he has been approved, he will receive the crown of life which the Lord has promised to those who love Him. Let no one say when he is tempted, "I am tempted by God"; for God cannot be tempted by evil, nor does He Himself tempt anyone. But each one is tempted when he is drawn away by his own desires and enticed. Then, when desire has conceived, it gives birth to sin; and sin, when it is full-grown, brings forth death.

Do not be deceived, my beloved brethren. Every good gift and every perfect gift is from above, and comes down from the Father of lights, with whom there is no variation or shadow of turning. Of His own will He brought us forth by the word of truth, that we might be a kind of firstfruits of His creatures.

James 1:12–18

This passage makes several important points.

God intends testing to be a blessing (James 1:12). We noted earlier that the same Greek verb *peirazō* is translated "to test" and "to tempt." James 1:12 should read: "Blessed is the man who endures testing." When God permits believers to experience stressful situations, His intent is to approve them, so that by enduring successfully they might win "the crown [reward] of life."

God is not the source of temptation (James 1:13). We may experience the intended test as a temptation and feel a pull toward sin. James wants us to know that God is not the source of that pull, although He is the shaper of the circumstances in which we feel the pull toward evil. "God cannot be tempted by evil, nor does He Himself tempt anyone."

The source of temptation lies within us (James 1:14). The pull toward wrong that we might feel in any circumstance is not inherent in the circumstance. The pull toward evil is rooted in our *reaction to* the circumstance. The temptation—the conflicting pull between wrong and right choices—comes from our own sinful nature and desires.

Giving in to temptation is a process (James 1:15). James used the analogy of conception, birth, and adulthood to describe how temptation can turn into sin. The initial desire to sin is conception. Submitting to the desire and doing what is wrong is giving birth. Continuing in sin is adulthood, which always ends in death. The implication of the analogy is that we need to control our response to temptation at the earliest stage, before desire gives birth to sin.

We are to see every experience as a good gift from God (James 1:16, 17). James wanted his readers to keep clearly in mind that "every good gift and every perfect gift is from above." Everything God brings into our life is intended as a good gift. When our desires are aroused and we are tempted, we're likely to see the situation we are in as a wholly negative thing. If, however, we learn to look at every circumstance as a good gift from a loving God, we are much more likely to see our situation in a positive light—as a test which God expects us to pass. How we view such situations may well be a crucial factor in determining how we choose to act.

God gave us new life that we might overcome temptations (James 1:18). James reminded his readers that God chose to give believers a new birth (He "brought us forth"), and His purpose in so doing was "that we might be a kind of firstfruits of His creatures."

In the Old Testament, firstfruits were the first crops to ripen. Those crops were brought to the temple and offered to God in thanksgiving for the harvest about to be reaped. James encourages believers to view themselves as the firstfruits of what God will do for His entire creation: He will free it from sin's grip and bring in righteousness. God intends the circumstances in which we feel tempted as tests; when we pass those tests, God's purifying work in our lives is displayed. Believers have the privilege of showing the world of human beings and angels what God will one day do for all.

Summary. We cannot blame Satan or God for our temptations, for the source of temptation lies within us. We are to regard every circumstance in which temptations arise as a good gift from God, as an opportunity for us to display the beauty of God's transforming power in our lives, not as an occasion intended to trip us up. What an encouragement it is when we experience temptation to realize that what God has done is to give us a fresh opportunity to rely on Him and experience His powerful presence in our lives.

JESUS IS PRESENT TO HELP US OVERCOME OUR TEMPTATIONS

We've seen that we are not to blame Satan when we give in to temptations, nor are we to blame God when we feel tempted. God shapes the circumstances in which temptation occurs, but He intends them as a test, a good and perfect gift. However, God does not stop there. He comes to help us when we are tempted.

We learned from Satan's temptation of Jesus that He faced each test in His human nature; that is, He relied on the same resources that you and I have when we are tempted. But Hebrews 2:18 goes beyond that to say: "For in that He Himself has suffered, being tempted [tested], He is able to aid those who are tempted." The One who overcame Satan's temptations is now ready to aid us when we are tempted! The writer of Hebrews explains:

For we do not have a High Priest who cannot sympathize with our weaknesses, but was in all points tempted [tested] as we are, yet without sin. Let us therefore come boldly to the throne of grace, that we may obtain mercy and find grace to help in time of need.

Hebrews 4:15, 16

Jesus sympathizes with our weakness (Hebrews 4:15a). As a true human being Christ was subject to every pressure common to humanity. He views our struggles sympathetically, not with contempt or condemnation.

Jesus "was in all points [tested] as we are, yet without sin" (Hebrews 4:15b). Some people have doubted that Christ could really understand our temptations since He did not have a sinful nature. In fact, Christ understood testing far better than we do. Imagine a contest between two people to see who can keep his head underwater longer. The first person goes under and, as pressure begins to build, pops up after 17 seconds. The second person goes underwater. The pressure begins to build, but he stays underwater. His lungs begin to ache, but he slowly exhales and stays underwater. The pressure becomes almost unbearable, and his lungs cry out for air, but he stays underwater. Finally, after nearly five minutes, he comes up for air. Which of the two truly understands what it means to resist the temptation to come up for air? Obviously, the person who experienced that temptation to the fullest.

This is how we are to understand Hebrews 4:15. Jesus, as a true human being, experienced the ultimate pressures that a human being can know, and he *never* sinned. Only Jesus can truly understand what it means to be tested to the maximum. Only the sinless Jesus truly understands the weakness to which flesh is heir.

Jesus invites us to come boldly to Him for mercy and help in time of need (Hebrews 4:16). One of Satan's more subtle traps is to convince us, after we have given in to temptation, that God must be disappointed and angry with us. But Scripture invites us to come to Jesus "boldly" for mercy. And it is mercy that we need when we have fallen short and failed God and ourselves. Why "boldly"? Because we are confident that we will be welcomed by a sympathetic Jesus and sure that He will not condemn, but forgive.

Hebrews 4:16 also invites us to come boldly to "find grace to help in time of need."

God does not intend for us to face tests and temptations alone! We can turn to Jesus, who has overcome temptation, for He will provide the grace we need to overcome temptation.

THE STRUGGLE CONTINUES: SATAN'S WARFARE AGAINST HUMANITY

The temptation of Jesus was simply the opening battle between Satan and Jesus in the Gospels. In fact, the last words of Luke's account of the temptation of Christ are: "Now when the devil had ended every temptation, he departed from Him until an opportune time" (Luke 4:13). Satan was not finished with Jesus. He would look for other opportunities to resume the struggle.

Satan still is not finished with Jesus or with Jesus' followers. The Gospels and the Epistles provide fascinating insights about how Satan and his followers work against believers today. A central passage in Ephesians gives us valuable information about Satan's underlying strategy. After we examine that passage, we'll look at every verse in the Gospels and Epistles that touches on Satan's continuing war against Christ and His followers.

SATAN'S BASIC STRATEGY IS TO CREATE CULTURES IN WHICH TEMPTATIONS TO SIN EXIST (Ephesians 2:1–3)

We noted earlier that Satan is a creature, and thus he cannot be omnipresent. Satan must work through his followers and through other secondary means. Ephesians 2:1–3 gives us a significant insight into the strategy Satan has adopted:

And you He [God] made alive, who were dead in trespasses and sins, in which you once walked according to the course of this world, according to the prince of the power of the air [Satan], the spirit who now works in the sons of disobedience, among whom also we all once conducted ourselves in the lusts of our flesh, fulfilling the desires of the flesh and of the mind, and were by nature children of wrath, just as the others.

"In which you once walked" (Ephesians 2:2). The word "walk" is frequently used in the Bible with reference to a person's behavior. Today we would use the word "lifestyle." This verse immediately focuses our attention on a lifestyle of "trespasses and sins."

"The course of this world" (Ephesians 2:2). The word translated "world" is *kosmos,* which is not used here in the sense of "the earth," or even "the inhabited earth." Instead, *kosmos* refers to human society, with all its tightly woven patterns of beliefs, values, and motivations that permeate institutions and find expression in individual lives. What Paul was saying here is that the unsaved have adopted a lifestyle of sin which is in accord with the sinful pattern of relationships embedded in human culture and society.

This is a crucial concept, and it has significant implications. When we looked at the role of demons in Old Testament times, we saw that demons were behind the religions of pagan peoples and influenced religious beliefs and practices. Daniel 10:13, 20 suggested that fallen angels serve as "princes" of nations and seek to influence political and social policies. Satan's basic strategy seems to be one of *shaping* cultures so that they appeal to, and promote the impulses of, humankind's sinful nature.

We see multiple examples of this in our own society. The lyrics of music targeted at young people incorporates thoughts and values that are repugnant to God; for example, those lyrics depict corrupt relationships between the sexes. Movies and television shows actively promote values that are contrary to God's values. Today there is an aggressive movement to paint homosexuality as an acceptable alternative lifestyle, with terrible consequences: Our society is marred by increasing gender confusion among young adults. Sexual abuse and sexual harassment have become so common that they are both mentioned constantly in the news. Christian values and Christian ministries are treated negatively, and Christian beliefs are distorted by the media.

Satan's strategy, of course, has a far more subtle influence upon our society. A pervasive, materialistic focus is exhibited in advertising which suggests that happiness can be found in a fragrance or in wearing a particular brand of jeans. Careers are chosen not on the basis of how they enable us to serve, but by the power or wealth or status they offer. Even the positive aspects of capitalism, such as the encouragement of hard work and self-reliance, are twisted to support other values. And the apparently altruistic ends of many social programs do more harm than good to individuals by making them captives to a paternalistic bureaucracy which robs individuals of personal responsibility and its rewards.

Another subtle influence of Satan's strategy is reflected in our language. The word "love," which ought to suggest the finest of human qualities, has been twisted to suggest the most corrupt concepts. Thus, "making love" now means nothing more than "having sex," no matter how casual or debased the actual relationship. Again and again, words that were coined to reflect the good and the godly, such as "gay," have been twisted to suggest that which is, or to indicate those who are, perverted.

Given the tremendous influence of the values that are institutionalized in the life and language of any culture, Satan hardly needs to approach individuals in person to achieve his ends.

"The prince of the power of the air" (*Ephesians 2:2*). In New Testament times, "air" designated earth's atmosphere, where, according to popular belief, demons reside. Paul used this phrase in a way every first-century reader would have understood: to identify Satan as ruler of the demonic hosts who are at work in human societies, influencing cultures to encourage lifestyles that appeal to humankind's sinful nature. Thus, Satan is "the spirit who now works" through culture and in those who disobey God.

REFERENCES IN THE NEW TESTAMENT TO SATAN'S CONFLICT WITH JESUS AND HIS FOLLOWERS

As we turn our attention to passages in the New Testament that speak of Satan and his attacks on Jesus and humankind in general, we need to keep clearly in mind Satan's basic strategy of corrupting human lifestyles through cultures.

Matthew 6:13. "And do not lead us into temptation, but deliver us from the evil one." This familiar petition is from the prayer Jesus taught to His disciples. Some interpreters assume that the first part ("And do not lead us into temptation") means "do not let us sin when we are tested." It is better to take the phrase as a warning against the kind of presumption which led Peter to claim he would never deny Jesus—just before denying Him three times (Matt. 26:34–47).

The second part ("But deliver us from the evil one") suggests that an individual's false evaluation of his or her own strengths is one of the traps Satan sets for human beings. The unsaved may be encouraged to suppose their good works commend them to God—but that is simply not true. The believer may be encouraged to imagine that his or her relationship with God guarantees freedom from sin—but that is simply not possible during this life. No one can live a godly life, except through a complete and humble reliance on the Lord.

Matthew 13:19. "When anyone hears the word of the kingdom, and does not understand it, then the wicked one comes and snatches away what was sown in his heart." Here, in a familiar parable, Jesus depicted Satan as one who "snatches away" the word when it is sown. The point of the parable is that Satan frantically works to distract anyone who hears the gospel and fails to grasp it immediately. Rather than let the hearer pause to think about the message, Satan brings in a hoard of distractions. These distractions need not be sinful; indeed, they may be "good." The fact is, however, that anything that occupies our thoughts and draws our attention away from God's message serves Satan's purpose of snatching away the word.

Nonbelievers and believers alike are vulnerable to that strategy. There are so many things to occupy our time these days—work, play, TV, sports, popular music. In a culture which constantly bombards us from every side with messages that invite our attention, Satan is all too successful in drawing attention away from God's Word.

Matthew 13:39. "The enemy who sowed them is the devil." In this parable, the servants of a man who owned a field asked whether they should pull up weeds, which looked much like young wheat plants. The owner replied that the two were to be allowed to "grow together until the harvest" (13:30).

In this parable and Jesus' explanation of it, we see another strategy of Satan. Satan promotes counterfeit religion today, just as he did in Old Testament times. The problem is that we cannot determine with certainty whether individuals within our own fellowships—or even those who appear to be adherents of a counterfeit religion—are true believers or not. Only God can do that. Yet all too often we take it upon ourselves to place some individuals in and others out of God's kingdom, and, in the process, we may harm those who truly do belong to Christ.

It is appropriate for Christians to hold onto and to contend for truth as Scripture presents it, but it is dangerous to assume that we can judge the relationship others have with the Lord. When we do judge and condemn others, we are doing Satan's work, not God's.

Matthew 16:23. "But He turned and said to Peter, 'Get behind Me, Satan! You are an offense to Me, for you are not mindful of the things of God, but the things of men.'" This explosive statement burst from Jesus' lips when Peter, out of the best of motives, urged Him not to take the path which led to the cross.

It's sometimes hard for us to realize that we are not competent to judge God's will for others. God's will is something each believer must determine for himself or herself, within the guidelines provided in Scripture. To set ourselves up as authorities to judge the choices others must make is to fall into another of Satan's traps. We can advise, but we cannot direct.

Mark 4:15. "And these are the ones by the wayside where the word is sown. When they hear, Satan comes immediately and takes away the word that was sown in their hearts."

Mark 8:33. "But when He had turned around and looked at His disciples, He rebuked Peter, saying, 'Get behind Me, Satan! For you are not mindful of the things of God, but the things of men.'" See the comments on Matthew 16:23, just above.

Luke 8:12. "Those by the wayside are the ones who hear; then the devil comes and takes away the word out of their hearts, lest they should believe and be saved." See the comments on Matthew 13:19, p. 215.

Birds devoured the seeds by the wayside.

Luke 11:4b. "And do not lead us into temptation, but deliver us from the evil one." See the comments on Matthew 6:13, p. 215.

Luke 13:16. "So ought not this woman, being a daughter of Abraham, whom Satan has bound—think of it—for eighteen years, be loosed from this bond on the Sabbath?" Satan's attacks on us are not simply mental. Here, Jesus referred to an arthritic woman, who had suffered with a crooked back for 18 years, as one "whom Satan has bound." Christ identified her as a "daughter of Abraham," which was a testimony to her true faith in the Lord.

As we will see in the next chapter, Satan and his followers can afflict us with illnesses and diseases. Even believers are subject to oppression by evil supernatural forces. Yet as we saw in our study of Satan's torment of Job, the Lord permitted what happened to Job for a purpose that was ultimately good. When we are overcome by a chronic physical problem, it's important to remember that even though Satan's followers may be involved, God intends to use the experience to accomplish something good—for us and for others.

Luke 22:31. "And the Lord said, 'Simon, Simon! Indeed, Satan has asked for you, that he may sift you as wheat.' " In biblical times wheat was sifted to separate the kernels from bits of chaff. Apparently, Satan was implying that Peter was all chaff and, as in the case of Job, asked God for the chance to prove himself right. This passage reminds us of several truths.

First, Satan is limited in what he can do to us. He must seek permission from God for any direct or extraordinary effort against us.

Second, Christ is on our side! Verse 32 reads: "But I have prayed for you, that your faith should not fail; and when you have returned to Me, strengthen your brethren." This verse seems to indicate that Satan was to be allowed to sift Peter. Rather than pray that Peter might be spared, Christ prayed that his faith would not fail. Christ prays for us in the same way—not that we should be spared testing, but that we might have the faith required to see us through.

Third, Christ seemed to indicate that for Peter there would be an initial, but temporary, failure ("when you have returned to Me"). In the end Peter would return, and then he would have the responsibility to "strengthen [his] brethren." Satan would have us believe that any failure on our part disqualifies us from all future ministry. Christ not only forgives our failures, but tells us that when we return to Him, He can use us still. We should never let Satan cast doubt on the amazing grace of our God.

John 8:44. Jesus directed strong words to "the Jews" (see 8:22). John did not use this phrase for anti-Semitic purposes. John was not referring to the Jewish people at all; instead, he used the phrase "the Jews" only with reference to the religious leaders who opposed Jesus at every turn. Thus, to "the Jews" Jesus said:

> "You are of your father the devil, and the desires of your father you want to do. He was a murderer from the beginning, and does not stand in the truth, because there is no truth in him. When he speaks a lie, he speaks from his own resources, for he is a liar and the father of it."

Why did Jesus say "You are of your father the devil"? He explained why in the following phrase: "and the desires of your father you want to do." Ultimately, every person gives allegiance either to God or to Satan. The one who is moved by the same selfish desires that motivated Satan to rebel against God, such a person knowingly or unknowingly takes his stand with the father of lies and is thus related to him. The person who submits to God as creature to the Creator, such a person chooses to please God and is thus related to the Lord. There is no middle ground.

One of Satan's choice strategies is to disguise rebellion as "freedom" and submission to God as "slavery." In fact, the opposite is true. As Jesus warned the Jewish leaders, "whoever commits sin is a slave of sin" (John 8:34). How tragic it is to be a slave to our baser passions, rather than to be freed by God to become all that we can be as a result of joyfully choosing to do His will.

John 13:2. "And supper being ended, the devil having already put it into the heart of Judas Iscariot, Simon's son, to betray Him." We have here an unusual event in which Satan may have been personally involved. Certainly this was a special and critical occasion, worthy of Satan's personal attention. We are not told how Satan suggested to Judas that he might betray Jesus for money, but the idea was certainly diabolical.

Some commentators have suggested that Judas never intended for his betrayal to lead to Christ's death. Judas may have thought that Christ would extricate Himself from the temple priests' attempt to have Him seized, as He had done before. In this case, Judas would have profited by 30 pieces of silver, and no harm would have been done. How clever it must have seemed! Judas' suicidal reaction to Christ's condemnation to death (Matt. 27:5) gives some support to this view. Yet Judas must have been sensitive to the explosive climate in Jerusalem and to the religious leaders' intense hostility toward Jesus. Surely, Judas would have known that his action, whatever his intent, was *wrong.*

We can never excuse an action by appealing to intent alone. We must evaluate every action morally. If we do so, and if we remain committed to doing what God says is right, neither Satan nor his followers will be able to divert us from doing God's will.

John 13:27. "Now after the piece of bread, Satan entered him [Judas]. Then Jesus said to him, 'What you do, do quickly.' " The phrase "entered him" is clearly related to demon possession, a topic we will take up in chapter 14. As we will see, it seems that once a person opens himself or herself to demonic influence, as Judas did to Satan (John 13:2), he or she becomes vulnerable to demonization. "Demon possession" describes a situation in which a person surrenders his or her will to an evil being, which enables the evil being to act through that person.

The phrase "Satan entered him" suggests that Satan at that moment took control of Judas and acted through him. Although demon possession cannot happen to a person who guards against and does not welcome demonic influences, it is a danger to which human beings are vulnerable.

John 17:15. "I [Jesus] do not pray that You should take them out of the world, but that You should keep them from the evil one." In

After the Passover supper, Satan entered Judas Iscariot (13:27).

Jesus' prayer for His followers, our Lord does not pray for God to remove them from the influences that swirl around them in this world. "World" (*kosmos*) denotes that pattern of cultural influences in which each human being is necessarily immersed. Satan influences and shapes human cultures to promote a godless lifestyle. We will never be able to escape from this "world" of Satan's influence, and Jesus does not wish for us to escape.

Jesus prayed that His followers might be kept "from the evil one." We do not have to succumb to the satanic influences in our world. Instead—through the Father's grace—we can remain true to God and, as Jesus did, live godly lives in a corrupt world. When we do so, we shine as beacons of righteousness and attract others to the Lord.

Acts 5:3. "But Peter said, 'Ananias, why has Satan filled your heart to lie to the Holy Spirit and keep back part of the price of the land for yourself?' "

One of the notable features of the earliest church was the generosity believers showed to each other. Some members of the church in Jerusalem even sold land or houses to help meet the needs of the poor (4:34–37). One couple in the early church wanted recognition for being especially generous; but, at the same time, they wanted to keep money for themselves. As Peter pointed out, it would not have been wrong for Ananias and Sapphira to have kept *all* the money (5:4). The property and the proceeds were theirs to do with as they wished. However, they decided to give some of the money and pretend that they had given all. Peter confronted Ananias, and asked, "Ananias, why has Satan filled your heart to lie to the Holy Spirit?"

Satan filled Ananias' heart to lie to the Holy Spirit, and Satan put it into Judas' heart to betray Christ for money (John 13:2). In each case, the reference is to an idea whose source was identified as Satan. The very character of each act—betrayal, lying, and deceit—bears the stamp of Satan's own character and personality. Whatever motivated Judas

and Ananias to carry out those actions, the original source was clearly satanic. Satan *invented* that kind of behavior.

The consequence for Ananias and his wife, after Peter openly confronted them with the truth, was severe: They dropped dead on the spot. The warning for us is that our culture is filled with many inducements to that kind of behavior. When we open ourselves to those types of influences, we become vulnerable to Satan—and subject to tragic consequences.

Acts 13:10. "And [Paul] said, 'O full of all deceit and all fraud, you son of the devil, you enemy of all righteousness, will you not cease perverting the straight ways of the Lord?' " These harsh words were directed against a sorcerer, a false prophet named Bar-Jesus, who actively sought to turn others away from the faith (13:8). Paul called him a "son of the devil," meaning that the sorcerer followed in the devil's footsteps and acted as Satan did.

When we run across others who actively contend against Christianity, it's important to recognize the source of their antagonism. Whether the opposition comes from a secular person committed to "science" or from a "religious" person who denies the deity of Jesus, open hostility to the gospel is a sign of satanic entrapment.

As Luke reported in Acts 13, Paul confronted and silenced the opposition. In 2 Timothy 2:25, 26 Paul advised servants of the Lord to correct "in humility":

those who are in opposition, if God perhaps will grant them repentance, so that they may know the truth, and that they may come to their senses and escape the snare of the devil, having been taken captive by him to do his will.

1 Corinthians 5:5. "Deliver such a one to Satan for the destruction of the flesh, that his spirit may be saved in the day of the Lord Jesus." Paul wrote to the Corinthians about an open scandal they had permitted to go on unchecked. A man calling himself a believer was openly maintaining a sexual relationship with his father's wife. Although Paul blamed the church for not disciplining this man, he also blamed the man himself. Paul's verdict was that the church should withdraw its spiritual protection and should actively pray for the man to suffer physical death.

The reference to delivering the man "to Satan for the destruction of the flesh" is rooted in the fact that our bodies return to dust (Gen. 3:19), and it reflects the tradition that Satan and Michael argued over the disposal of the body of Moses after he died (Jude 9). The worst that Satan can do to us is engineer our death; at most, all that Satan can ultimately possess of the believer is the empty shell of his or her body, as it dissolves into dust. Our personality, which is the conscious essence of the individual self, belongs to God, and He will guard us until the day of resurrection comes.

1 Corinthians 7:5.

Do not deprive one another except with consent for a time, that you may give yourselves to fasting and prayer; and come together again so that Satan does not tempt you because of your lack of self-control.

A group of people in the Corinthian church mistakenly believed that having sexual relations in marriage was somehow "unspiritual," and so they promoted total abstinence. Paul corrected them, teaching that both husbands and wives have a right to their spouse's body. While temporary abstinence for the specific purpose of fasting and prayer was acceptable, total abstinence was not. Couples were to resume normal sexual relations so that Satan would not tempt them.

This passage is important for several reasons. It reminds us that the natural functions of our bodies are not sinful in and of themselves. For instance, sex in marriage is intended to be a godly delight. Denying ourselves that which God provides—whether it be the enjoyment of proper food or amusements or sexual experience—is not wise, nor is it pleasing to the Lord. In fact, such self-denial can provide an occasion for Satan to tempt us.

We need to view Satan's temptations in this passage as involving far more than the sole temptation of sexual sin. The person who denies himself may well become proud of his "self-control," never realizing that pride is one of the worst sins encouraged by Satan. The person who denies herself certain foods may disdain others who enjoy them, without ever realizing that being judgmental is just as much a sin as gluttony. Satan is far more subtle than we imagine, for the ways in which he would trap us into sin are hardly as obvious as ways that seem to threaten us initially.

2 Corinthians 2:11.

"Lest Satan should take advantage of us; for we are not ignorant of his devices." In this passage Paul responded to word from Corinth that the person he had urged the Corinthians to discipline in his first letter had repented. The Corinthians were uncertain about how they should treat a repentant sinner. Should they continue to ostracize him and "make him pay"? Paul urged the Corinthians to forgive and comfort him, and Paul assured them of his forgiveness too (2:7). This is the context for Paul's reference to Satan's "devices," or "schemes."

What the verse suggests is that Satan has built into human thought and culture a pattern of multiple and equally sinful options. The church no longer ignores open and flagrant sin? All right, Satan will encourage the church to go overboard with discipline. If the church treats repentant sinners harshly, what a reason that is for others to hide their sins! And what an opportunity for the church to make the person who repented feel that God no longer loves him!

Paul's response is important because it reminds us that believers are like sheep prone to go astray. Only by freely forgiving each other as God forgave can the church become the close and loving community it must be in order to nurture spiritual growth. How delighted Satan would be if, in doing the right thing (disciplining open and persistent sin), believers developed a spirit of harshness and condemnation, for that would destroy the effectiveness of the church just as quickly as would a failure to discipline in the first place.

2 Corinthians 4:4. "Whose minds the god of this age has blinded, who do not believe, lest the light of the gospel of the glory of Christ, who is the image of God, should shine on them." Paul was referring here to "the perishing," those who do not respond to the gospel. Paul wrote that the "god of this age," another name for Satan, has "blinded" the ones who do not believe.

The reference to the gospel being "veiled" (2 Cor. 4:3) suggests how Satan blinds human eyes. Satan encourages the development of cultures in which so many interests and ideas attract attention that the gospel message seems dim and uninteresting. With so many exciting things competing for attention, nonbelievers have no interest in looking closely at the claims of Christ.

Today there are over 1,000 Christian radio stations in the United States. Yet how quickly a person searching for a news program or one of the "top 20" music stations turns past the religious stations! How subtly Satan shapes cultures to blind the eyes of men and women to the good news of Jesus Christ.

2 Corinthians 11:3. "But I fear, lest somehow, as the serpent deceived Eve by his craftiness, so your minds may be corrupted from the simplicity that is in Christ." The Corinthian church was comprised of various parties who claimed allegiance to different Christian leaders (see 1 Cor. 1—4). In 2 Corinthians 10, Paul wrote about competitive individuals who put down the apostle and compared him unfavorably to themselves or their favorite leader. Paul was not concerned for his own reputation; rather, he was concerned that the various parties, in emphasizing the distinctiveness of their group or their leader, would be "corrupted from the simplicity that is in Christ."

One of Satan's crafty schemes is to get believers to focus on the particular theological emphases of their leader or group. We may be Calvinist or Wesleyan, charismatic or non-charismatic, for or against the methods of the Christian Right. But unless we are careful, Satan will use these allegiances to distract us from centering on Jesus Christ and the gospel of salvation through faith alone.

2 Corinthians 11:14. "And no wonder! For Satan himself transforms himself into an angel of light." The apostle directed his attention to "false apostles," the "deceitful workers" who presented themselves as ministers of Christ. The presence of false apostles in the church should not surprise us, for even the dark angel presents himself as "an angel of light."

Satan often makes a pretense of taking the side of "righteousness." There are many examples of that today. Churchgoers may express the concern that Christians should recognize the "good" in other religions, that Christians should show "respect" for other faiths by refusing to "proselytize." We should send medical help to foreign countries, but should not suggest that their faith is any less valid than ours. Some churchgoers encourage the acceptance of the homosexual lifestyle, calling for compassion and understanding. Some churchgoers reject supersecessionism and renounce Jewish evangelism on the basis that Judaism's Old Covenant relationship with God is just as valid as Christianity's New Covenant relationship with God through Christ.

In all these, and many other things, "ministers of righteousness" (11:5) argue that their view is based on "Christian" values, such as love, compassion, acceptance, and respect for others. They appeal to Christian values, but they reject the clear teachings of Scripture. However "righteous" their arguments may appear, we can identify Satan's ministers by their rejection of the authority of God's Word.

2 Corinthians 12:7.

And lest I should be exalted above measure by the abundance of the revelations, a thorn in the flesh was given to me, a messenger of Satan to buffet me, lest I be exalted above measure.

Almost every commentator agrees Paul's "thorn" was a chronic illness of some sort, although they disagree about its nature. The verse reminds us that Satan, when God permits, can attack our bodies. Paul's insight about God's intent in permitting his suffering reminds us that God is so much greater than Satan that even the "harm" Satan does to us will be transformed into good.

Ephesians 2:1, 2.

who were dead in trespasses and sins, in which you once walked according to the course of this world, according to the prince of the power of the air, the spirit who now works in the sons of disobedience.

See the comments on p. 214.

Ephesians 4:26–27. " 'Be angry, and do not sin': do not let the sun go down on your wrath, nor give place to the devil." Anger is likely to flare up in us, but we must not allow it to control us. Conflicts with others must be dealt with immediately. Otherwise, Paul suggested, we "give place to the devil." The image here is one of warfare. Giving in to anger or other sinful emotions is like soldiers falling back before the advancing forces of their enemy.

Martin Luther once noted that he could not keep the birds from flying around his head (that is, feeling sinful emotions or having sinful thoughts), but he could keep them from building a nest in his hair (that is, taking control of his behavior). He was right. We do not have to give Satan any such advantage over us.

Ephesians 6:11. "Put on the whole armor of God, that you may be able to stand against the wiles of the devil." God has provided us with the resources we need to overcome Satan's influence in our lives.

1 Thessalonians 2:18. "Therefore we wanted to come to you—even I, Paul, time and again—but Satan hindered us." While Satan may be the active agent in making plans for ministry go amiss, ultimately God remains in control.

2 Thessalonians 2:9. "The coming of the lawless one is according to the working of Satan, with all power, signs, and lying wonders." In this chapter Paul wrote about history's end and the appearance of Satan's human agent called the "lawless one," or "Antichrist." Satan

The soldier's panoply (Eph. 6:11-17).

will use his supernatural abilities to support this agent with "power, signs, and lying wonders," that is, miracles intended to deceive.

Missionaries to many lands have reported encountering phenomena which served to keep pagans in awe of their witch doctors or sorcerers, but which the missionaries themselves could not explain. Such "lying wonders" are less frequent in the West, where Satan shapes culture to keep individuals in spiritual darkness. Here, however, Paul looked forward to a future time when Satan will unleash all his powers to attempt to capture the total allegiance of humankind.

In a society like ours, where most people doubt the existence of a personal devil, it suits Satan's purposes to remain in hiding. In other societies and in other times, it has suited Satan's purposes to manifest his malignant influence more openly and to dominate humans through fear.

2 Thessalonians 3:3. "But the Lord is faithful, who will establish you and guard you from the evil one." Paul was speaking of being "delivered from unreasonable and wicked men" (3:2). Throughout history, Christians have experienced persecution for their faith. Paul regarded the persecutors as agents of Satan who are doing his work. The word translated "establish" is *stērizō*, and it means "to remain firmly fastened." The Greek word for "guard" is *phulassō*, and it indicates protection. If we read Paul's encouragement against the backdrop of spiritual warfare, an appropriate image would be that of a walled city, unbreached by the swarming forces of an attacker.

Unreasonable and wicked men may persecute and even kill believers, yet the Christian colony God has established in a world dominated by Satan can never be overwhelmed. As Revelation 2:10 says,

Do not fear any of those things which you are about to suffer. Indeed, the devil is about to throw some of you into prison, that you may be tested, and you will have tribulation ten days. Be faithful until death, and I will give you the crown of life.

1 Timothy 3:6. "Not a novice, lest being puffed up with pride he fall into the same condemnation as the devil." In this passage Paul set out the requirements for the office of church elder. He warned that a new convert should not be selected, for he or she is less likely to understand his or her place in God's economy. A new convert is likely to become proud and, like Satan, step outside the will of God. Even the civil governments of the first-century world insisted that a person be tested by holding lower offices before becoming a candidate for higher office.

1 Timothy 3:7. "Moreover he must have a good testimony among those who are outside, lest he fall into reproach and the snare of the devil." This verse adds another qualification for the office of church elder. A well-established and good reputation is required of elders, for Satan delights in scandal and false accusations.

In a well-attested incident, Julius Caesar divorced his wife for what might seem to us a very innocent and minor indiscretion. Caesar, explaining his action, said, "Caesar's wife must be above reproach." How much more important that Christian leaders be above reproach, for Satan is intent on finding ways to defame our faith!

1 Timothy 4:1. "Now the Spirit expressly says that in latter times some will depart from the faith, giving heed to deceiving spirits and doctrines of demons." Two ascetic doctrines were specified as examples of the lies spoken by those who departed from the faith: the first forbade marriage, and the second commanded abstinence from certain foods. The danger here was one of abandoning grace in favor of a religion based on human effort.

Any requirements added to the Christian gospel by religious teachers are promoted by Satan. God's grace infuses the message of salvation by faith through the blood of Jesus Christ, and God's grace infuses the call to Christian living. We are invited to love God and to rely on His Holy Spirit to enable us to live godly lives. Augustine captured the secret of Christian living when he said, "Love God, and do as you please." If we truly love God, we will do what pleases Him.

1 Timothy 5:15. "For some have already turned aside after Satan." Paul encouraged young widows to marry again, rather than seek admission to the corps of widows who had the unique ministry of helping to guide the younger women in household management. Although they were subordinate to their husbands, wives in first-century society completely controlled the household, which might include slaves and servants, and that task was a greater challenge than we usually imagine.

Paul's concern was that widows under the age of 60 lacked the maturity and wisdom needed for their ministry, that they would "learn to be idle, wandering about from house to house, and not only idle but also gossips and busybodies, saying things which they ought not" (5:13). Paul already observed this in some churches, and he called it turning "aside after Satan." Thus, Paul's fear was that younger widows would turn away from their positive ministry and turn to destructive meddling. Before we teach others, we need to undergo the discipline of learning to *be* what we exhort.

2 Timothy 2:26. "And that they may come to their senses and escape the snare of the devil, having been taken captive by him to do his will." One of the ways in which a person in the first century might become a slave, someone forced to do another's will, was by being captured in battle. The image here is one of taking captives by snaring or netting.

This verse can be related to Satan's basic strategy: Satan enmeshes individuals in the numerous strands of beliefs and values in human society that reflect his own values rather than God's. Once enmeshed, the individual does Satan's will without even realizing that he or she is a slave and no longer free. Paul reminds us that to reach people who have been snared by Satan:

A servant of the Lord must not quarrel but be gentle to all, able to teach, patient, in humility correcting those who are in opposition, if God perhaps will grant them repentance, so that they may know the truth.

2 Timothy 2:24, 25

1 John 4:4. "You are of God, little children, and have overcome them, because He who is in you is greater than he who is in the world." In our survey of Satan's continual struggle against Christ and His people we've encountered a powerful and subtle being, whose well-tested strategies are designed to keep nonbelievers in his camp and to keep the people of God confused and unproductive. Yet Scripture never suggests that believers are outmatched, and the reason for that is stated in this verse: We have within us the Holy Spirit, God Himself, and God is far greater than the one who crouches in the world, intent on taking us unaware. And there is more. Satan is a *defeated* enemy whose doom is certain. We are on the winning side. As we will see, we have been equipped by God to win spiritual victories in our own lives here and now.

ANGELORE

MARTIN LUTHER'S HYMN

Martin Luther's most famous hymn is titled "A Mighty Fortress Is Our God." One of the stanzas of that hymn has lost much in translation. Here's what Luther affirmed as he contemplated our conflict with Satan.

> A mighty fortress is our God,
> A good weapon and defense;
> He helps us in every need
> That we encounter.
> The old, evil Enemy
> Is determined to get us;
> He make his vicious plans
> With might and cruel cunning;
> Nothing on earth is like him . . .
> But if the whole earth were full of demons
> Eager to swallow us,
> We would not fear,
> For we should still be saved.
> The Prince of the world,
> However fierce he claims to be,
> Can do us no harm;
> His power is under judgment;
> One little word can fell him.

1 John 5:19. "We know that we are of God, and the whole world lies under the sway of the wicked one." Earlier in this letter (2:16) John described the *kosmos* that lies under Satan's sway: "For all that is in the world—the lust of the flesh, the lust of the eyes, and the pride of life—is not of the Father but is of the world." The person who is "of God" must always guard against adopting the perspectives of sinful human cultures. The person out of touch with God craves to possess, values the things society deems important, and boasts about social status—and all these things are contrary to the perspective, values, and attitudes of God.

John reminds us that we know we are of God when we find ourselves gradually becoming different from those around us. An inner transformation which leads to a new and godly orientation in life is one sign that we are breaking away from the domain ruled by the wicked one.

THE DECISIVE BATTLE: HOW CHRIST DEFEATED SATAN

In the previous section we discovered that Satan is still active in our world, that he continues to weave the threads of culture that ensnare human beings, and that he is still intent on blocking Christ's work in the lives of believers. However, Scripture makes it clear that Satan is already a defeated enemy.

CHRIST DEMONSTRATED HIS POWER OVER SATAN IN HIS LIFE ON EARTH

Christ did not succumb to Satan's temptations (Matt. 4; Luke 4). Christ's initial victory over Satan was an important one, for it demonstrated that Satan could not deceive or trick Jesus, nor could Satan shake Jesus' commitment to do God's will. In that first direct confrontation, Satan was the one who fell back, unable to achieve a single objective.

CHRIST DEMONSTRATED HIS AUTHORITY OVER THE DEMONIC CITIZENS OF SATAN'S KINGDOM

Many stories in the Gospels deal with the direct conflict between Jesus and demons, and in each confrontation the demons are shown to be subject to Jesus (see chapter 14). Two illustrations from Luke establish the point.

Luke 4:41. "And demons also came out of many, crying out and saying, 'You are the Christ, the Son of God!' And He, rebuking them, did not allow them to speak, for they knew that He was the Christ." Jesus commanded the demons, and they were forced to do what He told them to do.

Luke 8:28, 29.

When he saw Jesus, he cried out, fell down before Him, and with a loud voice said, "What have I to do with You, Jesus, Son of the Most High God? I beg You, do not torment me!" For He had commanded the unclean spirit to come out of the man.

The man was possessed by many demons, not just one. Those evil spiritual beings were no match for Jesus. They recognized Him as the Son of God, and they were terrified of Him.

Jesus, during His life on earth, consistently demonstrated that He was superior to Satan and his fallen angels. Peter later described Jesus as someone who was anointed "with the Holy Spirit and with power, who went about doing good and healing all who were oppressed by the devil" (Acts 10:38). There was nothing the devil could do that Christ could not undo!

ONE OF CHRIST'S MISSIONS WAS TO PUT AN END TO THE DEVIL'S WORKS

With reference to His coming crucifixion, Jesus said, "Now is the judgment of this world [*kosmos*]; now the ruler of this world will be cast out" (John 12:31). In a similar vein, Jesus revealed that the ministry of the Holy Spirit would be one of convicting the world of sin, righteousness, and judgment: "of judgment, because the ruler of this world is judged" (John 16:11). Jesus' death on the cross demonstrated conclusively God's commitment to punish sin; and in that decisive event the doom of the universe's chief sinner, Satan, was sealed.

Jesus' mission as it regards Satan is described even more clearly in Hebrews and 1 John. John wrote, "For this purpose the Son of God was manifested, that He might destroy the works of the devil" (1 John 3:8). And Hebrews 2:14, 15 spoke of Jesus' incarnation as necessary "[so] that through death He might destroy him who had the power of death, that is, the devil, and release those who through fear of death were all their lifetime subject to bondage." From the very beginning Satan was clearly doomed, destined to be overcome and destroyed by Jesus.

Christ won the decisive victory on Calvary *(Colossians 2:13–15).* The apostle Paul wrote:

And you, being dead in your trespasses and the un-circumcision of your flesh, He has made alive to-gether with Him, having forgiven you all trespasses, having wiped out the handwriting of requirements that was against us, which was contrary to us. And He has taken it out of the way, having nailed it to the cross. Having disarmed principalities and pow-ers, He made a public spectacle of them, triumph-ing over them in it.

Satan and all the angels who fell with him are the "principalities and powers" who have had such a disastrous influence on our race from the beginning. The Cross displayed the redeeming love of God, powerful enough to give life to those who were spiritually dead and to wrest them from Satan's kingdom. In the power of the Cross, the utter futility of Sa-tan's effort to defeat God was publicly dis-played, and all Satan's pretensions of power and glory were shown to be hollow and empty. Satan is nothing but a creature after all.

Satan's doom will come in God's own time. The Bible depicts Satan as a condemned crim-inal, one who is free for a time, but only until the sentence, already passed, is carried out. Satan is still our active enemy, and we need to be on guard against him. The book of Revela-tion describes a day when the devil will be "cast into the lake of fire and brimstone" to be "tormented day and night forever and ever" (20:10). The judgment and the destiny of Sa-tan and his fallen angels will be examined in the final chapter of this book.

STANDING AGAINST SATAN TODAY

Although Satan is a defeated enemy, he is an active enemy. Peter warns us: "Be sober, be vigilant; because your adversary the devil walks about like a roaring lion, seeking whom he may devour" (1 Pet. 5:8). Scripture does more than simply warn about or describe Sa-tan's strategies; the Bible also provides instruc-tion designed to help us avoid the traps Satan sets. Thus, Peter continues: "Resist him, stead-fast in the faith, knowing that the same suffer-ings are experienced by your brotherhood in the world" (5:9).

Satan will use suffering in an attempt to shake our faith. We are to resist Satan's sugges-tions that some strange thing is happening to us when we experience suffering; we are to re-main steadfast, confident that God is in con-trol. Satan will fall back before those who have their confidence fixed in the Lord.

Throughout this review of Satan's present activities, many similar thoughts and princi-ples have surfaced. Three critical passages pro-vide overarching principles for us to apply.

PRINCIPLES DRAWN FROM THE TEMPTATION OF CHRIST
(Luke 4; Matthew 4)

Be aware of areas of human vulnerability. Sa-tan's first temptation was addressed to the physical nature of human beings. Although we must provide for our bodily needs, we are to be careful lest a concern to meet a physical need draws us away from God's will.

Satan's second temptation was addressed to the moral nature of human beings. People in every society value what they believe is "good," and are drawn to it. We must be care-ful not to let our desire to attain a good end lead us to adopt the wrong means; we must not put something that is "good" in place of God's will, which is always "best."

Satan's third temptation was addressed to the spiritual nature of human beings. We have a need for a personal relationship with God, yet we may often feel separated from Him, iso-lated and alone. We are to remember that our calling is to live a life of faith; we must remain confident of God's loving commitment to us. We should not demand that God "prove" His love to us. An awareness of these three av-enues of temptation may help us to become more sensitive to our personal vulnerabilities and thus better able to recognize occasions when Satan is tempting us.

Remember to take a stand on a word (rhēma) from God. When Satan tempts us to take a course of action, it's important that we have a specific word from God on which to take a stand. The word (*rhēma*) may be internal, our personal sense of being led by the Holy Spirit. Most often the word (*rhēma*) will be a verse or teaching from Scripture brought to mind by the Holy Spirit. If we have no such word to guide us, it's good to search the Scriptures and ask the Lord to lead us to the relevant truth.

PRINCIPLES DRAWN FROM JAMES 4:4B–10

This passage focuses on certain basic attitudes which dramatically affect our ability to resist Satan and evade his many traps.

Do you not know that friendship with the world is enmity with God? Whoever therefore wants to be a friend of the world makes himself an enemy of God. Or do you think that the Scripture says in vain, "The Spirit who dwells in us yearns jealously"?

But He gives more grace. Therefore He says:

"God resists the proud,
But gives grace to the humble."

Therefore submit to God. Resist the devil and he will flee from you. Draw near to God and He will draw near to you. Cleanse your hands, you sinners; and purify your hearts, you double-minded. Lament and mourn and weep! Let your laughter be turned to mourning and your joy to gloom. Humble yourselves in the sight of the Lord, and He will lift you up.

James 4:4b–10

Don't make friends with the world *(James 4:4)*. In the New Testament, the "world" (*kosmos*) represents human culture, woven through and through with the values, perspectives, attitudes, and motives that reflect Satan's character. If we are to resist Satan, we must decisively reject the cravings which drive the unsaved and consciously choose the values of God as revealed in His Son and in Scripture. There truly *is* a difference, so much difference "that friendship with the world is enmity with God."

Develop a spirit of humility *(James 4:5–7)*. The "humble" are contrasted with the "proud."

Pride was a central element in Satan's original sin. He wanted to live life on his own terms rather than submit to the Lord as the creature he was.

God is jealous of us: He yearns for us to be committed to Him fully. He is eager for us to adopt that spirit of humility which leads us to welcome His will and to follow it joyfully. Yet there will always be a struggle. In that struggle we are to consciously submit to God and to consciously resist the devil. When we do, the devil will flee from us.

Make a clear-cut commitment *(James 4:8–10)*. These verses seem harsh and unrealistic at first, until we note that verse 8 describes people who can't make up their minds; who try to live with one foot in the world and one foot in God's kingdom. Obviously, that is impossible. The things the world offers may be associated with joy and laughter, but they must be seen for what they really are—dark and oppressive causes for lamenting and mourning. When we humble ourselves, when we make a complete commitment to God and to the ways of His kingdom, He will lift us up.

What James advocated, then, was for us to nurture a relationship with God—which includes purging ourselves of the motives and values of this world, adopting a spirit of humility, and making a decisive commitment to Christ and His kingdom. A person who nurtures that kind of relationship with the Lord will have nothing to fear from Satan.

INTERPERSONAL PRINCIPLES DRAWN FROM EPHESIANS 6:10–18

This passage has been a favorite of Christians through the ages. An analogy forms the basis for a description of the basic equipment that the Christian faith provides believers so that they may "be able to stand against the wiles of the devil." The analogy is between spiritual resources and the panoply, or armor, of the fully equipped Roman foot soldier. The passage reads:

Put on the whole armor of God, that you may be able to stand against the wiles of the devil. For we wrestle not against flesh and blood, but against principalities, against powers, against the rulers of the darkness of this age, against spiritual hosts of wickedness in the heavenly places. Therefore take up the whole armor of God, that you may be able to withstand in the evil day, and having done all, to stand.

Stand therefore, having girded your waist with truth, having put on the breastplate of righteousness, and having shod your feet with the preparation of the gospel of peace; above all, taking the shield of faith with which you will be able to quench all the fiery darts of the wicked one. And take the helmet of salvation, and the sword of the Spirit, which is the word of God; praying always with all prayer and supplication in the Spirit, being watchful to this end with all perseverance and supplication for all the saints.

Ephesians 6:10–18

Paul emphasized the fact that we are engaged in a spiritual warfare with dark angelic hosts directed by Satan himself. He also described the equipment God has provided to enable us to battle Satan successfully.

While there is some debate about the meaning behind some pieces of God's armor, the best way to understand what the pieces of armor mean is to look within the context of Ephesians itself. Only when Paul mentions the "sword of the Spirit" does he give a definition—it is "the Word of God." The reason Paul provided a definition here is that "the Word of God" has not been treated earlier in Ephesians. Paul has already provided the information we need to interpret the other pieces of equipment successfully. If we do interpret "the whole armor of God" in this way, we can better understand how God equips us for our warfare against Satan and his hordes.

The belt of truth (*Ephesians 6:14*). Paul urged the Ephesians to put "away lying" and " 'Let each one of you speak truth with his neighbor,' for we are members of one another" (4:25). Openness and honesty gird us together; misunderstanding and hidden motives divide us.

The breastplate of righteousness (*Ephesians 6:14*). Paul insisted that there must not be even a hint of immorality or impurity among God's holy people (5:3). Righteous living is essential, for it guards our hearts and the hearts of others.

Feet shod with the preparation of the gospel of peace (*Ephesians 6:15*). More than once in this letter Paul stressed how the gospel brings peace, reconciles us to God, and makes us one. In Ephesians, peace is the bond which maintains the unity created by the Spirit. When that unity is maintained, Christ's church is able to move in full responsiveness to its Head.

The shield of faith (*Ephesians 6:16*). We maintain a confident hope in the reality and power of God. That trust extinguishes doubts. We are inadequate in ourselves, it is true; but our trust is in God, "who is able to do exceedingly abundantly above all that we ask or think, according to the power that works in us" (3:20).

The helmet of salvation (*Ephesians 6:17*). Salvation brings us a new life and a new identity. By keeping our identity as "Christ's people" constantly before us, our perspective of life is transformed. Satan's dreams of distorted relationships cannot cloud the mind of the person who grasps the full meaning of the salvation we enjoy in Christ.

The sword of the Spirit (*Ephesians 6:17*). Paul identifies the sword, a weapon used for attack and defense, as "the word of God." Here the term for "word" is *logos,* not *rhēma.* The entire revelation found in Scripture is our armory, from which we can select the appropriate weapon whenever we need it. The more we study the Bible, and the better we understand the Scriptures, the better equipped we are to do battle with Satan.

Praying always with all prayer and supplication in the Spirit (*Ephesians 6:18*). While Paul does not present prayer as a piece of armor, he reminds us that prayer is basic. As we put on any piece of "the whole armor of God," we should pray. In all we do, we seek God's will; and in all we do, we rely completely on Him.

SUMMARY

God truly has provided all we need to meet Satan's attacks victoriously. Luke's report of the temptations of Christ makes us aware of our vulnerabilities and teaches us how to rely on a word from God to protect us. James 4 teaches us the basic attitudes we need to develop if we are to watch the devil flee from us. Ephesians 6 describes an interpersonal dimension of God's resources: Paul exhorts us to stand against the devil and to stand together as we engage in spiritual warfare against evil.

Satan is a defeated enemy. Christ is triumphant. No matter how powerful Satan may be, in Christ we triumph over evil.

CHAPTER 14

KINGDOMS IN CONFLICT:

JESUS VERSUS DEMONS
Matthew—John

M artin Luther asserts:

If we would be Christians . . . we must surely expect and reckon upon having the devil with all his angels and the world as our enemies, who will bring every possible misfortune and grief upon us. For where the Word of God is preached, accepted, or believed, and produces fruit, there the holy cross cannot be wanting.

Larger Catechism

Satan's angels were active in the Gospels, where they are called "demons," "evil spirits," and "devils." Those fallen angels were also active in Old Testament times, as we saw in chapter 7. A brief review of what we learned about demons in the Old Testament will set the stage for the complete revelation about demons and their activities given in the New Testament.

DEMONS IN THE OLD TESTAMENT

REFERENCES TO DEMONS IN THE OLD TESTAMENT

There are only a few references to demons in the Old Testament. When demons are mentioned, they are always closely associated with pagan religions. Demons were believed to be very real supernatural beings, who lurked behind the idols of the deities worshiped by the pagans. God warned His people to keep away from pagan religions (Lev. 17:7; Deut. 32:17). Sacrifices offered at the worship centers set up by Jeroboam I of Israel for the worship of Yahweh were condemned because they violated God's command to offer sacrifices only at the temple in Jerusalem, where descendants of Aaron served as priests. Second Chronicles 11:15 explains more about what Jeroboam did: "Then he appointed for himself priests for the high places, for the demons, and the calf idols which he had made" (NKJV). Sacrificing to idols—no matter whether the idols were dedicated to pagan deities or to Yahweh—was equated with sacrificing to demons. Today the same spiritual beings crouch behind the false religions of our world and accept the worship which rightfully belongs only to God.

NAMES FOR DEMONS IN THE OLD TESTAMENT

Several different Hebrew words were used to refer to demonic beings. For instance, they were called *Shedhim*, "rulers" or "lords" (Deut. 32:17). *Sa'ir*, which means "goat," was also used to designate demons (Lev. 17:7). *'Elilim* identified the pagan gods in Psalm 96:5: "all the gods of the peoples are demons." Also, the word *'elohim*, which is usually rendered "God" or "gods," was sometimes used of demons, in which case it means "supernatural beings" (1 Sam. 28:13; Isa. 8:19).

In addition, several demon-gods of pagan peoples are mentioned by name in the Old Testament. *Gad* and *Meni* (Isa. 65:11) were the Babylonian demon-gods "Fortune" and "Destiny." *Qeter* (Ps. 91:6) was the demon-god "Destruction."

What is significant is that the Old Testament linked demons with pagan worship, false religion, or the occult, which was closely associated with the practice of many pagan religions.

DEMONS IN THE ANCIENT NEAR EAST

The very few references to demons in the Old Testament provide a fascinating contrast to the proliferation of demons and demon-gods in the Ancient Near Eastern cultures out of which the Hebrew people were called. The Sumerian, Assyrian, and Babylonian languages had hundreds of words for the various spirits, demons, and deities who infested those lands. Most of those demonic spirits and gods were regarded as hostile to human beings. Much energy was devoted to devising spells that would help persons avoid or reverse the harmful actions of demons.

At the same time, the Mari tablets indicate that messages from the spirit world, and especially from the deities worshiped in the land, were valued by rulers as sources of guidance. Those demonically inspired messages helped bind the people to their deities. The Mari tablets gave three different names to carriers of such messages: *apilu, assinuu, muhhu*.

The extensive literature on demons in the Ancient Near East makes it clear that evil spiritual beings seemed terribly real to ancient peoples. However, aside from the few references in the Old Testament just mentioned, demons played no such role in the lives of God's people. God clearly placed a hedge around Israel, and when the Israelites were faithful to Him, they were protected from Satan and his demon hordes.

DEMONS IN FIRST-CENTURY JUDAISM

JEWISH EXORCISTS WERE IN DEMAND IN THE FIRST-CENTURY ROMAN WORLD

Jewish exorcists were held in high regard throughout the Roman Empire in the first century. Acts mentions "itinerant Jewish exorcists" (19:13) and "seven sons of Sceva, a Jewish chief priest," who also performed exorcisms (19:14). It's clear from the context that those exorcists relied on the same kind of magical formulas found in pagan magical texts of the period.

JOSEPHUS CREDITED SOLOMON WITH TEACHING JEWS ABOUT DEMONS AND HOW TO CONTROL THEM

The first-century Jewish historian, Josephus, praised Solomon as the father of Jewish exorcism. Josephus described an incident in which a countryman of his—in the presence of the emperor Vespasian, his sons, and his military retinue—spoke Solomon's name, recited incantations supposedly composed by Solomon, and successfully drew a demon out the nostrils of a possessed man. Josephus said of Solomon:

God granted him knowledge of the art used against demons for the benefit and healing of men. He also composed incantations by which illnesses are relieved, and left behind forms of exorcisms with which those possessed by demons drive them out, never to return. And this kind of cure is of very great power among us [Jews] today.

Antiquities 8.2.5

THE *TESTAMENT OF SOLOMON* REFLECTS FIRST-CENTURY JEWISH BELIEFS ABOUT DEMONS AND EXORCISM

A fascinating book called the *Testament of Solomon,* which dates from sometime during the first to third centuries A.D., describes many beliefs about demons and Solomon. Scholars agree that these beliefs were undoubtedly common in the first century, when Josephus wrote. The *Testament of Solomon* provides a striking contrast to what we read about demons in the New Testament.

In chapter 2 Solomon, to whom God gave the power to control demons, questioned a demon named Ornias.

I said to him, "Tell me, in which sign of the zodiac do you reside." The demon replied, "In Aquarius; I strangle those who reside in Aquarius because of their passion for women whose zodiacal sign is Virgo. Moreover, while in a trance I undergo three transformations. Sometimes I am a man who craves the bodies of effeminate boys and when I touch them, they suffer great pain. Sometimes I become a creature with wings [flying] up to the heavenly regions. Finally, I assume the appearance of a lion."

In chapter 3 Solomon questioned a female demon named Onoskelis, described as having a very beautiful body with the legs of a mule. Onoskelis responded to Solomon's queries:

"I am a spirit which has been made into a body. I recline in a den on the earth. I make my home in caves. However, I have a many-sided character. Sometimes I strangle men; sometimes I pervert them from their true natures. Most of the time, my habitats are cliffs, caves, and ravines. Frequently, I also associate with men who think of me as a woman, especially with those whose skin is honey-colored, for we are of the same constellation. It is also true that they worship my star secretly and openly. They do not know that they deceive themselves and excite me to be an evildoer all the more."

In an interview with the demon Asmodeus, reported in chapter 5, Solomon learned the following:

"My constellation reclines in its den in heaven; some men call me the Great Bear, but others the Offspring of a Dragon. . . . So do not ask me so many things, Solomon, for eventually your kingdom will be divided. This glory of yours is temporary. You have us to torture for a little while; then we shall disperse among human beings again with the result that we shall be worshiped as gods . . . I am the renowned Asmodeus; I cause the wickedness of men to spread throughout the world. I am always hatching plots against newlyweds; I mar the beauty of virgins and cause their hearts to grow cold."

I said to him, "Is this all you do?" He spoke again: "I spread madness about women through the stars and I have often committed a rash of murders."

Later (chapter 19) Solomon was impressed that a prophecy of the demon Ornias had come true. He forced the demon to explain how he knew God's plan for the future. Ornias told him:

We demons go up to the firmament of heaven, fly around among the stars, and hear the decisions which issue from God concerning the lives of men. The rest of the time we come and, being transformed, cause destruction, whether by domination, or by fire, or by sword, or by chance.

A quote from Solomon's interview with a demon named Lix Tetrax (chapter 7) indicates the importance of incantations. Solomon himself had a seal of power, but ordinary men needed more to hold off or defeat hostile demons. Lix Tetrax, in addition to setting fields on fire and slithering into households to make them nonfunctional, was linked with a sickness called "day-and-a-half fever." He recommends that "men pray about the day-and-a-half fever, invoking these three names, 'Baltala, Thailal, Melchal.' " One of the demon's duties was to heal this fever when the three names were invoked.

OLD TESTAMENT AND PAGAN CONCEPTS REFLECTED IN THE *TESTAMENT OF SOLOMON*

A quick reading of the *Testament of Solomon* would seem to indicate that it dimly reflects Old Testament teachings about demons. However, pagan concepts common in both the Ancient Near East and the Hellenistic world are prevalent in the *Testament of Solomon,* which undoubtedly reflects the views of many ordinary people in first-century Palestine.

Biblical concepts in the Testament of Solomon. There can be no doubt that the Old Testament assumes the existence of demons. The major point of harmony between the *Testament of Solomon* and the Old Testament is found in the statement made by Asmodeus that "we shall be worshiped as gods." The Old Testament warnings against paganism and idolatry emphasized that behind every pagan god and its idol stood a demon, eager to direct the worship of human beings to himself and his leader, Satan, and away from the Lord.

Another point of harmony between the *Testament of Solomon* and the Old Testament is in the constant linking of demons to the occult. While the *Testament of Solomon* goes far beyond the Old Testament by associating specific demons with different signs of the zodiac, all occult practices are condemned as demonic in Scripture (Deut. 18:9–14).

A third point of harmony between the *Testament of Solomon* and the Old Testament is that demons are viewed as basically hostile to human beings and that they display this hostility in a number of ways.

Pagan concepts in the Testament of Solomon. Numerous assumptions about demons are common to the pagan mythologies prominent in the Ancient Near East and the first-century Roman world.

Demons have names that can be known. Supposedly, knowing a demon's name provided some level of control over him or her. Very few demons are named in Scripture (see Luke 8:30; Rev. 9:11). There is no suggestion in Scripture that knowing the names of demons has any relationship to power over them.

Demons may be of either sex. The preponderance of demons in the Ancient Near East were male, but there were a few female demons. Scripture knows only male angels and demons.

Demons can be bound or driven out by the use of incantations. Incantations are not called for in any exorcism reported in Scripture.

Demons specialize. Specific demons in pagan lore caused specific effects. There was a demon of the "day-and-a-half fever," and a demon who marred the beauty of virgins, and so on. Also, specific demons had to be called on in any attempt to reverse the effects of other demons.

Demons can tell the future. This element was strong in both Hellenistic and Mesopotamian cultures. The oracles of the Greek-speaking world and of the *apilu, assinuu,* and *muhhu* in the Mari tablets are so well attested that there seems to be truth in this claim. The *Testament of Solomon* explained how demons could know the future by suggesting that demons fly up into the heavens and "overhear" God's plans. It seems more likely that demonic predictions are based on observations of human behavior and information not available to the individuals to whom the prediction is made.

Demons can take on animal and human form. Two of the demons "quoted" in the *Testament of Solomon* claimed they could take on various forms when their intent was to deceive or harm human beings. It is possible that this tradition has historic roots in Genesis 6.

Demons are associated with dark and dangerous places. This association was strong in the demonology of the Ancient Near East; it goes back to Sumer and was carried on by other Mesopotamian cultures. Scripture associates demons with pagan places of worship, an association understandably absent in those cultures whose religions were dominated by demons.

THE GOSPELS AND ACTS SHOULD BE READ AGAINST THE BACKGROUND OF PAGAN SUPERSTITIONS ABOUT DEMONS

An example of how an understanding of popular beliefs about demons common in first-century Palestine can provide insights about biblical texts is provided by Mark 1:23–27. The passage reads:

> Now there was a man in their synagogue with an unclean spirit. And he cried out, saying, "Let us alone! What have we to do with You, Jesus of Nazareth? Did You come to destroy us? I know who You are—the Holy One of God!"
>
> But Jesus rebuked him, saying, "Be quiet, and come out of him!" And when the unclean spirit had convulsed him and cried out with a loud voice, he came out of him. Then were they all amazed, so that they questioned among themselves, saying, "What is this? What new doctrine is this? For with authority He commands even the unclean spirits, and they obey Him."

The bystanders were not surprised that a demon took control of a human being. They were not even surprised that such a demon was cast out of the man. What shocked the by-standers was the fact that Jesus *relied on His own authority* when commanding the demon to leave.

If a Jewish exorcist had been called in, he would have used an incantation that invoked

a variety of heavenly powers to cast out the demon. The Jewish exorcist described by Jose-phus held a "root that Solomon prescribed" under the demon possessed man's nose, "speaking Solomon's name and reciting the incantations which he [Solomon] had composed" (*Antiquities* 8.5.2). Such exorcists claimed no power of their own, but they did claim to have the knowledge needed to manipulate or control supernatural powers and so overcome demons.

However, Jesus simply said, "Be quiet, and come out of him!" And the demon did. Jesus relied on His own intrinsic authority, the power of His own word, and the demon was forced to obey. No wonder the onlookers were stricken with amazement. In their whole system of demonology, no human being had the authority to command demons; no one could make demons obey.

Christ's power over demons, which we take for granted today, was utterly revolutionary in a culture where demons were feared and human beings felt helpless against them. Not even the prophets of old, not even Moses, had cast out a demon! In casting out demons wherever He went, and in healing sicknesses caused by demons, Jesus provided unmistakable proof that He was indeed Israel's promised Messiah.

WHEN KINGDOMS COLLIDE

In chapter 13 we looked at direct confrontations between Jesus and Satan, and we also examined what the Bible teaches about Satan's continuing warfare against God's people. We noted that one of Satan's titles was "prince of the power of the air" (Eph. 2:2). John called Satan the "ruler of this world" (John 12:31; 14:30; 16:11). When Satan offered to give Christ the power and glory of all the kingdoms of the world (Luke 4:6), he told at least a half-truth. It's no wonder that Paul portrayed God's redemption of sinners in these words: "He has delivered us from the power of darkness and conveyed us into the kingdom of the Son of His love, in whom we

Jesus casting out demons.

have redemption through His blood, the for-giveness of sins" (Col. 1:13, 14).

DEMONS BELONG TO THE KINGDOM OF SATAN AND ARE SATAN'S WILLING SUBJECTS

The kingdom of Satan includes his super-natural subjects: the angels who fell with him, who are none other than the demons of the New Testament and the gods and demons of pagan religions. Matthew 25:41 speaks of "Sa-tan and his [fallen] angels." The possessive "his" indicates that Satan has authority over the dark hosts. The demons of the Old Testa-ment who set out to divert the worship of hu-man beings to themselves and to Satan were doing that dark angel's work.

When we read about Jesus' conflict with demons in the Gospels it is important to un-derstand that what is described is a clash of kingdoms. The kingdom of God, in the per-son of King Jesus, invaded a realm that had been controlled largely by Satan. Jesus' im-pressive victories over Satan and his demonic followers provided visible evidence that the historic moment of salvation was near.

THE SIGNIFICANCE OF THE CLASH IS SUMMED UP IN MATTHEW 12 AND PARALLEL PASSAGES

Jesus' stunning power over demons not only amazed the common people, it also shocked the religious leaders who increasingly opposed the Lord. When the common people began to wonder aloud about whether Jesus was the Messiah (Matt. 12:23), Jesus' oppo-nents had to come up with a plausible explana-tion for His healings and exorcisms. Matthew tells us what the religious leaders proposed:

> Now when the Pharisees heard it [that people were wondering if Jesus was the Messiah] they said, "This fellow does not cast out demons except by Beelzebub, the ruler of the demons."
>
> But Jesus knew their thoughts, and said to them: "Every kingdom divided against itself is brought to desolation, and every city or house di-vided against itself will not stand. If Satan casts out Satan, he is divided against himself. How then will his kingdom stand? And if I cast out demons by Beelzebub, by whom do your sons cast them out? Therefore they shall be your judges. But if I cast out demons by the Spirit of God, surely the kingdom of God has come upon you."

Matthew 12:24–28

❖

Jesus and the Pharisees.

Casting out "demons . . . by Beelzebub, the ruler of the demons" (Matthew 12:24). This explanation was based on the accepted notion that to control demons a person must call on some greater being(s) who could force the demons to leave the sick or the possessed alone. Jesus' powers were so obvious and so great that the Pharisees decided there could be only one explanation: The only being powerful enough to force his will on so many different kinds of demons must be the chief of demons himself! This accusation would have carried considerable weight, given the notions about demons current in the first century.

"If Satan casts out Satan . . . how then will his kingdom stand?" (Matthew 12:26). Jesus pinpointed a flaw in the Pharisees' reasoning. Satan had no reason to support the kind of massive attack on his kingdom that Jesus' actions precipitated. Never in Old Testament history did a single prophet, priest, or holy man cast out a single demon, or heal a single individual oppressed by a demon. Yet there Jesus was, performing such wonders daily, and in the process showing up demons as comparatively weak beings. If Satan wanted to extend the influence of his kingdom, he surely would not go about it in this way. To assume that Satan was the power active in Jesus' act of casting out demons would mean that Satan was at war against himself, and that is an absurd notion. Satan isn't about to destroy his own kingdom or reduce its influence over the minds and hearts of human beings.

"By whom do your sons cast them out?" (Matthew 12:27). We noted earlier that in the first century, Jewish exorcists were highly regarded throughout the Roman Empire. Jesus easily turned the Pharisees' argument against them. If it takes the prince of demons to cast out demons, doesn't this imply that their own sons were in league with Satan? This was a logical conclusion but one which the Pharisees, who believed firmly in spirits and the supernatural, definitely did not want to accept! While Jesus' remark showed how vul-

nerable the Pharisees' accusations against Him made the Pharisees themselves, Jesus let this point go in order to focus on what was really happening.

"But if I cast out demons by the Spirit of God" (Matthew 12:28). The power Jesus used against demons was, in fact, the power of God. The greater and more powerful One who forced the demons to obey Jesus was the Spirit of God Himself. How much more reasonable it was for Jesus' observers to conclude that God provided the power needed to cast out demons than to conclude that Satan was at war with his own followers.

"Surely the kingdom of God has come upon you" (Matthew 12:28). Jesus was not suggesting that the kingdom of God had already been instituted on earth. What Jesus did was to present Himself as the One whom God had appointed to bring in the eschatological kingdom. The kingdom is present in the person of the King, and Jesus' daily victories over demons made this fact absolutely clear.

Only the person who refuses to recognize the implications of Jesus' power over demons will miss or deny Jesus' implicit claim to be the Messiah.

THE SIGNIFICANCE OF DEMONIC ACTIVITY IN THE ERA OF THE GOSPELS

Matthew's report of the Pharisees' charge and Jesus' reply helps us understand the significance of the demonic activity described in the Gospels.

In the Old Testament demons are hardly mentioned, but in the Gospels they occupy our attention page after page. It is clear that something very unusual was happening; in fact, the Pharisees' accusation might reflect a striking increase in demonic activity during Christ's lifetime, especially during His years of ministry. What seemed to have been happening was that Satan marshaled his forces to oppose Jesus during His time on earth. Satan's opposition took many forms, but certainly it included the spreading of rumors like the one started by the Pharisees—that Jesus was in league with the devil.

THE SIGNIFICANCE OF JESUS' DOMINANCE OVER DEMONS

Jesus said, "But if I cast out demons by the Spirit of God, surely the kingdom of God has come upon you." Jesus' dominance over demons provided proof that the King had come and was present. The demons who oppressed and possessed human beings and made their lives miserable were being cast out. Clearly, when the King took His throne, there would be no room in His kingdom for the pain and suffering caused by dark spiritual forces. Thus, when Jesus cast out demons He not only presented Himself as the Messiah, He also demonstrated what it would be like for human beings to live in the kingdom of God!

JESUS' DOMINATION OF DEMONS CALLED FOR A DECISION FROM THOSE WHO OBSERVED

The evidence provided by Jesus' casting out demons was so compelling that it called for a decision from observers. After emphasizing His power over Satan himself (Matt. 12:29), Jesus told his listeners, "He who is not with Me is against Me, and he who does not gather with Me scatters abroad" (Matt. 12:30). One who saw what Jesus did should not hesitate, but should fully accept Him as the Christ.

After seeing Jesus cast out demons, there was no justification for sitting on the fence. Anyone who did not make a positive decision immediately had, by their hesitation, decided against King Jesus and His kingdom. There are only two kingdoms to which human beings, knowingly or unknowingly, can give allegiance. We can either be committed to Jesus, or we will fall under the power of Satan. Although we can learn a lot about demons by exploring references to them in the Gospels, the most important lesson the stories about Jesus and demons convey is that Christ is Lord—and we need to acknowledge Him as such, now.

EVERY CONFRONTATION WITH DEMONS IN THE GOSPELS

Each time we encounter demonic activity in the Gospels, the situation involves an incident in which Jesus, or His disciples, confronted and defeated them. This continues to be the central message of the stories about demons in the Gospels: Jesus—who mastered the forces of Satan, and who deserves our complete trust and allegiance—is Lord. At the same time, the stories about demons can help us develop a biblical understanding of the nature of these malevolent beings and their powers. So it is important to examine each reported incident to see what we can learn. This is especially important because, as we will see in chapter 15, demons are still active today.

Matthew 4:24.

Then His fame went throughout all Syria; and they brought to Him all sick people who were afflicted with various diseases and torments, and those who were demon possessed, epileptics, and paralytics; and He healed them.

The word translated "demon possessed" is *daimonizomai,* which means "to be possessed by a demon." Just what demon possession implies must be discovered from the texts in which the word is found (most frequently in the Gospel of Matthew), since there is no corresponding term in the Old Testament.

Here demon possession is listed among "various diseases and torments," including epilepsy and paralysis. While Matthew distinguishes between demon possession and the other named diseases, the inclusion of demon possession on this list suggests that it frequently involved physical weakness or chronic sickness. Whatever the nature or source of the "diseases and torments" of those brought to Jesus, "He healed them." No sickness—whether naturally or supernaturally induced—was too difficult for Jesus to cure.

Matthew 8:16. "When evening had come, they brought to Him many who were demon possessed. And He cast out the spirits with a word, and healed all who were sick."

Again the Greek word is *daimonizomai*, and, once again, demon possession is mentioned together with the healing of the sick. This time, however, more information is provided. The verb phrase "cast out" indicates that the demons had in some way entered the person who was possessed, that a demon or demons had taken up residence in or alongside the personality of the individual. Jesus forced the demon to leave the person, and in this way He freed the person from the demon's hold and from the damage the demon had been doing.

The fact that Jesus cast out demons with a word is also important. The verb phrase "cast out" does not imply that Jesus used a word or the name of power, as in an incantation; rather, the phrase describes the means Jesus used to expel the spirit: a simple command. Jesus spoke, and the demon was forced to obey Him. Whatever evil influence demons may have over human beings, they are unable to stand before Jesus Christ.

Matthew 8:28–32.

When He had come to the other side, to the country of the Gergesenes, there met Him two demon possessed men, coming out of the tombs, exceedingly fierce, so that no one could pass that way. And suddenly they cried out, saying, "What have we to do with You, Jesus, You Son of God? Have You come here to torment us before the time?"

Now a good way off from them there was a herd of many swine feeding. So the demons begged Him, saying, "If you cast us out, permit us to go away into the herd of swine."

And He said to them, "Go." So when they had come out, they went into the herd of swine. And suddenly the whole herd of swine ran violently down the steep place into the sea, and perished in the water.

Mark and Luke tell a story extremely similar to this one in their Gospels. Most commentators believe that Mark and Luke report the same incident, but that they chose to focus on one of the demon possessed men. From this report in Matthew's Gospel alone, however, we gather quite a bit of information about demon possession.

"Coming out of the tombs" (Matthew 8:28). In some cases of demon possession, normal interpersonal relationships are rejected. These demon possessed men left their towns and families to live in a desolate area of tombs, which the typical first-century person would have avoided, especially at night.

"Exceedingly fierce, so that no one could pass that way" (Matthew 8:28). In some cases, the demon possessed exhibit extreme hostility, and they might even violently attack other persons. In this case, the demonized men attacked anyone who even passed near.

"What have we to do with You, Jesus, You Son of God?" (Matthew 8:29). These demons certainly cannot be described as "influences" or as some unidentified mental illness. The demons used the men's vocal apparatus to speak. They not only spoke of themselves in personal terms ("we"), but also recognized Jesus. The demons immediately identified Jesus as the Son of God, even though He had just come into their district by sea, even though Christ did not provide the evidence He usually did to the people to whom He ministered.

We learn here that in some cases demons can and do speak using the body of the person they "possess." To that extent, at least, demons control the possessed person's actions. In fact, the impact of demon possession on the relationships and attitudes of these demon possessed men indicates that in severe cases, demons distort the mental and emotional stability of individuals and control their behavior.

"Have you come here to torment us before the time?" (Matthew 8:29). This question makes it clear that demons know the fate that awaits

Jesus sent demons into a herd of swine.

❖

them and recognize the ultimate futility of their struggle against God. It is a commentary on the character of demons that, despite this knowledge, they seem determined to bring as many human beings with them to destruction as they can, or at least to torment humans as much as possible here and now.

"Permit us to go away into the herd of swine" (*Matthew 8:31*). This request suggests two things. First, some demons seem driven to inhabit the physical body of a living being, especially that of a human. This is the only place in Scripture where there is any mention of demons possessing animals. Second, the reaction of the pigs, who dashed into the waters and were killed, suggests that there may be such a great difference between demons and animals that it is impossible for demons to possess animals successfully. As we will see in

chapter 16, there is a much closer correspondence between the nature of human beings and that of angels and demons. However, we can only speculate about this issue.

Matthew 9:32–34.

As they went out, behold, they brought to Him a man, mute and demon possessed. And when the demon was cast out, the mute spoke. And the multitudes marveled, saying, "It was never seen like this in Israel!"

But the Pharisees said, "He casts out demons by the ruler of the demons."

Here again the word *daimonizomai* is used. The symptom that Matthew emphasizes is muteness. In this and many other passages, we see that demons have the ability to do physical harm to the persons they afflict. When Jesus cast out the demon, the physical symptom went away and the man was cured.

The remark made by the bystanders ("It was never seen like this in Israel") reminds us that there is no parallel to Jesus' healing and exorcising ministry among the Old Testament prophets. This is the first mention of the Pharisees' theory that Jesus' power over demons was itself demonic.

Matthew 10:1, 5, 8.

And when He had called His twelve disciples to Him, He gave them power over unclean spirits, to cast them out, and to heal all kinds of sickness and all kinds of disease. . . .

These twelve Jesus sent out and commanded them, saying, . . . "Heal the sick, cleanse the lepers, raise the dead,* cast out demons."

ANGELORE

Mark I. Bubek suggests that the following symptoms "may indicate severe demonic affliction" (see *The Adversary,* 1975).

1. A compulsion to curse God.
2. Intense antagonism toward the Bible.
3. Suicidal or murderous thoughts.
4. Bitterness and hatred (toward the Jews, the church, a Christian leader, and so forth).
5. A compulsive temptation.
6. Vicious use of the tongue against others.
7. Terrifying feelings of guilt.
8. Physical symptoms with no medical explanation, which appear or pass suddenly—such as choking sensations, moving pains, or fainting.
9. Deep depression or despondency.
10. Panic and abnormal fears.
11. Clairvoyant or horrible, recurring dreams.
12. Surges of violent rage.
13. Doubt of personal salvation.

In this striking passage, Jesus gave His disciples power over demons. The Greek word for "power" is *exousia,* which is also fre-

* The phrase "raise the dead" is absent from some early manuscripts.

quently translated as "authority." *Exousia* carries the underlying sense of freedom of action. The greater a person's authority or power (*exousia*), the more freedom that person has to act without being limited by circumstances or by another person.

The Gospels make it clear that demons normally have power (*exousia*) over the person they possess, which causes the person to experience all sorts of mental and physical problems. Here, Jesus gave His twelve disciples authority over demons. With the power Jesus provided, the apostles could limit the freedom of demons to oppress or possess human beings. Verse 8 contains the instructions Jesus gave His twelve disciples concerning healing and casting out demons.

It is important to note that Jesus provided only the power to cast out demons. In the *Testament of Solomon,* Solomon was pictured as having authority to make the demons do his will, and so he forced them to help build the Jerusalem temple. There is no hint in the Gospels of any such authority being given to human beings.

In this passage the demons are called "unclean spirits." In the Old Testament "clean" and "unclean" denote ritual states. A person who was ritually "unclean" by virtue of, for instance, touching a dead body, could not participate in worship until he or she had been ritually cleansed. Usually, ritual cleansing was accomplished by washing with water and waiting a certain period of time.

In Jesus' time, the Pharisees observed strict rules of behavior—such as ritual washings before meals—which they associated with cleanness and uncleanness. However, the Old Testament prophets saw an analogy between ritual uncleanness and a person's moral state. A person who sinned and did evil was morally unclean and had no more right to approach God in this state than did the person who had violated ritual taboos. Thus, to call demons "unclean spirits" was to speak of their rejection by God and their evil moral nature. That is why many English translations simply translate the Greek term for "unclean spirits" as "evil spirits."

Matthew 11:18. "For John came neither eating nor drinking, and they say, 'He has a demon.' "

The reference here is to John the Baptist. In preparation for his ministry, John lived as a hermit. When John came out of the desert and began to preach, he was dressed in skins, and he ate only locusts and honey. In the first century, desert places and caves were assumed to be the homes of demons. The fact that John had chosen to live in such areas, together with his strange appearance and ascetic lifestyle, made him vulnerable to the charge of "having" (being possessed by) a demon. Rather than give honest consideration to John's uncomfortable call for repentance, the "children" of "this generation" used John's alleged demonization as an excuse for their own hardness of heart.

Matthew 12:22–28. See the comments on p. 235.

Matthew 12:43–46.

When an unclean spirit goes out of a man, he goes through dry places, seeking rest, and finds none. Then he says, "I will return to my house from which I came." And when he comes, he finds it empty, swept, and put in order. Then he goes and takes with him seven other spirits more wicked than himself, and they enter and dwell there; and the last state of that man is worse than the first. So shall it also be with this wicked generation.

In this fascinating paragraph, Jesus warned His listeners against a failure to respond favorably to His proclamation of the kingdom of God. "This generation's" failure to respond would leave their "house" empty and vulnerable to far greater oppression than they had previously known.

What is of interest here is the analogy Christ used to make his point. A demon may be cast out of a person, but as long as his "house" remains empty, that person is vulnerable to the demon's return. Only by opening one's life to God, by becoming a dwelling for the Holy Spirit, can a person, once demonized, be protected from future demonic attacks.

It is noteworthy that demons are again called "unclean spirits." This time the Greek word *ponēros,* "wicked," is used to describe them. Two Greek words are normally translated as "evil" in English versions of the Bible. *Ponēros,* is a stronger and more active word for "evil" than the other term, *kakos.* *Ponēros* is used of active rebellion and deep hostility directed against God, people, and anything which is good. The description of the unclean spirits makes it clear that "unclean" (*ponēros*) is used in a moral, not ritual, sense: These spirits are "wicked."

Matthew 15:22. "And behold, a woman of Canaan came from that region and cried out to Him, saying, 'Have mercy on me, O Lord, Son of David! My daughter is severely demon possessed.' "

The references to demon possession in the Gospels clearly indicate that demon possession had distinctive symptoms which distinguished it from ordinary sickness or disease. Moreover, the descriptions of demon possession provided in the Gospels suggest that the symptoms of demon possession ranged from relatively mild to extreme, as in the case of the demoniac of Gadara (see Luke 8:26–33). Note that the Canaanite woman described her daughter as being "severely demon possessed." (The symptoms will be summarized later in this chapter.)

Matthew 17:18. "And Jesus rebuked the demon, and it came out of him; and the child was cured from that very hour."

Matthew reports that a distraught father brought his son to Jesus and said, "he is an epileptic" (17:15). The physical symptoms were those of epilepsy, yet the father and the disciples were aware that the root problem was demon possession (17:19). The disciples had been unable to cure the child, but Jesus "rebuked the demon, and it came out of him." Jesus later explained that the disciples had been unable to cast out the demon "because of [their] unbelief" (17:20). This is the first time in the Bible that unbelief, best understood as a flawed trust in God, is mentioned as a condition for successful exorcism.

In His conversation with the disciples Jesus added, "However, this kind does not go out except by prayer and fasting" (17:21). The implication is that there are different kinds (ranks?) of demons, some of which are more difficult to exorcise than others.

Mark 1:23–27.

Now there was a man in their synagogue with an unclean spirit. And he cried out, saying, "Let us alone! What have we to do with You, Jesus of Nazareth? Did You come to destroy us? I know who You are— the Holy One of God!"

But Jesus rebuked him, saying, "Be quiet, and come out of him!" And when the unclean spirit had convulsed him and cried out with a loud voice, he came out of him. Then they were all amazed, so that they questioned among themselves, saying, "What is this? What new doctrine is this? For with authority He commands even the unclean spirits, and they obey Him."

It may seem surprising that a man with an unclean spirit was in the synagogue, gathered with other Jews to worship God. It is interesting that Mark did not describe the physical symptoms of the demon possession. Apparently, this man was accepted as "normal" by his coreligionists.

According to Mark 1:21, 22 Jesus was teaching in the synagogue. Finally, the demon could no longer stand to be in His presence, and cried out. The demons perceived Jesus' presence as an offensive attack ("Let us alone!"). Feeling themselves threatened and under attack, the demons cried out, thereby exposing their presence in the demon possessed man. The discomfort of demons in Christ's presence is typically expressed by questions similar to the ones raised here.

The demons recognized Jesus as "the Holy One of God." Some commentators have taken the expression, "I know who You are!" as a threat. This interpretation is based on the pagan concept that to know the "true name" of a being provides some level of control over that being. But that idea, so deeply rooted in pagan demonology, is a fiction to which real demons would hardly subscribe.

The demons are uncertain about Jesus' intentions, and they fear He plans to destroy them. The word for "destroy" is a form of *apollumi*. The literal meaning is "to kill," but the word was also used in the sense of "to lose" or "to suffer loss." Although the demon who spoke to Jesus may have eternal punishment in mind, it is also possible that the demon is speaking of "destroying" all the work performed in the person of the demon possessed man, in which case the demon would lose his place of residence. Another possibility is suggested by a demon's reference to "the abyss" in Luke 8. Jesus felt no need to answer the demon; He simply commanded the demon to leave. The demon did so after he "had convulsed" the man. Frequently, convulsions—or some other physical signs—indicate the departure of a demon.

The witnesses' reaction was rooted in the commonly accepted "doctrine" (that is, belief) that one must call on more powerful spirits to exorcise a demon or heal a sickness caused by demons. Jesus commanded, and the demons obeyed. Jesus spoke as one having authority in Himself, and by casting out demons Jesus proved He truly did have authority.

Mark 1:32–34.

At evening, when the sun had set, they brought to Him all who were sick and those who were demon possessed. And the whole city was gathered together at the door. Then He healed many who were sick with various diseases, and cast out many demons; and He did not allow the demons to speak, because they knew Him.

This Gospel text, among others, gives the distinct impression that there were an unusually large number of cases of demon possession during Jesus' time on earth. Here, the text says he "cast out *many* demons." The town of Capernaum, where Peter lived (1:21, 29), was an administrative center and the hub of the active fishing industry on the Sea of Galilee, but it was much smaller than our modern towns or cities. That the population included "many" demon possessed suggests unusual demon activity. It is likely that the rash of demon possessions was indicative of Satan marshaling his forces to resist Jesus' ministry.

The text states that Jesus would not allow demons to announce His identity. Jesus rejected the testimony of demons; He let His actions reveal His true identity.

Mark 1:39. "And He was preaching in their synagogues throughout all Galilee, and casting out demons."

Again, Mark gives the impression that demon possession was widespread in the Holy Land during Jesus' day. It would be a mistake to generalize from the Gospel reports and claim that demon possession is just as widespread or virulent in our time and society.

Mark 3:11, 12. "And the unclean spirits, whenever they saw Him, fell down before Him and cried out, saying, 'You are the Son of God.' But He sternly warned them that they should not make Him known."

The demons' reaction to Jesus was typical. Christ did not need to approach demons and identify Himself. The demons knew Jesus instantly, and they seemed compelled to unveil themselves by falling down before Him and announcing His identity.

Mark 3:14, 15. "Then He appointed twelve, that they might be with Him and that He might send them out to preach, and to have power to heal sicknesses and to cast out demons."

See the comments on Matthew 10:1, 8, on p. 240.

Mark 3:22–30. "By the ruler of demons He casts out demons." See the comments on Matthew 12:24–28, on p. 235.

Mark 5:1–15. "Then they came to the other side of the sea, to the country of the Gadarenes."

This story is repeated at length in all three synoptic Gospels. In Scripture repetition typically indicates significance. This incident is discussed at length in the comments on Matthew 8:28–33 (p. 238), and again in the comments on Luke 8:26–38 (p. 245).

Mark 6:7, 13.

And He called the twelve to Himself, and began to send them out two by two, and gave them power over unclean spirits. . . . And they cast out many demons, and anointed with oil many who were sick, and healed them.

See the comments on Matthew 10:1, 8, p. 240.

Mark 7:25–30.

For a woman whose young daughter had an unclean spirit heard about Him, and she came and fell at His feet. The woman was a Greek, a Syro-Phoenician by birth, and she kept asking Him to cast the demon out of her daughter. . . .

Then He said to her, ". . . go your way; the demon has gone out of your daughter."

And when she had come to her house, she found the demon gone out, and her daughter lying on the bed.

The Gospels record incidents of Jesus' healing at a distance, but this is the only report of Christ casting out a demon that was not in His immediate physical presence. The exorcisms performed by the disciples when they traveled two by two (Matt. 10:1, 8) were done in the power Jesus provided. The exorcisms we read about in the book of Acts were performed in Jesus' name and by His power, as are contemporary exorcisms. Christ does not have to be physically present to exert His authority over Satan or demons.

Mark 9:17–29.

Then one of the crowd answered and said, "Teacher, I brought You my son, who has a mute spirit. And whenever it seizes him, it throws him down; he foams at the mouth, gnashes his teeth, and becomes rigid. So I spoke to Your disciples, that they should cast it out, but they could not." . . . Then they brought him to Him. And when he saw Him, immediately the spirit convulsed him, and he fell on the ground and wallowed, foaming at the mouth.

So He asked his father, "How long has this been happening to him?"

And he said, "From childhood. And often he has thrown him both into the fire and into the water to destroy him. But if You can do anything, have compassion on us and help us."

Jesus said to him, "If you can believe, all things are possible to him who believes."

Immediately the father of the child cried out and said with tears, "Lord, I believe; help my unbelief!"

When Jesus saw that the people came running together, He rebuked the unclean spirit, saying to it, "Deaf and dumb spirit, I command you, come out of him and enter him no more!" Then the spirit cried out, convulsed him greatly, and came out of him. And he became as one dead, so that many said, "He is dead." But Jesus took him by the hand and lifted him up, and he arose.

And when He had come into the house, His disciples asked Him privately, "Why could we not cast it out?"

So He said to them, "This kind can come out by nothing but prayer and fasting."

There are several things we should note about this account in Mark.

The careful description of symptoms. The same incident is given much briefer treatment in Matthew 17:15–21. Matthew focused on the symptoms similar to epilepsy. Mark gives additional details. The symptoms of this demon possession were especially severe: The man's son was deaf and mute, and he had periodic seizures, in which the demon often threw him "into the fire and into the water to destroy him" (Mark 9:22).

The destructive tendency of this demon. The demon's hostility toward the son was so great that the demon tried to injure or destroy him, despite the fact that the son's body had become the demon's residence. As noted in the comments on Matthew 17:15–21, Jesus spoke of "this kind" of demon, indicating that there are different ranks or powers of the demons who oppress or possess human beings. This incident and that of the demoniac of Gadara suggest that there is a direct correspondence between the severity of the symptoms of demon possession and the rank or power of the demon involved.

Demon possession "since childhood." The father's answer that the son had been possessed "since childhood" is also significant. Missionaries frequently report that demonization runs in families. The children of parents who are demon possessed are particularly vulnerable to demon possession themselves. It is not necessary to suppose that this was the case here. What is significant is that a person apparently is susceptible to demon possession at an early age. Certainly, any child's early fascination with the occult must be seriously discouraged.

Spiritual preparation for exorcism? One of the most significant aspects of this account occurs in Jesus' answer to the disciples' question about why they could not drive out the demon. Christ answered, "This kind can come out by nothing but prayer and fasting" (Mark 9:29). It would be wrong to assume that there is anything special about prayer and fasting that gives a person power over demons, but this verse does seem to imply that, in certain cases, serious spiritual preparation for confrontation with a demon is vital.

The reason why preparation is necessary can be found in Matthew 17:20. Jesus first responded to the disciples' question by saying that they could not drive the demon out "because of [their] unbelief." We may need times of prayer and fasting to refocus our trust in the Lord so that we may go into any such confrontation with absolute trust in His power to expel the demon.

Mark 16:17. "And these signs will follow those who believe: In My name they will cast out demons; they will speak with new tongues."

There is a serious question about whether Mark 16:9–20 was in the original manuscript of Mark's Gospel. Regardless of the answer to that question, the accounts of the early ministry of the apostles and Saint Paul make it clear that these signs did follow Christ's resurrection. Today many people look confidently to the Lord and expect to see the same signs operative in contemporary missions and local church ministry.

Luke 4:33–35. "Now in the synagogue there was a man who had a spirit of an unclean demon."

See the comments on Mark 1:23–27, p. 242.

Luke 4:41. "And demons also came out of many, crying and saying, 'You are the Christ, the Son of God!'"

"And He, rebuking them, did not allow them to speak, for they knew that He was the Christ."

See the comments on Mark 3:11, 12, p. 243.

Luke 7:17b, 18.

Jesus came down from a mountain and stood with a great multitude of people from all Judea and Jerusalem, and from the seacoast of Tyre and Sidon, who came to hear Him and be healed of their diseases, as well as those who were tormented with unclean spirits. And they were healed.

It's clear from this report about people from outside the Holy Land, flocking to Christ for healing, that reports of the young teacher's wonder-working powers had spread everywhere. There was no real basis for anyone to doubt the identity of Jesus. The phrase "those who were tormented with unclean spirits" indicates that demon possession was a terrible burden for those possessed, as well as for their loved ones. It seems that once a person was possessed, he or she definitely needed help from someone else to expel the demon. No wonder people from the whole region flocked to Jesus.

Luke 7:21. "And that very hour He cured many of infirmities, afflictions, and evil spirits; and to many blind He gave sight."

John the Baptist was imprisoned and, as the weeks passed without Jesus presenting Himself as the military conqueror envisioned by the prophets, John began to have doubts. So John sent some of his disciples to ask Jesus, "Are You the Coming One, or do we look for another?" (Luke 7:20).

Rather than answer John's disciples directly, Jesus performed a variety of miracles and then told them to go back and tell John what they had seen. In His statement to John's

disciples, Jesus paraphrased Isaiah 61:1–3, which had been identified as a messianic prophecy in the first century. Isaiah announced that God had anointed (commissioned) a Messiah "to heal the brokenhearted, / To proclaim liberty to the captives, / And the opening of the prison to those who are bound" (Isa. 61:1).

Jesus' works of healing and freeing God's people from domination by demons would be proof enough for John that He was indeed the promised Messiah. However, this clear proof of Jesus' identity was ignored and rejected by the religious leaders, and finally by the people themselves.

Luke 8:2. "And certain women who had been healed of evil spirits and infirmities—Mary called Magdalene, out of whom had come seven demons."

Luke identified a number of women who followed Jesus and who supported his ministry financially. Mary Magdalene played a significant role in the Gospel story: she was one of the first to learn of the Resurrection. The mention of Mary Magdalene here is significant because it indicates that there was no remaining taint of demon possession, even though the spirit who possessed Mary was specifically described as *ponēros,* a "wicked," actively hostile spirit. Once the demons were cast out of Mary, and she had control of herself once again, there was nothing to prevent her from having a significant ministry to Christ and, later, to the church.

A person who has been demon possessed may be vulnerable to being possessed again (see the comments on Matthew 12:43–45), but if one commits oneself to Christ after being demonized, no taint that would be a hindrance to ministry remains.

Luke 8:27–37. The story about Jesus casting out demons in the land of the Gadarenes is told at length in Matthew, Mark, and Luke. Because it is so significant for any study of demons, Luke's account is repeated here:

And when He stepped out on the land, there met Him a certain man from the city who had demons for a long time. And he wore no clothes, nor did he live in a house but in the tombs.

When he saw Jesus, he cried out, fell down before Him, and with a loud voice said, "What have I to do with You, Jesus, Son of the Most High God? I beg You, do not torment me!"

For He had commanded the unclean spirit to come out of the man. For it had often seized him, and he was kept under guard, bound with chains and shackles; and he broke the bonds and was driven by the demon into the wilderness.

Jesus asked him, saying, "What is your name?" And he said, "Legion," because many demons had entered him. And they begged Him that He would not command them to go out into the abyss.

Now a herd of many swine was feeding there on the mountain. So they begged Him that He would permit them to enter them. And He permitted them.

Then the demons went out of the man and entered the swine, and the herd ran violently down the steep place into the lake and drowned.

When those who fed them saw what had happened, they fled and told it in the city and in the country. Then they went out to see what had happened, and came to Jesus, and found the man from whom the demons had departed, sitting at the feet of Jesus, clothed and in his right mind. And they were afraid.

This account contains several important themes:

The symptoms of demon possession (8:27, 29). Luke, a physician, identified a number of symptoms exhibited by the demon possessed man.

- He was antisocial. The man wore no clothes, and he refused to live in a house or in the company of other persons.
- He was violent. The man was apparently dangerous enough to others that he had often been seized, bound, and kept under guard.
- He had unusual strength. The man broke the bonds and fled into the wilderness.
- He demonstrated moral depravity. The man violated the norm of modesty and other norms of society.
- He was clearly and unmistakably not "in his right mind" (8:35).

- He demonstrated paroxysms or fits of rage. The man attacked anyone who came near (see Matt. 8:28).

The immediate recognition and fear of Jesus (Luke 8:28, 31). Demons respected and feared Jesus. They knew Him and immediately recognized His presence. They did not attempt to resist Him. No matter how great the number or the power of the demons who oppress human beings, they have no defense against Jesus. They *must* obey Him.

The primary fear expressed by the demons here was that Jesus would "command them to go out into the abyss." The Greek word for abyss is *abussos;* it is found only nine times in the New Testament, seven times in the book of Revelation, where it is translated "bottomless pit" (Rev. 9:1, 2, 11; 11:7; 17:8; 20:1, 2). The references in Revelation make it clear that the abyss is a place where some demons are presently confined and where Satan will be confined in the future. The demons with whom Jesus spoke were desperate not to have their freedom of action limited by such a confinement.

No other reference in the Gospels suggests that Jesus sent demons into confinement, rather than simply banning them from the person whom they had possessed. However, the question recorded in Mark 1:24 and Luke 4:34, "Did You come to destroy us?" may refer to that fate.

The possession of the man by a multitude of demons (Luke 8:30). Jesus asked the demon, "What is your name?" Jesus did not ask because He did not know the demon's name; rather He asked to instruct us. The demon's answer, "Legion," is explained by the phrase "many demons had entered him."

A fully staffed Roman legion contained 6,000 men. We should not conclude that 6,000 demons infested the Gadarene, but we can be sure there were many demons. Seven demons had been cast out of Mary Magdalene (Mark 16:9). Enough demons were present in the Gadarene for them to infest a large herd of pigs (Luke 8:33).

The complete restoration after the demons were cast out (Luke 8:35). The restored man was found "sitting at the feet of Jesus, clothed and in his right mind." With the demons gone, the man reverted to normalcy. The phrase "sitting at the feet of Jesus" implies the man was listening to and learning from Jesus, his teacher.

It is striking that when demons are cast out, there seems to be no residual effect. The Gadarene became normal again, and he no longer exhibited strange behavior. He was truly "cured."

Luke 9:1. "Then He called His twelve disciples together and gave them power and authority over all demons, and to cure diseases." See the comments on Matthew 10:1, 8, p. 240.

Luke 9:38–43. This passage contains Luke's account of the story about the father who begged Jesus to help his son after the disciples failed to cast out an evil spirit. See the comments on Mark 9:17–29, p. 243.

Luke 10:17, 18, 20.

Then the seventy returned with joy, saying, "Lord, even the demons are subject to us in Your name." And He said to them, . . . "Nevertheless do not rejoice in this, that the spirits are subject to you, but rather rejoice because your names are written in heaven."

Commanding demons. Luke 10 reports Jesus' commissioning of seventy disciples to preach, much like His commissioning of the Twelve recorded in Matthew 10. The seventy were excited about their power over demons when they exorcised them in Jesus' name. Luke makes it clear in his Gospel and in Acts that the believer can command demons in Jesus' name and they must obey.

"In Your name." The use of the (supposed) names of angels and other supernatural powers in pagan religious practices and magic was based on the assumption that the person who knew the true name of any such being could, to some extent, require that being to serve

him or her. The biblical belief which calls for prayer or exorcism "in Jesus' name" is rooted in a totally different concept.

In Hebrew thought the "name" is considered to reflect and capture something of the essence of the thing or person named. The *Expository Dictionary of Bible Words* (p. 454) says of prayer in Jesus' name:

To pray in Jesus' name means (1) to identify the content and the motivations of prayers with all that Jesus is and (2) to pray with full confidence in him as he has revealed himself.

Similarly, to cast out demons in Jesus' name means to identify our purpose and intent with those of Jesus and to rely completely on Him to act.

Don't rejoice that demons are subject to you (Luke 10:20). One of the dangers to any person who attempts an exorcism is a sense of personal power or pride, for that is at odds with a sense of complete reliance on Jesus. Demons are both evil and powerful beings; therefore, no one should be overconfident in an attempt to deal with demons, and demons should not be taken lightly.

Luke 11:14. "And He was casting out a demon, and it was mute. So it was, when the demon had gone out, that the mute spoke; and the multitudes marveled."

The demon was not mute, but its presence was evidenced by the possessed man's inability to speak. This symptom of demon possession is mentioned several times in the Gospels.

Luke 11:15–22. "But some of them said, 'He casts out demons by Beelzebub, the ruler of the demons.' "

See the comments on Matthew 12:24–29, p. 235.

Luke 14:24–26.

When an unclean spirit goes out of a man . . . he goes and takes with him seven other spirits more wicked than himself, and they enter and dwell there; and the last state of that man is worse than the first.

See the comments on Matthew 12:43–45, p. 241.

John 7:20. "The people answered and said, 'You have a demon. Who is seeking to kill You?' "

Demons were known to cause people to act irrationally, so the charge here should be understood as an accusation that Jesus was seriously paranoid for asking "the Jews" (that is, the Jewish leaders; see John 7:15), "Why do you seek to kill Me?" (John 7:19). This may well be an indication that the rumor spread by the religious leaders, that Jesus was in league with demons, was also taking root in the thought of some of the people.

John 8:48–59. "Do we not rightly say that You are a Samaritan and have a demon?" This passage reports a sharp conflict between Jesus and the Jewish religious leaders. They considered Jesus' teachings about salvation irrational (see 8:52), and thus the product of demonization. This conflict led Jesus to state plainly His identity as the deity of the Old Testament—Yahweh (8:57, 58). This revelation was rejected by the Jewish leaders, who "took up stones to throw at Him," the penalty for blasphemy.

John 10:20, 21. "And many of them said, 'He has a demon and is mad. Why do you listen to Him?'

"Others said, 'These are not the words of one who has a demon. Can a demon open the eyes of the blind?' "

Each mention of demons in John is for a similar purpose: Jesus is accused of "having" a demon and speaking irrationally. Irrational and "mad" behavior certainly is one of the symptoms of demon possession. Yet the healings Jesus performed—which in the other Gospels are closely linked with Jesus' casting out the demons who caused the illnesses—were contrary to everything the people understood about demonization. A demon might cause blindness, but no demon would

or could open the eyes of a man blind from birth (John 9:1–7). Such a healing is beyond the capacity of a demon, for a work that benefits a human being is totally out of character for a demon, who is by nature hostile to human beings. John's Gospel does not record many incidents in which Jesus cast out demons, but the few times John does mention demons, what he says is in complete harmony with what the other Gospels teach about demons and the symptoms of demon possession.

THE NATURE AND ACTIVITY OF DEMONS

The passages in the Gospels reviewed in this chapter provide the Bible's major contribution to our understanding about the nature and the activity of demons. We can summarize those teachings as follows.

DEMONS ARE PERSONAL BEINGS RATHER THAN MERE NEGATIVE INFLUENCES

The Gospels use personal pronouns when reporting dialogues with demons (see Luke 8:27–30); individual demons apparently have personal names, and groups of demons have "team" names (see Luke 8:30). Demons can communicate and hold conversations (see Luke 4:22–26; 8:28–30). Demons also have intelligence (see Mark 1:23, 24; Luke 4:34; 8:28), emotions (see Luke 8:28), and a will (see Mark 1:27; Luke 4:35, 36).

DEMONS ARE MORALLY PERVERTED AND EVIL BEINGS

Demons are called "evil spirits" (see Luke 7:31). The Greek word for evil, *ponēros,* indicates an active, virulent wickedness that expresses itself in doing harm to others. Demons are also called "unclean spirits" (see Matt. 10:1; Mark 1:23), which also has a moral connotation. These evil characteristics are described further in the Epistles, where demons are among the "spiritual hosts of wickedness" (Eph.

6:12) who infest our world and who inspire false teachers and false doctrines (1 Tim. 4).

DEMONS CAN ENTER AND INFLUENCE HUMAN BEINGS

Demons have the ability to control, or to influence, human beings. The Gospels report incidents in which demons caused mental derangement, including full-fledged insanity (see Luke 8:27–29) and suicidal mania (see Mark 9:22).

The Gospels also report that demons cause a variety of physical disabilities. These include muteness (see Matt. 9:32, 33; Mark 9:17–29), blindness (see Matt. 12:11), deformities (see Luke 13:11–17), and severe seizures (see Matt. 17:15–18; Luke 9:39).

Today believers are eager to admit the existence of angels and their active ministry in the world. It is clear from the Gospel accounts that dark angels are just as active in their efforts to thwart God's plans and harm God's people. We have no reason to doubt that demons are as active today as they were in New Testament times. In the next chapter we will look more closely at demon possession and Christian exorcism.

CHAPTER 15

EXORCISING DEMONS:

A CONTEMPORARY ISSUE

Acts—Jude

Accounts of angel encounters are enriching, and they warm our hearts when we read or hear about them. They're even more enriching when we experience them.

My wife, Sue, was praying one night for our son Matthew, who was just 19 and far away. She felt a strong compulsion to pray that God's angels would protect him from danger. As Sue prayed, she seemed to see an angel stretch himself out over Matt and shelter him, but she noticed that Matt's feet were still exposed. She prayed, "His feet, too, Lord," and as she prayed she could see angel wings stretch down and cover his feet.

Angel encounters are common in Sue's family. One night 21 years ago, her mother awoke from a sound sleep and saw a bright figure seated at the end of her bed. The figure told her that Sue, her pregnant daughter, would be all right, even though she wouldn't

be able to contact her. After receiving the message, Sue's mom lay back down and went to sleep. About a week later, Sue's mother got a phone call from Germany. A distraught voice reported that there had been serious problems with the delivery of Sue's baby. Before the voice could explain what had happened, the call was disconnected. Although Sue's parents tried desperately to reach someone in Germany, they could not get through. It was several days before they finally learned the baby had died and that Sue would be all right, even though she had nearly died too.

During those awful days of uncertainty, the memory of the angel's visit provided Sue's parents comfort and hope.

Today many people—Christians and nonbelievers alike—do not doubt the existence of angels; they accept stories about angel encounters as true. But what about reports of demons and demon possession? The Bible speaks about angels *and* demons. If we accept that angels are real and active today, we need to give careful consideration to the possibility that the same holds true for demons as well.

DEMON ENCOUNTERS TODAY

Demon encounters aren't spoken of as frequently as angel encounters. They are far less popular! Yet demon possession is real today. A pastor in Seattle—a friend and seminary classmate of mine—has, over the past thirty years, dealt with many cases of demon possession, and he has had a significant ministry in exorcising demons from many individuals. This does not mean that every sensational story about demons is true. However, my friend's experiences, as well as the experiences of many other trustworthy witnesses, provide solid evidence of demonic activity in the world today.

HOW CAN WE DIAGNOSE DEMON POSSESSION?

Study the stories of demon possession in the *Gospels.* The stories in the New Testament indicate that demon possession has a variety of symptoms. We know from those stories that in most cases the symptoms were obvious enough that the possessed individuals, or their families, were aware that they were demon possessed.

In a culture like ours it is very common for the cause of such symptoms to be misunderstood. The symptoms may be attributed to psychosomatic causes, or dismissed as manifestations of some type of mental illness. So the first step in recognizing contemporary cases of demon possession is to take the New Testament seriously and study the stories of demon possession for a better understanding of the symptoms we may see today.

Identify the symptoms of demon possession. In some instances there are no obvious symptoms of possession, as was apparently the case with the man worshiping in a synagogue and listening to Jesus' teaching. Finally, the demon

in the man could no longer stand the pressure of being in Christ's presence, and he identified himself by shouting out, "Let us alone!" (Luke 4:33–36, NKJV). This was an unusual case. The Gospel writers, more often than not, clearly described symptoms of demon possession.

The primary symptoms mentioned in the Gospels are:

(1) A demonstration of moral depravity. Either the thoughts or the actions of the person are focused on immoral behavior; and the person under the influence of a demon may say or do things he or she would not normally say or do.

(2) Indications that the person is not in his or her *right mind.* Such indications may include random or meaningless speech, a sense of deep depression, a paranoid suspicion of others, and so on. Demon possessed individuals, as well as their family or friends, may be seriously concerned about their sanity.

(3) Paroxysms, or fits of rage. The demon possessed person may frequently lose control and strike out against others verbally or physically.

(4) Unusual strength. When they are not acting like themselves demon possessed individuals show unusual strength, especially if others try to restrain them.

(5) Personality change. Strong shifts of mood are the cause of actions and words which seem out of character. A person who is normally quiet and polite may become loud and profane. A person who is normally open to spiritual things may suddenly resist them obstinately.

(6) Self-destructive tendencies. In severe cases of demon possession, individuals controlled by a demon may attempt to harm themselves. Typically, such individuals do not plan ahead to harm themselves; such a person may unexpectedly jump out into traffic or deliberately try to drown.

While there can be other causes for each of these symptoms, it would be wise for a person who exhibits several of them to at least consider the possibility of demon possession.

CONTEMPORARY REPORTS OF DEMON POSSESSION

The following are published reports of recent cases of demon possession. Note how these reports compare to the biblical stories of demon possession. Two accounts are taken from C. Fred Dickason's thorough study, *Demon Possession & the Christian* (1987). Two more come from Merrill Unger's book, *What Demons Can Do to Saints* (1991).

From Reverend W. L. McLeod, of Saskatchewan.

She related that while I was preaching she had felt some strange power rise up slowly inside her. She said, "I began to cut you in pieces and everything you said and stood for." Never before had she had an experience like this. She was greatly agitated as to why it should happen now. In talking with her I found she had had some involvement in the occult. She had allowed a friend of hers to display her occult powers in her presence. This had included the locking of doors without touching them. Out of curiosity she had also gone into a witchcraft shop. . . . She had a further involvement which she did not tell us about. This came out in a conversation with the unclean spirits who had invaded her life. I asked her if she would be willing to renounce the Devil and all his works, naming the areas of involvement. She was willing to do this. However, when we got to the place where I led her to say, "I now renounce the Devil and all his works," she was unable to do so. There was a struggle as she attempted to get the words out but couldn't. . . . Kneeling we went to prayer. Immediately the demon powers rose to the surface and took over. We then began to give her some advice on how to get rid of them. At once she was blinded and deafened. They didn't want her to hear the advice we were giving her.

From Dick Hillis, of Overseas Crusade, as told by a friend.

Hillis told me of one incident which happened while he was in China, before the Communist takeover, when one of the elders of his church, who was unquestionably a believer, became so demon possessed that his personality changed. He became vile and profane in his language and extraordinarily strong. Some members of the church locked him up in a room and sent for Hillis.

When Dick came in the door, this man became violent and a strange voice shouted, "I know who you are."

From a young woman in Dover, Delaware.

At seventeen I married a boy in my school who was not a Christian. My life became miserable, and I started to drink. At times I became so intoxicated that I would pass out. Under the influence of liquor I would make a fool of myself before men and curse my husband in front of them. I got to a point where I just couldn't stand myself.

One evening as I sat alone in my living room, the Lord began to speak to me. I was twenty-two years old. I asked God to forgive me for living in awful sin, and I rededicated my life to Christ.

Believe it or not, then began eighteen months of hell on earth for me. The very next morning I awoke terribly afraid. It seemed as if a great hand was around my heart, squeezing the very life out of me.

I began to study the Bible and pray and tried desperately to have fellowship with the Lord. I didn't know it then but during my years of sin and turning my back on God, I had been invaded by a demon. As long as I lived in sin and drunkenness, and did what the demon wanted, he didn't bother me. But the moment I committed my life to Christ, the demon made my life one long torture session. I was constantly obsessed by terrible feelings of guilt.

Awful fear gripped me. It is impossible for me to convey to any human being the horror of demonic fear. It hounded me when I attempted to read the Scripture or pray. It confused my mind when I tried to think about the things of God. I could take this torture for only about five or six days. Then you know what I would do—rather be compelled to do? I would get drunk.

Every time I got drunk or willfully sinned, the pressure and the fear would stop! I did this two or three times a month. I would ask the Lord to forgive me. Then presto—the torture would start again. I yielded to God, cried out to Him, read every book I could lay hands on dealing with the victorious life. But the pressure, fear, and torment only got worse. Things got so bad, in fact, that I began planning to commit suicide.

From a missionary to Mexico's Ohontal Indians.

This case has to do with a young man, an Indian. This young man began to manifest demonic symptoms by a sickness that showed no physical cause at all. A little while later I was called late one night. He had jumped into the well! After pulling him out, and then talking and praying with him and his family for an hour, I came to the conclusion that the problem was demonic.

When I finally left the house after another hour of counseling and praying, *a demon followed me out!* It was the experience of a real presence, evil, terrifying, yet hard to explain. I could literally sense that being trying to gain entrance to my life. My desire was to start in a headlong run. But, praise God, I didn't run. I stood my ground and prayed. For two or three days a constant battle raged, before the evil spirit quit and left me.

Then the young man, whose name was Fernando, got worse again. I went to see him and talked very frankly with him about his salvation. With tears he assured me that he was saved, but that he would go empty-handed into the Lord's presence, because he had little faith. Moreover, he was certain that he was going to die, because he had been so weak spiritually. He complained also that at times he saw specters around the room.

Two days later he had another attack. I and five other men went to see him. Standing at the head of his bed, I saw him suddenly looking wildly at something across the room and he cried out, "Why have you come to torment me?"

In an instant his voice changed (the demon taking over) and glaringly he turned to us, yelling loudly, "Who are you? I am stronger than all of you!"

With that he began to scream, curse, kick, and swing his arms violently. His strength was such that the six of us could not hold him down. Fortunately help soon arrived. At the end of two hours he quieted down somewhat, but it had taken eight to ten men at a time to control him. After two hours seventeen strong young men were worn out, yet he was still as strong as ever.

These outbursts would usually come at night. As a rule he slept all morning, and in the afternoon was more or less normal. At these times he would talk and act quite sanely. He was very sure that he was going to die as a chastening from the Lord, but equally certain he was saved.

Before the demon took control, he generally knew it and would say, "It is coming. Grab me!"

During these attacks, his voice would change completely (the demon talking through him). Even his face would be altered completely. Often he would under seizure attempt to injure himself.

From a case presented in a counseling class.

Ms. A. was still having problems, especially in the area of lust. She had very strong, almost overwhelming thoughts and desires in those areas.

In our first confrontation session, we contacted the demon of lust. It was done through the relaying of the thought method. She told me the thoughts she heard in response to my questions.

The counselee was not cooperative in that she would not let the demon speak freely through her. She herself said she felt the demons wanted to do this but she refused to let them, fearing she would be giving them control.

There were other demons we were able to touch upon—suicide, despair, death-despair, and resentment.

I attempted to concentrate on the one called lust. I asked for moral ground that it had upon Ms. A. Confession and application of the Word was made, and then telling the demon he had no ground to stay; a command was issued for the demon to leave.

When I tested, I found that the demon had not left. I asked why. The answer came back that it was too deep and strong.

During our second confrontation session, we were able to call to manifestation this demon. This time, I was able to get its rank, that of throne, and bind his entire kingdom to him. Ms. A. had a time of confession, confessing all known sin and desire in this area. She wanted it to go.

CAN CHRISTIANS BE DEMON POSSESSED?

Many Christians have argued that a believer cannot experience demon possession because, as the Bible teaches, the Holy Spirit is present in those who have trusted Christ (see John 14:17; Eph. 1:13, 14). Yet in each of the cases reported above the person troubled by demons was a believer.

Usually the demonization of believers seems to take place before conversion or during a period of time when the person is not living a Christian life. The best theological explanation for that is the fact that even after conversion believers still have the capacity to sin referred to in the New Testament as "the flesh." At the same time, believers have been given a new capacity to live for God and to please Him. Ephesians 4:21–24 (NKJV) speaks of both capacities in this way:

If indeed you have heard Him and have been taught by Him, as the truth is in Jesus: that you put off, concerning your former conduct, the old man which grows corrupt according to the deceitful lusts, and be renewed in the spirit of your mind, and that you put on the new man which was created according to God, in true righteousness and holiness.

Apparently, there is room in that dimension of human nature called here the "old man" for demons to take up residence, even though the Holy Spirit is resident in that dimension called the "new man." Just as the presence of the Holy Spirit in our lives is no guarantee that we will not choose to sin, His presence is no guarantee that demons will not enter Christians who dabble with the occult or choose a sinful lifestyle.

It would be wrong to assume that demon possession is widespread in our day, or to assume that demons lie behind every sin, every illness, every fit of depression, or every mental illness experienced by a Christian or non-Christian. But there is enough evidence provided in Scripture and in contemporary reports to make us aware that demon possession is a real possibility, should several of the symptoms listed above be present in our life or the life of a loved one.

EXORCISM IN THE ANCIENT WORLD

People who lived in cultures that readily acknowledged the possibility of demon possession or sickness caused by demons struggled to find defenses against their evil oppressors.

As noted in chapter 7, those defenses typically involved incantations and calling on gods or goddesses to purge the demon from the sufferer.

AN INCANTATION FROM ANCIENT BABYLON

Maqlu, written in cuneiform, contains the most significant of the Babylonian magical incantations, and it undoubtedly reflects traditions dating back to 3000–2000 B.C. in Mesopotamia.

Be off, be off, begone, begone,
Depart, depart, flee, flee!
Go off, go away, be off, and begone!
May your wickedness like smoke rise ever
    heavenward!
From my body be off!
From my body begone!
From my body depart!
From my body flee!
From my body go off!
From my body go away!
To my body turn back not!
To my body approach not!
To my body near not!
On my body abut not!
By the life of Samas, the honorable, be adjured!
By the life of Ea, lord of the deep, be adjured!
By the life of Asulluhi, that magus of the gods,
    be adjured!
By the life of Girra, your executioner,
    be adjured!
From my body you shall indeed be separated!

Another incantation from the same source includes instructions for the priest to follow while reciting the incantation.

You [the priest] recite the incantation,
  "Evil demon, to your steppe"
  all the way to the outer entrance;
then you encircle the entrances with parched flour.
You then enter into the house, and at the
  place where you performed the "burning" you
  libate water and recite the incantation,
  "I cast an incantation upon the assemblage
  of all the gods."
Thereafter you encircle the bed with flour paste and recite the incantation "Ban, ban" and the incantation "Adjured is the house."

AN INCANTATION FROM ANCIENT EGYPT

This spell, a charm for driving away the demon causing a headache, is particularly interesting because the magician, after calling on the gods to expel the malevolent spirit, then threatens to harm the gods if they do not do as asked (Joseph Kaster, *The Wisdom of Ancient Egypt,* p. 150).

As for the head of [name], born of the woman [name], it is the head of Osiris Wen-Nefer, on whose head were placed the three hundred and seventy-seven Divine Uraei, and they spew forth flame to make thee quit the head of [name], born of the woman [name], like that of Osiris. If thou dost not quit the temple of [name], born of the woman [name], I will burn thy soul, I will consume thy corpse! I will be deaf to any desire of thine concerning thee. If some other god is with thee, I will overturn thy dwelling place; I will shadow thy tomb, so that thou wilt not be allowed to receive incense, so that thou wilt not be allowed to receive water with the beneficent spirits, and so that thou wilt not be allowed to associate with any of the Followers of Horus.

If thou wilt not hear my words, I will cause the sky to be overturned, and I will cast fire among the Lords of Heliopolis. I will cut off the head of a cow taken from the Forecourt of Hathor! I will cause Sebek to sit enshrouded in the skin of a crocodile, and I will cause Anubis to sit enshrouded in the skin of a dog! . . .

Then indeed shalt thou come forth from the temple of [name], born of the woman [name]! I will make for thee the magic amulet of the Gods, their names being pronounced on this day.

This spell was to be recited over a piece of fine linen which had the names of several gods

inscribed on it, and the cloth was to be placed on the temples of the man with the headache. The papyrus sheet on which the spell was inscribed contained pictures of the gods to be copied on the linen: two jackals, four seated gods with human heads, four Eyes of Horus, and four serpents.

EARLY JEWISH INCANTATIONS

Alfred Edersheim (*The Life and Times of Jesus the Messiah*, pp. 775–76) identifies a number of magical formulas and incantations against demons that reflect first-century practices, even though they were written down later. He notes that the exorcism formulas "mostly consist of words which have little if any meaning." The following is an incantation against boils:

Baz, Basiya, Mas, Masiya, Kas, Kasiyah, Sharlia and Marlai—ye Angels that come from the land of Sodom to heal painful boils! Let the color not become more red, let it not farther spread, let its seed be absorbed in the belly. As a mule does not propagate itself, so let not this evil propagate itself in the body of [name], the son of [name].

Here is a simple incantation to exorcise demons:

Burst, curst, dashed, banned be Bar-Tit, Bar-Tema, Bar-Tena, Chashmagoz, Merigox, and Isteaham.

These few examples contrast significantly with the exorcism stories recorded in the Bible. The ancient magical literature makes it clear that people in antiquity were not only aware of demons and their powers, but were desperate to find release from their evil influence. Still, the writings on demonology from the ancient world offer no hope at all. In contrast, the New Testament offers hope to all.

THE NEW TESTAMENT ON THE EXORCISM OF DEMONS

In chapter 14 we looked at each of Jesus' encounters with demons in the Gospels. We saw that in every case the demons were subject to Christ and forced to do what He commanded. We also saw that Jesus even dele-

Egyptian magical items.

gated power to cast out demons in His name, first to the twelve apostles (Matt. 10:1–8) and then to 70 followers (Luke 10:1–20). In these cases, Jesus' followers were successful in casting out demons.

Edersheim makes an interesting observation: The Jewish rabbis did not challenge such miracles of Jesus, or even such miracles attributed to Jesus' followers after the Resurrection. Edersheim writes:

Egypt was regarded as the home of magic (Kidd. 49b; Shabb. 75a). In connection with this, it deserves notice that the Talmud ascribes the miracles of Jesus to magic, which He had learned during His stay in Egypt, having taken care, when He left, to insert under His skin its rules and formulas, since every traveler, on quitting the country, was searched, lest he should take to other lands the mysteries of magic (Shabb. 104 b).

Here it may be interesting to refer to some of the strange ideas which Rabbinism attached to the early Christians, as showing both the intercourse between the two parties, and that the Jews did not deny the gift of miracles in the Church, only ascribing its exercise to magic. Of the existence of such intercourse with Jewish Christians there is abundant evidence. Thus, R. Joshua, the son of Levi (at the end of the second century), was so hard pressed by their quotations from the Bible that, unable to answer, he pronounced a curse on them. . . . R. Ishmael, the son of Elisha, the grandson of that High-Priest who was executed by the Romans (Josephus, War 1.2,2) . . . agreed with R. Tarphon that nothing else remained but to burn their [Christian] writings. It was this R. Ishmael who prevented his nephew Ben Dama from being cured of the bite of a serpent by a Christian, preferring that he should die rather than be healed by such means (Abod. Zar. 27 b).

Yet what did the early Christians do when they healed or when they exorcised demons? To answer these questions, we need to continue with an examination of the demon encounters reported in Acts and the teachings about demons recorded in the Epistles.

EVERY DEMON ENCOUNTER IN THE BOOK OF ACTS

Acts 5:3. "But Peter said, 'Ananias, why has Satan filled your heart to lie to the Holy Spirit?'"

The mention of Satan here need not be taken as a literal reference to Satan himself; it could be a reference to the fallen angels Satan leads. The phrase "filled your heart" suggests influence, but it does not indicate the kind of control that we find in demon possession.

Common terms for demon possession in the New Testament include to have "a spirit of an unclean demon" (Luke 4:33), to be a person "with an unclean spirit" (Mark 1:23), to be "tormented with unclean spirits" (Luke 6:18), and to be "demon possessed" (Matt. 15:22). In Acts we will encounter phrases such as "tormented by unclean spirits" (5:16) and "oppressed by the devil" (10:38).

It seems likely that Ananias permitted himself to be influenced by demons without surrendering total control to them. It is of note that Peter did not cast any demons out of Ananias or his wife; rather, they were immediately judged by God and fell dead. The two were completely responsible for their own actions, and not (yet?) under demonic control.

Acts 5:16. "Also a multitude gathered from the surrounding cities to Jerusalem, bringing sick people and those who were tormented by unclean spirits, and they were all healed."

The report of the healings performed by Peter sounds much like those associated with Jesus' early ministry (see Mark 1:32–34). It is clear that the exorcism of demons did not cease with Christ's death. Jesus' followers continued to display power over evil beings.

Acts 10:38. "How God anointed Jesus of Nazareth with the Holy Spirit and with power, who went about doing good and healing all who were oppressed by the devil, for God was with Him."

Peter gave a quick review of the gospel message to Cornelius, a Roman officer. Peter identified Jesus as the one "whom God anointed . . . with the Holy Spirit and with power" and went on to state that Jesus used that power to do good and heal "all who were oppressed by the devil." Again, the reference to the devil should be understood to include his followers, the demons who tormented the ones Jesus healed.

The phrase "for God was with Him" is significant. Jesus' power—as He lived His human life—came from the Holy Spirit, and the flow of Jesus' power was uninterrupted because "God was with Him." John reports a saying of Christ which explains this intimate relationship: "Most assuredly, I say to you, the Son can do nothing of Himself, but what He sees the Father do; for whatever He does, the Son also does in like manner" (John 5:19). Jesus responded perfectly to the will of God, so that there was unbroken fellowship between the Father and the Son.

Acts 16:16–18.

Now it happened, as we went to prayer, that a certain slave girl possessed with a spirit of divination met us, who brought her masters much profit by fortune-telling. This girl followed Paul and us, and cried out, saying, "These men are the servants of the Most High God, who proclaim to us the way of salvation." And she did this for many days.

But Paul, greatly annoyed, turned and said to the spirit, "I command you in the name of Jesus Christ come out of her." And he came out that very hour.

There is much in this report of importance for an understanding of demon possession and exorcism.

"A spirit of divination." Luke identified this spirit by how it manifested itself in the girl's life. The spirit enabled the girl to predict the future with some success. So "spirit of divination" was the "functional" name of the spirit. In the Gospels we see spirits identified in the same way; for instance, a "mute spirit" (Mark 9:17), a "deaf and dumb spirit" (Mark 9:25), and so on. Interestingly, in stories of contemporary exorcisms spirits are often named in the very same way—by referring to how they manifest themselves in the possessed person's life.

"Paul . . . said to the spirit." Paul spoke directly to the spirit who possessed the girl; he did not address the girl. That seems to be the pattern

in reports of contemporary exorcisms also. Conversation is held with the person who is possessed, but at some point in the process the demon is addressed directly, and the demon speaks in turn.

"I command you." Paul recognized that he had authority over the demon, yet he was aware of the source of that authority.

"In the name of Jesus Christ." Paul lacked the intrinsic authority to command demons. He recognized that his was a delegated authority, so Paul named the one who had given it to him. Thus, Paul commanded the demon "in the name of Jesus Christ."

We saw in chapter 14 that the meaning of the phrase "in the name of" is significant. To pray or act in "the name of Jesus" means acknowledging His Lordship, acting in harmony with His will, and relying completely on His power.

The apostle Paul wrote about the

exceeding greatness of His [God's] power toward us who believe, according to the working of His mighty power which He worked in Christ when He raised Him from the dead and seated Him at His right hand in the heavenly places, far above all [demonic] principality and power and might and dominion.

Ephesians 1:19–21

Today Jesus, returned to glory, is seated on the throne of the universe, and He totally dominates all in the spiritual realm. There can be no question about His ability to exorcise any demon that might torment a human being.

"To come out of her." The purpose of Christian exorcism is to expel demons who take up residence in human beings and take over human personalities. The Gospels spoke of casting out demons (see Matt. 12:22–28) and described the result: the demon "goes out of" the person (see Matt. 12:43–45). Here the same language is used: After Paul commanded the demon, "he came out."

"That very hour." This is a strange phrase, unless some demons are able to resist leaving the person for a longer period of time. The demons exorcised by Jesus did not attempt to resist Him. Yet many contemporary stories of Christian exorcisms report the need for more than one session to expel demons successfully.

The story in Mark 9:17–29 is especially instructive. A father brought his son to the disciples to be freed from a demon. The disciples failed to cast out the demon. Apparently, the demon successfully resisted the disciples' best efforts, even though they spoke to it in Jesus' name. Later, when the disciples asked Jesus to explain why they had been unsuccessful, He told them, "This kind can come out by nothing but prayer and fasting" (Mark 9:29). It seems clear that some demons are so powerful, or have such deep roots in an individual's personality, that they do not depart the "very hour" in which they are commanded.

Acts 19:11, 12.

Now God worked unusual miracles by the hands of Paul, so that even handkerchiefs or aprons were brought from his body to the sick, and the diseases left them and the evil spirits went out of them.

Luke described these healings and exorcisms as "unusual." The Greek text says "not the common," or "not the typical." Luke wanted to make it very clear that we are not to view Paul's experience in Ephesus as a model, nor are we to expect the same thing in our day.

The reason for this out-of-the-ordinary manifestation of divine power can be attributed to the unique spiritual climate of Ephesus in the first century. Ephesus was the religious capital of Asia Minor. It featured the stunning temple of the goddess Diana (also called Artemis), which also served as a bank into which money was deposited and from which massive loans were often made to royalty. People from all over the Mediterranean made pilgrimages to Ephesus to visit Diana's temple and purchase religious medals and amulets. But worship of the goddess did not capture the hearts of the people of Ephesus like the practice of magic did. And the practice of magic involved a reliance on the occult and demonic powers.

The fact that Ephesus was the center of such activity led to the "unusual" manifestation of God's power through Paul. In truth, those "unusual miracles," which went far beyond the ability of magic to mimic, made a tremendous impression on the people of Ephesus. Acts 19:19 tells us that "many of those who had practiced magic brought their books together and burned them in the sight of all. And they counted up the value of them, and it totaled fifty thousand pieces of silver."

Luke also tells us that so many people in Ephesus became Christians that the profits of the craftsmen who made religious medals plummeted. A silversmith started a riot, claiming that "not only is this trade of ours in danger of falling into disrepute, but also the temple of the great goddess Diana may be despised and her magnificence destroyed, whom all Asia and the world worship" (Acts 19:27). It took a spectacular and extraordinary manifestation of Christ's power through the apostle Paul to touch the people of Ephesus, and the "unusual" healings and exorcisms did just that.

Acts 19:13–17.

Then some of the itinerant Jewish exorcists took it upon themselves to call the name of the Lord Jesus over those who had evil spirits, saying, "We exorcise you by the Jesus whom Paul preaches." Also there were seven sons of Sceva, a Jewish chief priest, who did so.

And the evil spirit answered and said, "Jesus I know, and Paul I know; but who are you?"

Then the man in whom the evil spirit was leaped on them, overpowered them, and prevailed against them, so that they fled out of that house naked and wounded. This became known both to all Jews and Greeks dwelling in Ephesus; and fear fell on them all, and the name of the Lord Jesus was magnified.

There are several interesting points in this report.

"Itinerant Jewish exorcists" (Acts 19:13). Luke's reference reflects the reputation some Jews en-

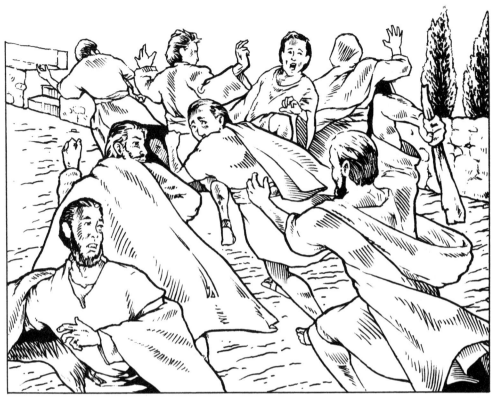

The sons of Sceva fled when attacked by the man with an evil spirit.

joyed as exorcists in the first century. One reason Jews were highly regarded as exorcists was the fact that they did not pronounce the name of Yahweh. People assumed that Jewish exorcists knew His true and secret name, which gave them such power that they could command Him to cast out demons. This is the only place in Scripture where the word "exorcist," *exorkistēs*, occurs.

"Call the name of the Lord Jesus over those who had evil spirits" (Acts 19:13). There is a significant difference between Paul's command for demons to come out "in the name of Jesus" and the practice described here. These Jewish exorcists attempted to use the name of Jesus in an incantation, like those quoted earlier.

"We exorcise you by the Jesus whom Paul preaches" (Acts 19:13). The Jewish exorcists

had no personal relationship with God through Jesus. Without such a relationship, they had no basis for calling on Him to act. The Jewish exorcists were using His name in a magical way. The demon admitted that he recognized Jesus and that he recognized Paul—but there was nothing about the seven sons of Sceva, no sense of the divine presence, that would lead the demon to recognize them. These Jewish exorcists had *no spiritual standing* that would give them a delegated authority over the demon.

"Then the man in whom the evil spirit was leaped on them" (Acts 19:16). As is typical, the demon possessed man displayed unusual strength when the demon took control. The seven sons of Sceva were beaten and stripped, and they fled into the streets.

"*And fear fell on them all*" (Acts 19:17). The Greek word translated "fear" here can be understood to indicate either fright or reverence. The report of this experience left the population in awe and caused the Ephesian Jews and Greeks to view Paul and Jesus with respect. That plus the "unusual" healings and exorcisms made it impossible for the Ephesians to dismiss Paul's message as just another superstition.

EVERY REFERENCE TO DEMONS IN THE EPISTLES

1 Corinthians 10:20, 21.

Rather, that the things which the Gentiles sacrifice they sacrifice to demons and not to God, and I do not want you to have fellowship with demons. You cannot drink the cup of the Lord and the cup of demons; you cannot partake of the Lord's table and of the table of demons.

In the first century most banquets held in private homes were dedicated to some pagan deity. Some Christians felt that it was all right to go to such banquets and to buy meat, which had been dedicated to a pagan god or goddess, from the markets behind pagan temples. They reasoned that since there is only one true God and the gods of the pagans do not exist, it made no difference whether they went to banquets or ate meat purchased from temple markets.

Paul reminded the Corinthians what the Old Testament taught—that the gods of the pagans are actually very real demons. Christians who showed their commitment to the Lord by taking part in the Eucharist were to avoid giving the impression that they were committed to demon gods by taking part in feasts dedicated to pagan deities.

Paul's advice was well balanced. If a first-century Christian was invited to a meal by a pagan, he or she should feel free to go. But if the pagan made it clear that meat dedicated to a deity was being served, the Christian should not eat it. On the other hand, if the pagan makes no mention of the source of the main course, the Christian could eat with a clear conscience without asking where the meat came from (1 Cor. 10:27, 28).

Interestingly, Paul explained that the reason for not eating was out of consideration for the *host's* conscience. In a culture where the norm was for an individual to worship several gods, Christians were to witness by their actions to the exclusive claims of Jesus Christ as the only way to God (John 14:6).

Colossians 2:15. "Having disarmed principalities and powers, He made a public spectacle of them, triumphing over them in it."

"Principalities" and "powers" are angelic ranks, like "colonel" or "major" in the military. The phrase is normally used in the New Testament Epistles of Satan's angels—the demons.

In this passage Paul was discussing the meaning of the death and resurrection of Jesus. He pointed out that through His cross Christ has given the believer new life and provided forgiveness of sins (2:13). In addition, Christ's death and resurrection "disarmed" Satan and his followers.

The Greek word translated "disarmed" is a double compound, *apekduomai,* which means "to strip" or "divest." The *Theological Dictionary of the New Testament* points out that the word "is meant to exclude any possible return to the old state." What Paul affirmed was that in His cross and resurrection Jesus firmly established Himself as Victor over demons, so that they are now a defeated enemy.

❖

EXORCISM AFTER THE APOSTOLIC ERA: FOUR CHURCH FATHERS

TESTIMONY FROM FOUR CHURCH FATHERS THAT EXORCISM WAS PRACTICED BEYOND THE APOSTOLIC ERA

Later Christians were powerful exorcists, "as you can learn even now from things done for all to see; for many persons possessed by demons, everywhere in the world and in our own city, have been exorcised by many of our Christian men" [Irenaeus]. "For some people incontestably and truly drive out demons, so that those very persons often become believers, those cleansed of evil spirits" [Tertullian]. "Let a man be produced right here before your court who, it is clear, is possessed by a demon; and that spirit, commanded to speak by any Christian at all, will as much confess himself a demon in truth as, by lying, he will elsewhere profess himself a god" [Origen]. "Traces of the Holy Spirit are still preserved among Christians, whereby they conjure away demons and effect many cures" [Cyprian].

Scripture tells us to "resist the devil and he will flee from you" (James 4:7). Satan is a defeated enemy, disarmed by Christ and divested of his powers against Jesus' people. It is on the basis of Christ's victory over Satan and his demons that the believer, who has been "made alive together with Him" (Col. 2:13), can exorcise demons today.

1 Timothy 4:1. "Now the Spirit expressly says that in latter times some will depart from the faith, giving heed to deceiving spirits and doctrines of demons."

We must remember that Satan and his forces do not need to possess individuals in order to corrupt Christians and blind the unconverted to the gospel. In chapter 14 we learned how Satan works to accomplish those goals indirectly by shaping culture to appeal to the sinful nature of human beings. First Timothy 4 suggests that Satan's demons work in the same way in the religious realm by seeking to distract the believer from the grace of God and to replace God's grace with an empty asceticism or with other equally futile approaches to Christian living (see 1 Tim. 4:2–5).

James 2:19. "You believe that there is one God. You do well. Even the demons believe— and tremble!"

James used sarcasm to remind his readers that there are different kinds of "faiths." One kind of faith is intellectual assent. In this sense, even the demons "believe." They know very well that God exists, and in their rebellion they hate and fear Him. The kind of faith James argued for is the faith of a person who commits himself or herself to God and trusts Him completely, and who consequently loves God and wants to obey Him. Only the second kind of faith establishes a personal relationship with God, brings Jesus into one's life, and enables the believer to command demons in Jesus' name.

James 3:15. "This wisdom does not descend from above, but is earthly, sensual, demonic."

The word translated "demonic" is *daimoniōdēs*, which means "devilish." It occurs only here in the New Testament. James pointed out that a person with bitter "envy and self-seeking" in his or her heart cannot disguise the fact that his or her attitudes are in harmony with those of demons rather than with those of God. What's more, those attitudes lead to "confusion and every evil thing." In contrast, God's kind of wisdom is marked by an approach to life which "is first pure, then peaceable, gentle, willing to yield, full of mercy and good fruits, without partiality and without hypocrisy" (James 3:17).

1 Peter 3:22. "Who has gone into heaven and is at the right hand of God, angels and authorities and powers having been made subject to Him."

Like Colossians 2:15, this verse reminds us that Jesus exercises authority over "authorities and powers," a phrase which usually indicates fallen angels and demons. The phrase "at the right hand" is an idiom which implies the exercise of authority. The text states specifically that angels and demons have "been made subject to Him." Because Christ rules from heaven, no demon can resist His will. Satan and his crew are defeated enemies.

References to demons in the Epistles remind us how vulnerable we are, if not to demon possession, then to adopting the attitudes of demons in our relationship with others, and thus falling victim to Satan's schemes.

EXORCISM OF DEMONS TODAY

We can distill a number of principles from the references to exorcism in the New Testament. We should be aware of those biblical principles and use them to evaluate reports of exorcism today.

BIBLICAL PRINCIPLES FOR THE EXORCISM OF DEMONS

The following principles can be discerned in the reports of exorcisms found in the New Testament.

(1) Christ has power over demons. During His life on earth Jesus commanded demons, and they were invariably forced to obey Him. Jesus delegated authority to cast out demons to His followers (Matt. 19:1, 8). After Jesus' death and resurrection, His followers continued to cast out demons in His name (Acts 16:18). Jesus is presently at the right hand of God, with complete authority over all angelic and demonic beings (1 Pet. 3:22).

(2) Trust in Christ as Savior provides a standing with God which enables believers to command demons in Jesus' name. Acts 19:13–15 reports on the efforts of exorcists with no personal relationship with God to use Jesus' name in casting out a demon. The exorcists were pummeled by the demon possessed man and had to flee.

An apparently contradictory verse is found in Mark 9. The disciples told Jesus: "Teacher, we saw someone who does not follow us casting out demons in Your name" (9:38). The text does not say that the person did not trust Jesus, but that he did not "follow" the disciples. We need to be careful to avoid concluding that simply because someone is not of our denomination or tradition, he or she is therefore not a true believer in Jesus.

(3) Spiritual preparation for confrontation with demons is important. Jesus told His disciples that a lack of faith prevented them from casting out a demon (Matt. 17:14–21; Mark 9:17–29). The practice of sin, or ignorance of the Scriptures—or anything which negatively affects the intimacy of our fellowship with the Lord robs us of the complete trust in Christ that is so essential in confronting demons.

(4) Demons are to be commanded to leave the possessed in the name of Jesus. There is no place and there is no need for rituals or incantations in exorcism. Exorcism is a confrontation between one or more demons and a believer representing Jesus Christ. Jesus' followers, both before and after His resurrection, won this kind of spiritual victory simply by relying on Jesus' authority and commanding demons in His name (Matt. 7:22; Luke 10:17).

(5) During an exorcism demons will speak through the possessed person. In most of the cases of exorcisms recorded in the Gospels and Acts where details are supplied, the demon speaks directly to the exorcist through the possessed individual. This phenomenon seems to be present in most contemporary reports of demon possession. Dealing with the demon directly is an important part of the exorcism process.

(6) Demons will resist being cast out. Demons who have taken up residence in a human being do not want to leave. The legion of demons who possessed the Gadarene asked to go into a herd of pigs (Mark 5:12; Luke 8:32). A demon successfully resisted being cast out by the disciples, but that demon could not resist Jesus (Matt. 17:14–21). Even Luke's comment that a demon left a slave girl "the very hour" when Paul commanded it to depart (Acts 16:18) indicates that in some cases demons successfully resist for much longer than that. Casting out demons may involve a lengthy and difficult spiritual battle.

(7) Demons of different ranks have the ability to resist exorcism. Jesus referred to the demon which the disciples could not cast out as "this kind" (Matt. 17:21). He explained that their failure was because of their lack of faith; and He told them that when they encountered "this kind" of demon, they would need the spiritual preparation of prayer and fasting (Matt. 17:21). There is no merit in prayer and fasting in itself. That exercise is recommended to sharpen the believer's focus on Christ and thus to strengthen the believer's trust in Jesus as preparation for the confrontation with demons.

(8) Demons will typically cause some physical symptom when departing. This is indicated a number of times in the Gospels by means of phrases such as "the demon threw him down" (Luke 9:42) or "convulsed him" (Mark 1:26; Luke 9:42). Apparently, the bond demons create with the individuals whom they possess includes a physical link which may cause pain when it is broken.

It is fascinating to see the principles we discerned in biblical accounts of exorcisms duplicated in contemporary reports of exorcisms.

CONTEMPORARY REPORTS OF EXORCISMS

Earlier in this chapter, we looked at several contemporary reports of demon possession. Each one of those stories also tells about the exorcism of the invading demons. The remainder of each story is provided here.

From Reverend W. L. McLeod, of Saskatchewan. Rev. McLeod told the story of a demon possessed young woman in his congregation. She had dabbled in the occult, and suddenly began to feel "some strange power rise up slowly within her," filling her mind with intense antagonism to the truths the pastor preached. We pick up her story at the point where the pastor and friends give her advice about how to get rid of the demons.

At once she was blinded and deafened. They did not want her to hear the advice we were giving her. . . .

She told us that for a while all she could see was Satan but that as we prayed she could suddenly see the blood of Christ. This was the stronger and the Satanic powers seemed to withdraw.

We then told her to pray to Jesus Christ and ask Him to completely deliver her. She did so and we all simply prayed and believed God for her. Suddenly all demonic activity ceased. The next morning I got a phone call from a very happy girl. She said simply, "I'm free."

From a young woman in Dover, Delware. This young woman began to experience demon inspired fear and terror only after she recommitted her life to Christ and began to study the Bible and pray regularly. Her torture continued and she could relieve it only by turning back to drunkenness, which she did "two or three times a month." The pressure, fear, and torment became so great that she "began planning to commit suicide." She tells the rest of her story:

At this point my health gave way. I was on the verge of a mental and physical breakdown.

At this desperate juncture I cried to the Lord, asking Him to show me what this awful thing was that stood between us. Just as clearly as if someone had spoken to me, this thought came to me. *You have a demon!*

At this time I knew nothing about demons, except that I believed no believer, such as I was, could be possessed by one. I knew though that God had spoken.

My first impulse was to tell my dear friend Shirley, who was a real student of the Bible. So I jumped in the car and drove to her house, telling her what had happened. She strongly disagreed with me, declaring that a Christian could *not* be demonized.

She suggested that we both go over to the parsonage and talk this over with Mrs. D———, the pastor's wife. This we did, and I told her the story. She and the pastor were aware of the torment I had been experiencing.

Mrs. D——— didn't say anything except that we should pray. The three of us knelt in front of her sofa. Mrs. D——— laid her hand on my shoulder and began to pray softly. I started to call on the Lord. At that moment the pastor's wife quietly commanded the evil spirit to come out of me.

When she did this, I began to feel a lurching inside me. I began to gag as though I were about to vomit. I couldn't catch my breath and had the sensation I was passing out, but actually it was the demon being expelled.

I was totally drained of strength and had to lie down and rest awhile. I felt as though the weight of two worlds had been taken off my shoulders and a new life was opening up for me.

The Lord has healed every wound in my heart and I know the abundant life He intends for His children to enjoy. I am balanced and secure. I'm in the hollow of His hand, and I'll never leave Him again. Praise God!

From a missionary to Mexico's Ohontal Indians. Fernando, the young man who was severely demon possessed, was convinced that he was going to die. His condition finally deteriorated so much that the missionary measured him for a casket. The report continues:

When his pulse became so weak that I could only get it at the jugular vein and the patient began to get cold, the end seemed very near.

While he was unconscious I heard him speaking as though to the Lord—very softly and reverently. Suddenly he opened his eyes, sat up, and spoke to me. He declared the Lord had given him "an hour." He wanted to see my wife (we had both often counseled with him) and all the members of his family.

When we were all assembled, his plea to us was, "Fear and serve the Lord. Take note of what happened to me."

At the end of the hour I expected him to die. When it passed, I asked him about it. He appeared puzzled, saying, "The Lord didn't say if it was an hour by a watch or what. I don't know!" He was sure, however that he had been told to testify for the Lord. This he did consistently and several came to know the Lord, and every one of these has remained true to the Lord to this day.

From a case presented in a counseling class. This case concerned a Ms. A, whose demons expressed themselves by driving her to lust, despair, and resentment. She too had considered suicide. She desperately wanted the demons to go.

I used a cassette player with a hymn of praise for the background. I began to read passages of praise from Revelation. I commanded the demon of lust to listen to the Word of God and the praise music. Ms. A.'s facial expression changed and she fell to the carpet holding her lower abdomen as if in pain. I commanded the demons in the name of the Lord Jesus Christ to stop causing her physical pain. It seemed to stop immediately.

I continued commanding, in the name of the Lord Jesus Christ, for the demons of lust to come out of her and go to the place where Jesus sends them. Her mouth opened and moved as the commands were being given, as if something was coming out of her. . . .

She later told me that as the commands were being given she felt them coming out of her.

She noted a real sense of relief after this occurred. We tested to see if the demon remained by commanding it to come to manifestation in the name of the Lord Jesus a number of times without any response.

In very significant ways, the reports of exorcisms in Scripture and these contemporary reports of exorcisms are similar. The demons of which the Gospels and the New Testament speak have not disappeared. Demons are real— and they, like angels, are present around us.

A TAPE-RECORDED CONFRONTATION WITH A DEMON

C. Fred Dickason, from whose book *Demon Possession & the Christian* (pp. 197–206) two of the reports above were drawn, has personally worked with some 400 demon possessed individuals. Fred has recorded a number of these counseling, or exorcism, sessions. One such session, in which he has a conversation with a demon, is included in this chapter as an example of what might happen in Christian exorcisms today. (The recording is duplicated here by permission.) The exerpt begins at the point where demons interrupted a counseling session and addressed Fred directly, in a voice very different from that of the counselee, Dottie. The demon's words are in italic.

"*They don't like you because you tell too much, and you talk too much, and too many people are getting convinced.*"

"Too many are getting convinced of what?"

"*We have been at war with you for too doggone long, and we are sick of it!*"

"Who is 'we'?" [Demanding]

"*What do you mean, 'we'? You know whom I am.*" [Angry]

"What is your name?"

"*Oh, come on!*" [Disgust] *You know my name. You named me. You named me last time I was here. You named me. You named me. So give me my name back.*"

"No, you tell me your name."

"*Oh, shut up!*"

"You're not Dottie, are you?"

"*I didn't say I was.*"

"What is your name?"

"*I will not tell you. I don't care. You've only got a few more minutes, and I will wait it out.*"

[Fred began to pray to the Lord that he might use the time wisely, and that the Lord would put pressure on the demon and not allow the demon to take evasive action.]

"*Oh, no! No, no, no, no, not Jesus, get away, get away, get away!*"

"The Lord Jesus will not get away. He's inside of Dottie."

[Prayer] "Lord Jesus, You're inside of Dottie; show Yourself to them in Your power, and cause them to stop this tormenting."

"Now I want your name, leading ranking spirit. You're a throne, is that correct?"

"*You know my rank; you know my name. Why do you ask me this over and over and over again? You know, you know, you know! You know too much!*"

"Then why are you afraid of telling me again?"

"*Maybe you have forgotten. And if you have forgotten, the game begins all over again.*"

"Oh, hardly. I could just name you all over again."

"*Oh, no!*"

"Oh, yes!"

"*No, you did that last time. You took everything away last time.*"

"Then why are you hanging around?"

"*I didn't say you got rid of me. I said you took everything away. There's a difference, you know.*"

"Confusion—is that your name?"

"*Sure. You named me!*"

"Did you confess last time that Jesus Christ was your victor?"

"*Sure!*"

"And that Dottie was your victor in Christ?"

"*Sure.*"

"Did you tell her you would obey and leave?"

"*Sure.*"

"Confusion, I command you to leave by the authority of Christ."

"When Jesus and Dottie agreed?"

"They haven't agreed yet."

"How do you know? Because you're not gone?"

"I'm interfering."

[Here, Fred prayed that the Lord would stop the demon's interfering and allow Dottie to be free. He praised the Lord that He is not a God of confusion but of order, and that He had given Dottie a mind not of fear but of love, and of power, and of a sound mind (see 1 Tim. 1:7).]

"Confusion, is Dottie God's child?"

"She's always been."

"No, not always. When did she come to know the Lord?"

"September 5, 1982, 7:30 P.M."

"Oh, you remember the day of your defeat?"

"She makes me sick."

[At this point Dottie, under the control of the demon, began to kick Fred's chair. Fred told him to stop, and reminded him of his position in Christ and His delegated authority.]

"You are under my authority."

"I know I'm under your authority. Rub it in! Come on!"

"You are under the authority of Jesus Christ. You are to respect Him and His servants! Now I want you to confess that you will leave today."

"We can play games again."

"This is no time to play games. You will have to face reality."

"I don't want to face reality. Fantasy is more fun."

"That's where confusion comes in, right?"

"Sure!"

"What do you deny Dottie?"

"Everything I can get my hands on."

"Including her personal dignity?"

"Oh, shut up, shut up, shut up!"

[Here, Fred reminds the demon that Dottie is made in the image of God and is important to Him.]

"Yes, but I put mud on it."

"Not so. The image has been restored. Ephesians 4:24 says that she has been recreated in righteousness and true holiness according to the image of God who created her. She is clean through the Word that Christ has spoken to her."

"No! I'm in her body. That can't be."

[The tape continues for some time. We pick it up again near the end.]

"Are you one of Satan's angels?"

"I was, but I'm not."

"And now you are one of his demons. And now you are going to have to leave Dottie."

"I know."

"Throne called Confusion, I command you to leave by the authority of Christ."

"I'll kill her first. You can't stop me from killing her!"

"Yes, I can. I forbid you to do it!"

"How?"

"Jesus forbids you."

"You can't do that!"

"Jesus did it."

"I'll make her—"

[At this point, Fred put a musical tape recording on her knee to symbolize her kneeling to Christ. He said . . .]

"You're kneeling in her body to the Lord Jesus."

"Don't touch me with . . . tape! I hate that song."

"You should hate that song. She is the daughter of heaven, and Jesus is the life of her."

"She was our princess!"

"She has been delivered from the kingdom of darkness into the kingdom of God's dear Son."

"She was ours! She was our temple!"

"You failed to keep her from trusting Christ."

"Yeah, Jesus desecrated her."

[Here, Fred called Dottie's personality back to talk with him. She affirmed her faith in the Lord and her delight in His presence. After another, shorter struggle, the demon admitted his defeat and left.]

CONCLUSIONS

There are several important conclusions we can draw from the Bible's portraits of demon possession and exorcism.

- Demons are real, personal beings who are active in the world today.
- Demonization has distinctive symptoms which are recognizable by anyone who has studied the Gospel accounts of demon possession.
- Demons look for opportunities to gain access to human beings. It is important to

avoid all contact with the occult, which is a primary avenue of contact with the demonic. It is also important to live a moral life. Christians who turn to sin are vulnerable to demon possession.

- Demons are a defeated foe. Christ has authority over them. Believers can command demons in Jesus' name and force them to depart.

- Despite the fact that Christ has triumphed, demons and demon possession should not be taken lightly. Those who have no contact with demons throughout their lives are blessed.

CHAPTER 16

LOWER THAN ANGELS:

HUMANS AND ANGELS COMPARED

Psalm 8; additional Old & New Testament passages

The pastor of the church I grew up in was a great big old man. When I was in fifth and sixth grades, on winter days I stopped at his house every morning on the way to school. I went downstairs, took the clinkers out of his furnace, and shoveled in coal for the day. The nice old man had one or two strange ideas. Whenever anyone died, he'd pat my shoulder and say, "Well, Lawrence, she or he is an angel now."

That idea hasn't gone out of style. As I write this, it's December. One of the Christmas movies touted this season is about "a country music singer who gets a chance to earn her wings and go to heaven after she died in an automobile accident." For some reason, many people aren't too clear on the distinction between angels and human beings. However, when we explore the Bible, we see that there are very important differences between humans and angels with regard to their origins and natures, their present ministries, and their future destinies.

THE ORIGINS AND CHARACTERISTICS OF HUMAN BEINGS AND ANGELS

THE DISTINCTIVE ORIGIN AND CHARACTERISTICS OF ANGELS

How the angels were created *(Psalm 148:1–5).* John 1:1–3 asserts that God created all things. Colossians 1:16 identifies Christ as the creator of both the visible world and the invisible world, and the latter specifically includes angelic beings. One of the Old Testament's clearest affirmations that angels were created by God, Psalm 148:1–5, tells us how they were created. Here the psalmist calls on all God's angels, all His hosts, and his "stars of light," to praise the name of the Lord, "for He commanded and they were created" (148:5). This verse teaches that God created all angels in a moment of time by His spoken command or word.

When the angels were created by God *(Job 38:4–7).* The Hebrew word for angels, *mal'ak,* means "messenger" or "ambassador." Special classes of angels are designated as cherubim, seraphim, and living creatures. There are a number of other terms used in the Old Testament to designate angels, such as "spirits," "holy ones," "heavenly hosts," "stars," "sons of the mighty," "sons of God," and "gods." When the Hebrew word *'elohim* is used of angels and translated "gods," as it is in Psalm 8:5, it has the meaning "supernatural beings."

Two of those names for angels are found in Job 38, a chapter which deals with God's revelation of Himself to Job. The Lord described the joy of the angels upon witnessing the creation of the heavens and earth. The Creation is described here in a series of questions, capped by the reference to angelic witnesses.

Where were you when I laid the
    foundations of the earth?
Tell Me, if you have understanding.
Who determined its measurements?
Surely you know!
Or who stretched out the line upon
    it?
To what were its foundations
    fastened?
Or who laid its cornerstone,
When the morning stars sang
    together,

And all sons of God shouted
    for joy?

Job 38:4–7

The Hebrew phrase "son of" is often used as an idiom to indicate membership in a class. Job used the phrase *"bebe 'elohim,"* "sons of god," in verse 7b to identify the "stars" of verse 7a. By doing so Job teaches that these "stars" belong to the class "sons of god," that is, the class "supernatural beings," or angels.

Psalm 148:1–5 thus tells us that angels were created directly by God. Job 38:4–7 adds that *"all* the sons of God" were created prior to the creation of the material universe, for angels had to exist already in order to witness that act with joy.

Angelic witnesses were present at the Creation.

Angels do not die (Luke 20:36). Jesus taught that humans who experience resurrection cannot "die anymore, for they are equal to the angels." The Greek word *isangeloi* is translated "equal to angels." It occurs only here, and it means "like angels in this respect." Humans who experience resurrection, like angels, cannot die.

Angels do not procreate (Matthew 22:30). This verse is a parallel to Luke 20:36. Here, Jesus is quoted as saying, "For in the resurrection they neither marry nor are given in marriage, but are like angels of God in heaven." Matthew used a different Greek construction, but the point is the same. With respect to marriage, the resurrected are "like angels of God." The reason why angels do not need to marry or procreate is, of course, that there is no need for reproduction in a population of beings who never die. God created all the angels at the same instant, and angels will exist forever.

Every angel who appears in the Bible is described as a male, which suggests that angels are all of one gender, or better, that angels have no gender. That is a reasonable assumption in view of the fact that angels have no need to procreate.

Angels are God's "holy ones" and they continually reverence Him (Psalm 89:5–7). This psalm exalts the Lord, and it provides a special insight about God's angels.

There are two groups of angels. The group who remained faithful to the Lord are referred to as God's angels (as in Matt. 22:30). The noun "holy ones" is built on a root which means "set apart," that is, "dedicated to the service of God." The other group of angels followed Satan when he turned to sin. This group is referred to in Matthew 25:41 as angels of the devil. Only the first group, the angels who remained faithful to God, are called His "holy ones."

The angels in each group made a choice and are now confirmed in that state. God's holy angels remain holy. These angels have not sinned and will not sin in the future. Satan's fallen angels remain rebels. These angels are and will continue to be hostile to God and to human beings.

Psalm 89:5–7 speaks of the holy angels and their relationship with the Lord.

> And the heavens will praise Your
>   wonders, O LORD;
> Your faithfulness also in the
>   assembly of the holy ones.*
> For who in the heavens can be
>   compared to the LORD?
> Who among the sons of the mighty
>   can be likened to the LORD?
> God is greatly to be feared in the
>   assembly of the holy ones,*
> And to be held in reverence by all
>   those around Him.

This psalm pictures God's angels gathered around Him, praising Him and bowing down before Him. Although these supernatural beings are powerful in their own right (they are "sons of the mighty," that is, mighty ones), they cannot compare to the Lord. Thus, the angels fear God (hold Him in awe) and reverence Him as they worship Him.

Angels are invisible (Colossians 1:16). Colossians 1:16 credits Christ with creating "all things," which includes all things "that are in heaven and that are on earth, visible and invisible." Among the invisible things Paul specifically names thrones, dominions, principalities, and powers, which are designations of different ranks of angels.

Angels are immaterial spirits (Hebrews 1:14). Angels do not have material bodies. Thus, they are called spirits. However, angels have personal identities and travel from place to place (see Dan. 10:20).

THE DISTINCTIVE ORIGIN AND CHARACTERISTICS OF HUMAN BEINGS

At each of the points noted above human beings are different from angels.

* KJV and NKJV read "saints" here, but most modern translations use "holy ones."

How human beings were created (*Genesis 2:7*). Genesis tells us how Adam was created: "And the LORD God formed man of the dust of the ground, and breathed into his nostrils the breath of life; and man became a living being." Eve was formed out of a rib taken from Adam's body, so she shared the same substance as Adam. This mode of creation differs significantly from that of angels, who sprang into existence at God's command. God was much more personally involved in the creation of the first humans.

When human beings are created (*Psalm 139:13–16*). All angels were created at one time, but God's plan for human beings was radically different. Theologians have argued over whether God designed human beings so that a new person comes into existence "automatically" when a male sperm fertilizes a female egg, or whether God creates the new "soul" directly and infuses it at conception. Psalm 139 makes it very clear that no matter which theory is correct, God personally superintends the creation of each new human being in his or her mother's womb.

David reflected on the wonder of how humans are created and wrote under the inspiration of God:

> For You formed my inward parts;
> You covered me in my mother's
>   womb.
> I will praise You, for I am fearfully
>   and wonderfully made;
> Marvelous are Your works,
> And that my soul knows very
>   well.
> My frame was not hidden from
>   You,
> When I was made in secret,
> And skillfully wrought in the
>   lowest parts of the earth.
> Your eyes saw my substance,
>   being yet unformed.
> And in Your book they all were
>   written,
> The days fashioned for me,

> When as yet there were none of
>   them.

Psalm 139:13–16

Angels were directly created at the same instant. Human beings come into existence through the natural process of procreation, generation after generation since the creation of our first parents.

Human beings experience biological death (*Romans 5:12*). Angels do not experience anything analogous to biological death; rather, they continue to exist as individual, self-conscious beings. In contrast, human beings experience biological death. The Bible's concept of "death" is complex; it has at least three main dimensions. Biological "death," of course, denotes the end of a person's life on earth. Spiritual "death" refers to a person's present state of sinfulness and separation from God. Eternal "death" describes the destiny of human beings who have never been reconciled to God through faith.

Angels are not subject to biological death. God's holy angels made a firm decision to remain faithful to Him, and so they are not subject to either spiritual or eternal "death." However, the angels who rebelled against God are subject to spiritual and eternal "death": They experience separation from God, and they will be punished for eternity at history's end.

Human beings procreate (*Genesis 1:27*). "So God created man in His own image; in the image of God He created him; male and female He created them." Unlike God's angels, who have no gender and who do not procreate, human beings were created as male and female and were intended to "be fruitful and multiply" (Gen. 1:28). This difference between human beings and angels is extremely important psychologically (if we can imagine a "psychology" of angels). Our sexuality affects our sense of personal identity, the way we approach many issues in life, the patterns of relationships in family and society, and indeed every aspect of our lives on earth. Although it is difficult, when we think about angels it is important not to superimpose on them notions rooted in human sexuality.

Human beings are sinful and they continually struggle with their desires to do good and temptations to do evil. God's angels decided to remain faithful to the Lord when Satan sinned and corrupted a significant number of the heavenly host. God's angels are now confirmed in their holy state; they have a pure and singular will to worship God and please Him. In contrast, the angels who followed Satan became demons. Satan's angels are confirmed in their sinful state; they have a corrupt and singular desire to rebel against God's will.

Human beings are in a vastly different situation. Even pagans have a moral sense and an innate appreciation of the good, as many ancient documents from Mesopotamia and from Egypt indicate. Despite that, all human beings sin and fall short not only of what God says is right, but of what they themselves believe to be right. Knowing right from wrong is no guarantee that one will choose the right!

This failure to do what is known to be right plagues believers as well as unbelievers. James points out that while every experience that God provides is intended as a "good and perfect gift" (1:17), our own sinful nature transforms many such gifts into temptations to sin. We are thus "drawn away by [our] own desires and enticed," a process which all too often "gives birth to sin" (1:14, 15). No wonder Saint Ignatius of Loyola told Ribadeneira that he wished "to be like the angels in not letting himself be distracted by any of his occupations, just as the angels do not cease to see God and rejoice in Him." Angels have no present experience which parallels our struggle to choose between good and evil, between God's will and something less.

Human beings are visible. Despite the various literary adventures of "the invisible man," hu-

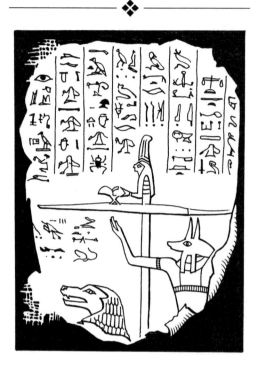

BIBLE BACKGROUND

EGYPTIAN MORALITY

Humanity's innate sense of morality is reflected in this passage from *The Book of the Dead*, which contains adaptations of material produced as early as 2700 B.C. The following so-called "negative confessions" were to be made to the gods of the underworld after a person's sins had been purged by magic (Joseph Kaster, *The Wisdom of Ancient Egypt*, pp. 138–139).

I have not done evil things.
I have not deprived a humble man of his property.
I have not vilified a slave to his master.
I have not inflicted pain.
I have not made anyone hungry.
I have not made anyone weep.
I have not committed murder.
I have not commanded to murder.
I have not caused anyone to suffer.
I have not fornicated or masturbated in the sanctuaries of the god of my city.
I have not added to the weight of the scale, nor have I depressed the pointer of the balance.

I have not taken away milk from the mouths
   of children.
I have not driven cattle from their pastures.
I have not caught fish with [bait of] their
   bodies.
I am pure! I am pure! I am pure! I am pure!

man beings live in the material universe, and our bodies are formed of its stuff. Through touch, taste, sight, hearing, and smell, our senses are designed to respond to cues from the physical world. The spiritual universe, which is above or alongside our own, is beyond our capacity to know with our senses, unless one of its inhabitants becomes available to our senses.

Angels seem to be aware of what is happening in both universes, the material and the spiritual. They observed God create the earth (Job 38:4–7), and they watched as God gave Moses the Law (Acts 7:53). An army of angels situated themselves between a Syrian force and God's prophet (2 Kings 6:17). Angels witnessed the birth of the Christ-child (Luke 2:11, 12). Even today, "angels desire to look into" the impact of the gospel in human lives (1 Peter 1:11, 12). Angels' awareness of events that take place in both the spiritual and material universes makes them vastly different from human beings.

Human beings have spirits, but they are not spirits. The word "spirit" is a slippery one because it has several meanings. On the one hand, angels are called ministering spirits. This means that angels are immaterial spirit beings, yet each one has a distinct identity and form. Typically, when we speak of a human being as having a "spirit," we mean that a human being possesses a consciousness and identity which transcends the body in which the "spirit" resides.

The Bible makes it clear that what we call "the spirit" of a human being survives biological death, and that each human individual retains self-consciousness and his or her own

personal identity after death. Thus, Paul speaks of dying and being with Christ (Phil. 1:23), and thus those who have died will return with Christ at His second coming (1 Thess. 4:14–17), at which time their bodies will be raised "spiritual bodies" (1 Cor. 15:44).

These passages suggest that in the resurrection we, like angels, will be aware of both the spiritual and the material universes. Rather than being limited to one, we will have the ability to live in both. Until then, however, human beings and angels remain distinctly different: Human beings are limited to life in the material universe; angels are spiritual beings who are able to sense and be aware of both the material and spiritual realms.

WHAT HUMAN BEINGS AND ANGELS HAVE IN COMMON

The previous sections of this chapter make it clear that there are significant differences between angels and human beings. However, there are also significant similarities between angels and humans. Although humans do not become angels when they die, we are nonetheless like them in many ways, even as they are like us.

Angels and humans are created beings. Humans and angels are creatures made by the same Creator. We owe Him our existence. Since we are God's creatures, we can only find fulfillment in doing His will joyfully. The first question in Calvin's catechism, "What is the chief end of man?" can be answered by human beings and by God's angels with the same phrase. Together, our chief end is "to glorify God and to enjoy Him forever."

Angels and human beings have individual identities. We human beings, as self-conscious beings, experience an awareness of ourselves as unique, distinct entities. The same can be said of angels. Angels too are "individuals"; each angel experiences a self-conscious awareness of self as a unique being.

Angels and humans are "persons." God made human beings in His image (Gen. 1:26). Thus, the Lord gave to Adam and Eve and their offspring those qualities which set humankind apart from animals. Of all the creatures on earth, only a human being has all of the following: a self-conscious, personal identity, emotions, intelligence, memory, will, the capacity to communicate, and the capacity to be aware of and to worship God. Angels share these qualities with us. This means that there is a closer relationship between human beings and angels than between humans and any other created being in all of God's universe. In all the universe, only humans and angels know what it is to be aware of God and to worship Him consciously and voluntarily.

Neither individual angels nor individual human beings will ever cease to exist. Jesus indicated that Satan and his angels are destined to spend eternity in what the Bible calls the "lake of fire" (Rev. 19:20; see Matt. 25:41). In contrast, God's angels will spend eternity worshiping and serving the Lord.

The Scriptures make it clear that the same options exist for human beings. Those who acknowledge God and respond in faith to His promise of life will spend eternity in God's presence, serving Him in exciting ways that they cannot begin to imagine. Those who continue along Satan's path and do not acknowledge and trust God will share the fate of Satan. Thus Daniel wrote:

> And many of those who sleep
> in the dust of the earth shall
> awake,
> Some to everlasting life,
> Some to shame and everlasting
> contempt.

> *Daniel 12:2*

In either case, the adjective "everlasting" is required, for while our bodies die, no individual personality will ever flicker out of existence and be gone. Each one of us will continue to exist, self-conscious and aware, throughout eternity. This, also, is something that angels and human beings have in common.

It's clear from this review of the differences and similarities between human beings and angels that angels and humans are distinct creations of God, not to be combined or confused. Although we share many wonderful qualities in common with angels, the differences between humans and angels are rooted in creation and the distinctive nature which God provided to each. Those differences are great and significant.

THE PRESENT MINISTRIES OF ANGELS AND HUMAN BEINGS

ANGELS ARE ACTIVE AS GOD'S MINISTERS   *(Psalm 104:4)*

Angels are committed to do God's will, whatever that may be. We can discern His will for angels in a number of Bible passages and verses.

Angels worship God constantly (Isaiah 6:3; Revelation 4:6–11). Many passages in the Bible call angels to worship or describe them at worship. Isaiah saw angels in heaven crying "Holy, holy, holy," as they surrounded God's throne. The most vivid portraits of angels at worship are found in the book of Revelation. John saw God on His throne, worshiped by angels who cry out:

> "You are worthy, O Lord,
> To receive glory and honor and
> power;
> For You created all things,
> And by Your will they exist and
> were created."

> *Revelation 4:11*

Surely the Creator of all things is worthy of praise.

Angels serve as God's personal messengers (Luke 1:28). The Greek word *angelos,* like the

Hebrew word *mal'āk,* means "messenger." Those words are used in Scripture to depict a very responsible individual, a kind of ambassador who represents the one sending him. Thus, one of the functions of angels is to serve as responsible representatives of God. No clearer picture of this function of angels is provided than in the story of the angel who came to Mary to tell her, "Blessed are you among women!" (Luke 1:28).

Angels protect God's people (Psalm 34:7). The psalmist tells us that "the angel of the LORD encamps all around those who fear Him, / And delivers them." Examples of this ministry of angels are listed in the Expository Index, p. 301.

Angels guide God's people (Genesis 24:7). Abraham promised his servant that God would send an angel to direct him to the woman the Lord had chosen to become Isaac's wife. Examples of this ministry of angels are listed in the Expository Index, p. 299.

Angels execute God's judgments (Psalm 78:49). The psalmist identified the source of the plagues visited upon Egypt by saying that God sent "angels of destruction among them." The Bible identifies many incidents in which angels acted as agents of divine judgment when sins were committed by God's people, as well as against God's people. Examples of this ministry of angels are listed in the Expository Index, p. 301.

Angels serve as God's army in the struggle against Satan and his evil angels (Daniel 10:20). An angel who brought a message to Daniel was in a hurry to leave. He told Daniel, "And now I must return to fight with the prince of Persia"—one of Satan's angels. Verses like this one suggest the existence of an invisible war, with different angels in each "army" assigned posts from which they influence the course of events and the history of nations here on earth. See the comments about this role of angels in chapter 17.

It is clear that the major services which angels render to God involves the guidance and protection of believers, as well as the punishment of the sins of believers and unbelievers alike. In serving God, angels serve God's people. Thus, Hebrews 1:14 says of angels, "Are they not all ministering spirits sent forth to minister for those who will inherit salvation?" The ministry that God has given to angels is not just one of serving Him, it is one of serving us!

BELIEVERS ARE TO BE ACTIVE IN SERVING GOD TODAY

Angels do God's will perfectly. We human beings fall short in our attempts to do God's will. Yet it is clear that there are some things that only we—as creatures who have been redeemed by God, who are His by right of creation and redemption—can do to serve Him.

Human beings are to worship God (John 4:23). Jesus taught that "the Father is seeking" human beings who will worship Him "in spirit and truth." Just as angels focus on the worship of God, we also are to worship and praise Him, both individually and corporately.

Jesus also made it clear that God must be worshiped in the way He prescribed. The common notion that adherents of all religions worship God is contradicted by Jesus and the Old Testament. The Old Testament taught that pagan religions are promoted by demons, who direct worship away from God and to themselves. There is only one way to approach God, for Jesus said: "I am the way, the truth, and the life. No one comes to the Father except through Me" (John 14:6).

God's search for worshipers begins, then, with the message that a relationship with God is available to all through faith in Jesus. The sins of the person who comes to God through faith in Jesus are forgiven; that person becomes a child of God and is assured of spending eternity in His presence.

Human beings serve God by sharing the gospel (Matthew 28:19, 20). Although angels are messengers of God, there is one message that angels are not allowed to share with human beings—the gospel. Angels announced Jesus' birth to the shepherds, and angels were present at the empty tomb on Easter morning to reassure Christ's puzzled followers. Still, the angel who appeared to the Roman officer, Cornelius, could only tell him to send for Peter, who would tell him what he must do (Acts 10:4, 6).

Jesus commissioned His human followers with these words: "Go therefore and make disciples of all the nations, baptizing them in the name of the Father and of the Son and of the Holy Spirit, teaching them to observe all things that I have commanded you." The initial proclamation of the gospel, the initiation of believers into the faith, and the instruction of new believers in the faith—all of these things have been entrusted to human believers. In those things angels have been given no role.

Human beings serve God by living righteous lives (Romans 8:3, 4). Although God's angels have been confirmed in holiness and gladly do His will at all times, human beings struggle with the constant pull of sin. God's Law provided a standard of righteousness, but it did not enable any person to live up to that standard—in fact, Scripture tells us that "all have sinned and fall short of the glory of God" (Rom. 3:23).

One of the great wonders of the gospel is that God, who declares us righteous on the basis of Christ's sacrifice for us, works in our lives here and now to enable us to live righteous lives. Romans 8:3, 4 tells us:

For what the law could not do in that it was weak through the flesh, God did by sending His own Son in the likeness of sinful flesh, on account of sin: He condemned sin in the flesh, that the righteous requirement of the law might be fulfilled in us who do not walk according to the flesh but according to the Spirit.

God's Holy Spirit is present in believers. When we rely on God, the Spirit enables us to live the kind of godly lives which fulfill God's righteous requirements, and thus we glorify our God. What a wonder that is! It is no wonder that holy angels do His will, but it is a wonder that born sinners can be transformed from within so that we do His will gladly each day.

Human beings serve God by using their spiritual gifts to minister to others (1 Corinthians 12). Angels are God's servants, and they minister to us. We human beings are God's servants, too, and we are called to minister to each other. First Corinthians 12:7 reminds us that a special gift is given to each believer by the Holy Spirit "for the profit of all." As we love and care for each other, as we freely serve one another, God uses us to enrich one another's lives.

While we are like the angels in that we are created beings called to serve God's people, the particular service we render is unique. No angel is able to nurture the growth of God's people in faith and godliness. No angel is able to model the love of God to others. Christians are called to nurture and to love.

We could list other ways in which human beings are to serve God. However, let us pause to highlight an important similarity between angels and redeemed human beings. Both are creatures, and both are servants of the Creator. Angels and human beings express their relationship to God through the worship of their Creator and through their service to God's people. Although the ways in which they serve God and others differ, humans and angels alike have the wonderful privilege of glorifying God by what they do—and what is more, the privilege of enjoying Him now and forever.

HUMANITY'S PRESENT RELATIONSHIP WITH ANGELS

Understanding the similarities and differences between the activities of humans and angels is important. However, it is also important to understand the present relationship between humans and angels. Too often that relationship has been misunderstood.

Angels are not under human control (Hebrews 1:14). Angels are "sent forth" by God "to minister for those who will inherit salvation." There is no suggestion anywhere in Scripture that angels are under the control of those to whom they are sent. Yet in some Christian traditions the notion persists that particularly holy people are "given" angels to serve them. For instance, it was said that Mother Agnes de Langeac "made her angel do as she wished." She "gave him" to help friends who traveled on dangerous roads, and so on. When Mother Agnes died, her guardian angel was supposedly on such a mission. He announced to the traveler, the superior of the Society of Saint-Sulpice, that an even greater angel was to be given to him to help him in his office.

Such stories make impressive hagiographies (stories about saints), but the notion that an angel can be made to do as a human being wishes has absolutely no basis in Scripture.

Angels are not to be called on to perform white magic. The distinction between "white" and "black" magic, mentioned in Hellenistic and Mesopotamian literature, is both ancient and simple: Black magic is intended to harm, white magic is not. The practice and basic tenets of magic have remained constant across the millennia. One of those tenets is that the person who performs magic can call on greater powers and, if correctly named, those powers can be enlisted to carry out the sorcerer's will.

ANGELORE

WHITE MAGIC SPELLS THAT CALL ON ANGELS

The following white magic spells come from Jewish and Christian sources (see Paul Christian, *The History and Practice of Magic* [1963], Vol. 2, p. 349).

> I, [name], servant of God, desire, and call upon thee, and conjure thee, Tehor, by all the Holy Angels and Arch Angels, by the holy Michael, the holy Gabriel, Raphael, Uriel, Thronus, Dominations, Principalities, Virtues, Cherubim, and Seraphim, and with unceasing

voice I cry, Holy, Holy, Holy is the Lord God of Sabaoth, and by the most terrible words: Soab, Sother, Emmanuel, Hdon, Amathon, Mathay, Adonai, Eel, Eli, Eloy, Zoag, Dios, Anath, Tafa, Uabo, Tetragrammaton, Aglay, Joshua, Jonas, Calpie, Calphas. Appear before me, [name], in a mild and human form, and do what I desire.

An incantation for exciting love with the help of Psalm 137:

> Pour oil from a white lily into a crystal goblet, recite the 137th Psalm over the cup and conclude by pronouncing the name of the angel Anael, the planetary spirit of Venus, and the name of the person you love. Next write the name of the angel on a piece of cypress which you will dip in oil and tie the piece of cypress to your right arm. Then wait for a propitious moment to touch the right hand of the person with whom you are in love, and love will be awakened in his or her heart. The operation will be more powerful in effect if you perform it at dawn on the Friday following the new moon.

Thus, it is not surprising to find that in black magic the sorcerer calls on demons, while in white magic the sorcerer calls on angels. However, the Scriptures make no distinction between white and black magic: *All occult practices are forbidden to God's people* (Deut. 18:10–14).

Angels are not to be prayed to or worshiped (Revelation 22:8, 9). In biblical accounts of angel encounters, angels have often been perceived as awesome beings. Even the apostle John was awed by an angel: "And when I heard and saw, I fell down to worship before the feet of the angel who showed me these things" (Rev. 22:8). The response of the angel puts our present relationship with angels in perspective: "See that you do not do that. For I am your fellow servant, and of your brethren the prophets, and of those who keep the words of this book. Worship God." (22:9).

Like the prophets and our fellow believers, angels are simply servants of God. Their supernatural powers may amaze us, and their uncloaked appearance may leave us awestruck, but angels are not to be worshiped. Nor are we to address prayers to angels.

We can appreciate and respect angels and especially those whom God sends to minister to us, as fellow servants of our common Lord. Like us, angels are creatures—only the Creator merits our worship, and only He can answer our prayers.

We can ask God to send His angels to help us (*Judges 13:8*). Manoah asked God to send the angel who had appeared to his wife to instruct the couple on how to bring up Samson, the son the angel promised them. Sue (whose true story I shared at the beginning of chapter 15) prayed for angels to protect her son, and she had a vision of an angel. Because we know that God is gracious in answering our prayers, and because we know from Scripture that angels guard, protect, and guide God's people, we can feel free to ask Him to send angels to us.

The important thing is that we should always maintain a clear focus on God, the one to whom we pray, as the ground of our hope. We are never to let our eyes focus on angels as if they were able to act independently of God, or as if we owed them the praise which rightly belongs to God alone.

THE FUTURE RELATIONSHIP BETWEEN HUMANS AND ANGELS

David expressed his wonder at the role God gave human beings in His plan:

> What is man that You are mindful of him,
> And the son of man that You visit him?
> For You have made him a little lower than the angels,
> And You have crowned him with glory and honor.

Psalm 8:4, 5

When we compare the limitations of human beings to the powers of angels, we may well wonder why David wrote that we were created only "a little lower than the angels." There is a passage in the Bible which promises

Angels serve among humanity.

that in the future believers will be catapulted *above* the angels. Throughout eternity there will be no comparison between the place granted believers and the place occupied by angels. That place is hinted at in Hebrews 1:14, for even today angels are "ministering spirits" whom God sends "to minister for those who will inherit salvation." Angels serve us.

In chapter 10 we examined Jesus' relationship to angels. We learned from Hebrews 1 that Jesus, the Son of God, is superior to all angels. Hebrews 2 explores Christ's impact on the relationship between human beings and angels.

THE DESTINY OF HUMAN BEINGS (*Hebrews 2:5–17*)

For He has not put the world to come, of which we speak, in subjection to angels. But one testified in a certain place, saying:

> "What is man that You are mindful of him,

Or the son of man that You take
    care of him?
You have made him a little lower
    than the angels;
You have crowned him with glory
    and honor,
And set him over the works of
    Your hands.
You have put all things in
    subjection under his feet."

For in that He put all in subjection under him, He left nothing that is not put under him. But now we do not yet see all things put under him. But we see Jesus, who was made a little lower than the angels, for the suffering of death crowned with glory and honor, that He, by the grace of God, might taste death for everyone.

For it was fitting for Him, for whom are all things and by whom are all things, in bringing many sons to glory, to make the captain of their salvation perfect through sufferings. For both He who sanctifies and those who are being sanctified are all of one, for which reason He is not ashamed to call them brethren, saying:

"I will declare Your name to My
    brethren;
In the midst of the assembly I will
    sing praise to You."

And again:

"I will put My trust in Him."

And again:

"Here am I and the children whom
    God has given Me."

Inasmuch then as the children have partaken of flesh and blood, He Himself likewise shared in the same, that through death He might destroy him who had the power of death, that is, the devil, and release those who through fear of death were all their lifetime subject to bondage. For indeed He does not give aid to angels, but He does give aid to the seed of Abraham. Therefore, in all things He had to be made like His brethren, that He might be a merciful and faithful High Priest in things pertaining to God, to make propitiation for the sins of the people.

Hebrews 2:5–17

BIBLE BACKGROUND

WHAT ARE HUMAN BEINGS
IN OTHER RELIGIONS?

Each religion must find some way to place human beings in the scheme of things. Their views of human origins provide the best way to evaluate the relative status human beings are thought to have in this universe and in eternity.

The *Enuma Elish,* which originated at least two millennia before Christ, describes the creation of man from the blood of a slain goddess. Tablet VI reads:

"Blood I will mass and cause bones to be.
I will establish a savage, 'man' shall be his
    name.
Verily, savage-man I will create.
He shall be charged with the service of the
    gods
    That they might be at ease!"

An even earlier Sumerian work, *The Atrahasis Story,* tells of the manufacture of human beings to take over chores the younger gods are tired of carrying out. Tablet I relates:

The Divine Assembly summoned the divine
    midwife,
. . . Mami the wise woman.
"Midwife the lullu!
Deliver Aborigines to labor for the Gods!
Let them bear the yoke.
Let them work for Enlil.
Let them labor for the Gods."

In early Egyptian theology, dating from at least three thousand years before Christ, the gods were only concerned with the Pharaoh. Joseph Kaster, in *The Wisdom of Ancient Egypt* (1993, p. 50), observes that "man, far from being the crowning achievement of creation, comes into being only incidentally, from the tears shed by Ra."

It is no wonder that with such views of the creation of human beings, none of the ancient religions held out much hope for the ordinary individual in the world to come!

"The world to come" (Hebrews 2:5). The writer of Hebrews looked ahead to a future in

which God's plan is fully worked out. Although angels are now far more powerful than the human beings to whom they are sent by God to serve, this will not be the case in eternity. The reason for that is this: God intended from the beginning to subject all of creation to human beings. One implication of God's plan is that there will be a radical change in the relationship between angels and human beings in the future.

"What is man?" (Hebrews 2:6–8). This utterly basic question was answered in humankind's creation, was affirmed in the Psalms, and is now explained in Hebrews 2.

In the beginning God said, "Let Us make man in Our image, according to Our likeness" (Gen. 1:26). In the Creation God shared something of His own nature with us. According to the same verse, God ordained for humans to "have dominion" over the material creation.

Despite the corruption of human nature in the Fall, a remnant of God's image and likeness remains (see Gen. 9:6; James 3:9). Thus, each individual human being is special, for he or she bears the image of the Creator. No individual stamped with the image of God can be dismissed as insignificant, nor can death mark the end of such a being's existence.

"That You take care of him" (Hebrews 2:6). Some ancient religions attributed a selfish motive to the gods who created human beings intentionally. "Savage-man" was created to serve the gods, to "labor for the gods," so that the gods might be at ease.

God's motive, as described in Psalm 8 and quoted in Hebrews 2:5–7, was totally different. The God of Scripture cared about and continues to care for human beings! We humans are special to Him, and although God created humans "a little lower than the angels," God "crowned him [humans] with glory and honor!"

"Put all things in subjection under his feet" (Hebrews 2:8). The writer of Hebrews, like the psalmist, was thinking of God's *intent* as ex-

pressed in Genesis 1:26. God created human beings to give them dominion over the entire creation. Before this purpose could be fulfilled, Adam and Eve sinned. Rather than having human dominion over creation, creation itself was corrupted. God explained to Adam the consequence of his sin (Gen. 3:17): "Cursed is the ground for your sake; / In toil you shall eat of it / All the days of your life." Human beings must now struggle with nature, rather than have dominion over it.

However, the fact that sin has made it impossible for humankind to "put all things in subjection" has neither changed God's original purpose, nor modified His intent! This, of course, was why the writer of Hebrews had to speak of the world to come. Even though "now we do not yet see all things put under him" (2:8b), in the world to come all of God's purposes for humanity will be achieved.

"But we see Jesus" (Hebrews 2:9, 10). The writer of Hebrews turned his attention to the question of how God is going to fulfill His purpose for, and in, humankind. He directs our attention to Jesus and to what Jesus did.

Jesus became a real human being; He "was made a little lower than the angels." The phrase "a little lower" in Greek can be translated as the NKJV has it here, or it can be translated "was made lower than the angels for a little while." The second reading is to be preferred here. Jesus, for a time, became a human being. He did this for a specific purpose—"for the suffering of death"—in order that "He, by the grace of God, might taste death for everyone" (2:9).

In so doing, Jesus became "the captain" of our salvation (2:10). The Greek word here is *archēgos,* which in various English versions of the Bible has been translated as "pioneer," "leader," and "champion." In the first century, *archēgos* was often used with respect to the founders of philosophical schools, who marked out the paths their disciples would follow. Jesus, who was made lower than the angels for a little while, has now been raised and returned to heaven, "crowned with glory and honor." Jesus is the author of our salvation, and He reveals what awaits us in the world to come as we follow the path He has marked out for us.

"For both He who sanctifies and those who are being sanctified are all of one" (Hebrews 2:11–13). This stunning passage of Scripture reaffirms the destiny God intended for humanity. Through faith in Jesus, who tasted death for us on Calvary, we are united with Him. We have become His "brethren" and His children.

This relationship effects a remarkable change in our destiny and in our relationship to angels. In Christ we are being restored to innocence; but more than that, we are being lifted up to participate with Christ in the rule of God's universe, just as God always intended. In Christ, we who are now temporarily lower than the angels will be, in the world to come, immeasurably higher than the angels.

We can diagram the relationships described in Hebrews 2 as follows:

In the original creation and now:
God

Angels
Humans

During Christ's time on Earth:
God

Angels
Humans, Jesus Christ

In the world to come:
God, Christ
Humans, in Christ

Angels

"He Himself likewise shared in the same, that through death He might destroy him who had the power of death" (Hebrews 2:14–18). The writer of Hebrews pointed out that Christ took on flesh and blood to make propitiation for our sins. "Propitiation," a significant theological term, refers to the satisfaction of the requirements of divine justice by the death of a substitute. Christ became a human being so that He might volunteer to die as full payment for our sins. In that act, Christ released us from the fear of death, which Satan uses so effectively. Now we are aware of our destiny, and death holds no terrors. Christ has come to our aid!

The writer of Hebrews made this additional observation: "For indeed He does not give aid to angels, but He does give aid to the seed of Abraham" (2:16). Human beings have been from the beginning, and continue to be in the present, the focus of God's loving concern. Angels are far less important in God's scheme of things than you and I. All who respond to God as Abraham did—with faith in His promise—are assured not only of God's aid now, but also of an eternity crowned with glory and honor as we fulfill the destiny that was in God's mind from the beginning of time.

THE DESTINY OF ANGELS
(Revelation 7:11)

Hebrews 2 made it clear that no change in status lies ahead for God's angels. However, Scripture does not outline the role of angels in the world to come. Angels, as Luke 20:36 made very clear, do not die. They, like us, will live endless lives dedicated to the service of God.

It is quite clear that many of the present ministries of angels will no longer be needed in the world to come. Angels will not need to guide, to protect, or to instruct us, for our powers will be far greater than theirs, and our knowledge of God far more pure. But one ministry of angels will never cease—the ministry of worship.

The book of Revelation hinted at this in a passage describing the presence of a great multitude of the saved, "Of all nations, tribes, peoples, and tongues, standing before the throne and before the Lamb" (7:10). The multitude praised the Lord, saying, "Salvation belongs to our God who sits on the throne, and to the Lamb!" Verses 11–12 immediately add:

All the angels stood around the throne and the elders and the four living creatures, and fell on their faces before the throne and worshiped God, saying:

> "Amen! Blessing and glory and
>   wisdom,
> Thanksgiving and honor and
>   power and might,
> Be to our God forever and ever.
> Amen."

What a wonderful destiny for God's angels, who will find everlasting joy in giving God the glory due His name (see Psalm 29:2).

CHAPTER 17

HISTORY'S END:

A LOSING STRUGGLE FOR SATAN AND HIS FORCES

Daniel; Revelation

Take a quick look around and you may get the impression that Satan is winning. The title of a recent book warns that our culture is *Slouching toward Gomorrah*. Yet the Bible maintains a strong and positive position: Satan is a defeated enemy whose fate was sealed at Calvary. There can be only one winner in the struggle between the angelic forces of God and the demonic hordes of Satan. Although the present battle between God and evil has rightly been called an invisible war, about which we are given few details, the final battle at history's end is destined to break through the boundaries between the spiritual and material realms, and that battle will be visible to all.

THE INVISIBLE WAR BEING FOUGHT TODAY

There are recurring intimations in Scripture about a war conducted by Satan and his demons against God and His angels. In that war Satan shows his hostility toward God by attacking human beings, who are the objects of God's love.

INTIMATIONS ABOUT THE INVISIBLE WAR IN THE OLD TESTAMENT

In Old Testament references to demon activity. In chapter 7 we saw that demons operated through the pagan religions of the ancient world. The goal of their activity was to direct worship away from God and toward themselves and Satan, and in so doing to keep human beings in spiritual darkness. Demons pursue the same goal today: Demonic beings are behind religions which present their deities and doctrines as a doorway through which humans can find access to the Creator.

In Daniel's report of fighting between God's angels and Satan's angels. Additional details about the invisible war are provided in Daniel 10.

Daniel related that for three weeks he prayed that he might understand a vision he had seen. At the end of that three-week period, an angel appeared in his natural fiery form and spoke to Daniel (10:5, 6). The angel explained that as soon as Daniel began to pray, God sent him to Daniel: "Now I have come to

Daniel and the invisible spiritual war.

make you understand what will happen to your people in the latter days, for the vision refers to many days yet to come" (10:14).

The reason for the three-week delay was that a powerful angel of Satan, identified as "the prince of the kingdom of Persia," held the messenger angel back. Finally, the archangel Michael, "one of the chief princes," came to help the messenger angel (10:13). Michael, more powerful than Satan's "prince of the kingdom of Persia," opened the way for the messenger angel to reach Daniel and carry out his mission. The angel also told Daniel that he was in a hurry to complete his mission: "And now I must return to fight with the prince of Persia; and when I have gone forth, indeed the prince of Greece will come" (10:20). This passage yields a number of insights about the invisible war between the forces of Satan and the forces of God.

First, it suggests that angels have ranks or powers similar to those of military personnel. God's messenger angel was held up by a pow-erful angel in Satan's army until an even more powerful angel in God's forces, Michael, ar-rived and overpowered him. While the anal-ogy to military ranks is clearly flawed, the concept that there is a hierarchy of angelic be-ings is clearly supported by this passage and New Testament passages, such as Ephesians 3:10 and Colossians 2:15.

Second, Daniel 10 suggests that a con-stant struggle between Satan's forces and God's forces is going on even now. The "prince of the kingdom of Persia" was intent on blocking the messenger angel from carrying out his mission. The messenger angel spoke of the need to "return to fight with the prince of Per-sia." We know little about what this kind of battle is like, but the imagery is powerful.

Third, Daniel 10 may well suggest that Satan has assigned some of his followers the task of influencing the course of nations. The passage speaks of a "prince of Persia" and a "prince of Greece." It also indicates that the archangel Michael was given special responsi-bility for the Jews.

While we do not have enough informa-tion to be dogmatic about the present nature of the invisible war fought between angels and demons, we do have enough to know that a cosmic struggle is going on even now between demonic forces committed to Satan and an-gelic forces committed to God.

INFORMATION ABOUT THE INVISIBLE WAR IN THE NEW TESTAMENT

The Old Testament indicates that Satan's demons wage war against human beings here on earth and that a struggle is going on in the spiritual realm. The New Testament provides much more information about Satan's war against human beings and how it is con-ducted.

The Gospels: Christ versus Satan (*Matthew 12:22–30*). In a critical passage in Matthew's Gospel, Jesus put His ministry of casting out demons in perspective: It was evidence of a clash of kingdoms. Jesus' exorcisms of demons marked the invasion of the kingdom of God into a realm where Satan had established *his* kingdom. Christ's victories over demons, who were forced to obey His commands, demonstrated God's compassion for the human beings being tormented. Satan demonstrated hostility toward God in his attacks on the human beings whom God values. Satan delights in crippling human beings by means of the physical and mental infirmities caused by his demons' efforts to control human behavior.

Satan versus humanity (*Ephesians 2:1–3*). Although the invisible war takes place in the spiritual realm, the primary battlefield is on earth. Satan's intention is to maintain control over human beings by any means available. Demon possession is only one of the many weapons in Satan's arsenal. Satan's tactical strategies are subtle: He influences human societies to incorporate beliefs and values which appeal to the sinful nature of human beings; and he encourages the design of religions which divert human beings from the knowledge and worship of the true God.

The believer's role in fighting the invisible war (*Ephesians 6:11, 12; 2 Corinthians 10:4*). The Epistles issue warnings about the attacks Satan will mount against the church and provide instructions for offensive and defensive spiritual warfare.

Satan will mount attacks on the church from within. Paul warned that "evil men and impostors will grow worse and worse, deceiving and being deceived" (2 Tim. 3:13). The best defense against attacks by those who creep into the church to corrupt the faith is to remain committed to the truths taught in Scripture, which thoroughly equip God's people "for every good work" (2 Tim. 2:17).

Peter warned that "there will be false teachers among" the people, teachers intent upon deceiving believers and destroying the faith (2 Pet. 2:1–3). He then described their motives, their lifestyle, and the characteristics of their teachings (2:4–22).

John warned his readers about "the spirit of the Antichrist, which you have heard was coming, and is now already in the world" (1 John 4:3). John provided a test to use against the emissaries of Satan. If they do not confess that Jesus Christ is the Son of God who has "come in the flesh," they are "not of God" (4:3; see 4:15). The full deity and true humanity of Jesus is a pivotal Christian doctrine.

Jude also warned against "certain men" who creep into Christian fellowships "unnoticed," who corrupt the grace of God, and who "deny the only Lord God and our Lord Jesus Christ" (Jude 4). Jude gave a careful description of such persons and urged his readers: "Keep yourselves in the love of God, looking for the mercy of our Lord Jesus Christ unto eternal life" (Jude 21).

In his invisible war against God, Satan will continue to employ his basic strategy of shaping culture to accomplish his goal. Satan will also try to infiltrate and corrupt the church. Therefore, we must continue to love Christ and retain our confidence in Him. Moreover, we must look with confidence to the Scriptures in order to equip ourselves to do God's will.

Believers are to mount attacks on Satan (*2 Corinthians 10:4*). Paul reminds us that although we are flesh and blood, that although we live in the material world, the struggle in which we are engaged is a spiritual struggle, one that involves encouraging others to give allegiance to God. In Ephesians 6:12 Paul claimed: "For we do not wrestle against flesh and blood, but against principalities, against powers, against the rulers of the darkness of this age, against spiritual hosts of wickedness in the heavenly places." In 2 Corinthians 10:3–5 Paul wrote:

For though we walk in the flesh, we do not war according to the flesh. For the weapons of our warfare are not carnal but mighty in God for pulling down strongholds, casting down arguments and every high thing that exalts itself against the knowledge of God, bringing every thought into captivity to the obedience of Christ.

The confrontation between the forces of good and evil continues.

In our battle against Satan for the hearts and the allegiance of those trapped in his kingdom, and in our battle for the full transformation of believers, we have been equipped by God with the Holy Spirit, faith, prayer, and truth. We are to rely on these spiritual resources and use them when we do battle with Satan.

Believers are to maintain their defenses against Satan's attacks (Ephesians 6:13–18). This passage, which speaks so powerfully of wrestling against "the rulers of the darkness of this age," gives a description of the armor provided by the Lord to enable us to "stand."

It is clear from these passages that Satan's war against God is an invisible one, that it is going on right now, and that we human beings have an important role to play in the present. However, the invisible war will come to an end. When it does, Satan and all his forces will experience total defeat.

SATAN'S DEFEAT IS PREDICTED IN SCRIPTURE

We met Satan in the first chapter of this book, where we learned about his origin. God created Satan as a cherub, one of the highest ranks of angels. His name then was Lucifer (Isa. 14:12). Inexplicably, Lucifer was not satisfied with his position, and he became determined to "be like the Most High" (Isa. 14:14). Lucifer resolved that he would live independently of God, in effect replacing God on the throne of His universe. In that moment Lucifer became Satan, and evil came into existence.

From that moment on, Satan set himself in opposition to God and dedicated himself to thwarting God's purposes. When God created Adam and Eve and placed them in Eden, Satan slipped into the material universe and successfully tempted the first humans to disobey God. As a result of that act of disobedience, our race became warped and twisted, attracted to evils which could only mean disaster for sinners and for all around them. Satan, as we saw in chapter 13, has struggled to retain his grip on humankind, weaving his evil influence into human culture to further his own purposes.

Even though we constantly see the consequences of Satan's handiwork—in the wars, the crime, the injustice, and the suffering that plague our planet—Scripture, from the very beginning, has portrayed Satan and his angels as doomed, defeated creatures.

SATAN'S FINAL DEFEAT HAS BEEN CERTAIN FROM THE MOMENT OF HIS REBELLION
(Isaiah 14; Ezekiel 28)

Two passages in Scripture describe the origin of Satan and introduce the problem of evil. In each of those passages Satan's final end is predicted.

Isaiah 14:12–15. Isaiah reveals what Lucifer "said in [his] heart" that transformed him into Satan. This revelation occurs in the context of an ancient funeral dirge, a dreary lament to be chanted over the dead.

Satan's declaration of independence from God (vv. 13, 14) is encapsulated by these two declarations (vv. 12, 15):

> How you are fallen from heaven,
> O Lucifer, son of the morning!
> How you are cut down to the
>   ground,
> You who weakened the nations!
> . . . .
> Yet you shall be brought down
>   to Sheol,
> To the lowest depths of the Pit.

Ezekiel 28:16–19. A similar pattern is found in Ezekiel 28. Following an extended description of Satan's original glory as one of God's cherubs (28:12b–15), Ezekiel provides a long prophetic description of Satan's fate, cast in the past tense to emphasize the certainty of its fulfillment. Here Ezekiel spoke "the word of the LORD" (28:11) and said (28:12), " 'Thus says the Lord GOD:

> "By the abundance of your trading
> You became filled with violence
>   within,
> And you sinned;
> Therefore I cast you as a profane
>   thing
> Out of the mountain of God;
> And I destroyed you, O covering
>   cherub,
> From the midst of the fiery stones.

> "Your heart was lifted up
>   because of your beauty;
> You corrupted your wisdom for
>   the sake of your splendor;
> I cast you to the ground,
> I laid you before kings,
> That they might gaze at you.

> "You defiled your sanctuaries
> By the multitude of your
>   iniquities,
> By the iniquity of your trading;
> Therefore I brought fire from your
>   midst;
> It devoured you,
> And I turned you to ashes upon
>   the earth
> In the sight of all who saw you.
> All who knew you among the
>   peoples are astonished at you;
> You have become a horror,
> And shall be no more forever.' "

Ezekiel 28:16–19

SATAN'S FINAL DEFEAT IS PREDICTED IN OLD TESTAMENT PASSAGES

Isaiah 27:1. In chapter 26 Isaiah looked forward to a future day when God will establish peace for His people (26:12). In that day, the prophet writes,

> Your dead shall live;
> Together with my dead body
>   they shall arise.
> Awake and sing, you who dwell
>   in the dust;
> For your dew is like the dew
>   of herbs,
> And the earth shall cast out
>   the dead.

Isaiah 26:19

Another prophecy associated with "that day" in the future has to do with Satan, who is described as a serpent (see also Rev. 12:9).

In that day the LORD with His
  severe sword, great and strong,
Will punish Leviathan the fleeing
  serpent,
Leviathan that twisted serpent;
And He will slay the reptile that
  is in the sea.

Isaiah 27:1

SATAN'S FINAL DEFEAT IS DESCRIBED BY JESUS

One remarkable feature of the Gospels is that Jesus' references to hell are recorded more often than His references to heaven. Matthew 25 provides Jesus' description of history's end: "When the Son of man comes in His glory, and all the holy angels with Him, then He will sit on the throne of His glory" (25:31). According to Jesus' description of that time, He will say to those who are condemned, "Depart from Me, you cursed, into the everlasting fire prepared for the devil and his angels" (25:41).

Two things are especially significant about this verse. First, "the everlasting fire" has already been prepared for the devil and his angels. Their future fate is fixed and certain. They run loose today, but at history's end God will condemn them to everlasting fire. Second, "the everlasting fire" was prepared by God "for the devil and demons." It is important to note that God did not design hell with human beings in mind. What God has had in mind for us from the beginning is made clear in Christ, who sacrificed Himself that we might be given eternal life (John 3:16).

God in Christ has done everything necessary to save human beings from suffering the fate He determined for Satan and his angels. Those who choose to disregard God's revelation of Himself, who fail to respond to God with trust, have chosen to be independent from God, the very independence which Satan craved. Tragically, they have also chosen Satan's fate. Satan's doom is sure. However, God has thrown open the door to salvation for hu-

man beings. God invites and urges everyone who will to enter.

VISIBLE ANGELS ARE ASSOCIATED WITH CHRIST'S RETURN AT HISTORY'S END

Matthew 25:31 says that Jesus will return "and all the holy angels with Him." Mark 8:38 speaks of the time when Christ will come "in the glory of His Father with the holy angels." Luke 9:26 speaks of Christ's return as a time "when He comes in His own glory, and in His Father's, and of the holy angels." A graphic description of Jesus' return is found in 2 Thessalonians 1:7, 8, which speaks of a time "when the Lord Jesus is revealed from heaven with His mighty angels, in flaming fire taking vengeance."

All of these passages indicate that angels will accompany Jesus when He returns to earth in glory at the end of time. Scripture clearly envisions a time at history's end when God's angels, now invisible, will become visible to all. In that day, the barriers between the spiritual and the material realms will break down, and what was once hidden will be unveiled.

VISIBLE WORKS OF SATAN AND HIS DEMONS ARE ASSOCIATED WITH HISTORY'S END

Two books of the Bible, Daniel and Revelation, are famous for their visions concerning history's end.

The contribution of Daniel. Daniel's visions are interpreted by angels in chapters 7—12. The predictions in Daniel 7—9 and the angelic revelation in 11:1–33 were fulfilled in exact detail in the centuries preceding Christ's incarnation.

One of the many striking predictions in Daniel 9 concerns a period of "70 weeks." The Hebrew text reads "seventy sevens." These "sevens" are to be taken as weeks of years, and thus the passage predicts 70 periods of seven years each, that is, a period of 490 years. Daniel 9:24 tells what is to happen at the end of that period of time:

> Seventy weeks are determined
> For your people and for your holy
>   city,
> To finish the transgression,
> To make an end of sins,
> To make reconciliation for
>   iniquity,
> To bring in everlasting
>   righteousness,
> To seal up [fulfill] vision and
>   prophecy,
> And to anoint the Most Holy.

At first glance it seems that this is a failed prediction. Yet Daniel 9 goes on to divide the 490 years into distinct periods. The period from the decree to rebuild Jerusalem until the coming of the Messiah was to be 69 sevens (9:25). After that "Messiah shall be cut off [die], but not for Himself" (9:26). Jesus died about A.D. 32. The same verse says that after the Messiah's death Jerusalem and its temple will be destroyed (9:26). This happened in A.D. 70, when Jerusalem was captured and burned by the Roman army.

Clearly, there is a gap between the end of the sixty-ninth seven and the final, or seventieth, seven-year period. Daniel 9 describes what will happen in the final seven-year period. In the middle of that period, "the prince who is to come" will introduce in the Jerusalem temple an "abomination" that "desolates." Jesus referred to this prediction when He was asked about His coming and "the end of the age" (Matt. 24:3). Jesus said that the end would be near "when you see the 'abomination of desolation,'" spoken of by Daniel the prophet, standing in the holy place [the temple] (Matt. 24:15). Therefore, according to Daniel, history's end—when God finishes transgression and puts an end to sin—still lies in the future.

Daniel 11:36—12:13 describes events that will take place on earth "at the time of the

end" (11:40). This passage is linked with Revelation 12:14 by the statement that

> At that time Michael shall stand up,
> The great prince who stands watch
>   over the sons of your people;
> And there shall be a time of trouble,
> Such as never was since there was a
>   nation.

Daniel 12:1

BIBLE BACKGROUND

DANIEL'S PROPHECY OF SEVENTY WEEKS

Sixty-nine Sevens of Years		Seventieth Week
(360 days each = 173,880 days)		
445 B.C. Decree to rebuild Jerusalem (Neh. 1–2; Dan. 9:25)	A.D. 32 Messiah cut off (Dan. 9:26)	A.D. ? Period of prophetic culmination

Support for this interpretation:

1. A gap of time is characteristic of Old Testament prophecy (see Isa. 61:1 and Luke 4:18–19).
2. Daniel 9:26 clearly predicts the Messiah's death.
3. Daniel 9:26 predicts events which took place in history a number of years after the death of Christ, specifically the destruction of Jerusalem under the Roman general, Titus, who later became emperor.
4. Christ related events of the seventieth week to history's end.
5. The apostle Paul describes events of the seventieth week predicted in Daniel 9 as yet future (2 Thess. 2:3–12).
6. The book of Revelation, in its description of history's end, specifically ties the victory of the archangel Michael over Satan to a 1,260 day period, the second half of the seventieth week (12:14).

The great contribution of the book of Daniel, then, is threefold. First, Daniel provides an accurate timetable for the appearance and the death of the Messiah. Counting from the issuance of the decree to rebuild Jerusalem, Jesus was crucified in the exact year predicted. Second, Daniel 9 makes it clear that a gap of indeterminate length lies between the time of Christ's death and the final seven-year period in which all prophecy is to be fulfilled. Third, Daniel 11:36—12:13 describes events that will take place on earth during that final seven-year period in ways that are clearly linked with Revelation's description of history's end.

The contribution of Revelation. While Daniel 11:36—12:13 describes the events that will take place on earth during history's final seven years, the book of Revelation describes the events that will take place in heaven. Daniel predicts that the archangel Michael will "stand up" during this period. Revelation shows us Daniel and all God's angels in their final struggle with Satan and his demons. The invisible war suddenly becomes visible to us through the visions which the apostle John recorded in the book of Revelation.

Throughout the history of the church, Christians have interpreted the book of Revelation in a variety of ways. There have been three main views of how the Revelation of John should be understood. In the early church Revelation was understood as prophecy, a literal description of events which will be fulfilled at history's end.

A second view also regards Revelation as prophecy, but understands its figures, symbols, and events as providing a description of the course of church history rather than history's end. This view was popular with the Reformers, who identified the evil creatures depicted in Revelation with Roman emperors, the pope, and the Roman Catholic Church.

A third view holds that the visions in Revelation are symbolic. Since Revelation is a piece of apocalyptic literature, its visions do not necessarily refer to literal events past or future; they are intended, rather, to reassure believers that God will triumph in the end.

Given the unmistakable link between Daniel and Revelation, and given the fact that Daniel's earlier prophecies were fulfilled precisely in striking detail, it's best to approach Revelation as prophecy—but prophecy that is difficult to interpret because the apostle John simply did not have the vocabulary to explain exactly what he saw. John was forced to attempt to convey truly cosmic events for which there were simply no first-century corollaries.

Some recent interpreters have been tempted to explain John's visions in modern terms, using the analogy of hydrogen bombs and biological weapons. That is surely a flawed approach. What we can understand of Revelation is clear: The disasters John described are caused by God, who at last acts through His angels to judge sin and to punish Satan and his demonic forces. Revelation, then, provides graphic and powerful images of the end of the invisible war.

THE END OF THE INVISIBLE WAR AT HISTORY'S END

For many centuries Christians have believed that the book of Revelation contains prophecy, that it presents a powerful and reassuring description of history's end, with the final triumph of Christ over Satan. Today many Christians continue to see Revelation as a description of the future, whose details are difficult to interpret, but whose major outline of things to come is clear.

If we place ourselves in this tradition of interpretation, in Revelation we can see the role God gives to His angels in winning the final victory. We can also see the final, desperate struggle of Satan and his hordes as they fight against their fate. The story told in the book of Revelation can be divided into several distinct segments.

THE INITIAL REVELATION (Revelation 1:1–20)

The apostle John was approximately 90 years old and in exile on the island of Patmos when he was given a vision of Jesus resplendent in His full glory as God the Son.

JESUS' MESSAGE TO THE CHURCHES
(Revelation 2:1—3:22)

Christ gave John messages which he was to relay to churches located in seven different cities in Asia Minor. Many commentators believe the spiritual condition ascribed to those churches provides a paradigm for the evaluation of local congregations today.

AN ANGEL CALLED JOHN TO HEAVEN TO OBSERVE WHAT WILL HAPPEN IN THE FUTURE
(Revelation 4:1—20:15)

John observed a "door standing open in heaven" and heard a voice saying, "Come up here, and I will show you things which must take place after this" (4:1). From this point on, John was an enthralled observer who saw God's plan for history's end unfold before him. John struggled to describe what he witnessed—the end of the war between good and evil, between God and Satan. This section of the book of Revelation can be divided into several subsections as we trace the future John saw.

Preparations were made in heaven *(Revelation 4—5)*. The first thing John saw in heaven was this: angels of all ranks bowing down and worshiping God, seated on His throne. Initially, they praised God as Creator.

> "You are worthy, O Lord,
> To receive glory and honor and
>   power;
> For You created all things,
> And by Your will they exist and
>   were created."
>
> *Revelation 4:11*

John then noticed a sealed scroll in God's hand. The scroll represents the fulfillment of God's purposes and history's end. At first no one was found worthy to open the scroll, but then John saw Christ step forward, "a Lamb as though it had been slain" (5:6). Christ took the scroll, and the whole company of heaven broke out in a new song.

> "You are worthy to take the scroll,
> And to open its seals;
> For You were slain,
> And have redeemed us to God
>   by Your blood
> Out of every tribe and tongue and
>   people and nation,
> And have made us kings and
>   priests to our God;
> And we shall reign on the earth."
>
> *Revelation 5:9, 10*

Christ the Redeemer is about to act, about to fulfill the promise implicit in Creation. He will establish His rule on the earth, and the redeemed will reign with Him. And so again the voices are raised in praise because at last God's power will be fully displayed.

> "Blessing and honor and glory and
>   power
> Be to Him who sits on the throne,
> And to the Lamb, forever and
>   ever!"
>
> *Revelation 5:13*

Angels inaugurated the last days by pouring out judgments on sinful humanity *(Revelation 6—8)*. We saw in chapter 3 that one of the ministries of angels is to judge sin and to punish sinners. Here, a dreadful time, predicted by Daniel and described by Jesus (Matt. 24), was launched by angels who opened a series of seals, each of which unleashed a terrible worldwide disaster.

The disasters described in Revelation 6 include war, famine, disease, cataclysmic earthquakes, and changes in the heavens. Those disasters were so terrible that men recognized God's hand and cried, "The great day of His wrath has come and who is able to stand?" (6:17). All those judgments which sin deserves, which God graciously withheld while inviting human beings to come to Him for salvation, were unleashed.

Revelation 7 describes a pause in the judgments, as 144,000 Jewish converts were set aside to evangelize the world during this period of terrible tribulation. But then Revelation 8 resumes the description of judgments, which involved the searing of a third of the earth and the death of a third of its creatures.

Demons were released and they turn against humanity *(Revelation 9—10)*. An army of scorpion-like demons were released from the Abyss to torment humanity (9:1–11). Then the four great fallen angels who were "bound" were released to make war on humankind (9:14–15). They were joined by an army of distorted demons with the heads of lions and tails like serpents (9:16–19). Despite the terror these evil beings evoked, the great majority of humankind refused to repent or turn to God.

❖

Demons released from the abyss.

But the rest of mankind, who were not killed by these plagues, did not repent of the works of their hands, that they should not worship demons, and idols of gold, silver, brass, stone, and wood, which can neither see nor hear nor walk. And they did not repent of their murders or their sorceries or their sexual immorality or their thefts.

Revelation 9:20, 21

Two great truths surface in this section. The first is that human beings truly have been so corrupted by sin that they choose to take Satan's side against God. The second is that despite humankind's hostility toward God, neither Satan nor his demons have any affection for human beings. Instead Satan and his demons take delight in the torments they can inflict on human beings, for in spite of our sins, we humans remain objects of God's love.

In Revelation 10 John tells us that he cannot reveal the next part of his vision. However, he does tell us that "in the days of the sounding of the seventh angel, when he is about to sound, the mystery of God would be finished, as He declared to His servants the prophets" (10:7).

Satan energized the Antichrist to enlist humankind on his side and direct man's worship to himself *(Revelation 11—18)*. In these chapters there are many references to the fulfillment of Old Testament prophecies, particularly those found in the last chapter of the book of Daniel.

In Revelation 12 Satan is described as "a great, fiery red dragon" who is incensed against a "woman" representing God's chosen people. Satan focused his antagonism on the Jews, "and war broke out in heaven" (12:7). This is how John described what he saw:

Michael and his angels fought with the dragon; and the dragon and his angels fought, but they did not prevail, nor was a place found for them in heaven any longer. So the great dragon was cast out, that serpent of old, called the Devil and Satan, who deceives the whole world; he was cast to the earth, and his angels were cast out with him.

Revelation 12:7–9

It appears that Satan and his angels will no longer have access to the spiritual realm; they will be cut off from heaven, and they will be locked with us in the material universe. However, that seems to infuriate and energize Satan rather than silence him. John pictures him as "having great wrath, because he knows that he has a short time" (12:12).

At this point, John saw a "beast" rising out of the sea. From his description (13:1) it is clear that this beast is the Antichrist of whom Daniel and Jesus both spoke. John wrote that "the dragon gave him [the beast] his power, his throne, and great authority"—the very things Satan had promised to Jesus if He would bow down and worship him (Luke 4:6–8). In return, Satan was given what he had always wanted—worship: "And all the world marveled and followed the beast. So they worshiped the dragon who gave authority to the beast" (13:3, 4).

The same chapter describes the emergence of another "beast," who is energized by Satan to perform "great signs, so that he even makes fire come down from heaven on the earth in the sight of men" (13:13). The miracles performed through Satan's supernatural powers deceived the rest of humanity, and people gladly showed their allegiance to the Antichrist by accepting his "mark" on their right hands or foreheads.

While Satan and his forces were at work on earth, God's angels were preparing a series of terrible, final judgments. John wrote: "Then

Christ victorious!

I saw another sign in heaven, great and marvelous: seven angels having the seven last plagues, for in them the wrath of God is complete" (15:1). Chapter 16 describes the terrible anguish caused by these plagues and the reaction of people who "blasphemed the name of God who has power over these plagues; and they did not repent and give Him glory" (16:10). Then demonic spirits were sent out by Satan, the Antichrist, and a third leader, the "false prophet," to enlist human rulers for a last great battle against God at a place called Armageddon (16:16).

The powers displayed by Satan and his followers, both demon and human, seemed to disturb John. So an angel explained the coming fall of those who worship Satan and the world system Satan wove so carefully (17:1–18). The angel said, "These will make war with the Lamb, and the Lamb will overcome them, for He is Lord of lords and King of kings; and those who are with Him are called, chosen, and faithful" (17:14).

Christ appeared with His army of angels and defeated the forces of Satan (Revelation 19). John graphically portrayed Christ as seated on a white horse, ready at last to intervene personally. John described the final battle in these words:

And I saw the beast, the kings of the earth, and their armies, gathered together to make war against Him who sat on the horse and against His army. Then the beast was captured, and with him the false prophet who worked signs in his presence, by which he deceived those who received the mark of the beast and those who worshiped his image. These two were cast alive into the lake of fire burning with brimstone. And the rest were killed by the sword which proceeded from the mouth of Him who sat on the horse.

Revelation 19:19–21

Satan was imprisoned, then released, and finally cast into the lake of fire (Revelation 20). With the battle decided, an angel seized Satan and locked him in what Scripture calls the Abyss, or "bottomless pit." Satan was kept

there for a thousand years, while Christ reigned on earth in fulfillment of many Old Testament prophecies (20:4).

At the end of the thousand years, Satan was released. Immediately, he set about to deceive human beings and enlist them on his side. Amazingly, Satan succeeded, and he gathered a great army to continue his fight against God (20:8).

However, this time God had had enough. Fire from heaven destroyed the human army, and "the devil, who deceived them, was cast into the lake of fire and brimstone where the beast and the false prophet are. And they will be tormented day and night forever and ever" (20:10).

Then the material universe itself dissolved, as ultimate reality was starkly revealed. God was on His throne, and the dead of all history were brought before Him for final judgment. All those who failed to respond in faith to God's revelations of Himself, and so did not have their names entered in "the Book of Life," are judged by their works—and con-

Satan defeated!

signed with Satan and his fallen angels to the lake of fire (20:12–15).

God created a new heaven and earth for perfected humanity *(Revelation 21, 22).* The final two chapters of Revelation contain John's vision of a new universe created by God and peopled by the saved, who now enjoy an intimate relationship with God in a place of purity and beauty.

The age-old struggle was over at last. Not only were Satan and his angels dealt with, but believers were resurrected and their natures were purified from every taint of sin. John summed it up for us.

They shall see His face, and His name shall be on their foreheads. There shall be no night there: They need no lamp nor light of the sun, for the Lord God gives them light. And they shall reign forever and ever.

Revelation 22:4, 5

And we can say with John (22:20): "Amen. Even so, come, Lord Jesus!"

EXPOSITORY INDEX

An expository index organizes information by topic and guides the reader to Bible verses and book pages which are critical to understanding the subject. It does not list every verse referred to in the book, but seeks to identify key verses. It does not list every mention of a topic in the book, but directs the reader to pages where a topic is discussed in some depth. Thus an expository index helps the reader avoid the frustration of looking up verses in the Bible or the book, only to discover that they contribute in only a small way to one's understanding of the subject.

This expository index organizes references to angels and to demons by topic. Topics and sub-topics are identified in the left-hand column. Key Bible verses and passages are listed in the center column under "Scriptures." The far right column identifies pages in this book where the topic is covered.

In most instances, several of the key verses in the "Scriptures" column will be discussed on the book pages referred to. Very often additional verses will be referred to on the pages where the topic is covered. Our goal is to help you keep in focus the critical Bible verses and passages. Similarly, the book pages referred to are only those which make a significant contribution to understanding a topic, not every page on which a topic may be mentioned.

Please note that material under sub-topics is sometimes organized chronologically by the sequence of appearance in Scripture, and sometimes alphabetically, depending upon which organization will be most helpful in understanding and locating information.

TOPIC	SCRIPTURES	BOOK PAGES
ANGELS (Good Angels)		
ANGEL OF THE LORD, THE		
A CLOAKED APPEARANCE OF GOD HIMSELF	Gen.16:7, 13; Ex. 3:2, 4; Judg. 6:12, 14	17–18
THE SIGNIFICANCE OF HIS NAME	Ex. 3:14, 16; Ex. 6:2	20–22
THE RELATIONSHIP OF JESUS TO THE ANGEL OF THE LORD	John 1:1–3; 8:58	23
OLD TESTAMENT APPEARANCES		
To Hagar	Gen. 16	23–24, 129
To Abraham	Gen. 22	24–25, 129
To Moses	Ex. 3—4	25–26, 132

TOPIC	SCRIPTURES	BOOK PAGES
To Balaam	Num. 22	26–27, 134
To sinning Israel	Judg. 2	27, 135–36
To Gideon	Judg. 6	28, 136–37
To Manoah	Judg. 13	28–29, 137
To David	2 Sam. 24	29–30
	1 Chron. 21	140
To Elijah	1 Kings 19	30, 141
	2 Kings 1	30, 141
Destroys an	2 Kings 19:35;	31
Assyrian army	Isa. 37:36	
To Zechariah	Zech. 1, 3	31–32
	Zech. 12:8	31–32

ANGELS
ANGELS ARE:

Created beings	John 1:1–3	49
	Job 38:4–7	268–69
	Ps. 148:1–5	273
God's servants	Ps. 103:19–21	146, 276
Invisible	Col. 1:16	48–49, 270
Limited spatially	Dan. 10:10–20	49–50
Organized in ranks	Dan. 10	181–82
"Persons"	1 Pet. 1:12	49–50
	Luke 1:27–38	274–75
Sexless	Matt. 22:30	50, 166
	Mark 12:25	167
	Luke 20:36	270–71
Spirits	Heb. 1:14	270
Undying	Luke 20:36	50, 166
	Matt. 22:30	167, 270, 274

ANGELS APPEAR AS:

Ordinary men	Gen. 18:1–5	34, 51
	Heb. 13:5	128, 153, 172, 184
Radiant beings	Dan. 10:6;	51
	Luke 24:4	

ANGELS ARE CALLED:

Angels	Ps. 104:4	48
Chariots	Ps. 68:17	145
Cherubim	Ezek. 9—11	48, 149
Gods	Ps. 8:5; Gen. 35:7	48, 144–45
Heavenly hosts	Ps. 148:2	48
Holy ones	Heb. 2:2	48, 89, 135–36
Living creatures	Ezek. 1, 3	48, 149

TOPIC	SCRIPTURES	BOOK PAGES
Promotes fear of death	1 Cor. 5:5;	219
	Heb. 2:14	
NAMES AND TITLES OF		
Accuser	Rev. 12:10	
Adversary	1 Pet. 5:8	
Beelzebub	Matt. 12:24–28	241
Destroyer	Rev. 9:11	
Devil, the	Luke 4:2;	216
	John 8:44;	
	Heb. 2:14	
Evil One	John 17:15	10
	1 John 5:18	222–23
God of this world	2 Cor. 4:4	221, 225–26
Great Dragon	Rev. 12:3, 9	292–93
Liar, Deceiver	John 8:44;	206
	Rev. 12:9; 20:3	
Lucifer	Isa. 14:12	7
Murderer	John 8:44	
Prince of power of air	Eph. 2:2	234
Prince of this world	John 12:31; 16:11	225
Ruler of demons	Matt. 12:24;	247
	Luke 11:15	
Satan	Zech. 3:1, 2;	5–7
	Acts 5:3;	
	2 Cor. 11:14;	
	Rev. 12:9	
Serpent	Gen. 3:1–13	5, 6
	Isa. 27:1;	288
	2 Cor. 11:3	
Spirit working in	Eph. 2:2	214
sons of disobedience		
Tempter	Luke 4:1–13	8–9
	1 Thess. 3:5	201–11
SPHERE OF ACTIVITY		
Earth	Job 1:7	115
	Eph. 2:1–3;	222
	1 Pet. 5:8	
Heavenlies	Job 1:6; 2:1;	116–17
	Rev. 12:10	
Limited by God's	Job 1:12; 2:6	117–19
permissive will	2 Cor. 12:7;	184–85
	1 Pet. 2:4	
Limited by our	Luke 4:9	210, 211
freedom of choice		

SCRIPTURE INDEX

(Bible references are in boldface type, followed by the pages on which they appear in this book.)

---------- ❖ ----------

THE "EVERYTHING IN THE BIBLE" REFERENCE SERIES

Every Covenant and Promise in the Bible. From the Old Testament covenants God made with Noah, Abraham, Moses, and David through the promises that still apply to our lives, this volume helps you develop a new appreciation for God's dependability and the power God's promises can afford to believers today. (Available)

Every Good and Evil Angel in the Bible. The Bible leaves no question about the reality of angels, even though humankind has not always been clear on their nature and function. This volume takes a thorough look at every mention of angels in the Bible—both those working for God and those working against Him. It also looks at the place of angels in the lives of contemporary believers. (Available)

Every Miracle and Wonder in the Bible. A God who created all that is certainly is capable of working miracles. Beginning with the miracle of Creation, this volume reviews God's wondrous works in dealing with His people. Major emphasis is given to the special evidences of God's activity in the Exodus, the ministries of Elijah and Elisha, and the ministry of Jesus. (Available)

Every Prayer and Petition in the Bible. The Bible is filled with evidences of prayers offered to God—some intensely private and others joyously public. Individuals are seen coming to Him with their requests and their complaints, their confessions and their praises. Three chapters look at the powerful prayers in the Psalms. Four chapters focus on Jesus' teachings about and practice of prayer. (Available)

Every Woman in the Bible (Available Spring 1999)

Coming soon

Every Man in the Bible

Every Name and Title of God in the Bible

Other titles are being planned.